Praise for Robyn
NOTHING BU

'Her great strength is to write history from
the inside...wonderfully entertaining.'
Age

'Annear's ironic approach and eye for minutiae
ensure a lively and fascinating story.'
Sydney Morning Herald

'A welcome addition to Australian history.'
Quadrant

'Annear evokes a carnival atmosphere...
highly recommended.'
Bookphile

'Successfully blends extensive research
and a lightness of touch.'
Australian Book Review

'A vivacious introduction to the actuality
of life on the goldfields.'
Weekend Australian

'So lively and descriptive, you'll think
you're reading a novel.'
Family Circle

Robyn Annear is author of *Nothing But Gold: The Diggers of 1852* and *Bearbrass: Imagining Early Melbourne*.

THE MAN WHO LOST HIMSELF

THE UNBELIEVABLE STORY OF THE TICHBORNE CLAIMANT

ROBYN ANNEAR

ROBINSON
London

Constable & Robinson Ltd
3 The Lanchesters
162 Fulham Palace Road
London W6 9ER
www.constablerobinson.com

First published in Australia by The Text Publishing Company, 2002

First published in the UK by Robinson,
an imprint of Constable & Robinson Ltd 2003

A copy of the British Library Cataloguing in
Publication data is available from the British Library

ISBN 1-84119-799-8

Printed and bound in Australia

10 9 8 7 6 5 4 3 2 1

This project has been assisted by the Commonwealth Government through
the Australia Council, its arts funding and advisory body.

For David and Rosie

CONTENTS

CAST OF CHARACTERS

Allport, Curzon	Claimant's Melbourne solicitor
Angell, Captain Henry	Friend of the Orton family
Arundells of Wardour	Aristocratic English Catholics; Alfred Tichborne's in-laws
Baigent, Francis	Tichborne family genealogist
Ballantine, Serjeant	Claimant's barrister at the civil trial
Baring, Georgiana	Leading supporter of the Claimant in the later years
Barraut, Jules	Servant to Roger Tichborne in South America
Berliner, Otto	Melbourne-based private detective; collected evidence for the Claimant's side
Bloxam, Harry	London importer, one of the Claimant's leading backers
Bogle, Andrew	Tichborne family servant, retired to the colonies
Bowker, Frederick	Solicitor to the Dowager Lady Tichborne
Bowker, James	Solicitor to the Hampshire Tichbornes
Bulpett, William	Hampshire banker and Claimant supporter
Burrows, Fred	Friend of the Claimant in Gippsland and Deniliquin
Burrows, Jane and John	Employed Tom Castro at Deniliquin
Butts, Truth	Son of a Sydney publican, became the Claimant's secretary
Castro, Don Tomas	Storekeeper at Melipilla, Chile
Castro, Pedro	His son
Castro, Tom	Claimant's colonial alias
Cater, Jack	Supporter of the Claimant, formerly a Wagga baker
Cockburn, Sir Alexander	Lord Chief Justice of England, presided at the Claimant's criminal trial

Cox, Charley ('Pocket-Book')	Publican, of Wagga, Hay, Jerilderie; finder of the Claimant's pocket-book
Cresswell, William	a.k.a. 'the Parramatta lunatic'; his identity was a matter of contention
Cubitt, Arthur	Proprietor of the Missing Friends Office, Sydney
Cullington, Francis	Solicitor for the Doughty estates
Davitt, Michael	Irish political prisoner and fellow-inmate of the Claimant
Denning, Inspector	In charge of the House of Commons Police
Dight, Jackie	Butcher; knew Arthur Orton in Hobart and Gippsland
Dobinson, James	Solicitor for the Tichborne estates
Doughty, Sir Henry	Roger Tichborne's uncle
Doughty, Kattie	Roger's cousin and sweetheart (see also Radcliffe)
Doughty, Lady	Roger's aunt, Kattie's mother
Fearne, William	Travelling photographer; knew Tom Castro in the Riverina
Foster, William	Claimant's employer at Boisdale, Gippsland
Gibbes, William	Tom Castro's Wagga lawyer
Gosford, Vincent	Steward of the Tichborne estates and friend to Roger
Hawkins, Henry	Second counsel for the defence at the Claimant's civil trial; Crown prosecutor at the criminal trial
Higgins, Robert	Employed Tom Castro at Wagga
Holmes, John	Claimant's London solicitor, 1867–69
Hopkins, Edward	Former Tichborne family solicitor; supporter of the Claimant in Alresford
Jury, Elizabeth (Lizzie)	Arthur Orton's sister
Jury, Mina	Wife of Frank Jury, the brother of Lizzie Jury's husband
Kenealy, Dr Edward	Claimant's counsel at criminal trial

METRIC CONVERSIONS

Some of the measurements in the book:

HEIGHT

5 feet 6 inches = 1.65 m

5 feet 7 inches = 1.68 m

5 feet 9 inches = 1.73 m

5 feet 9½ inches = 1.74 m

LENGTH

1 inch = 2.5 cm

16 yards = 14.6 m

DISTANCE

(to nearest 0.5 km)

1 furlong = 201 m

1 mile = 1.6 km

5 miles = 8 km

8 miles = 13 km

10 miles = 16 km

12 miles = 19.5 km

18 miles = 29 km

30 miles = 48 km

45 miles = 72.5 km

100 miles = 161 km

175 miles = 281.5 km

WEIGHT

(mainly the Claimant's; most to nearest 0.25 kg)

1 ounce = 28 g

1 stone (= 14 pounds) = 6.25 kg

3 stone = 19 kg

52 pounds = 23.5 kg

6 stone = 38 kg

120 pounds = 54.5 kg

11 stone 4 pounds = 71.5 kg

12 stone = 76.25 kg

12 stone 4 pounds = 78 kg

13½ stone = 85.75 kg

15 stone = 95.25 kg

16 stone = 101.5 kg

18 stone = 114.25 kg

19 stone = 120.75 kg

21 stone = 133.5 kg

27 stone = 171.5 kg

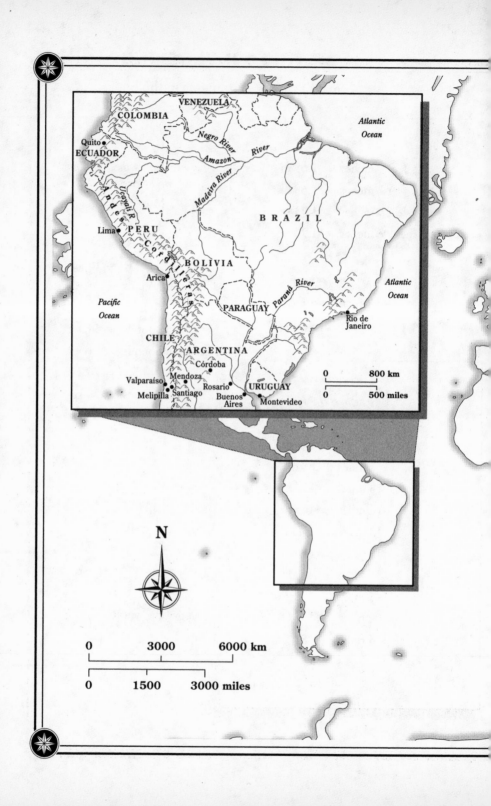

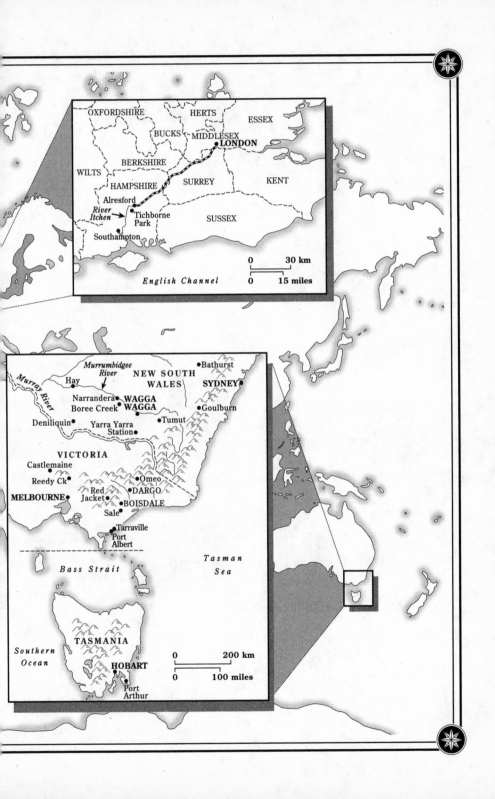

OXFORDSHIRE   HERTS   ESSEX
BUCKS   MIDDLESEX
LONDON
BERKSHIRE
WILTS
HAMPSHIRE   SURREY   KENT
Alresford
River
Itchen → Tichborne
Park   SUSSEX
Southampton
0   30 km
0   15 miles
English Channel

Murrumbidgee
River   NEW SOUTH   Bathurst
Hay   WALES   SYDNEY
Murray River
Narrandera   WAGGA
Boree Creek   WAGGA   Goulburn
Deniliquin   Yarra Yarra   Tumut
Station
VICTORIA
Castlemaine
Reedy Ck   Omeo
Red   DARGO
MELBOURNE   Jacket   BOISDALE
Sale
Tarraville
Port
Albert   Tasman
Sea
Bass Strait
TASMANIA
Southern
Ocean   HOBART
Port
Arthur   0   200 km
0   100 miles

PART ONE

ONE

TOM CASTRO OF WAGGA WAGGA

NOBODY knew what Tom Castro knew.

And up until August of the year 1865 nobody much cared.

Tom Castro butchered for a living at Wagga Wagga, roughly midway between Sydney and Melbourne. Wagga Wagga wasn't on the main route between those cities, nor was it near a goldfield or on the way to one. You couldn't even say it was on the scenic route. It was on a stock route and it's unlikely you'd have passed that way unless you had business in the stock trade. That was the trade Tom Castro had followed, one way or another, all the time he'd been in Australia.

Castro was a butcher of the Australian bush type. That is to say, he was a slaughterman who could dress meat in a rudimentary fashion. On the goldfields, on stations and in towns like Wagga, customers generally bought their mutton by the half or quarter, and cut chops and shanks and haunches to suit themselves.* Still, Tom Castro was regarded as a good butcher by Wagga standards: his meat was clean-cut and well-presented. Which is more than could be said of Castro himself.

'Loose and slommicking' is how one of his customers remembered him. At a shade over 5 feet 9 inches, he was a tallish man for his time, and solid-built, though he carried himself like an uneven load, all

---

* In the language of the Wiradjuri people, *wagga* means 'crow'—so that the name Wagga Wagga signifies a place of many crows. Whether for concision or because there are fewer crows nowadays, Wagga Wagga is commonly shortened to a single Wagga.

stooped and shambling. His hair he wore long and pushed straight back from the forehead, smoothing it with his lardy hands so often that it stank of slaughteryard pomade. A modest set of copper-tinged muttonchops framed his long, jowly face. His features were full and heavy, pastry-like, underhung by what someone described as 'a double chin, vacant'—a loose fold of skin waiting to be filled up. Every so often, one side of his face would clench in a kind of elaborate shiver, all the way from his eyebrow to the corner of his mouth. He had full, slack lips that hid the gap where three of his front teeth ought to have been. And he had a tendency to drool.

There was nothing about Tom Castro's heavy-lidded dark eyes to contradict the rest of his sluggish demeanour. But they noticed things.

Castro was employed—and had been for eighteen months, the longest he'd ever stopped in one place—by Robert Higgins, who owned the Australian Hotel in Fitzmaurice Street, Wagga's principal thoroughfare. The butchering business was 'attached' to the hotel; the slaughteryard and shop were at the end of the long rear yard. The shop, which went by the name of the Australian Market, was a rough skillion shed built of redgum slabs with a bark roof. An open verandah fitted with a bench and chopping block formed the shop itself, while a room behind served as office and sleeping quarters. Customers seldom came to the shop—the order boy did his rounds of a morning and most had their meat delivered—so there was no call for it to look flash. Just a hundred yards away, fringed with sprawling redgums, was the Wollundry Lagoon, a eunuch offshoot of the Murrumbidgee River. Tom Castro had started off with Higgins as slaughterman, but now he was foreman, which meant buying stock, collecting payments and keeping the books as well as running the shop. He had three workers under him, but still did most of the slaughtering himself.

During his first year at Wagga, Castro lived at the shop. He was, according to an acquaintance, 'deficient in the clothing line.' His entire wardrobe amounted to a shredded pair of moleskins, a couple of Crimean shirts and a lumpy grey-green pea jacket—all of them, and himself, unwashed and caked with muck. Even allowing that some degree of residual grime was unavoidable for a butcher in an age before disinfectant and running water, Tom Castro was a disgrace.

Evenings, for Castro, meant drinking, although not generally at the Australian Hotel. It was the domain of the squatters, the closest thing Wagga had to a gentlemen's club. The Commercial, half a block away, was more in Castro's line: rough and ready, with a bet and a brawl always about to happen. Some time around the middle of 1864, Castro started drinking at the Black Swan Inn at North Wagga Wagga. The main attraction at first seems to have been the billiard table, for all that Castro lost far more often than he won. Perhaps it was as consolation for losing at billiards that he found himself a wife at the Black Swan.

Mary Ann Bryant was nineteen and newly arrived from Goulburn when she came to the Black Swan as a domestic servant. Her employer's suspicions were aroused, a couple of months later, by the 'unnecessary amplitude of crinoline' worn by the young housemaid. Sure enough, Mary was in an advanced stage of pregnancy. She was delivered of a daughter, Annie, in the spring of 1864 and by Christmas she was betrothed to Tom Castro—who, though not the child's father, was prepared to take her on.

And Mary had a fair idea of what *she* was taking on. She'd seen Castro hit the brandy hard. She'd noticed—couldn't help it—the stink and the state of him. She'd seen him twitch and slobber when he got excited, and how people laughed about him when he was gone. She'd seen how he swaggered and would bet on anything: a game of billiards, the weight of a pig, you name it. Only once had Mary seen one of his wagers pay off, and that was when her baby was born. Tom bet on a girl. 'You came up trumps for me, Mary,' he said to her later. And it made him kind of fond of the kid from the start.

About six weeks before Christmas, Tom took a fall from his horse.

Castro Villa, the newlyweds' first home

His face was pretty badly smashed up (the doctor had to remove a piece of bone from his nose) and he convalesced at the Black Swan for a week. Mary washed his putrid clothes, and decided that she could do worse than Tom Castro. She'd never seen him whack anybody and although he drank, he didn't turn nasty with it. No one would call him a catch but she was no catch either, and she knew it. She was a meaty girl with dark hair and a cross expression. And a baby. But, laid up at the Black Swan while his swelling subsided, Tom watched Mary with her bub and the possibility of a different kind of life began to dawn on him.

Castro gave his age as thirty when he and Mary Bryant married at the end of January 1865. Both of them were Roman Catholics, but the ceremony was conducted by a Wesleyan minister. Castro told people that the Catholic priest had refused to marry them. According to the marriage certificate, he was born in Chile, the son of Tomas Castro, a merchant. He signed his name on the certificate, Mary marked hers with an X. Afterwards, Tom added an unusual touch to the festivities, insisting that the wedding party stop by the butchery so that he and his bride could be weighed. Just as if, said one of his mates, they were about to commence a prize fight. Mary tipped the scales at 12 stone 4 pounds, a whole stone heavier than her husband, occasioning hollers of 'Send her out to work, Tom!' and 'Feed him up, Mary!' Then the pair was tin-kettled all the way to their new home, a slab-and-bark hut set back in the paddocks between Baylis Street and the river, about ten minutes' walk from the shop.

When they first moved in just after Christmas, the hut's miserly bark chimney was peeling away from the wall, so Mary built a new one. It seems that her bricklayer father had lived just long enough to pass on the rudiments of his trade. Tom got hold of a couple of hundred misshapen bricks and she puddled up some clay in a washtub for the mortar. The chimney had turned out thick-set, like Mary herself, and

Fitzmaurice Street, Wagga Wagga. The verandah at the far left belonged to the Australian Hotel

not much above her height, but it drew well and that was no small blessing when you lived in a one-roomed hut with no windows. Tom named the hut 'Castro Villa'.

If people observed a difference in Tom Castro after his marriage, it was that he was cleaner. Mary made sure he had a change of clothes at least twice a week and, because she took in other people's washing, there was always a tub of leftover rinse water waiting for him to scrub himself down when he came in from work. She even bought him a comb. Tom's new life seemed to suit him. He started work at dawn most days, so he was free by midday to come home for dinner, followed by a nap with Mary and the baby. Mid-afternoon, he'd return to the shop to do the accounts and kill the next day's meat. He was still a regular drinker, now at the Prince of Wales in Fitzmaurice Street, handy to the shop. And Tom and Mary were both well known around the unlicensed grog-shanties in their neighbourhood.

The rest of his time Tom spent mucking about with horses. If there was one constant in his life in Australia, it was horses. He'd been whole weeks in the saddle when he was stock-riding, and long days on the mail-run. He'd even run-in brumbies for a while. These days, a good half of his pub talk centred on horseflesh, often ending up in a bet or a race, if not an argument. He was drawn to horse sales and race meetings, and he seemed to thrive on the haggling, the speculation, the deals. His own mount just now was a stringy, disappointed bay mare named Dolly. They were a mismatched pair, he and Dolly; but then, Tom Castro never looked quite right on any horse.

There were any number of horse-fanciers in Tom's circle of acquaintance: farriers, saddlers, feed-merchants, auctioneers, wheelwrights, and stockmen who came into town from outlying stations, or passed through on their way to and from the markets to the south. Tom was familiar with most of the stockmen, as well as the stations they worked on. He'd ridden stock on some of those stations himself, and at different times he'd bought stock from just about all of them, squatters' runs and smallholdings alike. Robert Higgins, Tom's master, was a squatter as well as a publican, owning a cattle station about a hundred miles down the Murrumbidgee. On a couple of occasions, he'd had Tom drove a mob of cattle to market in Melbourne—perhaps he sensed his slaughterman's itchy feet. When Higgins approached him to do the same in July 1865, though, Tom knocked the offer back. It didn't suit him to leave Wagga just then. But he knew the right man for the job.

Dick Slate was a drinking mate of his and a useful fellow to know, being, as Tom put it, 'open to do any odd job.' Sometimes he helped out at the slaughteryard, other times he drove the delivery cart or brought in beasts for killing. Slate headed off at the end of July to ride with a mob to Melbourne.

When he arrived back in Wagga a fortnight later, Slate brought with him a copy of a Melbourne newspaper, the *Australasian*, dated 5 August 1865. There was something in it that he was pretty sure would interest Tom Castro. Tom was lounging on a stump outside Castro Villa, enjoying a pipe, when Slate called by at about eleven on Sunday morning.

'You're up early,' he greeted Tom, swinging down from his splotchy grey nag.

'Just finished breakfast,' Tom puffed. 'How's Melbourne?'

Dick snorted with disdain. 'The same. Got something here though that'll interest you,' and he pulled the folded newspaper from his coat pocket. 'What do you reckon about that?' He handed the paper to Tom and tapped at a block of text on the front page.

A Handsome REWARD will be given to any person who can furnish such information as will discover the fate of ROGER CHARLES TICHBORNE. He sailed from the Port of Rio Janiero on the 20th of April, 1854, in the ship La Bella, and has never been heard of since; but a report reached England to the effect that a portion of the crew and passengers of a vessel of that name was picked up by a vessel bound to Australia, Melbourne, it is believed. It is not known whether the said Roger Charles Tichborne was amongst the drowned or saved. He would at the present time be about 32 years of age; is of a delicate constitution, rather tall, with very light brown hair and blue eyes. Mr Tichborne is the son of Sir James Tichborne, Bart. (now deceased) and is heir to all his estates. The advertiser is instructed to state that a most liberal REWARD will be given for any information that may definitely point out his fate. All replies to be addressed to Mr Arthur Cubitt, Missing Friends Office, Bridge-street, Sydney, New South Wales.

TWO

TEESH

THE Dowager Lady Henriette Tichborne had ever regarded her son's apparent loss at sea less as a tragedy than a vexation. All the evidence pointed to the *Bella* having sunk with no survivors, but she still preferred to believe, eleven years after the event, that Roger was hiding somewhere. And it was not an unreasonable suspicion, for the Dowager Lady Tichborne was just the kind of mother a son might feign death to escape from.

When she married Roger's father in 1827, Henriette was a girl of remarkable beauty: petite, dark-eyed, vivacious. The illegitimate daughter of an English gentleman and a Frenchwoman of (it was said) royal lineage, she had been raised in Paris. A brief sojourn with her father's family in Wiltshire had the desired result of Henriette's forming a match with an Englishman, James Tichborne. Perhaps the Tichbornes disapproved of the marriage, perhaps not; but from the outset Henriette bore a rancorous hatred towards her husband's family.

James was a younger son of an old Hampshire family. His eldest brother, Sir Henry, was the present incumbent of the Tichborne baronetcy.* As things stood, though, there seemed little chance of the title ever falling to James. True, Henry had managed to produce only a string of daughters (worthless in terms of the baronetcy) but

---

* A baronetcy is the lowest rank of hereditary title in Britain. Although he garnishes his name with the title 'Sir' and the appendage 'Bart.', a baronet is an elevated commoner, not a member of the peerage.

Henriette Tichborne in widow's weeds, c.1865

his brother Edward, two years older than James, came next in line. Not long married, Edward was as yet without issue, but any son of his would inherit the baronetcy ahead of James.

James' status as a younger son had its drawbacks: namely, narrow prospects and a limited income. But there were benefits, too—the freedom, for example, to make an unwise marriage. A tall, stoutish, sociable man, well-travelled and more than twice Henriette's age (she was just twenty when they married, he was forty-three), James Tichborne was too besotted to sense the trouble ahead. For the fascinating, flighty beauty turned out to be a tartar. At her insistence they made their life in Paris, where her demands took centre stage and James, cut adrift from his old haunts and associations, turned too much to drinking. Asthma, as well as inclination, made Henriette succumb to the life of a hothouse flower, swanning about their stuffy apartment on Rue St Honoré in a dirty old plaid dressing-gown with a hanky tied around her head. Both husband and wife had tempers— hers sniping, histrionic, accusatory; his explosive and (with Henriette, at least) quickly repentant—to which they gave full throttle. It was a bitter, shipwrecked kind of marriage.

Roger Tichborne joined the ménage in 1829. After him came two sisters who died young and a brother, Alfred, born in 1839. Roger grew up a coddled, sickly child. He suffered, like his mother, from asthma and was made to wear a dried pea inserted in an open, suppu- rating wound (called an 'issue') on his upper arm. It was an antiquated remedy even then, meant to act as an escape valve for the body's ill humours. In Roger's case it seemed to have no such effect, but he endured the irritation for six years before the pea was removed and the wound let heal. Both Roger's parents were Catholics, Henriette so devout that, in homage to 'our Blessed Lady', she dressed her elder son in a blue and white frock (called a *voue*) until he was twelve. At his mother's insistence, and against his father's wishes, he was raised as a French boy and schooled by a series of inept tutors. Roger Tichborne reached the age of sixteen ill-educated, friendless and barely able to speak a word of English.

In 1845 that all changed. Sir Henry Tichborne died and Edward stepped into the baronetcy. He still had no son, however, and his wife was past the age for child-bearing. James was next in line, not just for the title but for the fortune that went with it. In addition to the Tichborne properties in Hampshire, there were the Doughty estates, inherited by Edward from a distant relative some twenty years earlier. It was from the properties of the Doughty estates—many of them in the better parts of London—that the Tichborne family derived most of its considerable wealth. As a condition of inheritance, Edward had agreed to adopt the name Doughty, so that he now bore the name Doughty-Tichborne, as would all future heirs—including Roger. He was, however, generally known as Sir Edward Doughty.

James Tichborne looked at his son and wondered how on earth to prepare this foppish, mummsied Parisian boy for his future role as the master of Tichborne Park, to ride with the Hampshire Hounds and fit in at the Alfred Club—to be any sort of Englishman, come to that. He would require some degree of schooling, for a start, preferably in England. James wrote to Henriette's father, Henry Seymour, as an ally:

> the time appears to me as well as to others to be now arrived when it is absolutely necessary that he should go to school. This plan as you may suppose meets with the most violent & determined opposition from Henriette, & she abuses me with tears in the most violent manner possible, accuses me of being a Tyrant & wishing to be the death of the child. I have only to add that it will be the ruin of Roger if he remains with her any longer as she would render him totally unfit ever to go to school. The grand object she seems to aim at is to make a french man of Roger, this believe me I neither can or ever will submit to.

A plan was hatched. On the pretext of taking Roger to visit his grandfather in Wiltshire, James hustled the boy out of his mother's grasp and deposited him at Stonyhurst, a Jesuit school in Lancashire. Henriette was wild with rage. Her 'violence of temper' was such, James confided to his father-in-law, that 'I see all the hopes of my future happiness blighted & gone for ever.'

Henriette blamed her Tichborne in-laws for Roger's 'abduction' and she fired off letters around the family that boiled with vitriol. Something along the same lines must have reached the rector at Stonyhurst, as Roger himself wrote (in French) to rebuke his mother for her 'most unqualified indiscretion' in exposing 'the dissensions which exist between you and my family (as alleged by you)':

> it proves that you cannot keep family secrets, which is of the utmost importance to preserve the honour and character of any family. There is no end to what you say against my Uncles and Aunts. But it has always been unfortunate that you should fancy a number of things which have never existed, and which have only made you unhappy.

Plainly, Roger sided with his father—and realised that *he* was well out of it. Had Henriette but realised it, she had already lost her son.

At Stonyhurst, Roger was placed with the 'philosophers', a group of senior students for whom the college acted as a finishing school. He skimmed Latin, the French horn, mathematics, drawing and the sciences. But his chief object was to learn English, which he did pretty well, judging from his Stonyhurst correspondence. His letters reveal a young man growing in confidence and possessing a strong sense of propriety.

Roger's chief and most intimate correspondent during his time at Stonyhurst and afterwards was his aunt, Sir Edward's wife, Lady Katherine Doughty. Partially paralysed, Sir Edward was unable to write, so that it was Lady Doughty who took on the task of grooming Roger for the baronetcy and of providing him with the guidance and judgment, and even affection, that his own parents were ill-equipped to give. With them, he maintained a dutiful correspondence, but he was impatient of their squabbling self-absorption, and of his mother's demands. James fell out with the Doughtys in 1846 when they refused admittance to his abusive wife at Tichborne. After that, Roger saw his father only once—and his mother not at all—until after he finished his schooling.

During his three years at Stonyhurst, Roger spent his long summer vacations mostly with the Doughtys at Tichborne Park. Before his

Tichborne House and the River Itchen, where Roger failed to catch a single fish

first vacation a new wing was added to the rear of Tichborne House, with two rooms specially for the prospective heir. These he kept in such a state that Lady Doughty called them 'Stinkumalee' and joked about having them fumigated when he returned to school. She was less tolerant of his poor personal hygiene. 'Do pray be more particular about your dress and cleanly appearance,' she wrote. 'I know you despise the opinions of the world, but indeed you owe it to your family.'

Concerned not just for his mortal progress but for his 'eternal destiny', Lady Doughty exhorted Roger to confide in her, then castigated him for the slightest moral lapse. Nonetheless, he seems to have submitted to her probing with patience and candour. When she deplored the 'bad books' he read (racy French novels by Paul de Kock), he countered that she ought not condemn them on hearsay alone. So she searched out a pile of de Kocks he'd left behind in Stinkumalee, looked them over—then burnt them. It was rare, though, for Roger to defend himself. He seems to have recognised Lady

Doughty's remonstrations for what they were—an expression of love—though the time would come when he grew tired of her moralistic bludgeoning.

Roger left Stonyhurst at the end of summer term, 1848. Although, in writing, he could almost pass as English, in person he was still very much a Frenchman. He spoke with a pronounced accent, and his garbled idiom gave the impression 'that he thought in French and translated it into very bad English.' Three years outside of the Paris apartment had done nothing to flesh him out. He was still thin—cadaverously so, like his mother. In fact, one of his cousins called him 'an ugly likeness of his mother.' He had dark, lank hair that straggled over his face until he flicked it back with a jerk of his head. In conversation, he was animated and excitable, lapsing in and out of French, hands gesturing, thick eyebrows darting. In repose, he wore an expression that was melancholy, even pained—again, very like his mother's, it was agreed, only 'nicer…more kind.' A new acquaintance described it as 'a mixed expression of melancholy surprise and alarm, like a wild animal just caught.' His eyes were either grey-blue or the colour of forget-me-nots (depending on their observer's whim), above an ugly nose, slightly uptilted with open nostrils. From there down he was all narrowness: long chin and neck, champagne-bottle shoulders, concave chest and hips that were hardly there. He walked 'like a Frenchman' in short, quick steps, feet turned outwards, looking 'as if hung on wires.'

Roger wanted to travel to India when he left Stonyhurst. A career with the East India Company appealed to him, but his father forbade it and Roger was bound to comply with his wishes until he was twenty-one. In the end, it was decided that Roger should join the army. This meant a commission had to be bought and it was settled that he would join a cavalry regiment, the 6th Dragoon Guards, or Carabineers. After a brief visit to Paris bearing a case of his *maman*'s favourite Scotch marmalade, Roger returned home to Tichborne, ostensibly to study for the army entrance exam. In fact, the intervening months were spent bettering his acquaintance with the gentlemanly outdoors.

In the course of his country-house vacations he had developed a passion for hunting and field sports. He had his own horses and hounds, as well as the run of his Uncle Edward's gun-room, with the contents of which he made himself a hazard to the Tichborne tenantry. He wasted hours and ammunition shooting at random with a rifle (he said he was shooting at rooks), too close to the house for its inhabitants' comfort, and once he fired a shotgun at the door of a barn when a man was threshing inside. Brand, the Tichborne gamekeeper (Roger called him 'Bwand'), despaired of his carelessness with firearms. Nor was any cat safe with Roger and his dogs at large. For his amusement, he bought numbers of cats and tracked them on the downs around Tichborne. The dogs took this as a licence to menace any cat they should meet. Lady Doughty wrote to Roger after he left for the army: 'Brand tells me your dogs are such cat killers that he gets into great scrapes with old ladies especially if ever he walks them without a muzzle.' Others complained that Roger spoilt the fishing at Tichborne. Somehow, in spite of the most alluring flies, he never managed to catch a fish. He was observed to carry a chisel in his fishing kit.

He scraped through the army exam in July 1849 and joined his unit, the Carabineers' F-troop, on detachment duty in Dublin soon after. All were agreed that Cornet Tichborne was entirely the wrong make of man for the army.* There was the way he looked, to start with. His hips wouldn't hold up his sword-belt, his epaulettes fell down his shoulders and his calves were so slim that his boots slipped off. One of the soldiers in his command recalled that Cornet Tichborne's hair 'laid on his head just the same as a bundle of carrots.'

---

* A cornet (properly *cornet-à-piston*) was the lowest rank of commissioned officer in the cavalry.

No amount of drilling, it seemed, could make Roger carry himself like a soldier. Long hours on the parade ground made some improvement in the deportment of his upper body—gave him at least the illusion of a chest—but still he marched like a man whose legs 'did not belong to him.' His first commanding officer remarked of Roger's gait: 'he was what we would call of a horse, a bad goer.' On horseback, too, he was all over the place. While his seat was good enough for the hunting field, he could never master his mount sufficiently to ride well as a soldier. Military drill was all about maximum control with minimal effort. As his instructor explained: 'You should do the whole riding, just managing the rein with the little finger and the pressure of the leg.' Roger, in spite of extra drills and riding lessons, was a heavy-handed horseman.

Nor was he much better at handling the troops. His 'mild, little' voice, when he gave the word of command, came out as a high-pitched squeak and he had extreme difficulty in pronouncing the word 'attention' on parade. As a Frenchman, he sounded the '-tion' phonetically. He made a note in his memorandum book to remind himself that 'Ion and tion are pronounced—shun.' His fellow officers, mimicking his accent, called him Teesh. He was a perfect target for practical jokes. As a welcome to the regiment, his snuff was emptied into his teapot and many a morning he woke to find his shirts stuffed in the coal-box. Of course, it wasn't only Roger: with no war on, nor the prospect of one, practical joking was one of the chief features of army life. 'Sometimes we used to see a chest of drawers thrown out of windows,' recalled one carabineer, 'and we never bothered ourselves about it except they threw it on us, you know.'

By and large, Roger took the ragging, as it was meant, in good humour. There came a time, though, when certain of the officers noticed how Roger avoided another feature of army life—namely, the company of 'ladies of a certain character.' Next thing he knew, there was a 'low woman' shut in his cupboard and his brother officers were shoving tipsy camp-followers—as many as ten at a time—into his room as he prepared for bed. Roger remonstrated forcibly with his tormentors and, on the third such occasion, one of them asked, amid the scuffle, 'Do you truly object, on religious grounds?' 'Yes,' replied Roger, indicating a gold cross visible at the neck of his night-shirt. Next time, they put a donkey in his bed.

During his long stay at Tichborne, he had grown close to his uncle's estate steward, Vincent Gosford, whose office lay directly below Roger's rooms. Gosford was, in effect, manager of the Tichborne and Doughty estates and had been with Sir Edward since his succession. One suspects that Lady Doughty had recruited Gosford to share in the task of grooming her nephew. Fifteen years or more Roger's senior, and married, Gosford seems nonetheless to have extended a warm hand of friendship to the lad. He initiated him into some of the mysteries of the Tichborne finances, about which Gosford knew (and cared) far more than did any member of the family. Roger's letters to Gosford from Dublin demonstrate a keen sense of steward-ship over the family possessions. His uncle and father were in favour of selling some of their land holdings for a quick cash return; but Roger (via Gosford) used his authority to frustrate their plans, citing the entitlements of his future heirs. Roger valued Gosford more as a friend, though, than for his business advice. Gosford was the only person to whom he could sling off at Lady Doughty: 'She mentioned that she was going to the Queen's Drawing-room, and expressed a great wish that I should be with her. I am sure that if ever I thanked heaven for something it is at not having been able to go.'

In his darker moments too he confided in Gosford. Near the end of 1849, he wrote: 'I was thinking to myself that perhaps in some years hence I shall retire from the vanities of the world, and settle a mithantrop as a true Phylosopher.' Between chasing prostitutes from his bedroom and each day's fresh humiliation on the parade ground, Roger had found fortitude in Molière's *The Misanthrope* and

Chateaubriand's *René*. In his pocket journal, amid jottings about tailors and tobacco brands, he recorded this reflection:

> Happy the life of René he knew how to take his sorrows with courage, keep them to himself, retire from all his friends to be more at liberty to think about his sorrows and misfortunes, and bury them in himself. I admire that man for his courage, that is to say, to have the courage to carry those sorrows to the grave which drove him to Solitude.

THREE

BURN AFTER READING

ROGER was home at Tichborne for Christmas 1849 and celebrated his coming-of-age a fortnight later with a ball for the tenants and servants. At last he made the acquaintance of Sir Edward and Lady Doughty's daughter, his cousin Katherine, who had been away till now at convent school. Kattie was just sixteen and had never heard of a misanthrope. Who better to enlighten her than her cousin? His Byronic demeanour was just the thing to captivate a fresh-plucked convent girl, and in no time the beginnings of an 'attachment' were formed. Roger was fool enough to tell his aunt, before he returned to Ireland, of his affection for Kattie, hoping that she would approve. Lady Doughty was torn. She was prodigiously fond of Roger and wanted to see him happy—but not with her daughter. Thanks to their years of frank correspondence, she knew his flaws and self-doubts better than behoved a prospective mother-in-law and wrote to him on his return to Ireland:

> I ask you to reflect and think if a parent could be justified…in encouraging the affections of a person for their child who lives in determined opposition to the practice of their religion, who defies Almighty God, even in his holy Temple by not praying or even reading other works at the same time, and drowns thoughts of the future in drink and offends Almighty God by profane language. Could a young innocent being, full of religious feeling, be encouraged to risk her happiness in this life and, possibly, in the next by being united to such a man?

He commenced his reply submissively enough—'I am at present taking care of myself, a thing which I have never done before in my life…I hope, with the help of God, to become, before long, what you wish to see me.' But her specific charges he met with rather more spirit:

> I must say that I don't drink as much as you think, and even so I don't drink as much now as I used to do formerly, and besides that, in a moral point of view, I am very steady. It is perhaps surprising but it is the truth, and moreover I don't read profane books in Chapel, and moreover I never frequent loose society.

By the same mail, he sent to Vincent Gosford for a parcel of de Kock novels, for reading on the six and a half days each week not spent in chapel. Gosford shared Lady Doughty's apprehensions about her nephew's fitness as a suitor. 'His character was not formed,' he would later explain, 'his habits not precisely those which one would have liked to see in the husband of Miss Doughty.' He added, significantly, 'I felt more with Lady Doughty than with Roger.' That last would have come as a surprise to Roger. He poured out his heart in his letters to Gosford, thinking him an ally.

Roger would periodically write to his aunt that he had given up drinking spirits, sometimes even that he had abjured drinking altogether, for the sake of his marriage prospects. Each such resolution was followed, a short time later, by the admission of a significant lapse. For instance, after a couple of idle weeks quartered at Waterford on the Irish south coast, he wrote: 'We did not know what to do with ourselves all day long, so we used to drink very hard, only for the sake of spending the time.' Why did he have to tell his aunt, when it could only harm his cause? Was he baiting her, or was he just too honest for his own good?

In the spring of 1850, he was able to inform her that he had cut his tobacco consumption to one stick a week. What he didn't tell her was that the reduction had been ordered by the army surgeon. Roger was much addicted to pipe smoking—had been since his idle days under a tutor in Paris, when the café and billiard hall had been his classroom. At Stonyhurst, he'd smoked so furiously that the priests gave up trying to enforce the no-smoking rule in his case. He insisted, anyway, that his pipe smoking was medicinal—that it eased his asthma. Even among the Carabineers, Roger's tobacco intake was the stuff of legends, and he used to entertain the officer's mess with a parlour trick involving a house-fly, a glass tumbler and a lungful of pipe smoke. He fed his habit from a capacious sea-trunk stacked with sticks of very strong cavendish. But when his regiment was posted to Cahir, in rural Tipperary, his old 'cure' began to fail him. A near-fatal asthma attack put him on the sick list for more than a month and his commanding officer confiscated Roger's cavendish stash, rationing him to the aforementioned one stick a week.

Illness and the Carabineers' generous peace-time leave entitlements meant that Roger spent a good deal of time at home during 1850–51. He and Kattie grew more confirmed in their preference for one another, although Lady Doughty made sure Roger understood that he had no claim on her daughter's affections. She was free to form a more suitable attachment, should one present itself. Kattie appeared to acquiesce in her mother's wishes—submitting to the ballroom attentions of jolly young toffs—while secretly she vowed loyalty to Roger. Meanwhile, Sir Edward, incapacitated and grouchy, was kept in the dark about the uncousinly feeling between the pair.

When Roger came home for Christmas 1851, he brought news that his regiment was to be posted to India within a year. This was the reason he'd agreed to join the army in the first place. Travel. Adventure. Wild sport. For years, he'd relished tales of jungle exploration, big-game hunting, voyages round the Horn, all that. Those were tigers, not rooks, he'd been shooting at in the garden at Tichborne. India! But what about Kattie?

A week after his twenty-third birthday, in January 1852, Roger sought out Sir Edward in the library at Tichborne and asked his permission to marry Kattie. The interview was not a success. Sir Edward not only refused to consent, but forbade Roger to see his cousin again. Distraught, Roger bolted to his room to pack his bags, but slumped instead, head in hands. 'The idea,' he later wrote to Kattie, 'that I was obliged to leave the next day and not see you again, perhaps for years, was near bursting my heart.' Next thing, his aunt came softly knocking. Kattie wished to see him before he left. Late that night, after they parted, he wrote to her:

> I promise to my own dearest K. my word of honour that I will be back in england if she is not married or engaged towards the end of autumn of 1854 or in the month of January, 1855. If she is so engaged I shall remain in India 10 or 15 years in making wishes for her happiness.

Before the month was out, though, he was back at Tichborne. His uncle's health had taken a critical turn and Kattie had persuaded her weakened father to reconsider Roger's proposal. Sir Edward now agreed that the pair might marry, on certain conditions: that they wait three years (until Kattie was twenty-one), and that they obtain a dispensation from the Catholic Church, which frowned on first-cousin marriages. Lady Doughty reiterated that Kattie must remain free to receive other suitors. Moreover, their 'understanding' must remain a secret so as not to deter said suitors. Roger agreed. On the morning before he returned to Ireland, he penned a solemn note—a vow, or something like it—concerning his hopes for his and Kattie's future. He showed it to Gosford before sealing it well and entrusting it to his friend's safe-keeping.

In preparation for India, his regiment was to be posted to its headquarters in Canterbury. Roger narrowly escaped being rejected for foreign service. Not only had his health been increasingly bad (not just asthma: there was some suggestion of alcoholic poisoning or an ulcer), but his parents had written to his commanding officer urging that their son not be posted abroad. 'His poor father and I wished it,' Henriette would later write. 'He was still very delicate.' But Roger declared his determination to go and the medical inspection found him fit, even though, according to a fellow Carabineer, 'the slightest thing you had the matter with you, you were rejected by the doctor.' Under no circumstances would Roger accede to his parents' wishes—in this or in anything. When James urged him to leave the army and return to Paris, Roger wrote to Gosford: 'I know for myself (and I speak from experience) that the farther we are from each other the better it is for our mutual happiness.' A letter from Lady Doughty around this time also hinted at a rift between father and son. She told Roger: 'Your father never could believe you radically bad but…God only knew how he had suffered in mind & prayed for you.'

In spite of Lady Doughty's insistence on secrecy, by the middle of 1852 it was common knowledge in county and London society that Kattie was engaged to Roger Tichborne. Lady Doughty was furious. They'd spent the season in London and she'd done all she could to launch Kattie on the marriage market, only to discover that the girl was considered 'spoken for'. She demanded that Roger put an end to the rumours, which he did—though exactly how is unclear. At any rate, Lady Doughty afterwards wrote to thank him for his responsible behaviour. This episode marked a terminal cooling in relations between aunt and nephew. Roger, who so often had marked his candid epistles 'Private—burn after reading', determined to confide in Lady Doughty no more. To Gosford, he wrote: 'For my own part I will have nothing more to do with her in those private and confidential ways.' Thereafter he confined himself with Lady Doughty to safe topics like the weather.

Roger was permitted to pay just one visit to Tichborne after his return to England. Sir Edward, still lingering, had asked to see his nephew. If Roger had hopes of a further relenting, they were not to be realised. His ailing uncle held firm. On 22 June 1852, Roger and Kattie walked together in the grounds for the last time, and he presented her with this pledge, on crested notepaper:

> I make on this day a promise that if I marry my cousin Catherine Doughty this year, or before three years are over at the latest, to build a church or chapel at Tichborne to the Holy Virgin, in thanksgiving for the protection which she has thrown over us, and in praying God that our wishes may be fulfilled.

Soon after, the Carabineers' Indian posting fell through. It looked, for a time, as if they might instead be sent to the Australian diggings, to guard the gold escort wagons; but that too came to nothing. To make matters worse, Roger was laid low by an asthma attack so severe the regimental surgeon warned that another like it would kill him. Confined to barracks, steeped in disappointment, the last thing Roger needed was a visit from his mother. Yet a letter from Paris threatened just that. With Henriette's grudging approval, James was about to bring Alfred, now a robust and lively thirteen-year-old (such a contrast to Roger), to school in England. James planned to stay at Tichborne for a time and Henriette, knowing she was unwelcome there, proposed instead to visit Roger at Canterbury. On learning of her intention, he fired a letter back, affecting a tone of outraged propriety that was at least as impressive as anything his aunt could muster:

> It would be quite impossible for me, if you came to Canterbury to look after you. On all cases it would place you and I in a very false position to see you alone in this part of England and my Father in another. I cannot make out how you ever could think of such a thing. I hope that common sense will induce you to give up all ideas of coming over and that in future you will never think of such an absurd thing.

He ended with a half-hearted promise to visit her in the winter, and Henriette, much stung, remained in Paris. His father, too, wanted to see Roger and had written proposing that they meet at Tichborne. But Roger knew the Doughtys didn't want him there—nor had he any wish to be there (except to lay eyes on Kattie) or to see his father. James' visit was the first real attempt at rapprochement with Sir Edward since their blow-up six years earlier. A renewal of hostilities was on the cards as, from all accounts, James' temper had grown more 'hasty' in recent times. The Doughtys were most anxious to keep from James any knowledge of Roger and Kattie's attachment. According to Gosford, 'He had a most insuperable objection to intermarriage between such near relatives. Nothing would have obtained from Mr James Tichborne his consent.' Moreover, if James sensed that Sir Edward had in any way encouraged the relationship, 'it would have been like throwing oil in the fire. The same house would not have contained them.'

Roger was right to stay away. It transpired that his father already knew about him and Kattie—had done for a year. As expected, he blamed the Doughtys and, when Roger refused to come to Tichborne, raged and drank until he lapsed into smouldering ill-health. For Lady Doughty, it was like living with a landmine. She wrote to Roger on tiptoe: 'your name is seldom mentioned & tho your father is evidently in a very excitable humour, we all go tranquilly & he never speaks to me on any but general subject. These threatenings of blood to the head are certainly to be feared for him.'

Disgusted at the loss of his overseas posting, Roger decided to quit the army. If exile was to be denied him, then solitude would have to suffice. A cottage somewhere for the winter, with good hunting nearby, would suit him nicely. But when he advised Lady Doughty that he planned to find himself a place in Hampshire for the hunting season, she was aghast at his insensitivity. Could he not see that by settling so near his relatives and yet keeping aloof from them (as she insisted he must) he would be 'exposing both you and ourselves to the conjectures of others and making us all the subject of remarks'? Roger stood firm. 'It is fully my intention,' he wrote to Gosford, 'not to be nearer the house than 20 or 30 miles, and that they will hear of me no more at that distance than if I was in South America.' As a compromise, the Doughtys offered him the use of their former home, a respectable distance away in the next county. Roger accepted and, leaving the army at the end of October 1852, he spent his first four months of freedom at Upton, near Poole in Dorsetshire. With no pack of hounds in the neighbourhood, he had to make his own sport. Just a few hundred yards offshore from Upton, in Poole harbour, was a tiny island which, for his amusement, Roger stocked with twenty-five rabbits. Within a day of the rabbits' release, however, the island teemed with poachers and Roger became the talk of the county when he gave chase to a pair of them—first by boat and then on foot, drenched, through the streets of Poole. He'd have caught them, too, he told Gosford, but for the fact that his servant 'had as much idea of rowing as I have of flying.'

Upton was between tenants, but Roger was furnished with all the servants he required. John Moore, his valet, was a former servant of the Doughtys. Lady Doughty herself had recommended him. And there was Martha Fisher, known as 'the pretty laundress from Bath'. Roger used to gossip with her and the kitchen staff in the pantry and he tipped her handsomely on one occasion. She was surprised at the character of some of his launderables: shirts in candy stripes or patterned with stags, dogs' heads, capering Punches, even monkeys. Shirts like that, she thought, were 'an uncommon thing for gentlemen to have on.' What's more, he had handkerchiefs to match.

Shooting rabbits on an island the size of a tea-tray soon lost its thrill for Roger. Bigger islands and bigger beasts beckoned. Come spring, he would sail for South America. His books on the wild sports of Brazil and Peru had so convinced him there could be 'no sport equal to catching and riding wild horses' that he could barely wait to get his hands on a lasso. His parents objected when told of his plans, even though they must have known that they were wasting their breath. Henriette pulled out all the stops, exhorting him to think of *her* if he cared nothing for his own health. No objection could more surely have firmed his resolve. His mother was right, though, to be concerned about his health. The army surgeon had advised Roger, upon his discharge, that he must seek out a warmer climate or risk a fatal recurrence of his old complaint. He was still harbouring a bad cough; there was even a suspicion of consumption. He'd cut back on his pipe smoking, substituting for the trunk of cavendish a canister of Lundy Foot snuff.

Gosford joined him at Upton for a few days in February 1853 and Roger, keen to show off his bachelor's life, kept his friend up late, drinking brandy and water, smoking cigars, and playing at tuppenny toss and 'that horse-racing game.' He was the kind of drunk who liked to sing, and at two o'clock in the morning he launched into 'Come with Me to Fairy Land' (with its chorus that began 'I called for some rumpunch…') and 'We Won't Come Home til Morning'— songs, said Gosford, that he was 'fond of putting into practice.' They talked a little business, too. There was the matter of Hermitage Farm, not far from Tichborne, which Gosford believed would be a desirable addition to the estates. Gosford would talk over such a proposition with Roger before he would raise it with Sir Edward, let alone James Tichborne. Roger, he said, 'had thoroughly mastered the state of the family settlements' and 'knew ten times as much about them as his father ever did.'

Gosford also considered Roger 'a most peculiar young man' for his scrupulous management of his personal finances. He had a taste for small luxuries, as befitted his position, but was not extravagant and was particular about paying his debts. Like Gosford, he mistrusted lawyers in general and the Tichborne family solicitor, Edward Hopkins, in particular. Roger's will had to be finalised before he left for South America and he valued Gosford's advice on that score, since he was not inclined to rely on Hopkins for anything beyond the formalities.

From Tichborne, Gosford brought a letter from Lady Doughty and the news that Kattie was away from home, visiting her mother's family. The letter was an invitation—or, rather, a plea—to Roger to visit Tichborne before he left the country. Sir Edward was now very close to death, Lady Doughty wrote, and this would be Roger's last chance to see him alive. Roger sent his reply with Gosford: he regretted that his remaining time in England would not allow the pleasure, etcetera. Yet on his way to Southampton a week later, he detoured to Alresford, less than five miles from Tichborne Park, to see Hopkins about his will.

The truth was that Roger was thoroughly sick of the Doughtys: not just Sir Edward and Lady Doughty, but Kattie as well. After all, she was as spinelessly obedient to her parents' wishes as if she were nine rather than nineteen. It was her passivity that had drawn him to her in the first place, but not any more. She'd played her passive part, hadn't she, in her mother's desperate stratagems to find her a better husband than him? And, in spite of his pleadings, had she ever favoured him with a letter? Not once. 'I should never have thought of writing to him,' she said later. 'I knew my father and mother did not wish us to correspond.'

A brief, battle-racked visit to his parents in Paris, and Roger was away. He sailed from Le Havre on 1 March 1853, aboard *La Pauline* bound for Valparaiso in Chile. His mother, having exhausted her repertoire of emotional blackmail, wrote to her brother, Henry Seymour, a few days after Roger sailed:

> I am so unhappy about our dear Roger's departure that really I have not the courage for anything…you have no idea of my constant anxiety I am not fit for anything else but thinking over the perils of the sea certainly he did not conceive how very

unhappy his journey made us, or else he would not have undertaken it, he means to remain 18 months, and I really think that I can not have any peace or happiness, during all that time…Poor dear Roger. God may save him and bring him back to us.

FOUR

FOR THE SAKE OF KNOWING THE WORLD

TRAVELLING with Roger was his valet, John Moore, whose journal recorded the tedium of the voyage, broken only by the mysterious disappearance, one day in early April, of the ship's entire supply of cabbages. Roger suffered from chilblains and occupied himself, as usual, by shooting at things: porpoises, birds, even a floating bottle. When he tried to catch an albatross with a fishing rod, he ended up with the hook through his eyelid. He fancied himself as a naturalist and had half-learnt the craft of taxidermy from a book before he left, using rooks and rabbits for practice. Now he preserved the skins of the sea-birds he shot (or preserved them 'after a fashion', said Moore) to send back home for stuffing.

La Pauline reached Valparaiso in June and Roger set off immediately for Santiago. There a letter informed him that Sir Edward had died on 5 March, just four days after Roger's departure. His letter of condolence to Lady Doughty was short on sympathy and plainly expressed his relief at having escaped in the nick of time:

> I am not as you are perhaps aware of on very good terms with the whole of my family. All the causes of that disunion I know perfectly…All these different reasons make me thank Heaven that I was quite out of the way at my Uncle's last moments…It would have been quite impossible for me to have been able to keep my temper in the middle of all the different parties which exist in the different branches of the family. It would have been

moreover impossible to have put up with my Father and Mother's character.

Roger also wrote to Hopkins, the solicitor, asking that his allowance be increased, now that he was next in line for the baronetcy.

Moore was incapacitated by 'chest spasms' in Santiago, so that, after ten days' sightseeing and provisioning, Roger returned to Valparaiso without him. He'd found himself a new servant—a Spanish-speaking hotel waiter—and was none too sorry to leave Moore behind. Roger had come to think of him as Lady Doughty's spy. When Moore asked Roger what his relatives would think of his setting off into the wilds of South America with a servant unknown to them, he retorted: 'I wish they would care less for me and not interfere in my private affairs; it is I who pay, is it not?' For his part, Moore was not exactly sorry to see the back of Roger, since he had no wish 'to follow him in his wild schemes, which he will find, much to his cost, are wild indeed...But,' he wrote to Gosford, 'his present trip will, I believe, teach him a lesson, and prevent him taking a more foolish one.'

Roger's 'present trip' took him to Arica, near Chile's border with Peru, onwards to Lima and thence to Quito in Ecuador, with periodic plunges into the interior. Arriving back in Santiago on New Year's Day 1854, he found that Moore had set himself up selling Brandreth's Pills and cloudy ginger beer in a shop opposite the Hotel Inglese. Moore was astonished at the appearance Roger presented: 'he was covered with dust and dirt, and had a broken nose, which he said was done by riding a horse that no one else could ride in Valparaiso; he had on a bright, sailor's shiny hat, pea-jacket, and dirty yellow breeches of a yellow ochre colour, and long boots.'

Roger had no servant or luggage with him and seemed not to care when, or if, they turned up. At the urging of the hotel landlord, he took a bath, only to emerge dressed in the same decrepit outfit. He refused Moore's offer of fresh clothes, saying, 'Oh, I don't mind these ones.' Roger Tichborne had gone native. His staple diet was the *charqui an garbanzos*, a purgative dish of dried beef, beans and chillies. He'd cultivated a thin sniffle of a moustache (barely discernible under the dirt) so that he might better emulate the Byronic credo: 'I smoke, and stare at mountains, and twirl my mustachios very independently.' A ghostly wisp of fluff on the chin completed Roger's barbate credentials.

He stayed in Santiago for a fortnight, exploring the near countryside on restive horses and carousing by night at the Hotel Inglese.

Roger Tichborne at Santiago, January 1854

Among his new acquaintances was Thomas Helsby, an expatriate Englishman, who would later recall how ridiculous Roger looked when he returned from a morning's ride with a live guanaco (a wild relative of the llama) slung across his saddle. It was not just, said Helsby, that a pet guanaco was unheard of in Santiago; but the native horsemen were too proud to be seen carrying so much as a small parcel, let alone a struggling ruminant mounted on the pommel like a paramour. Helsby had a daguerreotype studio and, at Moore's urging, Roger agreed to have his portrait taken before he left Santiago. Moore saw to it that he was suitably spruced up, in light Kerseymere pants and waistcoat, dark frockcoat, and a spotted neckerchief worn bowtie fashion—although Roger refused to be parted from his lacquered straw sailor's hat and it was only Mrs Helsby's concern for the carpet and Mr Helsby's for his exposure that prevented the guanaco from appearing in the photograph as well. Roger posed for two portraits that day, the first with his waistcoat, the second without. On leaving Santiago, he asked Moore to send one portrait each to his mother and his aunt, and to take care of his guanaco. The portraits were sent, but the guanaco would fret and die on its tether outside Moore's shop. Moore wrote to Lady Doughty, informing her of her nephew's movements and complaining about a bill he'd left unpaid. 'Mr T. seems to be enjoying himself after a fashion,' he told her, 'and does not seem disposed to return to England for some time yet to come.'

From Santiago, Roger set off eastward, first over the treacherous Cordilleras to Mendoza and then across the Pampas, the vast plains that lie in the rain shadow of the mountains. With him went a string of pack mules, two muleteers and his latest servant, Jules Barraut. He was seven days making the crossing to Mendoza and on the second night, Moore heard of a severe storm in the mountains, with snow falling on the higher peaks. 'Mr T. would meet with much of it,' he told Lady Doughty, adding with a touch of spite, 'but it would only add interest to the crossing of the Cordilleras.'

Roger emerged at Buenos Aires in mid-February 1854, bearing tales of mules lost down mountain ravines, a painful case of saddle-rash and a gaucho outfit. The latter he sent home to Gosford for safe-keeping:

> There is everything complete, from the pure massive silver spurs to the saddle, bridle, saddle cloths, the dress for myself, in fact everything complete. I am very anxious that you should keep these articles locked up in your house, without saying a word about them to anybody till my return to England.

In the same crate he sent a mummified monkey from 'the tomb of the last of the Incas' and a 'collection of skins and very fine birds' which arrived in an appalling state. They were, said Gosford, 'very badly prepared' and he had to burn the lot of them.

Waiting for Roger at Buenos Aires was a letter from his mother, brimming with the usual puff and rancour. It ran to four pages: the first two carping on about a son's duties towards his mother, the remainder 'filled up with all kinds of imaginary fears, and a list of accidents, illness and sickness of every description which,' Roger admonished her, 'are quite unknown to any body but yourself.'

Sir James and Lady Tichborne were newly installed at Tichborne Park. Roger wrote to Gosford:

> I suppose that by this time you must have heard something about those Italian Princesses whom my mother is so anxious that I should choose one to marry. I have seen and known too well what is married life so as not to go and do the [...] to marry myself. I have done certainly a great many foolish things in my life but I hope to keep clear from that one at any rate.

Lady Tichborne was, to say the least, unhappy at leaving Paris. James felt the brunt of her displeasure and Gosford kept out of her way, knowing that she bore him (an evil agent of the Doughtys, or so she had long imagined) a particular animosity. Roger sympathised. His mother's 'disagreeable' character must, he wrote, 'make it a kind of hell for my father and every body in or about the house.' It was a hell Roger wanted no part of, and he instructed Gosford: 'It would be desirable in case my father should die during the time I am travelling to ensure her so much per year to live where she liked except at Tichborne: as it would be quite impossible for me to put up with her character.'

How long did he intend to keep travelling? Writing from Montevideo in March, he told Lady Doughty: 'I am very fond of the kind of life which I am leading, and as my health has always been very good it is not likely that I shall give it up in a hurry.' Actually, he was much bothered by rheumatism by the time he reached Rio de Janeiro a month later, and was ready to put South America behind him. Soon after landing at Rio, he heard that the *Bella* would sail for New York next day and he determined to go with her. However, a passport was required and, when he applied at the police office, Roger was told he must wait several days. He had resigned himself to taking a later ship when he chanced to meet the captain of the *Bella* in the billiard room of the Hotel de la Bourse. The ship's departure had been delayed and, what was more, Captain Birkett told him as the mood grew convivial, Roger need not wait for a passport. An arrangement was made.

Roger's servant, Barraut, sent his master's luggage on board the *Bella* early the next morning. Roger himself boarded soon after and Barraut, who was not going on to New York, visited him twice in the course of the day, bringing various items he had overlooked—a packet of dates, a hand-mirror, a jar of goose grease and a chisel. The *Bella* sailed at 6 a.m. on Thursday, 20 April 1854, with a crew of forty and Roger Tichborne her only passenger. Police delivered his passport to his hotel in Rio later that same day.

The *Bella* was to have called at Kingston, Jamaica, but she never made it that far. Six days after she left Rio, her longboat was found floating bottom up by the crew of the southbound *Kent*. There was no sign of bodies or survivors, but the presence of debris from the deck of the *Bella* indicated that this was the spot at which she had sunk. She must have met with a sudden accident, giving her captain no time to launch the longboat. Since there was no evidence of a collision, the *Bella* had probably been caught in a squall and her cargo of coffee, being carried too high, caused her to topple over and sink instantly. Captain Birkett, it was said, was a racer. Before he left Rio he'd declared that he would make one of the shortest passages on record—which he did, although not exactly in the manner he'd intended.

Jules Barraut learnt of the *Bella*'s loss on 4 May, but, thanks to Roger's subterfuge over his passport, it was a week or more before the British consul at Rio was able to confirm that he had been on board the missing vessel. It turned out that he had notified his bank's agent at Rio, so that funds could be forwarded on to New York. Word of the calamity finally reached Roger's family, via their London bankers, at the end of June. Perhaps it was an attempt to soften the blow, but the account they received of the *Bella*'s loss gave the family cause to hope that survivors might have been picked up and taken to 'Australia or elsewhere'. 'I am so glad you have this reasonable hope to cheer you,' wrote Lady Tichborne's sister-in-law. 'This account you send me indeed has an air of probability and we must not allow ourselves to despair. We shall all rejoice with you and Sir James if at last we hear from him even from Australia.' Lady Tichborne held onto that hope long after it ceased to be a reasonable one. She had so often predicted the worst, but when it finally happened she refused to believe it.

When six months had passed without word of him, Roger's other relatives accepted that he must be dead. Lady Doughty conceded that all hope was lost, but continued, as ever, to pray for her nephew's eternal soul. News of the *Bella* had soured the celebration of Kattie's engagement to Percival Radcliffe, and at their wedding in October

1854 one half of the congregation was dressed in mourning. In the early part of 1855, the Tichborne family lawyers made their own inquiries about the fate of the *Bella*. When they were unable to turn up evidence of any of the crew having been saved, Roger's will was proved and his insurance paid. But Lady Tichborne would still permit no memorial to her son to be put up in the family chapel.

Francis Baigent, antiquarian, genealogist and sycophant, was staying at Tichborne when word arrived of the *Bella*'s loss. Of a lowly but respectable Winchester family, he'd been introduced to Tichborne House as the son of Kattie Doughty's music tutor. Lady Doughty employed him to draw up the Tichborne family pedigree, and took a liking to the cultured young man with the glass eye. Of all the grand homes he visited, only at Tichborne was he welcomed as a guest; elsewhere he dined in the housekeeper's room. Baigent's mastery at the art of toadying enabled him to maintain—even to increase—his intimacy at Tichborne after Sir James' succession, while remaining one of Lady Doughty's closest confidants. He and Lady Tichborne had hit it off at once:

> Sir James and Lady Tichborne ever treated me in the kindest manner, and always spoke of me in such a way that a stranger would almost think I was their son. I have often been introduced to visitors at Tichborne House as one who knew more of the Family than even the members of the family themselves.

Sir James, in fact, was irritated by Baigent, but was happy enough to have him act as a sop and a flatterer to Henriette. At least he wasn't out to fleece her like those French maids ('a set of whores and robbers') she insisted on keeping.

Amending the Tichborne family's entry in the 1856 edition of *Burke's Peerage* to state that Roger had been 'lost at sea off the coast of South America,' Baigent chose his words carefully. 'I was never satisfied,' he said, 'to the evidence of his being drowned.'

I was wont to hold long conversations with Lady Tichborne, who was always impressed with the idea that her son had been picked up by some vessel going to Australia, and that he was there, still alive…I could not in any way weaken this impression, and she always said in reply, 'You will see that he will come home some day. I know my poor dear Roger is alive.'

Sir James couldn't abide such stuff and when she 'harped' on the subject would push her out of the room and lock the door. At the beginning of 1857 a sailor happened to called at Tichborne on his way home from Southampton, looking for a handout. Hearing that he'd been to Australia, Lady Tichborne asked whether he knew anything of the *Bella* and her crew, and he was happy enough to tell her (between mouthfuls of cold chicken and rum) what she wanted to hear. Yes, he believed he had heard something about some crew and 'a good many' passengers of a ship—it might have been the *Bella*, now he thought about it—having been picked up at sea and brought to Melbourne, a couple of years previously.* He even mentioned a survivor named Delafosse, who was still living at Melbourne. Baigent, visiting Tichborne, also quizzed the sailor and was inclined to believe him. But Sir James was scornful. Couldn't Henriette see the man had been duping her, just like her cursed maids and those nuns whose prayers she squandered money on? No, he would pay the sailor's story no notice, and she must do the same. Roger was dead. That was all.

Nevertheless Lady Tichborne wrote, on the quiet, to Delafosse asking whether Roger was known to him and, if so, 'Pray be so good as to let him know that his mother has written to you, and that a letter from him would be the greatest happiness we could have in this world.' Her letter to 'Monsieur Delafosse—Melbourne—Australia' went

---

* Perhaps he was thinking of the *Waterwitch*, which was wrecked off King Island, in Bass Strait, in October 1854. Eighteen passengers and most of her crew were saved by a passing clipper, and conveyed to Melbourne.

undelivered, but word soon got around among sailors on the tramp that they'd get a welcome from the old girl at Tichborne. Most of them had done a Melbourne run, or said they had, and a surprising number recalled having heard of the *Bella* and even of 'old Delafosse'. This went on until one afternoon in 1858 when Sir James found his wife serving cognac to seven sailors in the drawing room. After that, Brand, the gamekeeper, had instructions that roving sailors were to be 'moved on' before they reached the house. But Lady Tichborne sought them out, the way others did clairvoyants. She mawked about the docks at Southampton, and got in the way of the ropes when she sailed between London and Boulogne. She couldn't let a sailor pass without pressing half-a-crown on him and asking what (not if) he knew of the *Bella*.

For all Lady Tichborne's probing and prompting, nothing further came to light until 1860 when a rumour reached her that Roger was married and living in Argentina. Richard (later Sir Richard) Burton was just then leaving for Brazil to take up a position in the British consulate at Rio, and Lady Tichborne prevailed on him to make inquiries on her behalf. She even gave him a small package—containing a religious medallion and one of her four-page letters—for Roger, should they happen to meet. 'Being unable to find him,' Burton later said, 'I sent the present back.'

In June 1862, Sir James Tichborne died and was succeeded as baronet by his younger son, Alfred. Sir Alfred's wife now became Lady Tichborne, while Henriette was relegated to the minor ranks with the title of the Dowager Lady Tichborne. Alfred had made an advantageous marriage a year earlier to Teresa, daughter of Lord Arundell of Wardour and niece of Lady Doughty. To both families, the union represented a nice consolidation of assets. Only Lady Tichborne was less than pleased: she despised the Arundell–Doughty connection. But then Alfred had never filled Roger's place in her affections.

Roger's presumed death meant that Alfred, at fifteen, had become his father's heir. But Lady Tichborne insisted that Roger would one day return to claim his entitlement. She made sure Alfred understood: when Roger comes back, you must make way. And he believed her. He was an heir who would never inherit. From the age of fifteen, Alfred Tichborne was programmed for self-destruction. Think of a vice: he had it. And he was eccentric into the bargain. He contracted for a fantastic yacht to be built—with decks of inlaid mosaic and doors panelled with mother-of-pearl—in which he planned to set sail in search of Roger. It was to have cost £200,000 but, fortunately, bankruptcy intervened. He turned his attention then to a slightly less costly undertaking: the construction of a perfect sphere. Alfred wasted a good part of the Tichborne fortune before he even inherited it. The Doughty estates were far more extensive and more tightly bound up; but, given time, Alfred hoped to make his mark on them, too.

After Sir James' death, a fire sale was held at Tichborne in an attempt to bail Alfred out of debt. Pictures, books, livestock, guns and furnishings were sold, but only £1,600 was raised—not nearly enough. Alfred had wanted to sell Roger's gaucho outfit, but Lady Tichborne (to whom Gosford had entrusted it) would not let him have it. He was declared bankrupt soon after, and an itemisation of his debts included a jeweller's bill for £1,087, a black bearskin Chesterfield coat, a Mary-blue ribbed Cardigan coat, dressing cases worth £430, and more than £14,000 owed to money-lenders. He was at least as fiendish a pipe smoker as his brother, if his tobacconist's bills are to be believed. In the space of less than three months in 1861, Alfred blew 120 pounds of cavendish.

It must have been around the time of Alfred's bankruptcy that the Dowager Lady Tichborne decided that, if Roger were going to claim his entitlements, he had better do it soon. And she was free to seek for him vigorously, at last, now that her black-hearted husband was out of the way. She believed that Roger, wherever he was, had only been waiting for his father's death—waiting to assume his rightful role, not just as Tichborne baronet, but as his mother's protector. All that it would take was a signal from her.

> If anybody can give any clue of ROGER CHARLES TICHBORNE, and if there are any survivors of La Bella, they are requested to let L.T. know of them, at 1, Nottingham-place, Regent's-park. A handsome REWARD is promised for any well-authenticated particulars.

That notice appeared on the front page of *The Times* in May 1863, in English, French and Spanish. The Spanish version included the *Bella*'s date of departure from Rio and her destination, New York. In response, the Dowager heard nothing. But in the colonial columns of the same newspaper, two years later, her eye lit on a notice advertising the services of the Missing Friends Office (proprietor: Mr A. Cubitt) of Bridge Street, Sydney, Australia. The Dowager wrote without delay, asking Cubitt to inquire whether her son—a thin thirty-two-year-old, by her account—'was by chance in his neighbourhood.' 'He went away in 1853, only for the sake of knowing the world, and, most unfortunately, has never returned home.'

FIVE

FREAK OF FORTUNE

ADVERTISING for him in the colonial press, Arthur Cubitt adjusted Roger Tichborne's waistband, omitting the word 'thin' from the Dowager's description of her missing son. He supposed a man might change his shape in a dozen years or more.

Cubitt's advertisement was a rough enough fit for Tom Castro. He was getting on for thirty-two, most people would reckon him tall and, if you saw him after a wash, you could make out his hair as gingery fair. True, his eyes weren't blue, but they were a dark grey that might once have been blue. The 'delicate constitution' was a bit of a stretch, though there was that business of the twitch. But none of that explains why it was his friend Castro that Dick Slate thought of when he lit on the notice. In fact he'd said it, embellished, under his breath: 'Bloody Tom Castro.' Why was that, when maybe a quarter of the men of Slate's acquaintance might have fitted Cubitt's description of the missing man?

It was one of Tom Castro's stories that he was destined for 'better things'. One day (he'd tell his fellow-drinkers) he'd have the biggest butcher shop in Wagga and there'd be jobs for them all. Or else he'd buy the Australian Hotel or a stable of racehorses. Other times, when a creditor hauled him through the small claims court, he'd mutter that he was worth a dozen of them and that he'd buy their shop and chuck them into the street one day, you wait and see if he didn't. Whether grand or vengeful, though, his imaginings were always

Wagga-sized. As to the particulars of his prospective wealth and standing, he was vague—or, rather, secretive. When anyone asked where the money would come from or why, if he was so flash, he lived like *this*, he'd make a show of clamming up, hinting darkly that he came from better things and that better things awaited him.

Dick Slate had seen this performance of Tom's a good few times, and it had given him a laugh. Then, about a year earlier, there'd been an item in the *Wagga Wagga Express* that had interested Castro greatly. It was headed 'A Freak of Fortune':

> An old man, lately working at Mrs Stamp's hotel, Cockendina,* as gardener, appears to have come into not only a large fortune (in silver and gold, as vide ancient poetry) but also a noble title. The details of origin, etc., we know not, but learn from our informant that £1,000 has been deposited to the gardener's credit in a Sydney bank, and that further £15,000 are to be remitted from England by the next mail; and, strangest of all, this is to be the instalment of not only an annual fortune, but of the possession of the title of Earl Strafford.

Slate remembered how Tom had done his secret-like puffery, confiding half-turned away like he was watching to see nobody else was listening, even though you got the feeling he'd not be sorry if they were.

'That's what I am,' Tom said, nodding at the paper.

'What's that, a gardener?' Slate was ready to contradict his friend who, it was common knowledge, planted spuds eyes downwards.

'No, a bloody freak of fortune,' hissed Tom.

'Ah, so it's Earl Castro then, is it?' said Slate.

'Something like.'

Over the months intervening, Tom added little kindling hints that there was a title waiting for him and money too, if he wanted it, but that he'd had a bust-up with his family and had chosen freedom over

* Cookardinia, fifty-five kilometres south of Wagga.

fortune. It was pub talk, but he was careful who he tried it on.

Slate asked one time, 'So what's the missus reckon about being *Lady* Castro?'

'She don't know nothing about it,' Tom snapped, 'and don't you go saying nothing. Besides,' he added, 'Castro ain't my real name.' He laughed. 'You needn't tell Mary that, neither. She fancies being married to a South American feller.'

'Ha! I didn't reckon you really was a Mexican,' said Slate. 'But what about crossing them mountains with mules and wrestling panthers and all that?'

'Oh, I *been* to South America,' said Tom, and buried his nose in his beer.

Two doors up from the Australian Hotel was the office of William Gibbes, attorney, solicitor and conveyancer. Gibbes had been in Australia since the early 1850s, but had failed to prosper in the land of plenty. After ten years of unsuccess in Melbourne, Wagga represented a fresh start. He had taken over the Wagga law firm of a Mr Muggridge, complete with Fitzmaurice Street premises and a list of debtors that read like the electoral roll. One of the names on the list was Tom Castro.

Castro had owed Muggridge—now owed Gibbes—about £6 for professional services in connection with a couple of small claim cases in the local court. Gibbes

William Gibbes

took over the practice in the middle of July 1865 and about a month later (just a few days after Slate showed Tom the notice in the *Australasian*) he asked Castro to call on him over the matter of the money owed. Hearing that Castro had no hope of paying his debts, Gibbes suggested insolvency.

Castro had a think. 'How would it be if I came into money afterwards?' he asked.

'You'd have to pay your debts,' replied Gibbes.

'Then I won't do it.'

'You expect to come into some money then, do you, Tom?'

'Yes, well,' said Castro, 'I do, some day or other.'

Gibbes probed some more. What sort of money was Castro expecting? Did he mean money or property or both? The replies were gruff and inexplicit, but Gibbes gathered that his client believed himself entitled to some substantial property in England. Lawyers—even small-town colonial lawyers like Gibbes—were forever hearing tales of inheritances begrudged and legacies imagined; but Castro's manner made Gibbes take notice.

They next spoke on the subject ten days later. Outside, it was a clear, blowy September day, and Gibbes remarked that he'd give anything to be sailing on Sydney Harbour.

'You wouldn't say that if you'd ever been shipwrecked,' replied Castro.

Shipwrecked? Gibbes wanted to hear more, but Tom would only say it had happened not far from Rio de Janeiro and that he'd had enough of the sea.

'But you didn't go home?'

Tom flicked gravel from the sole of his boot with Gibbes' letter-opener. The story was much the same as he'd intimated to Slate: the title, the family bust-up. He wasn't interested in going home, he said. At least, not while his father was alive.

That evening, in their shingle-roofed cottage, Gibbes greeted his wife Lizzie with, 'What extraordinary things we come across in

Australia!' and proceeded to tell her about his client, a butcher, who came from a titled family and had survived a shipwreck.

Mrs Gibbes, who read the *Sydney Morning Herald* each day on her husband's behalf, felt a *ping* of recognition. 'That sounds like the fellow they've been advertising for,' she said.

William Gibbes was the first through the door of the Mechanics' Institute next morning. Propping the loose-bound folio of *Herald* back-issues on the sloping desk, he found what he was looking for on the front page of the 12 August edition.

Gibbes wet his lips. It *must* be him. The facts seemed to fit and the description was near enough. Roger Charles Tichborne, eh? The father dead (Castro would be glad to hear of it), leaving this missing Roger heir to all the estates—and a baronetcy. Well, thought Gibbes, not a bad morning's work. He copied down the notice, ending with the address of the Missing Friends Office in Sydney. Shutting his notebook, he smiled to himself. This is where my luck starts to change.

He hailed Tom Castro as the butcher was locking up for an early dinner. 'Have you seen the advertisements in the paper, Tom? Your family's looking for you.'

Castro bristled. 'What are you talking about? What advertisement?'

Gibbes pulled out his notebook. 'Shall I read it to you?'

'I can read it myself.' Actually, he barely could read Gibbes' scrawl, but he could make out enough to know what it was. 'That's nothing to do with me.' He handed back the notebook. 'I suppose that bloody Dick Slate showed it to you?'

'No, it was my wife who spotted it,' said Gibbes. 'Admit it, Tom. It's exactly like you told me: the shipwrecking...'

Castro cut him off. 'Just leave it, will you? I don't know nothing about it.' He shouldered the side of lamb he was taking home to Mary, and headed up the yard.

Gibbes hurried after him. 'Now, Tom...,' he began, but Castro threw back a look that stopped him. Gibbes watched him lumber off. 'I *know* it's you,' he said, in a voice that only the gatepost heard.

Days passed without Gibbes sighting Castro again. He's avoiding me, the lawyer thought. But when, a week later, he asked after Tom at the Australian Hotel, he learnt that the butcher had left Higgins' employ. Oh hell, thought Gibbes, I've lost him. He called at the Australian Market, where Pat Reardon, who'd taken Castro's place, said Tom was still living up Baylis Street, as far as he knew. He didn't know why Castro had given notice.

Gibbes had never been to Castro Villa, and he figured he'd better tread carefully now. So instead of heading up Baylis Street, he returned to his office. He might just catch the post.

Arthur Cubitt was hoping for word from New Zealand, where he'd heard that Roger Tichborne was in a militia regiment fighting the Maoris. Instead he got a letter from William Gibbes, an almost-forgotten acquaintance from his earliest days in Sydney. After pleasantries, Gibbes had written:

> Please let me know if you are in possession of any further facts respecting R.C. Tichborne than those mentioned in the advertisement—first, as to the peculiarity of his delicacy of health; secondly, as to the cause of his leaving home (England); thirdly, as to the nature of his education. I 'spotted' him, I think, some time ago, and could find him, I think, and if I could would urge him to disclose himself. He was hugely disgusted when he found I had detected him, and his real name has never passed between us. I should like the further particulars to enable me to be certain, that is quite certain, for I have scarce any doubt.

Gibbes' opening pleasantries had amounted to a swipe at his own less-than-brilliant career. Arthur Cubitt's colonial career had been nothing very splendid either. After five years with Henry Parkes'

Empire, Cubitt had set up his own news agency. The venture had not met with success, which was why, in addition to being the sole Australian agent for Miller & Richards printing presses and Snowgood's homeo-pathic preparations, he'd branched out into 'missing friends'. Replying now to Gibbes, he wrote that 'I have experienced the various ups and downs of a colonial adventurer, but I am happy to say the ups have preponderated. I should have been pleased,' he lied, 'could you have reported more favourably of your own career.' Turning then to 'the special purport of your letter in re. Roger Tichborne,' he told Gibbes:

> His mother's letter does not convey much on the points to which you specially refer, but she mentions the probability that he might adopt from feelings of pride an assumed name, and that his leaving home was from caprice, and not necessity…I beg of you to use every discretion, and, above all, to do nothing that might induce Mr Tichborne to retain his incognito; for rest assured that if he be so lost as not to desire a return to a position of comfort and afflu-ence, he will carefully avoid reference to any matters that may show not only what he is now, but what he ought to be.

A day or two after receiving Cubitt's reply, Gibbes stepped out of the grocer's to find Tom Castro leaning against a verandah post, smoking. Gibbes expected him to bolt, but instead the butcher raised his pipe and greeted his inquisitor with a slow, complicit grin. It was almost as if, thought Gibbes, he'd been waiting for me.

'Well, Tom,' began the lawyer, a trifle wary. 'Is it still Tom, or should I call you by your real name?'

'You mean this?' said Castro, and held out his pipe at Gibbes' eye level. It was a well-smoked black wooden pipe—a myall, they called it, after the wattle it was carved from—and scratched into the lower part of the bowl Gibbes could make out the letters RCT. He dropped the orange he'd bought for elevenses. Castro's grin just widened.

SIX

I CAN SAY NO MORE AT PRESENT

GIBBES retrieved his orange from the gutter and, with the offer of an open bottle, coaxed Castro to his office. Once there, he circled warily, mindful of Cubitt's warning. Tom said he was aiming to pick up some work in the horse-breaking line, maybe breed up a few for himself.

'You'll pardon me for asking, Tom,' interrupted Gibbes, seeing a chance, 'but your…that twitch of yours—a spill off a horse, was it?'

'I've always had it,' said Castro, 'since I was a kid. St Vitus' Dance, they called it—a nerve thing. It's a lot better than what it was.'

'It got in the way of your schooling, I suppose?'

Tom agreed that was so.

'You didn't get to Latin then?' Gibbes asked.

'No, but I can talk Spanish. Learned it in Chile.'

Gibbes could speak Spanish, too, and the pair of them launched into an animated exchange. Castro's side of it concerned mainly horses and places he'd been in South America, and he showed himself to be as elegant a speaker of Spanish as of his mother tongue.

The bottle on Gibbes' desk was half-empty before the lawyer eased the conversation—in English—around to the advertisement. He didn't let on that he'd been in touch with Cubitt, but he took Castro's re-appearance—and his carved pipe—as a sign that he was ready to show himself. Straight away, though, Castro turned chary.

'Come on, Tom.' Gibbes was exasperated. 'You were only waiting for your father's death, you said. And the baronetcy's yours now. What're you playing at? You as good as told me your name by showing me that pipe of yours.'

'Oh, that was just for devilment,' said Castro. Then, not looking up, 'Supposing I am the one in the paper, what would I have to do? Would it be like that gardener out Cookardinia that turned out an earl? They'd just send me the money and say "You're it"?'

Gibbes hadn't heard about the Cookardinia gardener. 'I don't rightly know,' he said, 'but they'd need to be certain of your identity and I should say that'd mean going home to England.'

'Bugger it then.' Tom was on his feet. 'I'm not going back.'

'But what about your family?' Gibbes almost said 'your mother', catching himself just in time. 'Don't you want to see them—at least let them know you're alive?'

'What, them over there?' Tom snorted. 'It's taken them this long to come looking for me. Anyway, I've got my own family here now. Me and Mary's expecting, you know, around Easter.'

'Well then think of the money, Tom, if nothing else. You've got debts left and right and, as things stand, you've got no hope of getting clear. Think how this money, your inheritance, could set you up— you and this family you're starting. You owe it to them, surely, to claim what you're entitled to. And even if you do have to go to England, you can always come back.'

Castro was back in his seat, biting a thumbnail. Gibbes could tell he was getting through to him at last.

'I understand how you feel, Tom,' he went on. 'Our mother country never did me any favours, either. Think of it like a gold rush, only in reverse. Go home, take what you're entitled to, and bring the spoils back here.'

This made Castro smile. 'You're talking to the wrong man there, Mr Gibbes,' he said. 'I never was one for gold-digging. But I see what you mean.' The lawyer had made it sound easy. Then Castro frowned.

'Don't know if I can face the sea again.' A pause while he chewed another nail, and finally he looked at Gibbes direct. 'I'd have to go by steamer.'

Gibbes kept his face straight and his voice steady. 'First things first, Tom,' he said. 'I'll write to Mr Cubitt in Sydney—he's an old friend of mine, as it happens—and find out how we ought to proceed.'

The bottle was empty by the time Castro left Gibbes' office. It was settled that Gibbes would write to Cubitt, telling him that their man had agreed to come forward on three conditions: that his identity not be revealed before the end of March (five months hence), that his marriage be kept a secret, and that, should he have to go to England, there'd be money to keep Mary in his absence. Gibbes agreed that, at this stage, discretion was vital. The Tichborne executors might well be disconcerted to learn how their baronet had spent his missing years. With luck—or rather, Gibbes told himself, with careful handling—the name Tom Castro need never reach their ears.

Gibbes wrote to Cubitt that same day. It might have been better if he'd let his head clear first, since the letter never reached its destination. No matter though, for in the next short while something happened that made Tom Castro swing around to embrace his destiny. Just ten days after his last, Gibbes wrote to Cubitt: 'He is so far changed from his original intentions that he is anxious to go.' An urgent reiteration that 'his present identity must be totally disconnected from his future' made the *something* behind Castro's change of heart sound almost sinister. Gibbes would later say of Castro: 'He delighted in making secrets and being mysterious.' But now *he* ended his letter to Cubitt: 'I can say no more at present.' Tom Castro's secretiveness was contagious.

The Dowager Lady Tichborne also had impressed on Cubitt the need for secrecy and she was likewise cagey about her reasons. Writing to her now, in December 1865, with the tidings 'that Mr Roger Tichborne is alive and well, [and] that he is now in this colony, within

600 miles of Sydney,' Cubitt reassured the Dowager that 'the secrecy you desire will be maintained…Mr T. will not probably reveal his own name, and when he leaves here will do nothing by which the public prints will know of his departure hence or of his arrival in England.'

Cubitt's main concern was money, both for the purpose of securing the Dowager's son and shipping him home and to cover the 'handsome' reward promised by Her Ladyship. 'Your son's circumstances,' he now explained to the Dowager, 'are of such a character that he has not even the means to come to Sydney, much less outfit and passage-money for his voyage home.' As to the question of the reward, Cubitt was careful to dismiss Gibbes as 'my agent', rather than as her son's discoverer. But the Dowager was infuriatingly vague about money. Since receiving her first letter in July, Cubitt had written monthly to acquaint her not only with the progress of his inquiries, but with the 'great trouble and expense' they were costing him. All the assurance he got, at first, was that the reward would be commensurate with the Dowager's happiness at having her son restored to her. Eventually, though, it became clear that she had no access to the Tichborne estates and little money of her own—just £40 a week, with which she ran households in both London and Paris. She expected that her son, on the strength of his name alone, would be easily able to obtain the funds for his voyage home, to be repaid once he came into possession of his estates. Roger's discoverer, she now told Cubitt, would likewise have to wait for his money.

The reward, by this time, was also the subject of wrangling between Cubitt and Gibbes. When he realised he was in danger of being sidelined, Gibbes wrote to Cubitt that 'I should feel myself justified in claiming the reward (on behalf of the real discoverer, my wife)' but that he would be satisfied with a half-share of, say, £250. Cubitt, who clearly had a far larger sum in mind, agreed with alacrity—figuring, presumably, to pocket the difference between Gibbes' meagre expectation and the actual amount of the reward. For the sake of appearances, though, Cubitt added that of course he would deduct his expenses from Gibbes' share. Now, if Cubitt was out of pocket over a few newspaper advertisements and ship-letters, it was Gibbes who bore the real trouble and expense of the hunt.

Since leaving Higgins' in September, Tom Castro had been knocking around doing odd jobs, mainly bookkeeping and slaughtering for other butchers. By Christmas, he was relying on Gibbes for the odd ten shillings and to keep his creditors at bay. He was a little uncomfortable about taking hand-outs, the lawyer could tell. Whatever he might once have been—and might yet be—he was now a man who was used to working for his living. But Gibbes (who, heaven knows, had little cash to spare) seemed to be fostering Castro's sense of entitlement. When he remonstrated with Castro about his improvidence, Gibbes was urging him, not to watch his pennies, but to look to his prospects. 'He was not an extravagant man,' Gibbes would later explain. 'He was a quietly conducted man; he was not improvident except he did not look out for his own interest.'

A letter arriving in the second week of January 1866 commanded Gibbes 'to send him on to Sydney by return of mail'—as if Castro were a parcel—so that Cubitt might satisfy himself as to his identity. The return of mail carried only Gibbes' reply: 'As for my showing him to you, mature reflection has shown me that to be out of the question without his consent, even if I could at present.' The problem was, he explained, that 'Sir R.C.T. has left his last place of abode! He has lately shown signs of restlessness; but I think he has not gone far as yet.'

The Castros had in fact moved into Dick Slate's old place. Tom liked it because it had a paddock with a rough bush-fenced corral, just right for horse-breaking. And, in truth, he *was* half inclined to bolt, to put himself beyond Gibbes' reach. But since he was only half inclined, he'd only half bolted. Slate had fully bolted, which was why they'd moved into his hut. He'd got himself involved in a job of dirty work—a cocked-up robbery that didn't quite amount to bushranging—and had shot through. Five days before Christmas, Slate and an accomplice had bushwacked a drunken farmer on his way out of Wagga. Pretending to be policemen, they'd emptied his pockets and taken off with the contents of his cart—a suitably festive load comprising three gallons of wine, two of rum, and eighteen pounds of currants—as well as his saddle and bridle. Was Tom involved? Probably not—he wouldn't have left the farmer's horse—but he'd undoubtedly shared in Slate's Christmas cheer.

Gibbes must have known that Cubitt was doing all he could to cut his 'agent' out of the deal; now he acted to outmanoeuvre his rival. Four days after informing Cubitt that their man had 'disappeared', Gibbes sat Tom Castro down at the desk in his office, with pen and ink and writing paper and a bottle by his elbow. The ostensible Roger Tichborne was writing to his mother. 'My dear Mother,' Castro began.

> The delay which has taken place since my last Letter, Dated 22nd April, 1854, Makes it very difficult to commence this letter. I deeply regret the truble and anxiety I must have cause you by not writing before. But they [the reasons] are known to my Attorney, And the more private details I will keep for your own Ear. Of one thing rest Assured that although I have been in A humble condition of Life I have never let any act disgrace you or my Family. I have been a poor Man and nothing worse. Mr Gibbes suggest to me as essential That I should recall to your Memory things which can only be known to you and me, to convince you of my Idenitity. I don't think it needful, My Dear Mother, Although I send them, namely, the Brown Mark on my side And the Card Case at Brighton...I do not wisch any person to know me in this Country When I take up my proper prosttrion and title. Having therefore made up my mind to return and face the Sea once more, I must request to send me

the Means of doing so, and paying a fue outstanding debts, I would return by the over land Mail. The passage money and other expences would be over two Hundred pound, for I propose Sailing from Victoria, not this Colainly, And to Sail from Melbourne in my own Name. Now to annable me to do this, my dear Mother, you must Send me…

There ended the first sheet of his letter. On the second sheet, which would later go missing, Castro asked for £400 and inquired after the health of his 'Grandad'. Gibbes' promptings are evident, not just in his suggestion that Castro remind the Dowager of shared secrets, but in the part about his 'humble condition of life'. The same point was made in Gibbes' own letter to the Dowager, dated the day after Castro's:

he has been following for some years [a] humble occupation, one totally incompatible with the position he is about to fill in life. His chief desire is that no person here should be able to identify him in his future station with him in his past one. I may venture that, lowly as he has been, he has not done anything of which he need be ashamed.

Gibbes introduced himself as 'his only confidant—not a voluntary one, I can assure you, so far as he is concerned,' alluding to the fact that he was her son's discoverer. In his letter, Castro had requested that the £400 be sent to Gibbes, rather than risk exposure by having it sent in his own name. On that point, Gibbes reassured the Dowager that:

in any communication you may favour me with you will have not only to rely on the honour of a man who is indebted simply to his profession for his title of 'gentleman', but of one who is as well born and connected as your own son. I should not make this remark except for fear you might imagine some 'low attorney' wanted to make money out of him.

By opening a correspondence between mother and son, establishing himself as her son's discoverer and protector, and even planning Castro's departure via Melbourne rather than Sydney, Gibbes aimed to undermine Cubitt absolutely. But such a scheme rather depended on Tom Castro's co-operation.

Now Castro signed himself 'Roger Charles Tichborne' a second time, at the foot of a letter to Arthur Cubitt:

> Mr Gibbes has no doubt made it known to you [he hadn't] that I have wrote to my Mother through him. I wish you to let me know what power my Mother has invested you with, or whether you have receved any advances from her. If you have not let me know what your charges are for advertisements, and ce., That I may settle them before leaving the Colonly. Has most likely of recepe of answer to my letter I may proceed to England via Melbourne. I don't wish my name or title to be known in Wagga. therefore Address your letter to T.C. post office Wagga-Wagga. You have no need to let Mr Gibbes know that I have Commucated with you. He seemed not to wish me to do so. For what reson I dont know. But most likely I shall find out.

Was this mischief or malice? Whichever, Castro's letter showed plainly enough that 'his only confidant' could expect no loyalty from him. Cubitt saw in an instant how things stood. He made no reply to Castro, but wrote the Dowager a carefully crafted letter: deadset and vulpine.

> Circumstances have come to my knowledge which convince me of the danger of entrusting any funds to the immediate charge of your son. Engaged in a menial capacity, involved in debt, and unable to leave the colony until these liabilities are settled, to say nothing of a most extraordinary indifference to take up his proper position in society, you may rest assured that a sudden acquisition to status and independence may have

dangerous results if funds be placed at his unlimited control; and I most seriously advise you, if you attach any value to the return of your son in the midst of his family, not to throw away the only chance of securing such a desire.

Back in Wagga, Castro's reputation was sinking in contradiction to his prospects. On the first day of February 1866, he procured a cow and a bullock by means that amounted to duffing. Pat Reardon, his successor at Higgins', had asked him to go and see about some cattle he was looking to buy. Tom had gone out to Gobbagumbalin and with the help of William Allen, who held a selection nearby, had cut a yellow cow and a red bullock out of the herd in a paddock below the homestead. He had the cow dead and skinned and the bullock penned in the yard behind the Australian Hotel when Dan Carroll, Sergeant of Police and Inspector of Slaughterhouses, showed up mid-afternoon. Their brands clearly showed the cattle to be the property of James Devlin of Ganmain. Caught red-handed, Castro none-theless managed to shift the blame, so that in the police court next day it was William Allen who was charged with cattle-stealing, with Tom Castro as a witness for the Crown. In the quarter sessions three weeks later, Allen was convicted and sentenced to five years' hard labour, leaving behind his four motherless infants. If Tom still harboured any doubts about renouncing the name Castro in favour of Tichborne, this must have put an end to them. In Wagga at least, Castro was a name hardly worth keeping.

SEVEN
THROW OFF THE MASK

CASTRO and Gibbes could only wait to hear from the Dowager—by the May mail at the earliest, Gibbes said. Castro didn't like the waiting. 'My being idle is drawing remarks from many,' he told Gibbes. 'And what to do I no not. I don't wish to leave the Town before we receve our letters from mother Which I hope will not be long first. But how to live in the meantime is what trubling me.'

He had no choice but to run up more debts—modest ones, for horse feed and groceries—and in March 1866 he prevailed on Gibbes to pay the midwife's bill. 'And believe me Sir,' he wrote, 'I am more like a Manick than a B of B.K* to think that I should have a child born in such a hovel.'

Mary had been delivered of another daughter, Mary Agnes Theresa. Castro had long been anxious over this event. Gibbes now noted how 'exceedingly gratified' Tom was to hear people say, and to observe for himself, that his daughter looked like him. It was not that he'd doubted his own paternity, he confided to Gibbes, but had there not been a strong resemblance, his mother 'would never have believed he was father of a child.'

Why ever not? asked Gibbes.

Castro, ever mysterious, only held up his little finger, indicated the second joint, and winked.

His calls on Gibbes for cash now came more frequently. At the

* Tom's abbreviation for 'Baronet of the British Kingdom'.

end of March he asked for £5, complaining about 'a slight Tuch of Sun stroke' sustained while crossing the racecourse the previous day. But, he assured the lawyer, he'd be down to see him shortly about 'regeratering' his daughter's birth. He referred to her as 'the Child', but she was generally called Agnes, to avoid confusion with her mother.

It's not clear how much Mary Castro knew up to this point about her husband's prospects. The chances are, if she suspected anything it was that Tom was involved in some commonplace shadiness, like thieving cattle or horses. Years later, he would say that he'd told her nothing and that 'she was too ignorant even to understand it, if I had.' But it's hard to credit that he could have resisted dropping broad hints to his wife about the change of fortune that awaited them. Unless he meant to leave her behind in Australia for good.

If time dragged in Wagga ahead of the May mail, Cubitt too despaired at how long it took to get an answer from England. He was still waiting for a reply to his letter of last December, in which he urged the Dowager to press the Tichborne executors to release funds for Sir Roger's return and his own reward. It was the middle of April before he got a reply. The executors, the Dowager told Cubitt, refused to advance money 'in the absence of satisfactory evidence as to his identity.' All she could offer was £40 to fetch her son to Sydney, and a rebuke to Cubitt:

> You must not wonder if the money is not paid beforehand, the more so as you do not give any details whatever about the person you believe to be my Son; you do not name even the Town where he is, and you do not say anything about the way he was saved from Shipwreck.

Although she had sent no money (and Cubitt bitterly assured her that £40 would not even reimburse his expenses to date), the Dowager had at least given him the means—or the hope—of raising funds at his end. 'The secret I mentioned in my other letters,' she told him, 'is now almost at an end, at least so far as it regards Roger's safety.' Cubitt wrote to Gibbes:

Things have now arrived at such a position that you must no longer remain silent, but aid me in bringing this search to a conclusion. I have promised you your share of the spoil, and as we are both interested, we must both work together. If you have really got the right man, both he and you must, so far as is necessary for the purposes of identity, throw off the mask.

Gibbes rode over to see Castro and reported back that 'Sir R.' was determined to wait for the Dowager's reply to his letter: 'He has not the slightest doubt of the executors sending him money, immediately.'

The anxiously awaited May mail brought no reply and no money. But a day or two later, a letter from the Dowager did arrive at Wagga. It had been sent care of Cubitt and he'd been holding onto it since the middle of April. It was written before the Dowager received Castro's letter—on the same day, in fact, as that letter to Cubitt in which she spoke coolly of 'the person you believe to be my Son'— and yet this man about whom she'd been told next to nothing she addressed with not a trace of uncertainty. 'My dear and beloved roger,' she began:

I hope you will not refuse to come back to your poor afflicted mother. I have had the great misfortune to lose your poor dear father and lately I have lost my beloved son Alfred, I am now alone in this world of sorrow I hope you will take that in consideration and that you will come to join me as soon as possible you need not be afraid about the money as you will have all the money necessary to pay your expenses, only come to see your poor *lonely* mother and remember the promise you made to your dear father before going away that if God called him to himself that you would then come back to be your Mother's protector certainly in that melancholy case and now that your poor dear brother is dead, I have no-body to look to but you.

Sir Alfred Tichborne had drunk himself to death three days before the Dowager's letter. He had been bankrupted a second time the previous year—had even spent time in debtors' prison—and still his debts had continued to mount. But now the haemorrhaging Tichborne estates were saved by Alfred's death, when his assets were frozen in Chancery.

Gibbes delivered Tom his letter. It was mid-morning and he was washing from a tin dish outside the hut door. He dried his face and arms before taking the letter from Gibbes. It was addressed to Roger Charles Tichborne and he knew straight off whose the handwriting was. One side of his face was seized with twitching, the worst Gibbes had seen it. Tom turned away as he opened the letter, and retired to the screen of a wattle sapling. When he emerged, Gibbes noticed his eyes were moist—though 'I cannot say whether it was shedding tears, or the effect of scrubbing himself with a good towel.' Tom handed the letter back to the lawyer, who read it through aloud. As he finished— 'and now that your poor dear brother is dead, I have no-body to look to but you'—and looked up, he saw Castro wince.

'I was very glad to hear you where quite well.' Tom began his reply to the Dowager's doom-laden epistle in the dutiful manner of a schoolboy. 'I was very sorry to hear of poor father and Alfred death. I Hardly know, my Dear mother, how you have borne the suspence of knowing my fate so long. You must not blame me, mother, for I believe fate had A gret deal to do with it.'

You must not blame me. Indeed, Castro told Gibbes, he'd never made a promise to return in the event of Sir James'

This gritty backyard portrait taken by Gibbes is the only visual trace of the unvarnished Tom Castro death. In the absence of a photographer in Wagga, Gibbes borrowed a calotype outfit from Healy's auction rooms and produced three shots of Castro, clumsily posed in the yard behind his office, squinting in the broad midday sun. Castro applauded Gibbes' skill as a lensman when he sent them with his letter to the Dowager. 'Speaking of Mr Gibbes,' he told her, 'he is the only friend I ever had since I been in Australia.'

Castro's only friend now found himself with much to do. Since the Dowager had ostensibly acknowledged him as her son, Castro was able—as Roger Tichborne—to approach bankers who might advance him the funds necessary to return to England. William Cottee, manager of the Australian Joint Stock Bank in Wagga, already knew him. Castro had for a long time supplied the bank with meat, as well as banking his employers' takings and keeping his own overdrawn account there. Cottee was more than surprised then, when Gibbes called at the bank one day early in May and confided the butcher's true identity. When Gibbes returned next day with Castro, introducing him as Sir Roger Tichborne, Cottee looked the butcher up and down, seeking some sign of good breeding that hitherto had escaped his notice. None was evident. He could keep books well enough, it was true. He wrote an untidy hand, but you couldn't count on that. Half of the bank's best customers were as bad; a quarter of them could barely write at all. Gibbes had already shown Cottee the Dowager's letter and some of Cubitt's correspondence, and confided in him the 'proofs' he had gleaned of Castro's true identity. Cottee, a betting man as well as a banker, was inclined to believe him. But why, he asked Tom, had he knocked around the colonies instead of going home? To which Tom is supposed to have made the lame and improbable reply: 'Well, it's a very jolly life.'

Castro was seeking enough money to pay his debts and take him to Sydney. Fifty pounds would do it. Cottee agreed and Roger Charles Tichborne signed a three-month bill of exchange for which Gibbes stood guarantor. Castro set about clearing up his debts. He was leaving Wagga for England early in June, he told people. To those who expressed surprise at his apparent change of fortune, Tom said his mother had died and left him a modest inheritance, which he was going home to claim. At least, mostly that's what he said, but as his departure drew nearer he seemed to be courting discovery among his Wagga acquaintances, just as he'd done with Gibbes six months before. He play-acted at secrecy, daring fellow drinkers to guess his real name and leaving clues like 'Sir R.C.T.' scrawled all about the place. One night at Cox's Squatters Hotel he boasted that when he came back from England, he'd build the fanciest butcher shop Wagga had ever seen, overlooking the Wollundry Lagoon, with a plate-glass front and a palm tree either side. He'd call it the Tichborne Meat Emporium.

Down at the lagoon end of Fitzmaurice Street was the bakery establishment of Messrs Cater and Monks. Their partnership broke up in May 1866 and Jack Cater, a steady man who'd done well out of Wagga, decided to return to his native England. Just before he left, he sold his delivery cart to Tom Castro and along with payment Tom handed him a letter marked 'Not to be opened until at Sea.' He was planning to leave Wagga himself in three weeks' time, Tom told him. The cart was to transport his family and their belongings as far as Goulburn, where he'd leave Mary and the girls with Mary's mother. He had his eye on a steamer, the *Kaikoura*, due to depart Sydney on 15 June. But there was still the small question of the fare.

Although Cubitt had explained to them the Dowager's inability to send the money for her son's return, Gibbes and Castro still had hopes that the June mail from England might bring the asked-for £400. When it didn't, they resorted to Plan B. Since winning Cottee's support, Gibbes had been busy floating Tom Castro—or, rather, Roger Tichborne—as an investment among Wagga's leading businessmen. Now Gibbes himself joined draper James Warby and storekeeper George Forsythe in standing guarantor for an advance of £500 from the AJS Bank.

Castro's new backers had taken some convincing. Gathered in Cottee's office at the bank, they questioned him about his family, his estates, and his life pre-Australia. Tom found this testing 'exceedingly disagreeable' and slumped in his chair, sullen and uncommunicative. His manner, said Gibbes, spoke strongly against the idea that he was thrusting himself forward in any way. Afterwards, he blew up at Gibbes for forcing him into such a position—he didn't just mean the questioning, but the whole business of asserting his identity. His inquisitors had managed, though, to extract a few details from between his gritted teeth. He was born in Dorsetshire, he told them, and had been schooled by the Christian Brothers, after which he had enlisted as a private in the 66th Regiment, the Blues. He'd only enlisted for a spree, he said, and had stayed with the regiment just thirteen days before deserting. In talking of his travels in South America he became rather more animated, especially in relating an incident involving mules and precipices. His account of the shipwreck was confused, but he did recall that seven members of the *Bella*'s crew had been rescued with him.

In spite of his surly manner, Castro's performance evidently satisfied Forsythe and Warby. As a final precaution, however, they required that he make a will favouring them with appropriate bequests. This Castro did. He specified in his will three properties which he said were his to dispose of, including Hermitage ('a small farm near Tichborne, in Dorsetshire'). This he bequeathed to his daughter Agnes, leaving another to 'Lady Hannah Frances Tichborne', his mother. To Annie Bryant, 'the daughter of my wife before her marriage with me', he promised an annuity of £200. Castro signed the will 'Roger Charles Tichborne' and his guarantors were satisfied. He had his fare; now he could go home.

EIGHT

THE REVERSE OF AN IMPOSTOR

WITH Cater's cart and a new whip to drive Cokey, the black mare Tom had just broken into harness, the Castro family set out from their place at North Wagga on 2 June 1866. Dick Slate, back in town but lying low, waved them off. They made slow and dicey progress; but after eight days on the road, they arrived at Goulburn. There Tom stopped for a couple of days—long enough to see Mary and the girls settled in with her mother and step-father, and to sell the cart—before setting off for the rest of his journey on horseback. But Tom Castro never did arrive in Sydney.

It was as Sir Roger Tichborne that he handed Cokey's reins to the ostler at the Metropolitan Hotel in Pitt Street. He'd long given up the idea of sailing by the *Kaikoura*—in fact, it left the day before he arrived—and he allowed himself a few quiet days to adjust to his new self. At the Metropolitan, at the tailor's and the tobacconist's he acted, as ever, with a mixture of theatricalised discretion and brazenness—still not sure, apparently, how much of himself to reveal. Gibbes had equipped him with a letter of introduction to the manager of the AJS Bank in Sydney and a warning to avoid Arthur Cubitt. But on his fifth day in Sydney, Sir Roger paid Cubitt a call.

Although he sported a new suit of clothes, his bearing was still far from that of a nobleman and Cubitt was wary. His first impression of 'this Roger Charles Tichborne' was 'a want of fixedness of purpose...I was unable to discover his absolute intentions with any degree of certainty.' Cubitt also marked his 'excitable temperament' and his twitching, which seemed to correspond with the Dowager's information about her son's nervous complaint. Nevertheless, he subjected Sir Roger to a severe line of examination and, before they left his office to dine, was pretty well convinced he had the right man. Was it Sir Roger's answers that convinced him, or something in his manner? Something like 'one little gesture' that had caught Gibbes' eye? Gibbes' wife had made to leave the room and the way in which Castro had opened the door, said Gibbes, bowing neither too much nor too little but with 'easy grace', was unmistakably that of a well-bred man.

After a late lunch at a Pitt Street pie shop, Cubitt went through the Dowager's letters, one by one, checking their meagre details against what Sir Roger knew. She had written that her son was educated by the Jesuits at Stonyhurst College, followed by two years as an officer in the Dragoon Guards. Quizzed now by Cubitt, Sir Roger repeated that he'd been taught by the Christian Brothers and attributed the discrepancy to the Dowager's poor grasp of details. But when her statement about his army career contradicted his, he exploded, 'I never was an officer. By God, I have a bloody good mind not to go near her at all when I go home.' Which, you must admit, was just how Roger Tichborne might speak of his mother. Cubitt must have felt so too, for he was emboldened to produce a letter addressed to Sir Roger from a Mr Francis Turville, private secretary to the governor of New South Wales.

Turville was well acquainted with the Tichborne family; in fact, he was one of the executors of Sir James' will. But he had never met Roger. The Dowager Lady Tichborne had written to Turville asking him to seek her son out and 'be a friend to him.' He, in turn, had entrusted Cubitt with the letter Sir Roger now held in his hand. As the Dowager had desired, Turville offered advice and friendship; more importantly though, he quoted at length from the Dowager's letter in which she professed no shadow of doubt that Cubitt's man

was her son. Here was the next best thing to an outright acknowledgment and it lifted spirits in the Missing Friends Office. Sir Roger
parted warmly from Cubitt, agreeing to meet again that evening.
Then he telegraphed Gibbes in Wagga: 'Identified by lady. Government
house sent letter. Acceptance all right.' Cubitt, meanwhile, pulled a
fresh leaf of quarto from his paper rack and commenced to write:
'My dear Madam,—After a long, anxious, tedious, and expensive
search, I have at length succeeded in discovering your son…'

Whether ingenuously or (more probably) not, Sir Roger had
conveyed to Cubitt the ill-will borne him by Gibbes. Cubitt felt it
necessary, therefore, to include a paragraph 'clearing myself of serious
imputations against my character':

> through the perfidy and deceit of one of my agents, who, with
> a view to acquiring gain for himself, has not hesitated to villify
> me in a manner disgusting to the feelings of any honourable
> man. Your son has been innocently dragged into a belief of
> these vile charges; but, with a candour and honesty which reflect
> the greatest credit, has promised without delay to remedy the
> injury already inflicted.

This Sir Roger did the next day. Supplied with a sheet of the same
paper, he assured the Dowager: 'I have found Mr Cubitt A very
different person to what he was represented to me.' Furthermore, he
told her, he had reached an 'arrangement' with Cubitt for the 'expence
and truble he been to.' In other words, learning of the relative ease
with which Sir Roger had secured £500 from the bank, Cubitt had
leaned on him for his share—the lion's share—of the reward. Sir
Roger promised to settle up with Cubitt before leaving Sydney. After
all, it was no more than he had promised Gibbes.

Cubitt and Sir Roger spent day after day together: at Cubitt's office
or the School of Arts of a morning, and sampling Sydney's wine shops
and hostelries most afternoons. When a week had passed, Cubitt

arranged a meeting between Sir Roger and Francis Turville, who
asked Sir Roger to describe his mother's appearance. When he saw
her last, said Sir Roger, she was 'stout, a very tall, large woman', not
unlike Mrs Butts, wife of the Metropolitan Hotel's landlord, in fact.
Turville was stumped. He could see not a speck of resemblance between
the burly woman who had just served them with tea and the sparrow-
like Dowager Lady Tichborne. But then Turville hadn't met Sir
Roger's mother until the late 1850s, by which time, he told himself,
grief and illness might have reduced her to a fraction of the woman
her son had known. Turville passed an hour in Sir Roger's company
and told his sister in England:

> I went yesterday to see Roger Tichborne. What an apparition!!
> And yet I think from his manner which is the reverse of that of
> an impostor, that he is the man. I noted, though I hardly like
> to write it, a look about the eyes and mouth which strongly
> reminded me of his father. His upper front teeth are all missing
> and he was, I can assure you, dirty enough, both in person and
> in dress for even a colonial butcher. His English too, a little
> butchery at times. His manner was nice and quiet…Why had
> he hidden himself in this way? He had always felt that he was
> a bad lot, and had been perfectly happy working for his bread
> as a common man. Even now, he should just go home to estab-
> lish his claim, see his mother, and then return to the colony
> where he means to live.

There it was again: *his manner which is the reverse of an impostor*. He
made so little effort to convince people of it that he *must* be Roger
Tichborne.

Soon after, a change of heart came over Sir Roger concerning the
family he'd left at Goulburn. A telegram to Mary was followed by himself
in the mail coach, looking better-heeled and better-fed than when she'd
seen him last. Now, at last, he told her who she'd married and what that

made her: Lady Tichborne, no less. He was taking her back to England with him, her and Agnes both. Annie (for all that he was fond of the kid) would have to stay in Australia with Grandma Payne: there'd be no place for her in the Tichborne family, he was afraid.

First things first, though. He and Mary had to get married again— properly this time, in a Catholic church. In her latest letter to Cubitt, the Dowager had demanded not only to know whether her son was married, but whether he was 'regularly' married:

> …as if it is not according to the laws the birth of the children will be disputed; you know yourself how important it is where there is entailed property, and if he married under another name even the marriage be legal, and also I wish to know whether he has been married according to the protestant religion; all those things are very necessary to know.

It was done. On 9 July 1866, Roger Charles Tichborne (gentleman) and Mary Ann Bryant were married by Father McAlroy at the Church of Sts Peter and Paul, Goulburn. Three days later they arrived back in Sydney with the overland mail.

Sir Roger's initial £50 advance was long since spent and during his first weeks in Sydney he'd drawn freely, but not extravagantly, on his £500. Now he began running up bills at a heavy rate. He took a suite of rooms at the Metropolitan to accommodate his household, hired a coach to show his wife the town and spent more than two years' Wagga wages on rigging out Mary and himself in a manner befitting their new position. A strange thing: the less 'butchery' he made himself, the more meaty he became. After a month of idle city living, he'd already gained almost two stone. A studio portrait taken at the time (so that the Dowager might see 'how greatly I have improve') shows his double chin and waistcoat beginning to fill out nicely.

In the third week of July an item appeared in the *Sydney Morning Herald* relating the 'singular' tale of Sir Roger Tichborne, who had lately

'How greatly I have improve'—*Sir Roger in Sydney, July 1866. He appears to
have been treated to a haircut after the event. Clumsy shading above the right
shoulder suggests that his hair originally hung below collar-length*

emerged from 'the obscurity of the Riverina' to claim his title and
estates. Within days, the story reached the Riverinal obscurity of
Wagga where it led the 'Local Intelligence' column in the *Express* of

21 July. It was headed 'Freak of Fortune', ratifying Tom Castro's boast of almost a year earlier.

> For some months past, a vague kind of rumour has been current in Wagga Wagga to the effect that a veritable British Peer was quietly residing, under an assumed name, in our midst. It was a rumour, however, to which very little credibility was attached, and was oftener the subject of jocular allusion than serious remark. It now turns out that, though not quite correct in form, it still approximated very nearly to truth...we really have been daily brushing up against a baronet for the last two or three years without knowing it. The individual to whom we refer has, up to the present time, been known to our townsmen only as 'Tom Castro,' and, during his residence amongst us, has occupied a very humble station in life. Recent events have disclosed the fact that his real name is not Castro, but Roger Charles Tichbourne, eldest son and heir-at-law to the late Sir James Tichbourne, Baronet, of Tichbourne Park, Hants. To the title and estates he now succeeds, together with an income of between ten and fifteen thousand pounds per annum. The history of the new baronet is rather a singular one. On or about the year 1854, being then quite a lad, and of rather a roving disposition, he quitted England in the ship 'Bella', which was, a few weeks later, wrecked off the port of Rio Janeiro. Young Tichbourne escaped to the land, minus his worldly goods, and then assumed the name of Castro, and as nothing was afterwards heard of him, it was believed he had perished, and, in the British peerages, he was reported dead. South American manners not being suited to his tastes, he again embarked on board a ship bound for Australia, and, in due course, arrived at Sydney. Being then without either money or friends, he was thrown entirely on his own resources, and experienced his full share of the rough vicissitudes of colonial life...

NINE

IS THAT YOU?

A DAY or two later, Sir Roger received unexpected callers at the Metropolitan. Michael Guilfoyle had been head gardener at Tichborne Park before migrating to Sydney in 1848. Now a successful and well-connected nurseryman, he read of Sir Roger in the *Herald* and came with his wife, Charlotte, to re-establish his link with the Tichbornes. Of course, he was curious, too. Guilfoyle recalled having met—or seen—Roger only once during his years at Tichborne Park. But he was well acquainted with others of the family and felt, like Turville, that he could recognise a real Tichborne when he saw one.

Sir Roger was at first flummoxed by his visitors. The name Guilfoyle meant nothing to him; nor could he recall the gardener at Tichborne. Guilfoyle also met a blank response when he asked Sir Roger about various of his relations. The Guilfoyles nonetheless left satisfied. Mr remarked on the likeness between Sir Roger and his uncle Robert Tichborne, particularly his voice and the back of his head, while Mrs thought his nose 'like his mamma's'. 'Yesterday,' Sir Roger told his mamma, 'one of Uncle Edward's Old servants call on me; he knew me has soon has he see me.'

One of Guilfoyle's questions had been 'Have you seen Bogle yet?' Sir Roger knew about Bogle. In one of her letters to Cubitt, the Dowager had revealed that 'there is a man of colour at Sidney who could tell you how the family stands, his name is *Bogle* and is quite black. Roger knows him very well, he was valet to Sir Edward Doughty.'

Andrew Bogle had been eleven years old when the young Sir Edward, then manager of a Jamaican sugar plantation, had 'taken a fancy' to him. In 1825, he went to England as Sir Edward's pageboy and later valet, a position he held until his master's death in 1853. Bogle took his family to Australia the following year, hoping that his sons might fare better than in England 'where the colour is against them' and where they would almost certainly end up servants like him. In Sydney, Guilfoyle helped set him up in a greengrocer's stall at the market which, together with a £50 annuity from Sir Edward's estate, gave Bogle a fair livelihood. His sons were settled now at their respective trades—one a Balmain barber, the other a musician—and Bogle, nearly sixty and widowed, dreamt of returning to England. People were 'more sociable' there, he'd decided; and he envisioned that, with his £50 pension, he could see out his years in the modest comfort of a Hampshire lodging house. But he couldn't afford the fare and Sir Edward's widow, to whom he wrote once a year when his pension arrived, had chosen not to apprehend his hints in that direction.

Now, though Sir Roger knew that Bogle was in Sydney, he—or rather, Cubitt—had been chary of seeking out the old servant because of something else the Dowager had written. 'I am afraid that man as soon as he has seen Roger will write it back to England immediately,' she declared, 'and I am afraid of the consequences which would be bad if not attended to.' If Bogle wrote to his patroness Lady Doughty he might blow the whistle on the Dowager's discovery of Roger. She did *not* want the rest of the family interfering. They had long dismissed her as mad, she knew, for believing Roger alive, and would do anything rather than admit she'd been right. And Lady Doughty—she was the worst of them. Alfred's widow, Tissie, was her niece, and those Arundells would be determined, the Dowager was sure, to keep a hold of the Tichborne estates. Cubitt, of course, was ignorant of these details; it was enough that Bogle sounded like trouble and he advised Sir Roger to avoid him.

Which is why Sir Roger was startled when, a couple of days after the Guilfoyles' visit, he found an elderly black man waiting in the yard of the Metropolitan Hotel. Sir Roger greeted him without hesitation—'Hello, Bogle, is that you?'—but then bolted upstairs on the pretext of changing out of his riding boots. Bogle waited (he was used to waiting) and after some minutes Sir Roger sent for him. Coming into the room, Bogle apologised: 'I came to see Sir Roger Tichborne.' Sir Roger just looked at him steadily.

'But you're not him, are you?' Bogle was incredulous.

'Oh yes, Bogle, I am.'

'But you've got so stout!'

'Well,' conceded Sir Roger, lighting his pipe, 'I'm not so slender as I was when I left Tichborne.'

But already Bogle began to see a resemblance to Sir Henry Tichborne, who had died falling from a horse in 1845. He told Sir Roger how things had changed for the worse at Tichborne after Sir Edward's death (didn't say, though, that Sir Roger's mother was the cause), how Gosford had advised him to leave and he'd decided to come to Australia. He still kept in touch with Lady Doughty, he said. Oh yes? said Sir Roger. How was she? And Bogle told him about Miss Doughty: how she'd married a Mr Radcliffe and had two children now, a boy and a girl if he recalled right, and another that had died. Bogle almost stopped himself as he spoke Miss Doughty's name, remembering, too late, how she and Mr Roger had been sweethearts and the trouble there'd been over it. But Sir Roger's face, through his pipe-smoke haze, never shifted from its look of steady interest.

Bogle called again the next day, and the next, and on the fourth day it was agreed that he would accompany Sir Roger to England. Bogle had proposed it at their first meeting; by their third, he'd sold up all his belongings and was dashed when Sir Roger told him he couldn't afford the extra fare. One of Bogle's sons agreed then to put up the money, on the understanding that Sir Roger would repay him.

So, within a week of their meeting, the old man joined Sir Roger's growing entourage in rooms upstairs at the Metropolitan Hotel. The household now included a nursemaid for baby Agnes and a young man whom Sir Roger called his secretary or protegé, the curiously named Truth Butts.

All this was costing money; but, just as the Dowager had predicted, Sir Roger found funds easy to come by once his identity became public knowledge. Stephen Butts, landlord of the Metropolitan and father of Truth, allowed him generous credit as well as cash advances. Butts reasoned that Sir Roger was good for business. After all, he spent nearly half of each day in the public house portion of the hotel, playing billiards and 'oiling his wig'. Plenty of folks came to the hotel just to lay eyes on him. And he was a likeable fellow, Sir Roger—very approachable, very natural-like for nobility. He'd even expressed interest in buying the Metropolitan.

Securing enough money to convey Sir Roger's entire party to England took time, causing their departure to be further delayed. Gibbes came up from Wagga to assure the Sydney bankers of his client's credentials (Cubitt having proved reluctant either to lend money or stand guarantor). For the bankers' satisfaction, Sir Roger made a statutory declaration, similar in detail to the newspaper reports except for its account of the shipwreck and his rescue. He now stated that the ill-fated *Bella* had been sailing from—not to—Rio, and with his seven fellow survivors he'd been picked up by the *Osprey*, which had landed them in Melbourne—not Sydney—on 24 July 1854. It was there, he said, that he'd assumed the name of Castro. Lordly living, it seemed, was restoring Sir Roger's memory by degrees.

'I was living pretty fast,' Sir Roger said, much later, of his time in Sydney, 'going about for pleasure and riding and driving.' He rode a hearty silver-grey colt named Quicksand, and out-paced a constable's hack in Macquarie Street when he looked like being slung for furious riding in the botanic gardens. Even so it was a sedentary life compared to what he'd known before, and a rather more lavishly victualled one, with all the trimmings—all the sauces and puddings and comfits—in abundance. He was in demand as a dinner guest among Sydney's elite, but he 'didn't care about that sort of thing' and always declined. He realised that it was as an object of curiosity that he was invited, like a performing bear or a tamed savage, and he wasn't about to give these colonial nobs a chance to gloat over his 'butchery' manners. It was his failure to turn up at a dinner in his honour that lost Sir Roger the support of the Guilfoyles shortly before his departure. They'd gone to considerable expense, hiring servants and napery, inviting some of Sydney's leading people (Guilfoyle's best customers among them), even organising fireworks in their harbourside garden. Michael Guilfoyle had made much of his connection to Sir Roger, going so far as to assure a money-lender: 'I could swear to him as I could to my own child.' Now the slight of Sir Roger's non-attendance caused Guilfoyle to reconsider his certainty.

Sir Roger's departure was finally fixed for 2 September, aboard the steamship *Rakaia*. Ten days before, Bogle wrote the letter the Dowager had feared. 'My Lady,' he addressed Lady Doughty, 'I send your Ladyship these to inform your Ladyship that Sir Roger & Lady Tichborne are in Sydney, also a little girl six months old, that they leave Sydney by the mail (Panama & NZ) on the second proximo, and I am going with them…Her Ladyship,' Bogle went on, meaning Sir Roger's wife Mary, 'is a native of Australia about 22 or 23 years of age.' These were the first tidings to reach England of the new Lady Tichborne.

In the final days before he sailed, Sir Roger settled up. To Stephen Butts he gave bills of exchange on Drummond's Bank in London totalling nearly £11,000: £10,000 as the purchase price of the Metropolitan Hotel and some £1,000 in monies owed. As promised, he paid Cubitt and Gibbes their rewards—£1,000 to the former and just £500 to his 'only friend'. When Cubitt wrote to inform the

Dowager of her son's impending departure, his own interests stood, as ever, at the forefront:

> On the subject of rewarding, this has been arranged with Sir Roger, and he has given me his bills on the Oriental Bank Corporation in London, dated so as to give him plenty of time to honour them at maturity. If the mail steamer arrives to her time he will have about three weeks to spare before they fall due. As Sir Roger no doubt will have many important engagements connected with his estates, in the midst of these he might by accident forget to place the funds in the bank to meet these bills. I am, of course, extremely anxious that no accident of this kind should occur, as it would injure my credit and reputation. It will not, therefore, be out of place to remind Sir Roger of this engagement.

Belatedly, he wished the Dowager 'a happy reunion' and expressed the hope 'that no difficulty will arise on your side of the globe in restoring him to his estates.' He might have added that, if it did, it would be no concern of his. Within days of receiving Sir Roger's bills, he sold them to a money-lender for four-fifths of their face value.

William Gibbes was in Sydney to see Sir Roger off. Uncomplaining, he paid for the three cabs that conveyed the party and their belongings to the docks, as well as for a pair of canvas deck shoes that caught Sir Roger's eye on the way, and a basket of fresh fruit. (Cubitt's *bon voyage* gift had been a half-bottle of Snowgood's Seasick Salve.) Gibbes even supplied a ha'penny for the weighing machine at the quay: Sir Roger always, it seemed, marked momentous occasions with a public weighing. The scale gave his weight as fifteen stone, the gain of fifty-two pounds since his Wagga wedding largely attributable to the ten weeks in Sydney. Back in Wagga, Gibbes wrote to tell the Dowager that her son was on his way and, almost as an afterthought, mentioned the existence of Sir Roger's wife and daughter. He extolled Sir Roger's 'unasked generosity' in rewarding him and, little thinking that his rival had received twice as much, stated that the £500—in the form of bills, like Cubitt's, redeemable on a London bank three months hence—'has far more than requited me for any services I have performed.'

Nobody knows what qualms or jubilation Sir Roger felt in leaving Australia and heading home at last. After the *Rakaia* pulled away from the quay, he stood pensive at the ship's rail for fully four minutes—until a magsman from second class claimed his attention with the offer of a game of cards.

TEN

AN IMPUDENT ATTEMPT AT EXTORTION

The new Baronet is in the prime of life, a portly gentleman, weighing 250 lb, but of an active, athletic frame, a great lover of horses and field sports generally, and notwithstanding his eighteen stone weight, he is withal a splendid rider, having apparently spent more of his life in the saddle than on foot. He is exceedingly kind and amiable, and possessed of that great requirement, common sense. Although not endowed with a large share of aristocratic polish, he will, we are sure, make a far better citizen and a more pleasant neighbour than many a more 'elegant gentleman'.

—*Panama Star*, 5 November 1866

Two months and three stone on, Sir Roger was just leaving Panama. He ought to have been nearly to England by now, but other things had claimed his attention. Between Sydney and Panama he'd gambled incessantly with three 'notorious blacklegs' in second class. The captain had tried to break up the rowdy junta by ordering that no first-class passenger was allowed in second class; but Sir Roger simply invited his friends up to his cabin instead. Travelling with him in first class were his wife, his baby daughter, and her Scotch nursemaid, Rosina McArthur. Down in second class were Truth Butts and Andrew Bogle. Butts' secretarial duties on board ship amounted to fetching cigars and tobacco and fresh bottles of brandy, and periodically running up on deck to settle wagers about the height of the waves or the fullness of the moon. Gout confined poor Bogle to his berth all the way to Panama.

The *Rakaia* reached Panama in the first week of October. In 1866 there was no canal through the isthmus that joined North and South America. Passengers travelling from Pacific to Atlantic had to disembark at Panama, cross the isthmus by rail and board an eastbound vessel. Sir Roger lingered at Panama. Cut adrift from his advisers, he was in at least three minds as to how he ought to proceed. To London? Or to France so that he could present himself directly to the Dowager in Paris? Or might he follow his fancy and join his shipmates bound for California? After a long month's prevarication, during which the *Rakaia* passengers dispersed east and west and his travel funds dwindled, Sir Roger settled on an intermediate destination: New York. From Aspinwall, the fever-ridden port on the Atlantic side of the Panama isthmus, they took the steamship *Henry Chauncey*. There was another month's lingering in New York. Sir Roger paid visits to Washington, Baltimore, and Philadelphia and, after borrowing $700 from his new friend Mr Galway, a New York provision merchant, was able to pay his hotel bill and launch his entourage on the final leg of their long journey home. They sailed aboard the *Cella*, bound for London, on 10 December 1866.

The Dowager Lady Tichborne, in Paris for the winter, had been expecting Sir Roger for more than a month. Gibbes' and Cubitt's letters informing her of his departure from Sydney had arrived in the second week of November, and Sir Roger ought to have arrived with them. For weeks now the Dowager's solicitor had had his man at the London docks watching every Atlantic arrival for Sir Roger and his family. And others were waiting for him, too.

When Bogle's Sydney letter reached Lady Doughty in mid-October, she sent copies to her daughter and to the executors of the Tichborne estates, telling them, 'I cannot help feeling agitated with this most strange affair.' Bogle's letter was not the first she had heard of it, however. The emergence in Australia of a person claiming to be Roger Tichborne had been generally known amongst the family for more than six months, the source of that knowledge almost certainly being the Bowker brothers. James Bowker of Gray's Inn, London, was the Dowager's solicitor, whilst his brother Frederick, of Winchester, was solicitor to Sir Alfred's widow, Lady Teresa Tichborne. Since March, Frederick Bowker had also represented the interests of a person whom the Dowager had failed to mention in her correspondence to Australia: Sir Alfred's posthumous son, Henry Alfred Joseph Doughty Tichborne. By rights, the infant was the new Tichborne baronet and heir to his father's estates. Imagine then the feelings of his family and the Tichborne executors when they learnt that the Dowager claimed to have found the long-lost Roger.

'I am afraid the whole business is an impudent attempt at extortion.' That was the stated opinion of James Bowker when he read his client's first letters from Gibbes and Castro, in March 1866. Forwarding Castro's letter to the Dowager in Paris, Bowker drew her attention to many discrepancies between the writing style of Roger Tichborne (of which he had numerous examples on file) and that of the man from Wagga.

The Dowager defended her new-found son against Bowker's suspicions. 'If he had lived among savages these last 12 years,' she told him, 'it is possible he should have forgotten English or at least that he should not write it as correctly as one could wish.' Her brother, Henry Seymour, when she showed him Castro's letter, also expressed grave doubts and remonstrated with her against acknowledging him as her son. 'And her answer to me,' reported Seymour, 'was that she was ready to swear to him without ever having seen him.' That readiness was evident in her correspondence with William Gibbes.

> I think my poor dear Roger confuses everything in his head, just as in a dream, and I believe him to be my son, although his

statements differ from mine…I fancy that the photographics you sent me are like him, but of course after 13 years' absence there must be some difference in the shape…

When the Dowager showed James Bowker the photos sent from Wagga, he failed to see any likeness to the Roger Tichborne he had known. But she recognised the chin, she said, and 'was prepared to swear that it was her son in any court of justice whatever.' Bowker pointed out that her recognition alone would not be sufficient to restore her son to his position and estates; he would also be required to answer 'some questions'. The Dowager sniffed at that. Roger would never submit to it, she said. And to Gibbes she simply lied: 'My solic-itor told me that they cannot keep Sir Roger out of his possessions for one hour when he has been identified.'

Once Sir Roger was in Sydney, reports of sightings filtered back to the circle of interested Hampshire persons: Lady Doughty, Francis Baigent, Lady Teresa Tichborne, and others who had known the young Roger. Most of the Sydney correspondents, while in no position to identify Sir Roger, were inclined to give him the benefit of the doubt; so that, by the time Bogle's letter arrived, Lady Doughty felt 'this person must be Roger but the circumstances altogether make it a painful event in the family.'

Baigent, despite his involvement in some of the Dowager's earlier wild-goose chases, was less ready to suspend disbelief. He had grown estranged from the Dowager in the years since Sir James' death, but remained on close terms with Lady Doughty and the incumbent Tichbornes. He wrote to a friend:

There is something so very droll about this story of the discovery of Roger Tichborne as to make it perfectly laughable, not to say ridiculous; certainly people are very credulous but in a case like this they ought to give their minds a little reflection—surely it does not bear looking into?…I do not believe for one moment that the person in question is the son of the late Sir James Tichborne.

Francis Cullington of the London firm Cullington & Slaughter, solicitors to the Doughty estates, was the first to use the word 'impostor'. 'I fear it must be a deep plot,' he warned Lady Doughty, 'and that we should protect the Infant Sir Henry and all interested in the family.'

At the beginning of November 1866, the text of Bogle's Sydney letter found its way into the *Hampshire Chronicle*, accompanied by a sceptical commentary on the affair of 'the *soi disant* Roger Tichborne.' The story went on to appear in newspapers all over England in the ensuing weeks and inside a month it had crossed the Atlantic to half fill a column in the *New York Herald* on the very morning of Sir Roger's departure. It was drawn to his notice by a fellow passenger, a W. H. Stephens, who was himself a journalist with the *Herald*. Until that very moment, half a day's steaming from New York, Sir Roger had not allowed of the possibility that he might be branded an impostor. Rough weather was already causing the *Cella* to buck violently from swell to swell; but that was not the only reason he felt ill.

He would emerge from that journey, as he'd done from others, with a new identity. The difference was that, this time, it would not be one of his own making. There could be only one living Tichborne baronet and, for now, the infant Sir Henry was it. To establish his right to the title and estates, Sir Roger would have to prove his identity. Meanwhile, he might call himself Sir Roger Tichborne, but there were those who would insist that he was Castro or some different person altogether. The name by which he would be most widely known—the new identity that awaited him in London—was the Tichborne Claimant, or just the Claimant.

When Christmas approached with still no sign of any person calling himself Sir Roger Tichborne, those waiting in England began to suppose that either he wasn't coming or had decided to meet the Dowager in Paris. Lady Doughty's view was that 'some competent person'—*not* the Dowager, in other words—ought to be stationed at the docks to recognise the Claimant (or not) upon his first landing. As it was, when the *Cella* berthed at Victoria Dock in London, those who might have watched for the Claimant were occupied elsewhere. It was mid-afternoon on a snowbound Christmas Day.

From the docks, the Claimant took his family straight to Ford's Hotel in the West End, the Tichborne family's usual bolt-hole in London. He went out for a while after dinner, purportedly to scout for the Dowager's London address and ascertain whether she was in town. Her house in Beaumont Street had been in darkness, he told Mary next morning; it looked as if his mamma must still be in Paris.

'Then why were you gone so long?' snapped Mary. It had been past midnight when he got in.

'Just re-acquainting myself with the old place.'

He packed himself and his family off, later that day, to the relative seclusion and economy of Gravesend, twenty-five-odd miles east of London near the mouth of the Thames.

When James Bowker arrived at his office two days after Christmas, he found a note from his man at the docks, informing him of the Claimant's arrival. Bowker swore. He telegraphed the Dowager and made for Ford's Hotel, hoping he wasn't too late. What if the Claimant had already left for Paris? That damned woman would recognise him whoever he was, if only to spite the rest of the family—never mind that she might perjure herself in the process. At Ford's he found only Bogle and Butts—one ill, the other ignorant—whom the Claimant had left behind. They couldn't say, didn't know, where he'd gone. Paris? Perhaps. No, he hadn't gone to Hampshire, they were sure, as he'd promised to take Bogle with him. Well, at least that was something, thought Bowker; the Dowager would be apoplectic if the Claimant went to Hampshire before he came to her.

The Claimant travelled down to Hampshire by train two days later. Since Roger Tichborne had last been there, the railway had extended to Alresford, within two miles of Tichborne Park; so it was at Alresford that the Claimant alighted with his travelling bag, 'RCT' stamped in gold below the clasp. At the Swan Inn in Broad Street, he gave his name as Taylor. The Swan's landlord, Edward Rous, that evening accepted the bulky stranger's offer of a cigar in the parlour. Was it possible, wondered the Claimant, to visit Tichborne Park? Rous, as it happened, had served twenty years as clerk to Edward Hopkins, who had only recently retired as solicitor to the Tichborne estates. Tichborne House was at present occupied by a tenant, he said, a Colonel Lushington. What exactly was his interest? asked Rous. He had come over on the ship with Sir Roger, explained the Claimant, and as he himself was a journalist, he naturally took a great interest in the affair. What was Sir Roger like? Rous wanted to know. Alresford was abuzz with the business. For weeks now they'd been expecting to see Sir Roger any day, and folks round these parts had set their views as to whether or not the fellow who'd come forward was the real man. He should know, chuckled Rous, there'd been enough rows over it in the bar of the Swan. Someone was even running a book on it. Well, said the Claimant, the feller he'd met on the boat had struck him as the real Simon Pure. There'd been an old black servant with him. Bogle? asked Rous. That was him, said the Claimant. Well my, said Rous.

By evening's end, Rous was fairly certain it was Sir Roger he had been smoking with. Rous had remarked that he'd heard that Sir Roger had got quite stout. Oh yes, replied the Claimant, I should say he's a man of about my size. Taking a look at him then, Rous had been startled to make out a shade of likeness to Sir Alfred about the lower part of the face. And hadn't Sir Edward and Sir James both been big men? Sir James in particular had got terrifically stout. They drove out together next morning, Rous and the Claimant. Rous had planned to offer a saddle-horse from his stable, but realising that none of his mounts would be sturdy enough to carry the big man (the needle on the scales at Waterloo Station had flickered past nineteen stone), took him instead in the gig.

Tichborne Park was in the direction of Winchester, set in hard, flinty, fox-hunting country close to the source of the Itchen River (to which the Tichborne family owed its name). The house itself consisted of two storeys, seven bays and an unremarkable porch. Built in 1803, it had replaced a structure dating from Saxon times, of which only a small lake—the vestige of a moat—remained. Beyond the house, on rising ground, stood the village of Tichborne; higher still, and visible for miles around, was the little square-towered church—properly the Tichborne family chapel.

Colonel Lushington was away from home, so the Claimant had to content himself with viewing Tichborne House from the outside and strolling for a bit in the grounds. He seemed deep in thought, Rous observed, and when he spoke it wasn't to ask questions as a visitor would have done, but rather, to point out (tentatively, it was true) the rooms that had been Roger's and to inquire whether the downstairs office was still in use. As they left the Park, he asked about the fishing and Rous replied he believed it had improved after Roger left. The Claimant smiled at that, and Rous challenged him. 'You're Sir Roger, aren't you?'

'You've got me there, Mr Rous,' the Claimant conceded, after a moment-and-a-half's hesitation. He still loved keeping secrets. 'But, for God's sake, don't let on.' He didn't want people recognising him yet, he said; not until he'd seen his mother.

Back at Alresford, he summoned Bogle by telegram and drew attention to himself by attempting to hide the lower part of his face in a handkerchief.

Bogle arrived by train first thing next morning and was recognised as soon as he set foot on the platform. He was hailed and stopped repeatedly on his way to the Swan, everyone greeting him with the wondering words: 'Then it's true…?' Bogle was the Claimant's canary, lowered down the pit first in case of deadly gas. Their brief meeting at the Swan was the first time Bogle had seen the Claimant since boarding the *Cella* in New York. Bogle was buoyant at the welcome he'd received and the Claimant, too, took heart from it. There was a New Year's Day mass at the Tichborne parish church, to which he sent Bogle to further test for fumes. Emboldened by Bogle's warm reception, the Claimant repaired to the bar of the Swan and bought a pint of ale for an old blacksmith, John Etheridge. Etheridge had seen a lot of the young Roger. In fact, it was he who'd given the lad the idea of taking a chisel when he went out fishing—'just as a lark, like.' When he judged the moment right (when Etheridge accepted a second pint), the Claimant asked, 'Do you think I could be Sir Roger?'

The old man nearly coughed up his anchovies. 'If you are, you've turned from a race-horse to a cart-horse.' Then he realised that the Claimant was serious. 'No!' he declared, 'I'll be damned if you are.'

The Claimant consoled himself by drinking Etheridge's untouched second pint.

Outside the church after mass, Bogle was greeted warmly by, among others, one of Roger Tichborne's cousins and the bailiff and his wife. Where was Sir Roger? they asked, and was it really him? Indeed it was Sir Roger, replied Bogle, and he was about to leave for Paris to see his mother (which is what he'd been told to say). He was asked the same questions when he called, with the bailiff, at Tichborne House. As a young maid, the housekeeper had been terrified of Bogle, but now she was pleased to show him over the old place and point out the changes since his time. (There was less on the walls than there had been: the result of Sir Alfred's fire sale.) Arriving back at the Swan after dinner, Bogle found a small crowd waiting for him, all wanting to hear about Sir Roger, and a few even wanting to hear about Bogle.

By now, the news was abroad that the Claimant himself was in

Alresford. Bogle's presence suggested it and Etheridge's account of the lardy pint-buyer tended to confirm it. The Claimant was alone in his private sitting-room at the Swan when a slim, excited gentleman burst in. He was momentarily nonplussed at the sight of the Claimant. Then, 'Are you Roger Tichborne?' he demanded.

'I am,' replied the Claimant in a muffled but dignified voice. He had covered his face with his hands. 'Now get out.'

The intruder introduced himself as Frederick Bowker, solicitor to the Tichborne family and its estates, and he stated his business bluntly: 'I came to tell you to mind what you're about.' But there he faltered. It was disconcerting, presenting an ultimatum to a man with his face covered. 'You say you *are* Roger Tichborne?'

'Get *out*,' the Claimant repeated, behind his hands.

So Bowker finished what he'd come to say. He had fought hard to preserve the estates from the excesses of the wastrel Sir Alfred and he was not about to see them handed over to an impostor. Any question of entitlement to the property, he told the top of the Claimant's untidy head, must be decided in a court of law. He hesitated again. 'Do you understand?'

'Get out!' said the Claimant again, his voice rising.

'Goodbye then, sir,' said Frederick Bowker and did as he was bid, shutting the door with a resolute click.

The Claimant and Bogle took the train back to London next morning. With time to spare while he waited for a connecting train to Gravesend, the Claimant stepped into the Continental Hotel, London Bridge, where he made the acquaintance, across a billiard table, of a commercial traveller for Allsopp's the brewers named Joseph Leete. The Claimant happened to mention that he was just back from Australia, causing Leete to remark how he'd heard the heir to the Tichborne estates had lately returned from that part of the world. As it happened, he'd known Sir Alfred Tichborne rather well himself.

'Well, *snap!*' declared the Claimant, 'So did I. In fact, he was my brother.'

Their game having been ruined anyway by a sideways flourish of the Claimant's cue on the word *snap*, he and Leete retired to the privacy of a booth curtained in by cigar smoke.

By noon next day, 3 January 1867, the Claimant had himself an attorney: John Holmes, of 25, Poultry. His speciality was commercial law and Allsopp's ranked among his larger clients—which is how Leete came to recommend him. Holmes had read about Sir Roger, of course, in the papers. Otherwise, all he knew of the Tichborne family and its affairs was that one of his clients had lost out badly over the late Sir Alfred's bankruptcy. The Claimant's case must have appealed to Holmes as a challenge. But, more immediately, the man himself appealed. The butcheriness was still there, but it was more thoroughly intermixed now with hints of cultivation and an expansive generosity of nature. In the space of six months the Claimant had transformed from a buffoon and cattle-duffer to a gentleman's idea of good company. Now his incessant talk of horses qualified him as a keen sportsman, his social awkwardnesses and odd mannerisms were classed as eccentricities, and his tall tales of life on the Australian frontier held listeners enthralled. In short, he had become that most desirable of clubland drinking companions: a gentleman who had lived.

ELEVEN

THE LONG-LOST MAN

BY telling the Claimant, in effect, *I'll see you in court*, Frederick Bowker had unwittingly shown him how he ought to proceed. Holmes' first act on the Claimant's behalf was to apprise Bowker formally of his client's claim on the Tichborne estates. His second was to inform the newspapers of his client's triumphant visit to Alresford, where he had (according to the Claimant) been rapturously acknowledged as Sir Roger Tichborne by townsfolk and tenantry alike. Lady Doughty's solicitor complained, 'The *Daily Telegraph* placarded it all over Town yesterday, and had half a column about it, and a sensational leading article on it to day. It is well done to prejudice the public mind in his favour.' Holmes' commercial nous, as well as his contacts in Fleet Street, were already shaping up well against Bowker's provincial pluck.

The other Bowker, James Bowker, the Dowager's man in London, had a letter from her: 'I am afraid he will find snares laid in his way in London, and I am very desirous that he should come immediately. I am his best friend. Alas very few people are my poor Roger's friend. I wish I could draw him away from London where he has so many enemies.' These sounded like her 'imaginary fears', the kind that, as the Roger of old had wearily pointed out to his mother, 'are quite unknown to any body but yourself.' But it was true that opposition to the Claimant was growing. The Tichborne family and its supporters had not set out to oppose him; to begin with, they had merely wanted to be certain that he was who he said he was. But his behaviour so far had given them cause for suspicion, chiefly in that he appeared to acquiesce to the Dowager's wishes and to avoid the very people with whom Roger had been most intimate. Hearing that the Dowager had instructed her solicitor that the Claimant was on no account to go near 'a certain relative' (meaning Lady Doughty), Baigent observed, 'If Roger is what he was when I knew him, he will not easily be led from his own view of things.' But there was the problem, apparently: neither Roger nor his view of things were what they had been.

Francis Cullington was the Tichborne family's eyes and ears in London. Calling at Ford's Hotel in search of the Claimant, he had struck up an acquaintance with Truth Butts. The young man was glad to have somebody to talk to (Bogle was away, and wasn't much company in any case) and even gladder to have dinner bought for him. For although he'd been promised £500 a year as Sir Roger's secretary, he told Cullington, he'd seen no more than £10 of it yet. Butts did happen to mention that Sir Roger had forgotten how to speak French. 'This looks suspicious,' noted Cullington. He left Butts with a £5 note and a message for his master that his friends and relations were eager to see him and 'speak as to his identity.' When, on returning from Alresford, the Claimant learned that his secretary had been fraternising with the enemy, Butts was dismissed from his service. He would remain in London for more than a year, badgering the Claimant to pay his passage back to Sydney, but he never turned against his old master—perhaps because he had nothing to tell.

Thinking to shield Lady Doughty, Cullington confided his battle plans to her son-in-law, Kattie's husband, Percy Radcliffe. 'Mr Bowker is satisfied it is not Roger Tichborne,' he told Radcliffe after the Claimant's Alresford visit. 'I expect Mr Gosford in Town this afternoon and hope we shall be able to confront him.' On 5 January, a Saturday, Cullington went to the Clarendon Hotel, Gravesend, with Roger's old friend Vincent Gosford and James Plowden, the husband of a Tichborne cousin, and asked to see Sir Roger Tichborne. He was out, they were told, and his wife would not see them. So they took the landlord into their confidence (intimating, for good measure, that the man he knew as Sir Roger might have trouble settling his hotel bill) and were shown to a private room to await word that their quarry was in sight. It was late in the evening when the landlord rushed in to say Sir Roger had just arrived in a cab:

> We ran down the corridor to meet him. Mr Plowden addressed him as Sir Roger Tichborne when he covered his face with his hands (he wore a foreign large peaked cap) and rushed up stairs as fast as possible, before we could see his face, and shut himself in his bedroom.

They sent a waiter up with Gosford's card, asking if the Claimant would see them. In the circumstances, the reply that came back was remarkably civil: 'Pardon me Gentlemen for not seeing you but i did not wish any one to know where I was staying with my family and i am much anoyed to find you all here.'

'We are using every means to ascertain if this be Sir Roger,' Cullington told Percy Radcliffe, 'but from his conduct I think most people would doubt it.'

Not the Dowager Lady Tichborne. She wrote to the Claimant from Paris in the first week of January showing not a mote of caution or doubt: 'I trust you will live with me; I will pay all your expenses…you have no better friend than your mother.' James Bowker, the Tichborne solicitors, and her own brother, Henry Seymour—all had urged her to come to London so that she might identify the Claimant in company with others of her relatives and friends. She refused. It looked as if the Claimant would leave for Paris any day now, and all were anxious that the Dowager should not be alone when they met. Baigent's concern, as he explained to Lady Doughty, was that:

> looking continually at the photographic portrait sent from Australia, might she not get it so impressed upon her brain that

such was her son's present appearance, so that when this person
actually came, the resemblance in the photograph should induce
her to acknowledge him as her son.

Her acknowledgement, once made, would be difficult to unmake, as
a mother's recognition of her son must carry considerable weight
even in a court of justice—and even if, as her brother said, she was
as mad as a haddock.

James Bowker, the Dowager's solicitor, left London on Monday
but arrived in Paris too soon. On Tuesday, he dared to remark on the
generally held belief among her relatives that the Claimant was an
impostor, at which she summarily dismissed him from the management of her affairs. So the Dowager had her way. The Claimant
arrived in Paris late on Thursday, 10 January, in company with his
attorney John Holmes. They put up at the Hotel de Lille et d'Albion,
not far from the Dowager's apartment. Next morning, Friday, a
message informed her that her son was too ill to come to her; she
must come to him instead.

'This was all very cunningly arranged by the Pretender,' Cullington
fumed to Percy Radcliffe, 'but how she could have been so foolish
and ill advised as to go alone I cannot conceive.' Cullington, it seems,
had a man on the spot in Paris: a source of intelligence so efficient
that a bulletin reached London by the Saturday post, tracing events
right up to the point at which the Dowager entered the Claimant's
hotel. 'Unfortunately,' he wrote, 'my information from Paris ends
like a chapter in a Romance—up to the last moment of post no one
could say what her ladyship's opinion is of him. I cannot believe she
can be deceived or would recognise a son in an Impostor.'

The next chapter in the romance opened with the Dowager's
admittance to the Claimant's suite. Sir Roger's health was worse,
Holmes told her; he was too weak even to stand. Holmes ushered
the Dowager into the dimly lit room where a large figure lay on a

bed, fully dressed, his back to the door, and a handkerchief covering his face. The Dowager approached, touched the back of his neck. 'Oh my dear Roger, is it you?' He let the handkerchief drop and half-turned to face her. He was shaking and in tears. 'Oh my dear Roger,'

'Oh, my dear Roger, is it you?' *The Claimant in Paris, following the Dowager's recognition, January 1867*

she said again, and cradled his head awkwardly in her bony arms. 'Where are your wife and child?' she crooned. 'What is your little girl's name?'

'Oh Mamma,' he sobbed.

According to Vincent Gosford, Roger Tichborne had never called his mother 'Mamma'. Gosford was just one of a contingent whom Cullington, on hearing of the Dowager's recognition, proposed should go immediately to Paris and force an interview with 'Castro'—enlisting, if necessary, the assistance of the British ambassador and the Prefect of Police. His contact at the Foreign Office, however, advised him that the embassy could play no part in such a scheme; nor was it likely that the French police would involve themselves in what was, after all, a civil matter.

Before Cullington could dream up a new plan of attack, notices appeared in all nine of London's daily newspapers stating that Sir Roger Charles Doughty Tichborne had been recognised by his mother 'and the two most distinguished English physicians in Paris.' The medical men had been called, in the first instance, to treat the Claimant's illness; then, at Holmes' suggestion, they had conducted an examination for such scars and oddities as the Dowager recalled her son having possessed. She listed a lump behind one ear from a fall at the seaside, scars at his ankles where he had been bled during an asthma attack, the distinctive mark of the 'issue' on his upper arm, as well as a peculiarity (it would later be claimed) the checking of which required the Claimant's trousers to be unbuttoned. Both doctors declared themselves satisfied as to the correctness of Sir Roger's identity. The Dowager was unequivocal: 'His features, disposition and voice are unmistakable...'

'Would the real Sir Roger have instructed his solicitor to make such a Parade in the public papers?' asked Cullington. But the Claimant's opponents were not averse to using the press either. The day after Holmes' publicity blitz in the London papers, a writer in the *Hampshire Independant* warned:

> But, though Sir Roger Charles has returned, according to the acknowledgement of his mother, it would not be safe to assume for one moment that he will be permitted to enter on the undisputed possession of the family estates. To all present appearances he will have to fight a stubborn foe in the law courts.

It was, in effect, the Tichborne family's public declaration of war. Two days later Frederick Bowker wrote to Holmes: 'Our instructions are to deny emphatically that your client is the person he represents himself to be and to leave him to adopt such measures as he thinks proper.'

The Claimant's most pressing concern upon arriving back from Paris was to find a place to live. His unwelcome visitors at Gravesend had been right when they hinted to the landlord of the Clarendon that he was unable to pay his bill. Nor had the bill at Ford's been paid yet, and Bogle was still lodging there at the Claimant's expense. To make matters worse, his bills of exchange on Drummond's and the Oriental Bank had come back to haunt him. The Tichborne family held accounts at neither bank—never had done—and the bills had been presented to him for payment. And all the while he'd been steadily running up other debts, keeping his small reserve of ready cash for cab fares and booze.

Holmes had been a help. Apart from paying their fares to Paris and advancing the Claimant the cash to clear his bill at the Clarendon, Holmes had promised that soon they would set about finding some men with money and clout who would support him in his claim. Holmes had even invited the Claimant and his family to stay at his house in Croydon while they looked for a place of their own. The Claimant had in mind a property of a substantial kind, not just for the sake of his position, nor even because Mary was expecting again, but because the Dowager was to live with them; and hadn't she said, 'I will pay all your expenses'?

Bogle would be living with them, too. Reports of the Claimant's Alresford visit, Cullington told Lady Doughty, indicated that Bogle was undoubtedly 'in the plot'. Up to that point, Cullington had allowed the possibility that Bogle was an unwilling dupe, or even that her Ladyship's letter from Sydney had not been written by him at all. But there he had been in Alresford, acting as his master's scout, proclaiming the Claimant's bona fides to anyone who'd hear, and telling 'a pack of lies', declared Cullington. When Bogle's annuity fell due in January, he was flat broke. He had seen no more money from the Claimant than a grudging thirty shillings wheedled for a cheap, warm coat when they last parted at Paddington station. He still had his sights on quiet lodgings and 'sociable' company, and to that end he wrote to Lady Doughty, advising where his £50 draft ought to be sent. His letter was forwarded to Francis Cullington, who sent a clerk round to Ford's Hotel with the reply: Bogle's annuity was suspended 'until after the law affair respecting Sir Roger is settled.'

'Great caution must be used, and secrecy about Roger's past life…' Once the Dowager had identified the Claimant and it was apparent he would proceed with his claim for the estates, his opponents became still more concerned at the prospect of his gaining inside intelligence about the Tichborne family to aid him in 'this Imposition'. He would glean a good deal (already had done, they feared) from Bogle, not to mention the Dowager herself. It was vital then that the family and its supporters remain tightly sealed against him.

Francis Baigent had been among the first to assert that the Claimant could not be Roger Tichborne. The very idea he'd dismissed as 'ridiculous'. But on 2 February 1867, he changed his mind. The Claimant had returned to Alresford at Holmes' insistence, to garner favourable

Francis Baigent

witnesses—people who would swear to his being Sir Roger. Perhaps it was curiosity that made Baigent agree to meet the Claimant for tea at the Swan. After all, nobody else on the family's side had got a look at him yet with his face uncovered. But Baigent's sycophancy may also have played a part. True, he was linked with the supporters of the young Sir Henry, not just by his intimacy with Lady Doughty but through his godmother, the present Lady Arundell. But what if the Claimant, and not the infant, turned out to be the real baronet? Which way then would Baigent jump?

His decision was made when he instantly, upon meeting the

Claimant, recognised him as the true Roger Tichborne. Nobody knows exactly what it was Baigent saw with his one good eye. Later he spoke of the accuracy with which the Claimant was able to describe Tichborne House and its grounds as they had been prior to 1853, as well as his detailed knowledge of the family. More than any of that, though, it was the man himself Baigent recognised. Beneath the butchery accretions and extra flesh, Baigent detected something—he couldn't say what—that left him utterly convinced.

He wrote without delay to Lady Doughty. 'It is Sir Roger Tichborne himself.' Her chilly reply offended him. 'From the tone of your note,' he wrote back, 'it is painfully evident that the news has been most unwelcome.' He rebuked Her Ladyship for allowing herself to be prejudiced against the Claimant and told her: 'I fully approve of every-thing he has done since his arrival in England; nothing could be more open and straightforward.' When, after a fortnight, he had received no reply, Baigent wrote again, one last letter to his long-time patroness. This time he seemed to taunt her, almost to threaten her: 'You must be in a dreadful state of mind—in a most painful position—far worse than you can realize. …how different things would have been at this moment had you answered my last letter.'

A London acquaintance, a retired military man, replied on Her Ladyship's behalf: 'You have taken a very great liberty with Lady Doughty in writing to her in that manner.' Those words tolled Baigent's excommunication from the Tichborne family circle.

The Claimant's next appointment at Alresford after winning over Baigent was to dine with Edward Hopkins, the long-time Tichborne solicitor. He recognised the Claimant too, having been primed by Cater, the baker, late of Fitzmaurice Street, Wagga. Cater's ship had been almost home before he remembered the letter Tom Castro had given him to open at sea. It began thus: 'At any time when you are in England should you feel inclined for a few months' pleasure, go

to Tichborne Hall, Tichborne, Hampshire, enquire for Sir Roger
Charles Tichborne and you will find one that will make you a welcome
guest.'

It was some months before Cater acted on the invitation. When a
letter inquiring after Sir Roger Charles Tichborne arrived at Alresford
at the beginning of December 1866, the postmaster thought Edward
Hopkins the best person to deal with it. Hopkins wrote back to Cater,
asking his business, and Cater duly replied:

> I presume, Sir, you and others in Alresford have read the romantic
> career of this Sir Roger as copied from the 'Wagga Wagga
> Express'. He has frequently come to my house and we have had
> many a comfortable chat together, but I do not recollect that
> he ever alluded to his former or future greatness, but remained
> incognito throughout. Still from these conversations I know a
> great deal of his Colonial life...

He quoted the substance of Tom Castro's letter, and Hopkins eagerly
asked that he might see it for the purpose of comparing the handwriting
with Roger's. Cater replied:

> I regret, Sir, I cannot conscientiously send you Sir Roger's letter
> of invitation to me, as it contains matter of a private nature,
> known only to ourselves, and which he has strictly charged me
> not to make known to any one; but suffice it to say, this matter
> is quite of a Colonial character, and would not, I think, in any
> way prove his identity.

In fact, there was nothing in Castro's letter that wasn't, by that time,
known or at least guessed at in England. The 'matter of a private
nature' amounted to this: 'But on no account Memsion the name of
Castro. Or allude to me being a married Man. Or that I have being
has A Butcher. You will understand me I have no doubt.'

Hopkins shared Cater's view of the affair, and declared himself enthralled by 'this, the most romantic of all stories.' He invited the Claimant to stay with him for the rest of his week at Alresford and even extended the privilege of fishing in his private stream. According to Lamb, the fishing-tackle man in Alresford, the flies the Claimant chose were precisely those favoured by the young Roger. But there was a difference in what he did with them: the Claimant proved to be a superlative fly-fisherman. His years in Australia had taught him something useful, then.

Hopkins' defection to the Claimant's side was a severe blow to the family. 'I fear,' Cullington told Radcliffe, 'he will furnish the Claimant with all the information he requires about the title and Estates.' Retired life had hitherto been a disappointment to Hopkins. But now he wrote to the Dowager's brother, Henry Seymour, with whom he was on good terms, urging him to come down to Alresford and meet the Claimant. 'I am perfectly satisfied that the more you hear and perhaps the more you see the more certain it will appear to you Sir Roger is the long-lost man. I cannot express how much respect I have for Sir Roger's truthfulness and entire absence of guile.'

TWELVE
A SHEAF OF AFFIDAVITS

HENRY Seymour came down to Alresford, but would not be convinced. To begin with he spoke in French to the Claimant, who couldn't understand him. Then he brought a smartly dressed man in from the garden and demanded, 'Who do you think this is?' Was it one of his uncles? hazarded the Claimant. No, it was an old Tichborne servant, dressed up to trick him. Next, Seymour produced an antique-looking letter and asked if the Claimant recognised the handwriting. He didn't. 'Good God!' exploded Seymour, 'You don't know your own father's handwriting?' But what sealed it was that the Claimant insisted on calling him 'Uncle' when, because they were so close in age, the young Roger had never called him anything but plain Henry.

Hopkins implored Seymour as he saw him out, 'Don't be in a hurry to decide.' He lowered his voice. 'You saw him twitch?'

'For God's sake, Hopkins…' Seymour began, then just shook his head.

The Dowager had declared that 'they cannot keep Sir Roger out of his possessions for one hour when he has been identified.' But he had not been identified by those who really mattered: namely, the trustees of the Tichborne and Doughty estates. The Tichborne estates, much diminished as they had been by the profligacy of the late Sir Alfred, were held in trust now for his infant son. Under the terms of Roger Tichborne's will, which had been put into effect eighteen months after his disappearance, the Doughty estates were left in trust for the purpose of paying off substantial encumbrances on the Tichborne estates. Until those encumbrances (£100,000 and growing) had been acquitted, no one could gain access to the Doughty estates or their income of £14,000 per year—unless, that is, it could be proved that Roger Tichborne was *not* dead, since it was only by his will that the Doughty estates were thus locked up. Likewise, if Roger Tichborne were alive, the baronetcy would revert to him and the Tichborne estates must be released from trust.

Now the scramble for evidence began. The Court of Chancery, when it came to decide whether the Claimant was entitled to the estates, would require proof of identity. In the absence of fingerprints, dental records or DNA testing, sworn testimony would form the basis of the Court's examination. Hopkins and Baigent rated as prize witnesses, and affidavits declaring their recognition of the Claimant as Sir Roger were now added to those of the Dowager and Bogle. Within six months, Holmes' sheaf of affidavits in his client's favour would swell to almost forty. Frederick Bowker, meanwhile, was also seeking out former acquaintances of Roger Tichborne, beginning with his fellow officers in the Carabineers. He urged them to rack their memories for anything that might aid 'in resisting the attempt of a person passing by the name of "D'Castra" who has just arrived from Sydney and states he is the long lost Mr Roger Chas. Tichborne.' Much useful testimony was gleaned, such as that of Colonel J. M. Custance: 'The Mr Tichborne in the 6th Dragoon Guards with me (commonly called TEESH in the Regt.) was a little wretched unwholesome looking young man about 5 feet 6 or at most 7, very pale thin and dirty looking and apparently not likely to grow.'

On the Claimant's side, two former soldiers would act as his entree to the Carabineers network. Thomas Carter and James McCann both had been servants to Roger Tichborne during his time in the army. Carter came forward unbidden to recognise his old master, followed soon after by McCann. Before long, both men were enveloped in the Claimant's burgeoning household—one as valet, the other as groom—where they proved invaluable in drawing many more Carabineers to the Claimant's side.

Even back in Wagga, the Claimant's stinting on details about his past had appeared to be an involuntary phenomenon. His loss of memory he attributed to delirium after the *Bella* shipwreck and to his subsequent headlong career as a rough-rider. But his supporters in England were well qualified to aid in recovering his memory. The Dowager, for a start: what didn't she know about Roger's childhood? She had boxes of stuff stored away in Winchester, some of which she fetched up to prompt the Claimant's powers of recollection. When she produced the gigantic silver spurs and stirrups of the gaucho outfit Roger had sent home from Brazil, the Claimant recognised them without a flicker of hesitation. In fact, so delighted was he with these mementoes of his ride across the Pampas that he kept them about the drawing-room as ornaments and a hazard to small children. In the same box was Roger's old army uniform, into which the Claimant attempted to squeeze himself. While it was not a kind fit—or any kind of fit—it seemed at least to have been made for a man of his height and length of arm, only 'thinner in person' than he found himself at present.

Edward Hopkins, as Cullington had feared, was only too happy to re-acquaint the Claimant with all that he'd forgotten about the Tichborne family's estates. Bogle liked to reminisce about life at Tichborne House in Sir Edward's time, while the army men, Carter and McCann, took turns at reminding their master of his time in the Carabineers. But it was Baigent who sought to coach the Claimant's memory in a systematic fashion. Already he knew every wrinkle of the Tichborne pedigree, and this, together with a précis of all living relatives, he compiled into a bound folio for the Claimant to study. Further sleuthing by Baigent resulted in lists of students and priests who had been at Stonyhurst in the late 1840s and of Roger's fellow officers in the Carabineers, complete with their present rank and place of residence. Baigent was only too ready 'to do anything I could for him.'

His efforts, however, were largely wasted on the Claimant, who mulishly resisted being coached or questioned and whose palpable lack of interest in finding out what he'd forgotten seemed expressive of the view that *he* knew who he was and he didn't have to prove it to anyone.

For their part, the trustees of the Doughty estates, represented by Francis Cullington, urged the Claimant to meet with those who were best placed to recognise him—family members and close friends of Roger's, like Vincent Gosford. Even Holmes pressed his client as to the necessity of such a meeting, but the Claimant resisted. His mother did not want him meeting those people, he said. 'Those people' had at their helm Percival Radcliffe, the husband of Roger's beloved cousin Kattie. Radcliffe had a strong motive for not wanting Roger Tichborne alive (or possibly two, if you counted jealousy of his wife's old sweetheart). As things stood, if the young Sir Henry Tichborne should die without offspring, Radcliffe's wife would eventually inherit the Doughty estates, while the Tichborne estates, entailed on a male, would come to their son. An extant Roger Tichborne—not to mention his children—would dislocate the lineage.

At the beginning of March, Holmes agreed with Cullington that the Claimant would meet family members at Tichborne when next he was in Hampshire. But Percy Radcliffe was sick of waiting. Together with his wife, Vincent Gosford, a Tichborne aunt and another cousin, Radcliffe arrived unexpectedly at the Claimant's new home at Croydon. For once the Claimant did not hide his face, but seems to have resigned himself to confronting his opponents at last. He had, after all, been in possession of Baigent's Tichborne family compendium for long enough to have made at least a desultory study of its contents. Radcliffe entered the house alone. Shown into the drawing-room, he had the presumption to close (to slam, the Claimant said) the door to an adjoining room where the Dowager was seated. He then proceeded to fetch the rest of his party in, one or two at a time. Radcliffe first brought in a woman, her face muffled in a heavy veil. 'You recognise this lady?' he demanded.

'Is it my cousin Katie?' The Claimant was tentative and spoke softly, suppressing his anger, perhaps, at the intrusion. All his visitors that day noticed in his voice something approximating a French accent.

At Radcliffe's instruction, two more veiled women were shown in. 'Your cousin and your aunt,' he told the Claimant, by way of intro- duction. Now the Claimant was confused.

To the elder of the women he stammered, 'Lady Doughty?' while his eyes darted from one to the other of the younger women. Could he have been expected to recognise Katherine Radcliffe even without the subterfuge of a veil? A well-rounded woman of thirty-three, she bore little resemblance to the girl Roger had last seen at Tichborne fifteen years earlier. 'There are so many veils,' he murmured, faintly stricken.

Now the woman who had first entered the room—the one he had taken for Kattie—stepped over to the window and lifted her veil. '*Now* say who I am,' she challenged the Claimant.

He said nothing, just shook his head.

Then, 'Tell me who *I* am,' demanded the older woman, flinging back her veil too. It was not Lady Doughty, but Mrs Nangle, another of Roger's aunts and the mother of Carrie who was standing unveiled by the window.

Still shaking his head and not looking at any of them, the Claimant said feebly, 'I don't know. I don't know.' He looked ill.

'You're not Roger Tichborne,' Mrs Nangle sneered. 'You're nothing but an Australian navvy!' And, having said what she'd come to say, she swept from the room with Carrie at her elbow, both of them calling back, 'Goodbye, Mr Castro!'

Seeing the Claimant's distress, Percy Radcliffe was almost apologetic. 'Gosford is outside,' he said. 'May I bring him in?'

The Claimant gave a helpless shrug.

Things were somewhat more dignified after that. The one woman who remained—it was, in fact, Kattie—sat and silently observed the Claimant from behind her veil while he talked with Vincent Gosford. Gosford, the former Tichborne steward and Roger's closest friend, treated the Claimant cordially. He called him 'sir' and seemed sincere in his questioning. The Claimant responded with gestures and monosyllables but, had circumstances been different—had he not felt himself skewered—he might have warmed to Gosford.

The interview ended badly. As the visitors stood to take their leave, Percy Radcliffe rattled off a question in rapid French, ending, '…*n'est ce pas?*' When the Claimant said nothing, Radcliffe insisted, '*N'est ce pas*, Monsieur Castro?'

'Damn you, sir.' The Claimant's voice was a tight growl and his fists were bunched. 'You are no gentleman.'

At that, Radcliffe gave an involuntary bleat of laughter, and the Claimant went for him. Percy Radcliffe burst through the drawing-room door backwards, just managing to keep upright. The Claimant was breathing hard; one side of his face twitched like a flapping blind. But he was slumped, defeated-looking. Evidently judging himself safe, Radcliffe got in one last thrust. 'No gentleman? That's ripe.' Then, to his wife, 'Come, my dear,' and she edged past the Claimant, head lowered. Gosford was the last to leave. He almost offered his hand, but checked the gesture and instead gave the Claimant a brisk nod and a look, a momentary hesitation, that just might have been regretful.

'I do not think I spoke for a few moments, because I was so scared with his appearance that I could not conceive the idea of his coming forward as Roger.' That is how Gosford would later recall his first impression of the Claimant that day. Gosford was struck by his 'very rough mass of neglected hair' and felt that 'his whole appearance bore out the description of a rough, seafaring person.' His way of speaking, in as much as Gosford could make it out, was 'altogether that of a person of very low station.' Carrie Nangle's first impulse upon seeing the Claimant had been, she said, 'a sort of uncontrollable laughter,' so that she was thankful to have been wearing a veil. Behind *her* veil, Katherine Radcliffe had scrutinised the Claimant almost unblinking the whole time she was in the room. She had known the young Roger Tichborne more intimately than had any of the others except perhaps Gosford, and she saw in the Claimant a decided likeness to her cousin Roger about the eyes, eyebrows and forehead. His voice, too, reminded her of Roger's. But she noticed that he spoke her name as Katie; Roger had always called her Kattie. Only one person knew her as Katie, she said, and that was the Dowager. Gosford told Holmes so in a letter, a day or two after the visit, and he asked whether they—himself and Mrs Radcliffe—might meet again with the Claimant. As yet, said Gosford, they were nothing like persuaded that he was Roger Tichborne, but if they might speak with him some more…

It was too late for that. Gosford's letter crossed in the post with one from Holmes to Percy Radcliffe, condemning the 'great impropriety' of his conduct and informing him of the Claimant's determination to hold 'no further intercourse' with any of the Tichborne relations. Cullington, the Doughty solicitor, replied on Radcliffe's behalf. His letter concluded as Holmes had known it must: 'The only mode of avoiding litigation was the recognition of your Client as Roger Tichborne, and, as it is now perfectly certain that he is not so, the responsibility of litigation must rest upon your Client, if he still persists in asserting his claim.'

He did.

THIRTEEN
I CANNOT REMEMBER

THE litigation Holmes would launch on the Claimant's behalf comprised two bills of complaint in the Court of Chancery against the trustees of the Tichborne and Doughty estates. Before those bills were filed, however, Holmes had a good deal of work to do.

He badgered his client incessantly, urging him 'to go among your friends and Brother Officers without delay,' pointing out to him 'the growing difficulties of your Case arising from your disinclination to see your Brother Officers' as well as 'the uncertain feeling existing in Alresford because of your absence.' Holmes was anxious to secure 'a better class of witnesses than you have got at present.' From the Carabineers, his client's supporters to date were principally enlisted men, not officers. Bogle was a servant. Hopkins, Baigent and Rous had something like the respectability Holmes was after, but what he really sought were people of rank, and with money. Of course, there was the Dowager. But she was part of the problem.

She had objected to the Claimant's meeting the Tichborne relatives and she continued to object to his going down to Hampshire. The place was full of enemies, she insisted. The Claimant found himself racked between her demands and those of his lawyer. At one stage Holmes threatened to drop the case unless the Claimant ignored his mamma's injunctions against going to Alresford. On another occasion, the Dowager triumphed by offering the Claimant £300 not to go, and Holmes was forced to telegraph those waiting at Alresford that

his client had a sore throat and could not travel. When Holmes asked
her to hand over Roger's South American letters, the Dowager prevaricated. First she said they were in storage at Winchester, then in Paris,
then that they were lost.

The Dowager had been living with the Claimant since mid-February
1867 at Essex Lodge, a large house in the south London suburb of
Croydon. It wasn't large enough, though, for the Dowager's peace
of mind. She may have recognised the Claimant as her son, but she
did not recognise his manners, or like them much. 'They must be
savages in Australia to have made him so rough,' she confided in
Rosina McArthur, the nursemaid. One of the savages he had brought
with him, in the shape of his wife, Mary. She and the Dowager did
not exactly warm to one another. Jack Cater, the Claimant's old Wagga
friend who lived with them at Croydon for a time, remarked on Mary's

Mrs Claimant—Lady Tichborne, née *Mary Ann Bryant*

sliding down the stair railings and how she felt smothered by her idle life. 'I'd prefer to tuck up my skirts and scrub the floors,' she told him, 'but I mustn't do anything that will shock my genteel servants.'

The Claimant's trail of bad cheques and promissory notes continued to catch him up. Holmes now had an uphill job to keep his client out of prison. Essex Lodge and all its furnishings were rented in the Dowager's name to prevent their being seized in lieu of payment by the Claimant's debtors. Even so, it was an almost weekly occurrence for a posse of burly men to push their way into the house and attempt to carry off the sofa or the dinner setting or the linen. The Claimant would have been a considerable drain on his mamma's purse even without the backlog of bad debts, since his tastes grew more lavish by the day. From his scrubby myall pipe he had graduated to chain-smoking Cuban cigars, much to the injury of his health. He told a friend, 'I have given up buying retail for I have to buy Wolesale now but the Dr. have put me on short allowance lately they only allow me twenty a day now But I take care to get largest cigars I can.'

He kept a muster of fine horseflesh in the stables at Essex Lodge and a small menagerie about the place: a pug, a mute canary, and a hutchful of rabbits for eating. The household was well-victualled, with the Claimant himself taking responsibility for the daily butcher's order. Veal was not to be sent at any time, he instructed the butcher, and pork only when it was small. Liquor, like cigars, was bought and consumed in wholesale.

It was all was too much for the Dowager. After only a month at Essex Lodge she complained to her priest, 'I am tired of the life I am leading there with Roger. Too much noise and too much expense.' Rosina McArthur observed that, although the Dowager's manner 'was that of an affectionate mother to her son,' the Claimant and his mamma 'did not seem to agree very well.' The Claimant himself insisted it was the air at Croydon that didn't agree with her. Whatever the real reason, she left Essex Lodge in April for a London hotel. She continued to advance the Claimant money and pay what bills she could, and the pair kept up an almost daily correspondence. She signed herself 'your only sincere friend.'

'I have got about thirty pounds, Mamma dear but that you see Mamma dear is not sufficient.' In one excruciatingly wheedling letter, the Claimant managed to squeeze in the words 'Mamma dear' or 'my dear Mamma' twenty-six times in less than a page. Those genuflective 'dear Mammas' expressed the shame and desperation of a man who hated to grovel. 'It almost drives me mad to think I cannot pay my way without taking your money,' he wrote. 'Had I known it before I left Australia I would have never wrote or come home to have caused you so much trouble and to have been such a drag on your purse.'

Often he would implore the Dowager 'not to worrit yourself to much,' but then, himself beset with ill-health and debt, he wrote:

> I am beginning to get very tired of so much worrat. I try to keep my spirits up but I cannot, I find. I begin to wander very much at times. I have no doubt another few months will find me in A Lunnitick Asylum. I wish my dear Mamma you was here to give me your advice oh how much happier it would have been for me to have remained in Australia my dear Mamma only for the pleasure and comfort of having you near me.

All that smoking and his removal from the curative colonial ozone had done the Claimant's health no good at all. His badly inflamed throat, though painful, was also a cause for congratulation when Dr Lipscombe of Alresford declared that he had treated the young Roger Tichborne for the very same complaint. The Claimant was troubled too by tapeworm. The agony in his bowels kept him bedridden for weeks in the spring of 1867; he even feared that he might die. 'I thought I was agoing a hunting in another country,' he wrote to the Dowager after an especially bad night. His waxing weight can't have helped. In May, the precision weighing machine at the Crystal Palace clocked his mass at more than twenty-one stone. Mary (or 'Lady Roger'), approaching her confinement, was no longer sliding down the bannisters. The child, a boy, was born in May and 'regerestered', at the Dowager's instruction, under the name Roger Joseph Doughty Tichborne.

The Claimant was as much concerned over the state of the Dowager's health as his own. 'You no my dear Mamma,' he wrote, 'that if anythink was to happen to you I have no other friend in this world therefore my dear Mamma you must take care of yourself for my sake as well as your own.' He knew full well that without her he would be lost. When she was laid low by asthma, he confided to Holmes his concern about the 'disposition' of her property if she should die. The lawyer urged her to make a will, but she resisted. Not long afterwards, William Bulpett, a Hampshire banker, agreed to lend the Claimant £5,000 for his legal costs on the condition that the Dowager insure her life. This she flatly refused to do. Put baldly then, the Dowager was worth more to the Claimant alive than dead. No wonder he told her, 'It is great importance you look to your health.'

The Claimant was increasingly aware of having forfeited his freedom. He hadn't reckoned on the web of obligation that ensnared him. As he told his mamma when she offered to have a Paris acquaintance—a stranger to him—swear to his identity: 'if I had one false witness it would ruin my Case. And my Friends would never forgive me.' When he wrote in May to his former 'only friend' William Gibbes at Wagga, there was a homesick cast to the letter. He rattled off a long list of those he wished to be remembered to, plus 'any others you know to be my Friends.'

The Claimant's twelve-year absence—from the sinking of the *Bella* to his emergence at Wagga—was the main topic on which he was examined in a hearing before the Lord Chancellor at the end of July

1867. Held in the hall of the Law Institution in Chancery Lane, the hearing considered the Claimant's bills of complaint against the Tichborne and Doughty estates. More specifically, it considered whether or not the plaintiff was, as he claimed, Roger Tichborne. Thirty-seven affidavits said he was, while the defence stated that it could produce as many witnesses to swear that he was not. Only two witnesses were, however, examined at the hearing: the Claimant himself in support of his claim and Vincent Gosford opposing it.

Since their meeting in March, Gosford had grown set in his resolve that the Claimant was an impostor. This was due in no small part to the Claimant's professed ignorance of the contents of the so-called 'sealed packet' left with Gosford by Roger Tichborne in January 1852. When Gosford met the Claimant, the packet was one subject he felt unable to broach in front of Mrs Radcliffe and (more particularly) her husband Percy. So he wrote to Holmes seeking his client's recollection of a sealed document concerning Kattie Doughty, and the answer came back: Sir Roger knew nothing about it. But Holmes sensed its importance and arranged a meeting with Gosford. He emerged little the wiser: Gosford's lips, like the packet, were sealed. Holmes did find out, though, that Gosford had destroyed the document some time after Roger's disappearance. Hearing of that seemed to tweak the Claimant's memory. Actually, he told Holmes, he recalled the thing perfectly well.

'You remember it?' said Holmes, excited. Here was a breakthrough. 'Then you remember what it said?'

'Of course.'

But then a pause lengthened into a silence. Holmes pressed and ranted and cajoled, but the Claimant would not tell. It wasn't important, he insisted. In the days leading up to the Chancery hearing, Holmes again urged him to divulge the details of the sealed packet, but without success.

The Claimant's barrister, Serjeant Ballantine, warned his client that he'd better not turn sulky or indignant when questioned at the Chancery hearing.* Ballantine's examination of the Claimant, which opened the proceedings at the Law Institution, touched but lightly on Roger Tichborne's young life and dwelt at rather more length on the twelve lost years, as detailed in the Claimant's own affidavit. Questioned about his sojourn in Australia, he might almost have been back in the bar of the Black Swan Inn at Wagga.

> When in Australia I was a good deal in the saddle. We hunted the Kangaroos, the Emu and the Dingo (a native dog). I was a very good shot you know. I used to make shooting and hunting expeditions into the interior and was often absent by myself for a month at a time. I have been in the mountains four months at one time you know without seeing the face of any human being. I was very fond of that sort of expeditions. They were my principal hobby for years after my arrival in Australia.

He claimed to have been of temperate habits—'not touching wine or spirits'—during much of his time in the colonies. And he produced his own drawing of a bucking horse, to illustrate how he'd been thrown onto his head that time at Wagga.

Not surprisingly, the cross-examination was less concerned with his colonial life than his early years. Chapman Barber, for the defence, was a flaccid sort of cross-examiner; even so, the Claimant said afterwards that he 'would not stand another examination like that for worlds.' It was high summer and the hall of the Law Institution was crammed beyond its capacity. The stifling heat added to the Claimant's discomfort during his inquisition.

To almost every question concerning his life pre-South America he replied 'I do not know' or 'I cannot remember.' The 'great difficulties caused by your defective memory' were the subject of 'a very

* The title *Serjeant* was short for Serjeant-at-law, at that time the highest rank of barrister in England.

earnest discussion' that evening between the Claimant and his legal representatives. There was even a fear, when Baigent raised the alarm next morning that the Claimant had not been home or heard of all night, that the cross-examination had had 'a prejudicial effect' on him. Hadn't Ballantine remarked, on first meeting him, the melancholy cast of his expression? But a dragging of the Thames was averted when he arrived at Holmes' office, looking only slightly more rough-cast than usual, in good time for that day's hearing. He had indeed been drowning his woes in the shadow of a bridge—at the Continental Hotel by London Bridge, to be exact.

His two days in the witness seat were over, anyway. Now it was Gosford's turn. Barber's examination focused almost entirely on the sealed packet as a crucial test of identity. Ballantine's ability to cross-examine Gosford on this subject was hampered by the Claimant's refusal to disclose his version of the packet's contents. All Ballantine could effect was a swipe at Gosford's credibility. Some years before, Gosford had been dismissed as steward of the Tichborne and Doughty estates. There had been 'irregularities' in his management of rent monies, some of which had ended up in his private bank account, though Gosford argued that those sums were merely a convenient float from which he paid outgoings on the estates. The family was inclined to believe him, but the Doughty trustees had insisted on his dismissal. Without references, Gosford had been unable to secure another position and he still owed money to the estates. Since Gosford was in the family's debt, Ballantine sought to imply, he was obliged to lie for them. There was only Gosford's word, Ballantine told the court, that the contents of the sealed packet had been identical with a note given by Roger to his cousin Kattie—a note now in the possession of the family's solicitors.

Gosford did not flinch. Not only had he seen the document written, he told the court, he had read it again before putting it to the match some two years after the loss of the Bella—'I did not think it proper that it should fall into other hands or under other eyes.' Besides, he pointed out, there were circumstances other than Roger's supposed death—he alluded to Kattie's marriage—which had by then rendered the contents of the package useless. Gracious, capable and direct, Gosford presented as the antithesis of a perjuror. Moreover, he had given the Claimant every opportunity to prove himself. Ballantine had to admit it was his client's demur that looked bad.

At the end of the three-day hearing, the Vice-Chancellor pronounced that he could not settle the case on the evidence before him. It would have to proceed to trial in the Court of Common Pleas. The Claimant's lawyers and supporters were bluntly of the view that his pig-headedness had cost him the chance for an early resolution. At Holmes' office around tipple-time that afternoon he was urged, in more forceful terms than previously, to divulge the contents of the sealed packet, especially by William Bulpett, the Hampshire banker. The Dowager having refused to insure her life as security for a £5,000 loan, Bulpett had eventually agreed to advance the money—and had brokered further loans from his well-heeled acquaintances—on the condition that the money, plus an equivalent amount as a 'bonus', would be repaid when the Claimant succeeded to the estates.

Bulpett now brought his fist down on Holmes' desk so hard that the ink-stand cracked. It was less the blow than the threat that went with it that persuaded the Claimant, finally, to write down his version of the infernal sealed packet. It took him less than ten minutes, pausing only once to bite his lip and stare hard at the shattered ink-stand. When he'd done, he pushed the paper away as if he wanted nothing more to do with it. Holmes took it up and commenced to devour it. But before he was halfway through, he wrenched his eyes away. 'Are you sure?' He was incredulous. The Claimant flung him a mutinous look. Holmes drew in his breath sharply. Well, he thought, this changed everything.

Bulpett, when he'd read it through, clapped the Claimant's shoulder in congratulation. 'But damn it, Sir Roger, why didn't you tell us this before? We could've routed that scoundrel Gosford—routed the lot of them!'

The Claimant kept his voice low, but he was shaking. 'Nobody else must know about this. I've given you what you want, but I will not allow…'

Bulpett was ready to object, but Holmes cut him off. 'Sir Roger's right. This is'—he searched for the word—'inflammatory. We must keep it to ourselves for now. And this,' brandishing the paper, 'we must keep safe. You're certain that's all, Sir Roger?'

The Claimant nodded miserably. 'Isn't it enough?' His voice was as heavy as a sinking ship.

Next day, double-sealed with string and wax, the paper was locked in a box at the Bank of England, and Holmes, thinking perhaps the dam had broken, gave the Claimant a book fitted with lock and key, for the purpose of writing 'a detailed story of your life.'

During the Chancery hearing, Ballantine repeatedly objected to his client's being crowded about and stared at. 'I never saw such a scene,' he said. 'It is perfectly scandalous, like what one reads of in the Backwoods of America.' Among the pressing crowd were many Tichborne relatives and acquaintances, including Lady Doughty, for whom this was the first opportunity of seeing the Claimant. There were gasps and laughter when he lumbered into the hall on the opening day. The reaction of Mrs Greenwood, an elder cousin of Roger's, seems to have been typical:

> Until I saw him at the Law Institution I always had doubts. I wavered according to the rumours I heard. I changed like a weather-cock from day to day. When I saw him at the Law Institution I never doubted it for a moment. I was disappointed almost to find that there was not anything of Roger Tichborne in the person when I saw him.

John Moore, who had cared for Roger Tichborne's guanaco in Santiago thirteen years earlier, was also in the goggling horde. Moore was considered one of the family's trump cards, having told their lawyers all he could about Roger's travels in South America. He attended the hearing merely for the purpose of hammering down the nail of his certainty that the Claimant was a fraud. Moore gasped, along with the rest, at the improbable size of the Claimant when he first appeared; but after that, he settled down to stare. All that first day he stared and, though he observed the twitch and discerned a certain likeness about the eyes, he saw nothing to convince him that this was his old master. He came back next day to hear the Claimant's cross-examination and right at the end, as the exhausted Claimant struggled to his feet in the witness box, Moore had an epiphany:

> He got up from his chair and went to the further end of the room, where the light was on his face. I saw him laugh, and I may say almost cry. I was astonished, and I went away and pondered over the matter and said to myself, 'You really must be Roger Tichborne.'

From the first week in January 1867—less than a fortnight after his arrival in London—the Claimant had been under the scrutiny of a detective. This was John Whicher, short, pock-marked and tenacious, a former policeman now in the pay of the infant heir's uncle, Lord Arundell. As the months went by, Whicher spent much of his time trying to uncover who—if not Roger Tichborne—the Claimant was. His list of possibilities initially included John Moore and several others of the Tichbornes' ex-servants. Whicher traced them all, eliminating those who were unarguably dead and recruiting others, like Moore, as allies. By the time of the Chancery hearing, the family suspected that the Claimant was an illegitimate Tichborne—a 'natural' son of either Sir Henry, Sir Edward, Sir James or their youngest brother, Robert.

Whicher had often taken potential witnesses to the Claimant's house, where they waited opposite the doorway, sometimes for hours, to catch a glimpse of him. Compared to that, the Law Institution hearing was ideal for an identity parade, and at least some of those staring and pressing in on the Claimant during those three hot days did so at Whicher's bidding. 'Three people have been planted by that window to stare at my Client,' Ballantine objected at one point.

But the detective's breakthrough came in the autumn of 1867. On the third Saturday of October, Holmes was at his office, worrying over an anonymous letter which had arrived that morning. Signed 'A Friend', it warned that exposure of the Claimant was at hand and that Holmes would do well to distance himself. He was just adding it to a file of similar correspondence when his overworked chief clerk, Mr Stevens, announced that there was a Mrs Tredgett in the outer office saying she had information for Sir Roger's lawyer. Stevens showed her in, a broad, bustly woman, ruddy-faced and evidently not at ease in a solicitor's office. Her reticent manner was offset by her volume, which, along with her accent, marked her out as a native Londoner. Mr Holmes would beg her pardon, she hoped, but she thought he ought to know that Mr Whicher, a detective, had called on her and her sister, Mrs Jury, some short time ago—they lived in Wapping, a street apart—showing them a photograph of the Claimant and asking after their brother who had killed cattle in Whitechapel Market. Mr Whicher had tried to make out that their brother was passing himself off as Sir Roger, and her sister and her just thought, said Mrs Tredgett, that Sir Roger's people ought to know.

'This brother,' said Holmes, 'what's his name?'

'It was Arthur, our youngest, he was asking about.'

'Arthur what?'

'Well, that Whicher got it wrong, didn't he?' Mrs Tredgett's length of delivery matched her volume. 'Called him Horton. But it's Orton. Arthur Orton.'

FOURTEEN

THE FAT BOY

SIXTY-NINE High Street, Wapping was home to the Orton family and centre of their little empire. George Orton was a butcher and provision merchant to the shipping trade. On 20 March 1834, Arthur was born, George and Mary's blessed last, their twelfth in less than fifteen years.

Wapping High Street faced the Thames, but was hulked over by the warehouses that rimmed the London Docks. The Ortons' shop and house was close to the dockyards entrance where crowds of men gathered every morning in the meagre hope of picking up a day's work. Compared with them, George Orton was secure, even prosperous. In the early 1840s, his eldest son, Thomas, consolidated the provisioning side of the business by marrying a greengrocer's daughter, then opened a branch of Orton's Shipping Butchers in Lower East Smithfield, a mile or so west of the Wapping shop. Lower East Smithfield was a narrow one-cart street running down from Ratcliffe Highway to the Thames and, like Wapping High Street, it skirted the docks—in this case, St Katherine's Docks. Close by was Dundee Wharf, where Scottish ships disgorged their cargo. It wasn't long before the Ortons were importing highland cattle and ponies from the Shetlands to sell at Smithfield Market. An old brewery in Great Hermitage Street (midway between Wapping High Street and Lower East Smithfield) was converted into a depot, complete with stables, byres and stockyards.

These three places, with the teeming streets and docksides between, formed the core of young Arthur's world. He went to Mr Knight's school in Great Hermitage Street from the age of six, and spent Wednesday half-holidays at the depot and in the streets, riding Shetland ponies with his schoolmates. Other times they'd play rounders in Red Mead Lane, between the dock walls, and in summer would dive off coal barges in the Thames below Wapping Old Stairs or bathe in the apron of the London Docks until the watchman chased them away. On summer Sundays they ventured upriver to the swamp-lands of Battersea Fields, the haunt of gypsies and vagabonds. The Battersea Sunday fair featured every kind of disreputable fun, from horse and donkey races to fortune-telling, dancing girls and pigeon-shooting matches at the rowdy Red House tavern. But the docks themselves— Arthur's front and back yard—were his greatest source of entertainment. Once he and a friend discovered there were two tigers on board a ship moored in St Katherine's Dock. Cadging an armload of beef shins from Arthur's brother, they were thrilled to watch the great silken beasts crunch the bones into splinters. When the keeper left, though, the boys taunted the tigers with the remaining shin-bone, so enraging them that one almost broke out of its cage. Arthur Orton was nearly done for then and there.

One night when he was nine, a fire broke out at Hartley's Wharf and the flames caught hold of shops in Wapping High Street, reaching to within three doors of the Ortons'. All who were at home joined in the bucket brigade; all except young Arthur. He'd been wrenched from sleep into a scene writhing with flames higher than houses, squealing horses, familiar voices made strange with panic, and, most terrifying, the drawn-out crash of a ship's mast toppling, followed by a spume of boiling steam as the end of Hartley's Wharf dissolved into the Thames. Clad only in his nightshirt, Arthur stood gaping in the road until his sister Lizzie, Mrs Jury, happened to notice and took him back to her house in Globe Street.

Some weeks later Arthur was sent home from school after shattering two slates and dropping his teacher's Word Expositor, cracking its spine, all within the space of a morning. His hands weren't working properly, he said. It was certainly true, Mr Knight had noticed, that Arthur seemed to have lost control of his handwriting. He'd never had a good hand, but lately its defects had been more those of the infirm—trailing-off and shaky—than the usual blots of a Wapping schoolboy. He seemed unable to sit still, too, even under threat of the cane. Mr Knight's school had only just recovered from the ravages of a scarlatina outbreak, to which Arthur had been one of the first to succumb. What pestilence had the wretch brought to school with him this time, the teacher wondered. He needn't have worried: what ailed Arthur wasn't contagious. It was St Vitus' Dance.

People said it was the fright that did it, but the scarlet fever might just as easily have been to blame. Before another week had passed, Arthur was well in St Vitus' grip. Like a badly strung marionette, he jerked and twisted uncontrollably. His hands clenched and unclenched, his arms made sudden thrashes, his shoulders heaved about and his face was seized by monstrous grimaces. Nor were his legs to be relied upon. Only when he slept was he still. His left side was the worse affected and his poor face on that side hung slack between convulsions. It made it hard to chew, and his cheeky, quick way of talking turned slow and slurred. Arthur was excused from school for a good long while.

Sitting on the step of his father's shop or hanging about the docks, he became something of a favourite among the tradesmen and rivermen. During his convalescence, Arthur's parents moved with their three youngest boys to the shop at Lower East Smithfield. George Orton provisioned the New York passenger liners which had lately removed from the London to St Katherine's Docks, and it suited him to live close by. Arthur took to spending part of each day at the shipsmith's next door, helping Walter Leaver to weigh out bags of nails and generally getting in the way. He was forever spilling things and could hardly be relied on to make a fair measure. But he never tired of playing with the scales. On his tenth birthday, he calculated that he weighed the same as six links of anchor chain and a pound sack of brads. He spent time, too, under the feet of Charley Lawrence, the sail-maker, two doors down, or glued to the boxy window of Parnell's, the optician's across the way, where a ship's compass was kept on display. Arthur was fascinated by it and used to enrage Mr Parnell by scraping a magnet across the window glass to make the needle move.

The rest of his time he spent on and about Dundee Wharf and the ships moored there. All the ship's captains and lightermen knew that the 'stout-built, sprawly lad, dressed in a butcher's frock' was George Orton's youngest lad. He was reckoned by some of them to be 'a little bit cracked'. As one of the lightermen put it, when young Arthur laughed 'he laughed all over his face.' The arrival of a ship carrying Shetland ponies was a big occasion for him. He shuttled back and forth between the wharf and his father's shop, clutching fistfuls of his frock and even stuffing some of it in his mouth in his excitement. And as the ponies were landed, he'd grab one, jump on, and, holding on tight round its neck, belt pell-mell up Dundee Wharf to dry land.

The children of Wapping nicknamed him Slobbery Orton because he dribbled out of the slack side of his mouth. All the Ortons had nicknames. Charley, the second boy, was known as Humpty for his hunchback. William, who favoured a claw-hammer tailcoat, was Gentleman Orton. The other boys shared the name of Bullocky and collectively the family was known as 'the Buffalo breed'. They were, one of their neighbours remembered, 'what we would call an awkward-made lot': broad-framed, lumbering and splay-footed.

Aside from Slobbery, which never really caught on, Arthur's nickname was The Fat Boy, after a character in *The Pickwick Papers*. Dickens' Fat Boy was a lad 'of astounding obesity', so obsessed with food that even his romantic attentions were viewed with suspicion ('there was enough of the cannibal in the young gentleman's eyes to render the compliment doubtful'). Arthur Orton was not as big as all that, but he was a lump of a boy—'lubberly', as they said—and was inclined to indolence even before illness slowed him down. Other boys used to laugh about having the street made wider for him. Will Syrett, one of his tormentors, would long recall the 'funny games' they used to play on The Fat Boy. 'We waited for Arthur coming round the corner, put him in a hamper, tied him down, and rolled him over and over.' No one who saw him ever forgot his 'slounging' walk or his straggling hair, the colour of 'a light Bath brick'. He was a scamp—'thick-headed and bright in mischief'—who brimmed with nonsense and 'never would give you a straightforward answer.' Eliza Kemmenoe, who lived in the street called Wapping Wall, summed up her former playmate: 'He was not a regular wit, but he was not a fool.'

A month after his fourteenth birthday, Arthur Orton was issued with mariner's ticket number 373719 and apprenticed to Captain George Brooks, master of the brig *Ocean*. Four of Arthur's brothers had gone to sea before him. Now, in 1848, it was the turn of the youngest Orton. It had been nearly five years since the fire at Hartley's Wharf, but still the twitching and shaking persisted—not as bad as they had been, but bad enough. In fact, had Captain Brooks not been a business acquaintance of Arthur's father, he would never have taken the lad on. Even aside from the nervous complaint, he didn't exactly strike you as energetic. A liability, more like, thought Captain Preston, who would be commanding the new apprentice on his first voyage.

The last Wapping saw of The Fat Boy, he was lounging on a rail as the *Ocean* sidled out of St Katherine's Docks bound for Antwerp, in ballast, to take on a cargo of gin. His mariner's ticket gave his hair as light brown, his eyes as blue, the marks on his person as 'none', and his height as 'growing'. To the captain's wife he looked 'fair and stout—a nice-looking lad.' In the course of his maiden voyage, Arthur

Orton distinguished himself as a sculler but not much else. It was in a South Sea anchorage that the slothful apprentice incurred his captain's wrath with an act which, recounted over rum, would raise a laugh on many a voyage thereafter. All hands but Arthur were ashore when a canoe pulled alongside the *Ocean* bearing a catch of muddy-green crabs. Fancying a change from ship rations, Arthur procured himself a lively-looker in exchange for half a plug of tobacco. There was a good fire in the galley stove and the ship's kettle was boiling on top, but Arthur couldn't find a saucepan big enough to hold his crab. Hurried calculations told him that he'd have plenty of time to cook the crab and boil the kettle afresh before the captain got back. No sooner had he slipped the thrashing crustacean into the kettle, however, than Captain Preston appeared over the ship's side, ravening for a cuppa. What could Arthur do but, avoiding the worst of the bubbling grey scum, fill the teapot out of the kettle with the crab still inside. Three minutes later, the captain burst into the galley, looked in the kettle, then frogmarched Arthur to the side of the ship and whipped him with a convenient rope-end. Captain Preston wrote home to his master, George Brooks, stating that it had been a mistake to apprentice young Orton. He didn't mention the crab.

Arthur landed back at St Katherine's Docks at midwinter 1851. On almost his first day ashore he called at the shipsmith's in Lower East Smithfield and found his old friend Walter Leaver taking his dinner break, as he always did, seated in the broad-bummed dish of the scales.

'My word, young Arthur, you've grown.' Leaver scattered crumbs as he tipped nimbly to his feet. 'Have yourself a seat,' he invited.

Arthur slung his rump into the swaying tin dish, laughing. 'It's just like being at sea.' The spring balance strained and the needle spun around like a fairground attraction, until it clocked his weight at thirteen-and-a-half stone.

'What'd they feed you at sea?' Walter Leaver wanted to know.

'Can't say as I've known many sailor boys what come back stouter than they left.'

Stouter he may have been, but they no longer called him The Fat Boy. Arthur was now seventeen. The change of air, or the passage of years, had done him good. All that remained of his affliction was a slight stammer and a startled kind of twitch, mainly about the eyes. He still had the downy cheeks of a boy, but with his size (he'd sprouted to 5 feet 9½ inches) and his gruffened voice he passed as a man and fixed himself as a regular at Scheider's Thames-side public house, the Gun. He liked a drop of 'dog's nose'—a pennyworth of gin and a ha'penny of beer.

His parents were back living above the shop in Wapping High Street, and Arthur swapped his canvas sailor's outfit for a butcher's blue frock and corduroys. But in truth Arthur had little inclination for his father's trade. The livestock side of the business was far more to his liking. Somewhere on his travels he'd learned a thing or two about rough-riding and, for want of a proper mount, he beleaguered the Shetland ponies in the yard at Great Hermitage Street. He also took to carrying a coil of rope with which he lassoed dogs and school-boys in the High Street. He outdid himself one morning by pinioning a coal-porter—sack and all—from a distance of twenty-five feet.

At Christmas 1851, Arthur began 'walking out' with Mary Anne Loder, the fifteen-year-old daughter of a tugboat captain who lived just around the corner from the Ortons' shop. A shy girl, she let Arthur talk all he wanted and believed most of what he said. He had ideas that didn't include a sailor's life, though his father had made it clear he'd be going back to sea just as soon as it could be arranged. In the meantime, the youngest Orton ran deliveries and errands between the butchery and the docks. Once his father sent him, in company with an interpreter, to transact the sale of some Shetland ponies to the master of a Spanish vessel. Arthur had picked up a little Spanish in his travels, and now he got the idea of becoming an interpreter himself. He talked to Mary Anne of having cards printed and even sketched out a rough design on the back of a butcher's bill. He'd call himself Arturo, he said, as a sign to Spanish sea captains that he was next to being a Spaniard himself.

The business cards of Arturo Orton, mercantile interpreter, never were printed. On 23 November 1852, Arthur was issued with a new mariner's ticket and was taken on, as a favour to his father, by Captain William Storre of the *Middleton*. The ship's owner, T. D. Chapman of Hobart Town, had commissioned the purchase of two Shetland ponies, and Arthur was engaged to care for them on the voyage to Van Diemen's Land. He had other livestock on board to care for, too, and some to kill, in his capacity as ship's butcher. Arthur was not unhappy. He was under no indenture this time and would be free to stay at Hobart Town, if such was his fancy. The parting from Mary Anne was tearful on her part, less so on his. He gave a tentative undertaking that, should he decide to settle at Hobart Town, providing it was a decent enough place, he would send for her.

With that, Arthur Orton sailed from Wapping for the second and last time. He was nearly nineteen years old and was headed for Australia at the height of the gold fever. As if that weren't enough, he had six caged ferrets as company for the entire voyage.

FIFTEEN

MACKENZIE THE DETECTIVE

Detective Whicher had arrived at Wapping and the Orton sisters by the scenic route, via the Australian colonies. He was not the only detective on the case.

John Mackenzie, a tall, wind-blown Scot, had first-hand knowledge of the colonies, having just returned thence after an absence of many years. Wily, ruthless even, he was trained in the law and versed in the bush. In February 1867, when it was clear that the Claimant intended pursuing his claim, the solicitors to the Tichborne estate hired Mackenzie to investigate the erstwhile Tom Castro on Australian soil. Mackenzie sailed for Sydney at the beginning of March.

The Claimant's own solicitor, John Holmes, had not long completed the task of extracting from his client an account of his missing years. It amounted to a great many mismatched, tangled, frayed and stumpy bits of story. By leaving many of the more peculiar scraps to one side, Holmes managed eventually to draft an account that made something like sense. He read it aloud to his client, noting his amendments and additions, and had one of his clerks write it up in the form of an affidavit, which the Claimant then signed. That statement formed the basis of his examination at the Law Institution hearing. Copies were made—dozens of them—for distribution to would-be supporters, so it was no surprise that Mackenzie, by the time he sailed, knew where his quarry said he'd been and what he said he'd done during

John Mackenzie

his eleven years and ten months in the Australian colonies.

He had landed in Melbourne on or about 24 July 1854. (A lapse into delirium after the wreck of the *Bella* meant that he had little recollection of his rescue or of the voyage to Melbourne.) All that had survived of his possessions was a ring bearing the Tichborne family seal, which he sold at a store in Elizabeth Street, not far from the Roxburgh Castle Hotel where he lodged for two nights. In wandering about the town, he was drawn to Row's Yard, a horse market in Bourke Street. Some brumbies were being auctioned and, when a bushified gent asked whether he could handle one, naturally he said yes. Impressed by his readiness, William Foster offered him work as a stockrider on his station in Gippsland. It was, Foster assured him, 'a jolly life, with plenty of hunting, fishing and shooting.' Agreeing to enter Foster's service, he called himself Thomas Castro in honour of a fellow he'd known in Chile.

He stayed eighteen months at Foster's Boisdale station and about the same on the remote Dargo run, then spent six months in the town of Sale. After that, he broke in horses at the Mitchell River for a while before drifting to the Omeo diggings. He moved north from there to southern New South Wales, stopping about a year at Deniliquin, then crossing the Old Man Plains to Hay, doing a few months on the Boree Creek–Narrandera mail run. After that, he went partner in a butchery at Tumut for half a year or so, then meandered to Wagga Wagga where he stayed for the next four years.

Taking that account as his guide, Mackenzie set about backtracking Tom Castro: from Sydney to Goulburn to Tumut to Wagga, on through Boree Creek, Narrandera and Hay, then south to Deniliquin. With him he carried a letter in which the Court of Chancery had authorised the Tichborne solicitors to draw on the estate (otherwise quarantined for the infant heir) to meet the expense of his investigations. It was an important-looking document, phrased in florid legalese on crested letterhead, and Mackenzie flashed it around to give the impression that he was conducting impartial inquiries on the Lord Chancellor's behalf.

The detective had a full beard but, for the sake of hearing the kind of talk that is best heard in barber shops, he had it trimmed in every town. For the same reason, he did the rounds of the public houses, where he kept himself to watered-down whisky but otherwise spent freely of the infant heir's inheritance, in the name of cultivating informants. He cosied up to local newspaper proprietors, taking them into his confidence—or letting them think he had—and they duly made sure the whole district knew that Mr John Mackenzie was in town 'specially to make enquiries respecting our old friend Tom de Castro, the claimant of the Baronetcy of Tichborne.' David Griffith Jones, of the *Deniliquin Pastoral Times*, was particularly obliging. In August 1867 he devoted an entire column to an inflammatory report based on information supplied by Mackenzie. 'In these parts he said he had served his time in London as a butcher, and had given all kinds of versions of his previous life.' Not content with denouncing 'de Castro' as an impostor, the *Pastoral Times* assured its readers that he was impotent, his wife a whore, his children bastards, and the Dowager Lady Tichborne 'weak-headed'.

Francis Baigent had an old schoolfriend, Edwin Twynam, who was now a solicitor at Hay. Of Mackenzie's visit to that town, Twynam wrote, 'I cannot understand what Mackenzie the Agent was about, but he has not proceeded in the usual way to get evidence so as to perpetuate same—He seems rather to have been listening to the Gossip or Yarns as we call them of the loafers about the place.'

But Mackenzie knew what he was about.

William Gibbes was beginning to fear he'd been taken for a fool. Tom Castro had left him embarrassed and in debt, with a worthless promissory note in lieu of a reward. The triumph he'd felt when news of his famous client first appeared in the papers had long since dissolved. Now, Gibbes knew, a good half of his acquaintances regarded him as a dupe. He still *wanted* to believe in the Claimant, but it was getting harder to do so. Over the course of many hours in Gibbes' office at Wagga, Mackenzie took the lawyer's doubts and kindled them. Systematically, he contradicted every statement Castro had made about the Tichborne family, its estates, and Roger's early life. The revelation that broke Gibbes' resolve—that Roger had been an officer in the Carabineers for three years, not a private in the Blues for thirteen days—was no more or less significant than any other of Mackenzie's contradictions; it was just a case of too many straws and a camel's back.

Later, Gibbes would deny that he'd declared, 'That being the case, I hope you will give the scoundrel fifteen years on the roads,' but he admitted, 'I did use strong language.' He changed his mind again almost before Mackenzie left the town. He'd let himself be bluffed and bullied and…what had he done? In a long letter of contrition he told the Claimant: 'Mackenzie pitched such a plausible yarn that even I was shaken for a short, very short, time.' But the harm was done. He had allowed the detective to examine and copy freely from all his papers relating to the case, including his own detailed statement—written at John Holmes' request—of his dealings with Tom Castro. Holmes could only deplore Gibbes' weakness and 'the disastrous effect' it might have on his client's case.

Wherever he went, Mackenzie particularly sought out butchers who might have known 'de Castro'. At Wagga, Joseph Emlyn told him how he'd heard from a butcher down Deniliquin way that Castro's real name was Henry Horton and that they'd slaughtered together at Whitechapel Market in London. Mackenzie reported the same to Dobinson & Geare, London solicitors for the Tichborne estates, who duly instructed Detective Whicher to follow up Emlyn's story. That was at the end of September 1867, and just a couple of days knocking around the East End meat markets led Whicher to the door of Mary Ann Tredgett (*née* Orton) in East India Road, Wapping.

The Monday after his visit from Mrs Tredgett, John Holmes learnt from his agent at the Shipping Registry that the Tichborne solicitors had been inquiring after the *Middleton*. 'Ever heard of it?' Holmes asked the Claimant when he called at Croydon that evening. Predictably, the answer was no. But when Holmes told him about the latest identity attributed to him by his opponents—'this Arthur Orton'—the Claimant laughed.

'Well, I ain't him; but I knew him. We was working together for a time—at butchering, you know.' Orton had been at Wagga when he left, the Claimant said, and, for all he knew, was still there.

'So there'd be others at Wagga who'd know him?' asked Holmes. He needed witnesses who could point Orton out as a person distinct from the Claimant.

'Well, he didn't always go by his right name…' The Claimant thought for a moment. 'Jack Cater, though—he'd know him.'

Cater, the former Wagga baker, was due to visit Croydon in the next few days and the Claimant promised Holmes that he'd sound him out about their mutual acquaintance. That he did, and Cater pronounced himself perfectly willing to swear to an affidavit that he had known and served bread to Arthur Orton, a pock-marked man quite distinct from Tom Castro, the Claimant.

Affidavits were one thing. What they really needed, Holmes knew, was to find this Arthur Orton.

At the close of the year 1867, the Claimant's side hired a detective of their own in the colonies. Otto Berliner, retired policeman and proprietor of the Private Inquiry Office in Melbourne, was the man retained for the task by Sedgefield & Allport, the solicitors acting for the Claimant in Australia. The Tichborne solicitors had, by this time, crossed off every name but Arthur Orton's from their long list of possible identities for the Claimant.

After Deniliquin, Mackenzie leapt across to Gippsland, in southeast Victoria, where he had the good fortune to renew an old acquaintance. As a young man in the colonies, he had, for a time, been employed on a sheep run in the Monaro district of New South Wales, in company with a rascally, horse-mad drover by the name of Matthew Macalister. Now, when Mackenzie inquired at Sale about Mrs Foster, widow of the late Mr William Foster of Boisdale, he was corrected: 'You mean Mrs Macalister.' The widow had married Mackenzie's old hut-mate.

In the Claimant's account of his Australian life, the Gippsland chapter pivoted on Boisdale station, just to the north of Sale. For his first three years in Australia, he'd lived and worked either on the station itself or—still on the Boisdale payroll—away in the mountains on the Dargo run. Mackenzie knew from experience that station managers kept a record of all but their most itinerant workers, so he figured that Castro's name ought to appear in three years' worth of Boisdale's store accounts and wage books—and that somebody ought to remember him.

As Mackenzie had hoped, there were station records stretching right back to 1854, and they were piled, waiting for him, on a table in the parlour the first day he rode out to Boisdale. They'd already

TOM DE CASTRO, THE CLAIMANT OF THE TICHBORNE BARONETCY. *576*
[FROM A RECENT PHOTOGRAPH.]

Mackenzie's mugshot—the Claimant as he appeared in the Illustrated Australian News. *The* 'de *Castro' betrays Mackenzie's intervention*

been through them, Matthew Macalister told him, and he'd be damned if there'd ever been a Castro on the Boisdale payroll. And Sara was certain she'd never heard the name.

'How are you at recollecting faces?' asked Mackenzie, addressing Sara Macalister, and he produced from his case a portrait of the Claimant.

'Oh, but we've already seen that. It's the one that was in the *Illustrated News*, isn't it?' The mugshot Mackenzie had handed her was a framed engraving from the *Illustrated Australian News*, based on the Claimant's Sydney portrait.

'But do you recognise him?'

'Oh yes, I know the face. He was here, right enough.' Sara Macalister was enjoying herself. 'But his name wasn't Castro—it wasn't Tom, even. As soon as I saw the picture, I remembered he was called Arthur something.'

This was early in August 1867. Mackenzie's letter relating Emlyn's story of Henry Horton, the Whitechapel butcher, was still in the mail-steamer on its way to London. It would be six weeks yet before Detective Whicher transformed Henry Horton into Arthur Orton. So 'Arthur something' rang no bells for Mackenzie.

'What about the books?' he asked, indicating the stack on the table. 'Could you not find the name there?'

There were, Sara Macalister explained, perhaps a hundred names listed in the station's quarterly accounts during the period when the Claimant was supposed to have been at Boisdale. But there were only two Arthurs. One was an Arthur Graham, listed as a shearer for two seasons, 1857 and 1858. The other was Arthur Orton.

Orton. Horton. Mackenzie was making connections. 'He wouldn't've been a butcher, I suppose?'

'He'd've done some butchering, certainly. But then, so do most of the stockmen.' Sara Macalister felt Mackenzie's interest quicken. 'Oh yes,' she said, archly, 'he was a stockman. Just like this Castro's supposed to have been.' She turned to the account books and opened the top one to a marked page. 'The dates don't match exactly, but,' nodding at the Claimant's portrait, 'that's him, I'm certain.' She and Mackenzie set to examining the station books.

Mackenzie was a fortnight in Gippsland, and, at the Macalisters' insistence, he made Boisdale his base. He visited pastoral stations all over the district. Often the Macalisters accompanied him, introducing him to their neighbours and relations and to old hands who might recall the man in Mackenzie's picture. His main prompts now were the portrait and the name Arthur Orton. If one didn't work, he'd try the other; and he had no qualms leading witnesses from a tentative recognition of the portrait to a sworn certainty that it was Arthur Orton.

By the time the Claimant's man Otto Berliner commenced his inquiries in Gippsland months later, the ground had been thoroughly plundered by Mackenzie. Berliner's portrait of the Claimant was different from Mackenzie's, being a copy of one of the Wagga photographs. It showed the Claimant leaner than his Sydney portrait, and in his working clothes—a closer fit, surely, to how he'd have looked as a stockman. But when Berliner called at Boisdale, Sara Macalister barely glanced at the portrait he handed her. It was, she stated flatly, a likeness of 'our old butcher' Arthur Orton. Berliner wrote to Holmes in London:

> Mrs McAlister, late Mrs Foster, is a strong antagonist in this case, and appears to be on friendly terms with Mackenzie…She is plainly spoken, a bitter woman, but at the same time both clever and playful with men in general…there is something which makes her conduct so strange and so base.

While Berliner was going over cold and hostile ground, Mackenzie was making an unexpected detour from his itinerary. Evidence had emerged in Gippsland that Arthur Orton had come to Boisdale, not from Melbourne but from Hobart Town. Up to this point, Mackenzie's investigations had been dictated by the Claimant's version of events. But now, aboard a steamer heading south from Melbourne, the detective exulted: he'd stepped off the Claimant's map.

Back in London, as 1868 began, John Holmes was hearing for the first time about Mackenzie's progress in Gippsland and the unanimous recognition there of the Claimant as Arthur Orton. Clearly it was now critical to the Claimant's case to locate this man Orton.

Mrs Tredgett, on her latest visit to Holmes' office, had happened to mention that Arthur had written to her from Fremantle the previous August. The pity was, she'd sent the letter on to their brother George in Singapore. Holmes had written to George Orton, requesting the letter's immediate return; now he wrote to government officials in Western Australia, inquiring as to Arthur Orton's whereabouts and situation. If he were at Fremantle, Holmes knew, there was a fair chance the man was a convict. In due course, George Orton would write from Singapore to say that he'd mislaid Arthur's letter, and the Comptroller of Convicts in Western Australia would advise that he had no convict named Arthur Orton in his charge—though, of course (he would add, trying to be helpful), the man might be using an alias. Holmes could have spat.

He had arranged for Mrs Tredgett and her sister, Mrs Jury, to meet his client and was relieved when both women stated categorically that they had never seen the Claimant before (except for the portrait Mr Whicher had shown them, and that, said Mrs Jury, had been a very poor likeness) and, for good measure, that he was no relation of theirs. The Claimant was reserved and gracious throughout the interview and insisted, when Mrs Jury complained of her loss of time and her good-for-nothing husband, that Holmes give her £3 on his account.

Holmes sent instructions to his agents in Australia to seek out

Arthur Orton at all costs. Gibbes replied that he'd never heard Orton's name before, and couldn't find anyone at Wagga who had. Berliner, on the other hand, heard of nobody *but* Arthur Orton. 'It appears very strange, he wrote, 'that Sir Roger was not known by the name of Castro in Gippsland. Everyone seen up to the present identifies the photograph of Arthur Orton.'

Berliner had collected numerous affidavits which bore out the Claimant's account of his Gippsland career and even supported his identity as Sir Roger Tichborne. But all were predicated on the inescapable conclusion that the Claimant, whilst in Gippsland, had gone by the name of Arthur Orton—'and it is unexplainable to me,' Berliner told Holmes, 'why Sir Roger did not instruct you of the fact.'

The day he received Berliner's parcel from Gippsland, Holmes spent many hours 'considering the effect of such an extraordinary position of things.' The Claimant assured his fraught attorney that he had never been known as Orton and had gone by no other name than Castro during the whole of his time in Australia. He couldn't explain how it was that Gippslanders had confused him with this man Orton. 'I urged upon you the importance of being very explicit,' Holmes noted darkly in his bill of costs where he made a record of the interview.*

Troubling reports from Gippsland were also reaching the ears of the Claimant's most influential supporters. William Bulpett had by this time staked thousands of pounds on the Claimant and was alarmed when a Gippsland acquaintance advised him to have nothing more to do with the case. Holmes had the task of appeasing Bulpett and the rest. 'Nothing whatever has occurred to lead me to doubt the truth of any of Sir Roger's statements respecting his identity,' he

---

* Holmes' dealings in the case would later be summarised in his bill of costs, with every conversation, every action, each new revelation and set-back painstakingly detailed. Throughout the document, Holmes addressed his client as *you*, creating an impression of intimacy and, often, of accusation.

assured them. But when he confided to Curzon Allport, his counter-part in Melbourne, that 'all the Counsel and friends of Sir Roger believe he is keeping back part of his history,' Holmes undoubtedly spoke for himself as well.

The next Australian mail brought a clipping, courtesy of Allport, from the *Hobart Town Mercury*. 'We understand Mr Mackenzie has ascertained,' it read, 'as the result of his investigation, that the Australian claimant, who was known in New South Wales as Tom Castro, is identical with a young man named Arthur Orton, who early in the year 1853 arrived in Hobart Town, from London, in the ship *Middleton*.'

The Claimant, when Holmes tracked him down at a pigeon shoot near Basingstoke, swore it wasn't so. But he did admit, at last, that he had known Orton in Gippsland. Protesting, he let Holmes haul him back to 25 Poultry, where a fresh affidavit was wrung out of him:

> I knew the Arthur Orton referred to in such paragraph very well indeed in Gippsland about 1855 and again in Wagga-Wagga in 1865. I first became acquainted with him when I was at the Dargo station. It was from him I learnt to slaughter and dress meat. He was the son of a butcher in Wapping. The face of the said Arthur Orton was pitted with small-pox.

The pock-marks were confirmed by Orton's sisters, as was his depar-ture on the *Middleton* for Hobart Town—the last they had seen of him. Holmes raged at his client, 'But why did you not tell me of this?'

'I didn't see as how you needed to know.'

Holmes managed not to seem like a desperate man when he met, a short while later, with William Dobinson, the Tichborne estates' London solicitor. In fact, if Holmes' record of the meeting is to be believed, he faced his opponent with conviction: 'Pointed out to him I believed both he and his Clients were entirely misinformed by the witnesses in Australia as to your being Arthur Orton.'

Still adrift in Gippsland when the news washed across Bass Strait, Otto Berliner informed the *Gippsland Times* 'that although Sir Roger whilst in humble circumstances in Gippsland assumed the name of Arthur Orton, he was by no means identical with the butcher of that name in Hobart Town.' He planned to make his own inquiries in Hobart Town, which he was confident would establish a clear distinction between the Arthur Orton of that town and Arthur Orton of Gippsland. The *Gippsland Times* concluded that 'in a few weeks, through the exertions of Mr Berliner, we may expect that the mystery attached to the case will be cleared up.'

SIXTEEN

A SMALL THIN HEART

It appears that the other side are trying to make out I am not
myself but a person named horton.

It wasn't the first the Dowager Lady Tichborne had heard of it; but
it was the first time she'd heard it from the Claimant himself. Through
her brother, Alfred Seymour, the Claimant's opponents had made
sure she learnt of anything that might erode her support for the big
man. Seymour had warned her, too, that if the Claimant were found
to be an impostor she might be charged with perjury or as an acces-
sory to fraud. Late in 1867, he'd sent his wife to impress upon her
that the Claimant's success would mean the displacement of the young
Sir Henry—that he'd be pushed well down the line of succession by
the spawn of the Claimant and his common colonial wife.

There are signs that the Dowager was rattled. Could they really
say she'd perjured herself? she asked her solicitor. After her visit from
Mrs Alfred Seymour, she sought the Claimant's assurance that, when
he succeeded to the estates, he would grant £50,000 to the son of the
late Sir Alfred.

The Dowager knew, a full month before the Claimant apprised
her of it, that the evidence from Australia made it look as if the man
she'd acknowledged as her son was nothing more than a London
butcher, Orton by name. And that his wife (as the Deniliquin paper
had spelt out) was 'a common servant of a certain class, who previous

to marrying de Castro had succumbed to the attentions of several men, by one of whom she had a child.' The Dowager was troubled already about what kind of man her son had become. She had recently paid the passage home of his children's nurse, Rosina McArthur, after the young woman confided that the Claimant's persistent sexual advances had culminated in an attempted rape, a charge he denied. Of course, his opponents knew nothing of that episode.

John Holmes stayed at home on 25 and 26 December 1867—his first days off in more than eleven months. Not long before, he had learnt that at least three hundred witnesses would be called in opposition to his client's claim. He calculated that, including those being procured in Australia, his own side could count on something like a hundred. They needed more. But the Claimant continued to resist when Holmes proposed visits to out-of-town witnesses or to France 'for the purpose of seeing whether the French language would return to you or not.' Francis Baigent, his most loyal supporter, despaired that 'he pays so little attention to letters it is disheartening to write to him.' And his memory showed little sign of improving. He confessed to Holmes, 'I never remember a person after meeting them'—not at all what his solicitor wanted to hear. Baigent complained, 'The Baronet is acting more foolish every day.'

The Claimant had a small but solid band of financial backers at the end of his first year in England. Guildford Onslow, like William Bulpett, was the principal of a Hampshire bank, as well as being a member of Parliament, and he had ridden to the hunt with Sir Roger's father. Harry Bloxam (known as 'Blocky') was a wine importer specialising in Spanish sherry, but he did a lucrative sideline in money-lending and 'bill-discounting'—buying and selling promissory notes at less than their face value. Charles Hingston, another importer, came to the case as a friend of Holmes. The odd one out was Colonel Franklin Lushington. His tenancy of Tichborne Park meant that the case to be heard in the Court of Common Pleas was filed as *Tichborne v. Lushington*; but the Colonel himself, impressed by the Claimant's familiarity with the furnishings of Tichborne House, was firmly behind him. All except Lushington were speculators by profession. They believed in the Claimant, but they were backing him for a win, at extortionate rates of interest. A loan of £6,000, for example, was to be repaid at £18,000. Another, brokered by Bloxam, secured £250 at ten per cent interest, to be paid quarterly, with £500 payable if the Claimant secured the estates. The loans came so dearly to him, Bloxam bluntly explained, because 'very few people believe in your identity.'

After a year on the case, Holmes' bill stood at £1,823 4s. 4d. He had seen nothing of the money raised, except as it passed through his hands. Some of it—too much—went on keeping debt-collectors at bay; Holmes' staff and the battery of agents collecting evidence had to be paid; witnesses were reimbursed; there were bills from the printers who copied affidavits and from the London School of Photography for copying photographs of the Claimant for circulation to potential witnesses; there were train fares and cab fares and stamps and telegrams; and there were the fees of the barristers hired to defend John Holmes' client against the barrage of debt claims he faced.

Holmes endlessly urged his client to reduce his expenditure. But debts attached themself to the Claimant like filings to a magnet. When he moved to a larger house in Croydon, his former landlord laid a claim for 'delapidations of furniture' during the Claimant's tenancy of Essex Lodge. The most persistent of his Croydon creditors was Mr Hammam, from whom he hired his linen and cutlery and whom he eventually fobbed off with a bill of exchange for £1,000 in payment of his £150 account. Of so little value were the Claimant's promissory notes that, if Hammam were lucky, a bill-discounter might give him one-tenth of the bill's value. Most of the Claimant's creditors, however, received nothing and it was their claims that led Holmes to complain to his client of 'the difficulty of keeping you out of prison on account of your debts.'

Not only were Holmes' exertions unpaid, they were unthanked. The Claimant and the Dowager sniped at what they regarded as his inaction. By March 1868, it was too much for Holmes. He unlocked his office early on Saturday, 7 March. There was a letter he had to write. 'Sir,' he began:

> The great labour and anxiety which I have undergone during the last twelve months in the transaction of your business has so weakened my health that it has become an imperative necessity for me to ask you to be good enough to relieve me of further conduct of it…

He had the letter signed and blotted when a knock announced his clerk with a telegram. *Don't open that telegram*, shrilled the unheeded chorus of Holmes' better judgment. The yellow slip advised that the Claimant was in the French port of Boulogne, lying low (as low as a fat man could) while the latest storm of debt blew over. Holmes looked from the telegram to the letter he'd just written, and held his head. Now was not the time to back out. With a heave of regret, he pushed the letter under his blotter. Holmes was back on the case.

The Claimant had learnt that he was about to be arrested in connection with one of his debts and, with the Dowager's encouragement, had decided to put himself beyond the law's reach. She had assured him that she would settle matters in his absence but, after a 'very long discussion' with Holmes, confessed herself alarmed at the desperate state of the Claimant's affairs. Holmes spared her nothing: the dishonoured bills mounting up at Mr Bulpett's bank and the great harm his disappearance would do if his enemies should hear of it. He even saw fit to acquaint her with a claim for compensation lodged against the Claimant by a woman named Elizabeth Reeves. Holmes' record of the Reeves claim is inexplicit, but references to 'the assault' and 'the state of her health' suggest a sexual misdemeanour, if not worse.

At a meeting in Alresford of the Claimant's principal supporters, the means were found to settle Elizabeth Reeves' claim and those of the Claimant's most pressing creditors. Edward Rous, of the Swan Inn, was despatched to Boulogne to fetch the fugitive home. Rous and the Claimant arrived back in London on Thursday, 12 March, to the news that the Dowager Lady Tichborne had died that morning in her drawing room at Howlitt's Hotel, with her head on the sofa.

Later, the Claimant would eulogise her as 'everything that was kind and good...if she had been an angel she could not possibly have done more for me.' But for now, he was all business. He proceeded straight to Howlitt's where, at Holmes' instruction, he 'took possession immediately of his late mother's boxes and papers,' as well as of her carriage and horses from a livery stables close by. He also 'took possession' of £73 which the Dowager had about her when she died. An inquest next day declared the cause of death to have been atrophy ('she had a very small thin heart'). Both the Claimant and Alfred Seymour were present at the inquest, and each accused the other of killing the Dowager, or having had her killed. However, two doctors stated emphatically that, whilst 'any excitement might have caused the heart to stop its action,' they had found no evidence of violence nor any trace of poison. At Holmes' office after the inquest, the Claimant asked his solicitor to ascertain the whereabouts of the family silver.

The Dowager was buried at Tichborne. Inside the chapel, the stone relief of a boy and his guardian angel ought to have comforted the Claimant, but seemed instead to mock him. He wept all through the service, then tussled with Alfred Seymour for the position of chief mourner in the funeral procession. In the end, two processions followed the casket out of the chapel into the tiny yew-hemmed churchyard. Detective Whicher was observed by the gate, pointing out the Claimant to a plain, stoutish woman, who dropped into a faint. In short, there was plenty to entertain the newspaper-reading public.

In spite (or perhaps because) of being pressured to make a will in the Claimant's favour, the Dowager had died intestate. For the past year, she had given him an allowance of £20 a week—half her income. How was he to manage now, with his benefactress dead and her estate in limbo? The Claimant's supporters met at Alresford after the funeral and a subscription was mounted, 'to assist you in your present destitute condition.' Holmes headed the list of subscribers who pledged £100 each, and the Claimant ended up with an annual income of £1,400. As his side of the bargain, he was required to sign a 'special Agreement in reference to your future conduct.' Which he did, willingly. After all, he was £400 a year better off.

But if the Dowager's money was replaceable, she was not. Her acknowledgment of him had been the bulwark between the Claimant and his opponents. Who should better know a son than his own mother? Weak-headed she may have been, but nobody ever doubted that her testimony could sway a court. Those boxes and papers the Claimant had taken from her hotel on the day she died, however, went some way towards filling the gap. Holmes spent many hours 'perusing and considering and arranging' the nearly two hundred letters between young Roger and his mother, which he found in one of the boxes. There was valuable correspondence too shedding light on the Tichbornes' life in Paris and the row over Roger's schooling, as well as other matters concerning which the Claimant's recollection had failed him. But most precious of all was a large gilt case containing a daguerreotype of Roger Tichborne as a young man, wearing a straw hat.

Holmes studied the portrait, rapt. It was the first likeness he had seen of the young Roger, and naturally he compared it with his client's present appearance. They were not much alike in breadth, that was certain. But now Holmes could see for himself the resemblance, attested to by many witnesses, about the eyes and the upper part of the face. Yes, it was the same dreamy eye. And, Holmes smiled, his client still had the eccentric sense of style which showed in the young Roger's choice of headgear. At first, the Claimant recognised the portrait as one he'd had taken at Southampton after he left the army. But a short time later, at Alresford, Edward Hopkins produced a lacquered straw sailor's hat and asked if the Claimant remembered it. He'd sent home it to Sir James from South America, Hopkins prompted. Why yes, replied the Claimant, turning it in his hands; in fact he believed he'd had his portrait taken wearing that very hat. And indeed, the Dowager's daguerreotype was one of the two Roger posed for in Santiago, with his shiny hat and his spotted necktie and his pet guanaco frolicking just out of the frame.

A place not far from Santiago had featured in the Claimant's affidavit to Chancery, in a brief account of his acquaintance with the original Tomas Castro. He'd stayed at Castro's inn in the village of Melipilla, thirty miles from Santiago and twice that distance from Valparaiso. He couldn't recall exactly how long he had been there—a few weeks— but he had been made to feel welcome. There had been shooting parties after wild pigeon and quail, Castro had given him the run of his stables and had introduced him to the lasso, and he'd found fellow- ship with an English doctor, John Hayley, who lived in the village with his Chilean wife. He had assumed Castro's name in Melbourne, the Claimant said, for no better reason than that the name of his host at Melipilla had been the first that came to mind.

Back in August 1867, when Holmes was just beginning to appre- hend the full sprawl of the case, he had judged it wise for his client to renew his acquaintance with Don Tomas Castro. Under Holmes' direction, the Claimant wrote this remarkable letter, signing it, as of course he signed everything, 'Roger Tichborne':

> Dear Sir and Esteemed Friend,
> I presume I am about the last person in this world from whom you would expect to receive a letter. But, dear friend, you know

full well that in this world we can never tell what we may one day have to do. What I have now to say is, that I have just returned to England, that is, in December last; and for the space of many years, and through neglect, I failed to write to my friends. I have got very fat, almost as fat as Don Ramon Azocar. On arriving in England I found that my property was, as it still remains, in the hands of my relations, who dispute my identity, and therefore, my right to the same...

Be good enough to present my remembrances to Dr Juan Hayley, the English doctor, and his wife Dona Clara and her sister Jesusa. And my respects to Dona Natalia Salmento or, as I used to teach you that I called her, Misses Castro. Please also to remember me to Don Ramon Alcalde, Dona Hurtado, and my old godfather as I used to call him, and to the Senorita Matilde. And also to Don Jose Maria Berenguel and his brother Jose Miguel...I was entirely forgetting a very old friend of mine, I mean Mr Toro Don Jose, the husband of your sister-in-law at Concumen.

I have another strange thing to tell you, and I do not doubt but that you will think I took a very great liberty, and that is that I assumed and made use of your Christian and surname, and that during the sixteen [sic] years I was in Australia I was only known as Thomas Castro. I likewise gave out that I was a Chilian, but they could easily see this is not the fact. I can however, assure you, my dear friend, that I never dishonored your name, or even your prowess on horseback during the time I was over there...

This was less than a month after the Claimant's cross-examination at the Law Institution, during which his recollection of his childhood, family life, school years, and army career—the first twenty-three years of his life, in fact—had failed him almost entirely. Yet he was able to recall the names of more than a dozen Chilean villagers whom, by his own reckoning, he had known, thirteen years earlier, for just three weeks. The Claimant's supporters were delighted at this sign that the fog was lifting. Baigent wrote: 'To me it seems wonderful that Sir Roger should remember all those names…'

The reply, when it came, was not from Tomas Castro, but from his son, Pedro. His father, he explained, had 'unhappily lost his reason.' Moreover, many of those named in the Claimant's letter were now dead:

> But Dona Maria Lagos, widow of my said godfather remembers you. I showed your letter to Don Juan Hayley the English doctor and to his wife Dona Clara Nories. The former retains no recollection of you; it is true that owing to intemperance his memory is gone; the latter does and is ready to declare so…Don Jose Miguel Valdivieso is at the present time Regidor of the Municipality of Melipilla. Directly he read your letter he went into an account as to who you were, of your stay in this place &c. &c., expressing great pleasure at hearing from you.

It was even more gratifying to hear that Dona Francisca Ahumada, mother of the fat Don Ramon Azocar, 'still preserves a curl of your hair.' The not-so-welcome news conveyed by Pedro Castro was that Severo Barra, an agent for 'the other side', had been inquiring about Roger Tichborne's stay in Melipilla. It looked as if the Claimant had been outmanoeuvred yet again.

SEVENTEEN
ARTURO HORTON

OF the purported three hundred witnesses whose evidence the Claimant's opponents intended to bring to the Court of Common Pleas, nearly half lived in the colonies and a handful in Chile. Holmes, likewise, had a growing list of witnesses who were oceans away from Westminster. By early 1868, it was clear to both sides that the expense of bringing so many witnesses to England was beyond them. The alternative was for the court to authorise commissions to go out and, under its oaths and offices, take evidence from far-flung witnesses. The expense would still be borne by the parties to the case, but it would be nothing like the cost of a hundred or more return passages. Legal representatives of both parties would examine and cross-examine witnesses under the scrutiny of two local commissioners. The resulting evidence would be considered at the trial in just the same way as the testimony given in court.

Since the case hinged on the question of the Claimant's identity, it was crucial that he should accompany the commissions to Chile and Australia. Mackenzie and Berliner knew only too well the limited value of photographs as a means of identification. Some people refused even to look at them—as if photography were one of the dark arts—while others made excuses like, 'I'm a very poor judge of likenesses,' or even, 'I do not understand these things.' Holmes seemed surprised when the Claimant readily agreed to go with the commissions, 'in order to prevent mistakes and your being sworn to as Arthur Orton.'

This was June 1868, and it heartened the Claimant's supporters no end that their man was willing to face witnesses and clear up the confusion over Orton. As Baigent told Rous: 'Sir Roger's task is quite easy—he has only to go out to Australia and the whole affair will fall to pieces.' The Chilean commission wasn't scheduled to begin until November but, at Holmes' suggestion, the Claimant was to call at Rio on the way, 'to ascertain if any one now there knew you.' He would sail at the beginning of September.

The Claimant needed a new will before he left. There was a third child to provide for now: James Francis, born in June. After the Dowager's death, the Claimant had moved with his family down to Hampshire, to the Old Post House in Broad Street, Alresford. No sooner had he had the doorways widened than he lost another of his most valuable supporters when his new neighbour, Edward Hopkins, suddenly died. With him went his fishing right and his matchless knowledge of Roger and the Tichbornes. The Claimant kept finding excuses now to go up to London—to be anywhere, in fact, but where his wife was. His Hampshire friends knew how he felt: they avoided the Old Post House for the same reason. They'd long considered Mary a regrettable choice of wife for a baronet and a liability to his cause. In front of visitors, she'd bawl abuse and throw things at her husband—a pair of bellows once, another time a warming pan. Even so, she wielded some influence over him, they were sure. How many times had they heard her snarl at him, *You promised me*'? And the way she spoke to them: as if they weren't paying the rent and keeping her in shot-silk taffeta, and as if they didn't know where she'd come from. It was demeaning to have to address her as Lady Tichborne. Still, his supporters had to admit, where her husband was concerned, she did have cause to complain. Between themselves, they muttered darkly about his 'drinking and whoring'.

They were determined that he would be well chaperoned on his trip abroad with the commissions. As well as a servant named Rayner and William Hall, a barrister, he would travel in company with Holmes' no-nonsense chief clerk, John Stevens, acting among other things as 'paymaster'.

On 8 September 1868, the day before the *Oneida* sailed, Holmes and his client set off together by train from Alresford. Mary said nothing untoward—nor threw anything, except for a baleful glare at Holmes as her husband kissed the children goodbye. As he watched the Claimant heave himself into the train, Holmes wondered how on earth he would manage abroad. Eight months he would be gone, four or more of them at sea, with hundreds of miles of inland travel. As if in answer to Holmes' thoughts, the Claimant produced from his pockets a loud handkerchief, a cigar like a table-leg and a quarter-pint of whiskey. He swabbed his face with the first, trimmed and lit the second, uncorked the third, and settled himself across three first-class seats for the twenty-mile journey to Southampton.

At the docks next morning, Holmes handed the Claimant his new will. He signed without reading a word. The will bequeathed John Holmes £1,000 on top of any monies owed him, gave him lifetime use of Upton (part of the Doughty estates) and £1,000 a year as land agent, as well as £500 as the will's co-executor. Charles Hingston and Colonel Lushington were also named as significant beneficiaries, while others of the Claimant's supporters stood to receive lesser bequests. Did the Claimant know what he'd signed? Did he care?

His opponents predicted that he would seize this opportunity to escape. Once beyond reach of the English courts, they figured, he would cast off his unravelling imposture and simply not return. Among his supporters, there were those who feared something similar. But Holmes wasn't one of them. He suspected that the Claimant thrived on it all—not just the lavish trappings, but the pitched drama as well. And what impostor would agree to revisit, in person, his fabricated past? Holmes' optimism was fortified by his release from the daily

Charley Orton

burden of the man himself. His buoyant spirits lasted exactly four
weeks, until 7 October when he learnt that Charles Orton had made
a 'confession' that the Claimant was his brother, Arthur.

Through Holmes' agency, Charles Orton had met the Claimant
earlier that year and had sworn that the big man was not Arthur, nor
any member of the Orton family. An out-of-work butcher, Charley
had insisted on being paid ten shillings 'for loss of time' on each
occasion Holmes made contact with him. Now he presented himself
to the Tichborne family solicitors, determined, he said, to tell 'the

whole truth': for more than a year the Claimant had paid £5 a month for his silence.

Confronted by Holmes over his about-face, Charley protested that the Claimant—his brother Arthur and none other—'had told him to deceive every one.' Charley's wife had been uneasy all along and, when the Claimant failed to pay for a continuance of fraternal loyalty during his long absence, 'Esther said if I did not say it was Arthur she would tell all in Court and I should be transported.' Then Charley told Holmes the last thing he wanted to hear:

> that Arthur Orton previously to going out in the Ship *Middleton* to Hobart Town, was on board the Ship *Ocean* and went in her to Valparaiso, remained in Chili sometime, returning home but a short time previously to going to Hobart Town, and he then spoke a little Spanish.

Poor John Holmes. He had counted on his client's first-hand knowledge of Chile and his intimacy with the inhabitants of Melipilla as a cast-iron proof—if not of his identity as Roger Tichborne, then at least of his *not* being Arthur Orton. Could Charley's word be trusted, though? Holmes sent a line to Mrs Tredgett, asking her and her sister 'to favor me with a call.'

Mrs Tredgett and Mrs Jury, when they heard what their brother Charley ('that cowardly cur') had said, professed themselves 'much surprised'. But they confirmed that their youngest brother had indeed been in South America. Holmes listened, incredulous, to their account: how, following the episode with the crab and the captain's cup of tea, Arthur had absconded from the *Ocean* at Valparaiso and found refuge with some kind folk for months or perhaps years; and how, on the mountain crossing to Buenos Aires, he'd eaten monkeys and rescued a dangling mule from a precipice. Holmes felt like crying. Hadn't he heard the Claimant recount the same tale in recollecting *his* journey across the Cordilleras? A visit to the Seamen's Registry the following day supplied the duplicate of the mariner's ticket issued to Arthur Orton when he joined the *Ocean* for its voyage to Valparaiso in 1848. According to the Orton sisters, their brother had arrived back in Wapping aboard the *Jessie Miller* in the middle of 1851. There was a Joseph M. Orton on the crew-list for the Valparaiso–London voyage: just like Arthur, he was a sixteen-year-old Londoner who had last served on the *Ocean*. When Holmes compared Joseph M.'s ticket with Arthur's, he saw that the signatures were all but identical.

The Claimant had been in Chile. So had Arthur Orton. The Claimant had eaten monkeys in the Cordilleras. So had Arthur Orton. The Claimant had been at Boisdale and at Wagga. So had Arthur Orton.

The very next week brought a letter from Pedro Castro, and it was as if he had divined Holmes' worst fears—

> No one has known here the true Arturo Horton; and, although Sir Roger bore that christian and surname, he himself communicated to Don José Miguel Valdivieso, and to other persons, that they were not his own; that he belonged to the English aristocracy; and that in England he played with the Queen's children.

Holmes was sitting down but could've sworn that the chair legs staggered. Had he received the same letter a fortnight before, he'd have cursed Severo Barra for 'planting' Orton's name on South American witnesses, as Mackenzie had done in Gippsland. Not now, though. Even supposing Barra had been asking about Arthur Orton, that didn't explain the villagers' accounts of this 'Arturo Horton'. If it was the runaway sailor Orton they were recalling, what of his aristocratic pretensions? But if it were Tichborne, why had he called himself Arthur Orton? Racking his brain for something that would serve in lieu of an explanation, all Holmes could come up with was that both men had been at Melipilla, years apart, and that the villagers' failing memories had run them into one.

Such evidence was sure to emerge at the Chilean commission. What, Holmes wondered, would the Claimant's counsel make of it, since they had no inkling that Arthur Orton had ever been in Chile? The difficulty and anxiety that awaited them in Santiago was, said Holmes, 'something I do not like to think of.'

Through the Australian winter of 1868, the search for Arthur Orton had continued. Holmes' inquiries in Western Australia having drawn a blank, he placed two notices in the Wagga Wagga press: one offering a reward for Orton's present address, the other calling on Orton himself to come to the aid of 'his old friend Tom Castro.' William Callaghan, landlord of the Pastoral Hotel in Fitzmaurice Street, came forward with two unclaimed letters addressed to Orton. Both were in the same hand and postmarked London.

When he opened them, Holmes found they were from Mrs Jury, who wrote to inform her brother that she had heard from his friend, Sir Roger (she had not yet met the Claimant), and had received photographs from him of Arthur and his family. Holmes thundered down to Wapping where, 'after very much discussion', Mrs Jury tremulously produced a slim bundle of letters. Even then, she was reluctant to hand them over to Holmes. She had promised to destroy them, she said.

EIGHTEEN

THERE IS SOMETHING WE DO NOT KNOW

THE six letters were written in a feigned hand—or rather, two feigned hands, both unmistakably the Claimant's. In the first letter, dated Gravesend, January 1867, he had stated that he was in communication with Arthur Orton and promised to send Mrs Jury a likeness of her brother and his wife and child. The signature on that letter was 'W. H. Stephens'; the rest were signed 'R. C. D. Tichborne'. Towards the end of 1867, he had confided to Mrs Jury that he was paying Charley Orton and Mrs Tredgett £5 per month for their secrecy and offered to include her in the arrangement. The letters mentioned photographs. Where were they? asked Holmes. From a drawer in the sideboard Mrs Jury produced a carte-de-visite. Holmes recognised it immediately. It was the Claimant in Edward Rous' garden at Alresford, taken in September 1867. There had been two photographs, said Mrs Jury. The other one, showing his wife and child, she had sent to George in Singapore.

'But this is Sir Roger,' said Holmes, flapping the pocket-sized portrait.

'Yes, well,' said Mrs Jury sheepishly, 'I was confused, like. I took it for a likeness of Arthur.'

'And is it like him?' Holmes asked.

'Well, it's like,' she conceded, 'but not so like as what I first thought.'

Holmes asked about the £5 per month.

'I don't know nothing about that. I never saw no five pound—only

Mrs Tredgett   *Mrs Jury*

them few shillings you give me, Mr Holmes.' And the secrecy? 'So far as I can tell, it was something to do with Arthur—something he'd done, like. Nothing to do with Sir Roger. It's just that him and Arthur was friends, he said, and he'd promised to look out for us.'

Holmes called next on Mrs Tredgett. She was alarmed at what her sister had told him, and still more alarmed to see the letters that Holmes now brandished. Mrs Tredgett had done as the Claimant had bid, and burnt hers (most of them) before he left for South America. Like her sister, she denied having been paid by the Claimant— except for the odd shilling or two—and stood by her statement that he was not her brother. Rather, she said, he had been sent by Arthur as 'a sort of benefactor to the Orton family.' She then recounted her acquaintance with the Claimant, from the beginning.

On Boxing Day 1866—the day after the Claimant arrived in London—Mrs Tredgett heard that a cigar-smoking stranger had been asking after her the previous evening at the Globe public house. According to the Globe's landlady, Cecilia Fairhead, he had first tried the Ortons' old house, 69 Wapping High Street, which he'd found closed up and billed 'To Let'. Drawn by the beckoning gleam of the

Globe, the well-muffled stranger had called for a sherry and, being Mrs Fairhead's only customer on Christmas night, had invited her to join him by the fire. He had shown great interest in the past and present inhabitants of the High Street, asking after a good many by name. In fact, said Mrs Fairhead, he had seemed to know more about them than she did. Among others, he had asked about the Orton family, expressing polite regret upon hearing that old George and Mary both were dead. Would Mrs Fairhead know where he might find their daughter, Mary Ann? he'd asked. That'd be Mary Ann Tredgett, the landlady had told him; Charley Orton would know—he lived not far up Hermitage Street. The stranger had replied sharply that he did not want *him*, just Mary Ann's address. Something in his collar-muffled mien had prompted Mrs Fairhead to ask if he were an Orton himself, at which he'd smiled and said no, just a friend of the family. At Mrs Fairhead's insistence that he was very like the Ortons, he'd said, 'Do you think so?' and called for another sherry. The landlady had fetched her married daughter in from next door then, and sent her around the neighbours to find out where Mary Ann Tredgett lived.

On Boxing Day morning, Mrs Tredgett heard all this, second-hand, from the neighbour who had supplied her address. No stranger having appeared in the course of the morning, she headed down to the Globe after dinner. While she was gone, the same bulky, muffle-headed stranger whom Mrs Fairhead had described called at Mrs Tredgett's house in East India Road. His insistent knocking caught the attention of a neighbour, to whom he presented a visiting card which read *William H. Stephens, Australia*—the *Australia* added by hand—and a letter addressed to 'Miss Mary Ann Orton, 69 High Street, Wapping'. Like the landlady of the Globe, Mrs Tredgett's neighbour inquired whether he was a relation of the Ortons, to which 'Stephens' replied, 'No, but I'm a great friend of Arthur Orton's.' Moreover, he said, he was the editor of an Australian newspaper and one of the wealthiest men in the colonies. He was on his way to Ireland to report on the Fenians, and had promised his friend Orton to deliver a letter to his sister.

When Mrs Tredgett returned he was gone; but this letter awaited her:

> Wagga Wagga
> Nw SW
> June 3rd/66
>
> My Dear and beloved sister. it is many years now since I heard from any of you. I have never heard a word from anyone I knew since 1854. But my friend Mr Stephens is about starting for England. And he has promised to find you all out, and write and let me know all about you. I do not intend to say much because he can tell you all about me. Hoping my dear sister you will make him welcome has he is a dear friend of mine so good by Arthur Orton.

Beneath his name, he'd fashioned a peculiar symbol:

·◯:C·

M

which experts would later identify as a *rubrica*, or signature mark, the use of which was commonplace in the Spanish-speaking world. The letter, dated the day after Tom Castro's departure from Wagga, had in all probability been written by the Claimant on the voyage from New York—after he'd made the acquaintance of the real W. H. Stephens, an American newspaperman bound for Ireland to report on the Fenian uprising. Certainly, that would explain a curious letter the Claimant received from Stephens early in 1867: 'I am so sanguine of your success and of course my part in it which we arranged on board the *Cella*, that I shall quietly await events.'

At any rate, Mrs Tredgett was convinced not just that the letter was bona fide, but that the mysterious caller really was her brother, Arthur. She told all her neighbours as much—and her sister, and their brother Charley—and immediately wrote to 'My dear brother', enjoining him to come back to Wapping and show himself. She addressed her letter, as per instructions on the reverse of his card, to 'R.C.T., Post Office, Gravesend'. In reply, he assured her she was mistaken to think him her brother, explaining that his friend Arthur was still living in Wagga, under an assumed name. However, if Mrs Tredgett wished to write to her brother, 'Stephens' would be happy to forward the letter. Exactly how he characterised the bond between himself and Arthur Orton, or what explanation he gave for Orton's incognito is not clear, since Mrs Tredgett burnt the letter. He had, however, enclosed 'a likeness of your brother's wife and child'— actually the Claimant's own wife and baby daughter—and the other Orton sister, Mrs Jury, immediately wrote asking 'Stephens' if she could have one too. Alas, he hadn't another to spare, but he assured her that:

> your brother is a very great friend of mine, and one who is regard as a brother, and have likewise promised to send him all the information I can about his family. I cannot call on you at present, but will do so before long…My future address will be R.C.T., Post Office, Liverpool. Hoping to have the pleasure of making your, the acquaintance of my friend's sister before long…

The Claimant would later deny that he had ever intended to 'make the acquaintance' of members of the Orton family: 'I merely wished to find out what I wanted to know, and have nothing more to do with them.' That was why he directed future correspondence to Liverpool— a place to which he had no intention of going. That put an end to his communication with the Orton sisters until the middle of 1867, by which time half the population of Wapping had figured out that the enigmatic W. H. Stephens was identical with the Tichborne Claimant of newspaper notoriety. He was still living at Gravesend, so that it was a simple matter for Charley Orton to track down his brother's 'great friend' and put the bite on him. Thereafter, the Claimant—as R. C. D. Tichborne—resumed his correspondence with the Orton sisters.

Most of this Holmes pieced together in the course of one interminable morning at Wapping. Now, at last, he understood the substance of a long-standing rumour, to the effect (as he had reported it to his client) that 'you went upon your arrival in England somewhere and were immediately recognised as the son of a person not Sir James Tichborne.' What Holmes couldn't understand was what the Claimant had thought he was about.

'There is something in this Orton business I cannot unravel,' wrote Francis Baigent on being apprised of the latest twist in the Claimant's story, 'there is something we do not know.' He and others at a meeting in Alresford 'unanimously felt that Sir Roger could not succeed against the strong points of resemblance between himself and Orton.' But the reluctance of the Claimant's supporters to relinquish their conviction (or, in the case of most, their investment) proved stronger still. For the time being, they contented themselves with writing to the Claimant in Chile, impressing upon him sternly 'the important necessity of your disclosing every circumstance of your life, so that your whole history might be proved beyond a doubt.'

November's post from Melbourne brought a large envelope from William Gibbes containing a copy of Tom Castro's Wagga will. This was tardy, to say the least. The Claimant's opponents had been familiar with the will's contents for more than a year, ever since their man Mackenzie had momentarily turned Gibbes' head. Word had reached Holmes, early in 1868, that Castro had named a Captain Henry Angell, from Bridport in Dorsetshire, as his executor, and that the Captain, sought out by Detective Whicher, had recognised in a likeness of the Claimant's photograph the same Arthur Orton he'd known as a boy. The Claimant swore that he'd never heard of Angell and had certainly not named him in his will. But now Gibbes' copy of the will revealed that Mackenzie had told the truth: Angell was named as co-executor with another Bridport man, John Jarvis.

Next to emerge from the packet was a stiff wedge of paper: photographic copies of a rough assortment of handwritten pages. According to the covering letter, they were samples of Arthur Orton's handwriting, gleaned from sources in Hobart and Gippsland. Holmes cast an eye over the one on top. 'At first sight,' he remarked, with unconvincing equanimity, on the Claimant's file, 'the handwriting of Arthur Orton was much like yours.' His head hurt as shook the tar-paper packet empty.

Out plopped an envelope addressed, in the Claimant's hand, to 'Alfred Smith, Pastoral Hotel, Wagga Wagga, Nw SW'. It had occurred to Callaghan, the landlord, that this, the third unclaimed letter yellowing on the shelf above his bar, might also be connected with the Tichborne case. And so it proved to be. It was from Mary Ann Tredgett, acquainting her brother with twelve years of family news and the advent of 'Mr Stephens'. This was the letter which the Claimant had offered to pass on to his pseudonymous friend Arthur Orton.

Jack Cater, the quondam Wagga baker, had now opened a shop at Cranford, west of London, a 'diabolical place' to which he wished he'd never come. Cater alone had been able to confirm the Claimant's story that there had existed at Wagga a distinct, albeit incognito, individual named Arthur Orton. He had sworn that Orton was a stooped, pock-marked man who'd sometimes kept company with Tom Castro. Detectives, newspaper notices, offers of a reward—all had failed to attract a skerrick of further corroboration, let alone proof, of Orton's presence at Wagga. Now the envelope addressed to 'Alfred Smith' seemed as if it might offer a clue. Had he known Orton by that name? Holmes asked Cater. Cater's reply was a stunner. No, he'd never heard of Alfred Smith; but then he'd never heard Arthur Orton's name at Wagga either—hadn't heard it at all until he was staying with the Claimant at Croydon.

'You remember him,' the Claimant had told him. 'Used to off-side for me at Higgins', then went as groom to Charley Cox at the Squatters'.'

Cater had dimly recalled the man he meant. 'Big fellow, keen on horses, terrible bad skin?'

'That's him.'

'But wasn't that Harry Osborne?'

'Might've called himself that. Went by different names, you know.' The Claimant tapped his nose with a forefinger. 'But he was Orton, all right.'

And Cater had bought it. It was solely on the strength of that conversation, he now admitted, that he had sworn to having known Arthur Orton. 'Cater's letter carries out our suspicions,' noted Holmes. 'This makes his Affidavit useless.'

It was nine weeks now since the Claimant had sailed east. Nine eventful, dispiriting weeks for Holmes. 'Depend upon it,' he wrote to Curzon Allport, his Melbourne counterpart, 'neither you nor I have got the *whole truth* about Tichborne yet—he is full of cunning and deceit…[and] he is not so simple-minded as he is thought to be.'

But Holmes still called the Claimant 'Tichborne' because, strange to relate, he still believed in him. He had to.

NINETEEN

THE MISSING EXHIBIT

Home sweet Home, there's no place like Home—
Good-bye, and be damned to you.

So began the Claimant's journal of his voyage to South America in
the autumn of 1868. On board the *Oneida*, he amused himself by day
with shooting and fishing; after dark, he played cards. He drank and
smoked cigars at all hours, and grumbled about his throat or the state
of his giblets.

Holmes' chief clerk reported from the island of St Vincent, in the
Caribbean, that his client was 'quite well and full of spirits.' 'The only
thing he complains of,' John Stevens went on, 'is the extreme heat—
this may perhaps tend to reduce him in size. I hope it will.' The
Claimant himself, however, wrote telling Francis Baigent that he was
'desperately unwell.' These contradictory accounts made Baigent
apprehensive. 'I should like to know the rights of such statements,'
he told Edward Rous. 'I think it may be because he is resolved not
to go on to Australia.'

The Claimant had made a solemn undertaking—an affidavit, for
what it was worth—that 'it is my positive intention…after the execu-
tion of the Commission in Chili to proceed direct from thence to
Australia for the like purpose.' By the time the *Oneida* reached
St Vincent, he had modified his travel plans. For the foreseeable future,
he informed his wife, letters might reach him at the Hotel de la Paix

in Buenos Aires. He had decided he needed a holiday: 'the truble and anxiety I have had to go through in getting up my Case its been enough to kill anyone and would have done me I expect had I not been smoke-dried and preserve with Whisky.'

He told nobody else of his intentions—not even his journal, which trundled on with little pause for reflection and not the least sign of scruple. Nor would his supporters learn of the Claimant's plans from his wife. They never saw her letter from St Vincent, and subsequent letters, when she would show them, had passages scored out and entire pages missing. 'She is so charry about it,' said Baigent, 'that she will scarcely turn away her eyes from the letters when she shews them.' Mary's ill-will towards her husband's supporters so irked Baigent that he urged that she be given 'no more tin—no, not a shilling.'

From St Vincent, the *Oneida* made for Rio. If he felt some unease at revisiting the scene of his shipwreck, the Claimant's journal gave no sign of it. But then he was rather distracted, at that time, by the dark-eyed daughter of a plantation owner who had just joined the ship. After Rio the ship called briefly at Montevideo, and when it berthed at Buenos Aires two days later, the Claimant announced that he was leaving the *Oneida*. He had resolved to retrace his old journey across the Pampas and the Cordilleras, and would, he said, meet up with his legal men in Chile in good time for the start of the commission. Stevens and Hall, the barrister, were not at all happy with this arrangement; but what could they do? The Claimant would not be dissuaded, and they had no intention of joining him. Tales abounded of travellers murdered by the natives of the Pampas plains, who were at that time aggressively resisting dispossession. Stevens and Hall couldn't afford to hang about arguing the point. So they went on by steamer, agreeing to meet the Claimant at Santiago in a month's time.

According to a contemporary guidebook, 'Buenos Ayres is essentially a pleasure-seeking place.' The Claimant twice visited the racecourse in the ten days he was there. He attended performances at six of the city's two dozen theatres, and became a fixture in the clubs favoured by British expatriates. He was favourably received by, among others, the editor of the *Standard and River Plata News* and by consular officials, including Wilfred Blunt, who had been at school with Alfred Tichborne and discerned a point of resemblance in the Claimant's thick eyebrows. 'His huge frame and coarse manner seemed to conceal reminiscences of aristocratic breeding as authentic perhaps, it was not saying much, as Alfred's,' wrote Blunt. 'I treated him, there-fore…in the light of a young man of decent birth gone woefully to seed.'

The Claimant left Buenos Aires at the beginning of November, taking a steamer up-river to the inland port of Rosario. Of the over-night voyage, he noted, 'Sleeped in company of about five thousand cockroaches, smoked three cigars, which drove them all away, and very near suffocated three young ladies in the next cabin.' It is clear from his journal that the Claimant regarded this as the start of his real journey. For all that he liked his fat cigars and silk handkerchiefs, he missed the rough-and-ready outdoorsiness of the life he'd lived in the colonies.

Awaiting him at Rosario was a letter from Captain Richard Burton, the famous hunter of the Nile's source, agreeing to the Claimant's proposal that they might, for safety, travel together across the most hazardous stretch of the plains. Having completed a dull consular posting in Brazil, Burton was about to mount an attempt on the unconquered Mount Aconcagua, the highest peak in the Cordilleras. Burton agreed that they should rendezvous at Córdoba, roughly halfway between Buenos Aires and Santiago, on the edge of the frontier. The group would be five strong, 'so altogether we shall make up a strongish party, equal to most mountaineers.' Thanks to a sequence of Chinese whispers that likely originated with the Claimant himself, his arrangement with Burton had taken on a glamorous aspect by the time it surfaced in the British press: 'Sir Roger, it seems, left Rosario in company with Major Rickards, the Hon. Constable Maxwell, and Captain Burton, in quest of "a mine of fabulous wealth" in the Indian territory. It is supposed that Sir Roger has either been sacrificed by the Indians, or that he has succeeded in establishing his right to the mine.'

An uneventful journey by train and coach brought him to Córdoba, on Friday, 13 November 1868. Burton was not expected for at least a week. The Claimant took a room at the Hotel de Paris, overlooking the Plaza San Martin, and amused himself with the proprietor's two daughters ('very nice girls'), on the pretext of brushing up his Spanish. On 23 November, by which time Burton ought to have arrived, the Claimant was gripped by spasms while promenading in the Plaza— it was the tapeworm turning. Staggering into the nearest shop, a French hatter's, he was revived by a swig of Dalby's Carminitive and a new starched corduroy sunhat. But when there was still no sign of Burton at the end of the month, the Claimant sold all eight of his horses, donned his new hat, and set off back to Buenos Aires. He was already two weeks overdue for the hearing in Chile, but his journal reads like an account of a holiday cut short.

The hundred-mile journey by stagecoach from Córdoba to Villa Nueva turned out to be more eventful than his entire trip so far. The coach tipped over a bank just two miles out of Córdoba, and was no sooner upright again than the leading horses stumbled, breaking their harness. The Claimant, fortunately, carried a spool of fishing line in his trunk, and the cobbled harness saw them safe to the next *posta*. But, as they made ready to depart, their seven fresh horses bolted: 'In less than two minutes all the horses, coach, and passengers laid on the Pampas in a heap.' The Claimant helped lasso more horses and the coach set off once again, but after just a short distance the fresh horses 'nocked up', and the passengers were stranded all night on the Pampas. The Claimant insisted that the ladies sleep in the coach while he and the other men made do with the roadside. The journey continued in an episodic fashion until, just a few miles short of their destination, a fist fight broke out on the driver's box. The horses bolted, the coach ended up in a hole, and the driver and his assailant continued their brawl on terra firma. Drawing his revolver, the Claimant threatened the coachman with its contents if he did not mount his box and proceed. Three days into its two-day journey, the coach limped into Villa Nueva.

Burton and his expeditioners were already installed in the town's Hotel Orientale when the Claimant arrived in a state of excited dishevelment at breakfast time on 2 December. Popular legend had the pair carousing together on a month-long binge ('They were a strange and disreputable couple') when they actually spent a mere day and a night in one another's company at Villa Nueva. Burton would later recall that the Claimant seemed 'very gentlemanly', inasmuch as he showed no emotion regardless of whether he won or lost at cards. It was a compliment of dubious value—the more so since Burton himself, addled by alcohol and low living, was likened at that period to a wild beast.

Arriving back in Buenos Aires the Claimant was grieved to find not a single letter waiting for him.

> Just been damning one of the waiters up hill and down dale to ease my mind a little…I suppose Mr Holmes stoped my wife from writing to me. Just broke my gold pen against the edge of the table. I have another, so no matter.

He was nearly a fortnight at the Hotel de la Paix, chivvying the waiters and still toying with the idea of proceeding to Chile by ship. But after he was floored by abdominal spasms one day at the racecourse, his doctor advised an immediate return to England and he was free to take up the offer of his new-found friend, the captain of a London-bound steamer, of a private cabin, and visiting privileges with a tiger on its way to the London Zoo. Even so, he was sorry to leave Buenos Aires, not least because he was believed there. At a farewell dinner, the editor of the *Standard* presented him with a paddle from a native canoe.

The Claimant paid ten sovereigns at Montevideo for a ton of ice to suck during the voyage home. His throat had given him trouble the whole time he'd been away and no amount of whiskey and cigar smoke seemed to take the edge off it. Clear of Rio and skirting the Bermuda Triangle, he celebrated the new year—1869—by cracking a bottle of champagne, and his birthday (that is, Roger Tichborne's, 5 January) by cracking two. He dosed himself between bottles with Kitchener's Peristaltic Persuaders, and when they called at the Caribbean island of St Jago he was well enough to go shooting. After that, though, his spasms grew daily worse until the Persuaders took effect, mid-Atlantic, and he passed a tapeworm an inch thick and sixteen yards long! We know the parasite's exact dimensions because its host not only recorded it in his journal, but wrote heartily of it to several friends. He even preserved a portion in a bottle of gin as something to show the children, along with the paddle and a tiny St Jago parrot.

It was the beginning of December when word first reached John Holmes of his client's divergence from the agreed plan. This notification was followed by fortnightly reports of his non-arrival in Chile, of the commission's starting without him, and of the troubling evidence that emerged there.

From Melipilla, John Stevens wrote that while none of the villagers had known Roger Tichborne, they well remembered Arthur Orton. 'It is a mystery,' wrote Stevens, 'which cannot be explained without Sir Roger's personal appearance.' The Melipilla witnesses all recalled 'Arturo' as a plump youth of sixteen or seventeen, with a 'moist and pouting mouth,' curly hair, light brown inclining to red, and bad teeth. Tomas Castro, released from the madhouse, gave evidence that Arturo was 'never a good horseman'—a judgment that would have crushed the Claimant, had he been there to hear it. The commissioners heard that the young Arturo *had* spoken of belonging to a noble English family; however, under questioning, Mercedes Azocar conceded that the boy's poor command of Spanish might have misled his listeners:

> He used to say his father was a butcher (*'carnicero'*), and, as he spoke such bad Spanish, we imagined him to mean (*'cancillero'*) Chancellor, but he would answer, 'You don't understand; my father gives this to the Queen'—taking up a piece of meat…He used to say that he was what we thought meant trumpeter, but afterwards discovered to be the last grade on board a ship.

According to another witness, José Guzman, Arturo had claimed to have been at school with the Queen's children.

'He was given to boasting then?' surmised the defence counsel.

'No,' Guzman insisted, 'on the contrary; he spoke with such simplicity that we often could not help believing it.'

The Claimant and his supporters were later critical of the way witnesses at the Chilean commission were led by the defence, particularly by the detective, Severo Barra. According to a friend in Santiago, Barra 'has the reputation of being a scoundrel; he will take up any dirty case, will do any mortal thing for money.' As for the witnesses themselves: 'This kind of native can be bought for a trifle and can lie to perfection.' A former British government agent in Chile was dubious of statements by Melipilla witnesses that they had sheltered Arturo for almost a year. They were a snobbish people, he said, who might extend a few days' grudging hospitality—but no more—to a runaway sailor boy.

John Stevens and William Hall, the Claimant's counsel in Chile, found the locals hospitable enough. 'Life is very easy here,' wrote

Stevens; 'the people seem to dream away their time.' Melipilla had but one inn, with just a single tiny bedroom for guests. Stevens and Hall were obliged to share the room with the legal team for the defence, an arrangement made only slightly more seemly by a canvas screen dividing them. So cramped was it, in fact, that all five men had to step into the garden each morning to dress.

The evidence of witnesses who'd met Roger Tichborne during his short time in Chile in 1853 seemed to concur that he had never been to Melipilla. From what was known of his travelling routes and schedule, it was impossible that he could have reached the village except by a protracted detour, or stayed there for longer than three days. It seems curious that both sides at the Chilean commission should have persisted in asking witnesses about a young *Englishman* in Chile, since Roger Tichborne had been a Frenchman in all but name. Both sides produced photographs, however, to assist their cause. The missing exhibit was the Claimant himself.

'All is lost,' Francis Baigent wrote to Holmes on 25 January 1860. He'd had a letter from the Claimant, dated 23 November—the day of his spasm attack in the Plaza at Córdoba—confiding his intention to return to England 'secretly'. This time it was Holmes who felt the worm turn. 'To my mind,' he told Edward Rous, 'it shews that the writer is possessed of the deepest cunning and subtlety.' He called a meeting at Alresford, three days hence. Arriving at Alresford station on 28 January, he was met by Baigent bearing a telegram and a kit-bag. The telegram was from the Claimant, who'd just landed at Falmouth, and Baigent was on his way to Basingstoke to meet him. Would Holmes join him? Holmes would not.

Instead, he sat up late in his room at the Swan Inn, writing his client 'a long and special letter…requiring your full explanations and giving you notice that unless they are satisfactory I shall at once decline to act as your Solicitor.' But when, next morning, he met the Claimant off the train and presented him with the letter, no explanations were forthcoming. The Claimant brushed him aside—*'Just leave me, can't you?'*—and took Rous' fly to the Old Post House, with its roomy doorways and his family waiting.

Holmes stayed at Alresford just four hours more. Baigent told him what he'd learnt: about the Claimant's ill-health, about natives and bolting horses, about the thing in the gin bottle. He was flushed as he told it all and wore a half-fearful look of appeal, as if willing Holmes to believe it; because if Holmes believed, then he could too. But this time Holmes did not believe and the Claimant refused to see him, so he took the two o'clock train back to London. Late in the evening of that long, long day, he wrote to his colleague, Curzon Allport, 'Under the advice of Counsel I have withdrawn from the Tichborne Case.'

PART TWO

TWENTY

LONG ARTHUR

HAVING dishonoured his pledge to accompany the Australian commission, the Claimant was not woken by the bells of St David's Church, Hobart Town, on the Sunday before proceedings began. Alfred Wyatt was. His room on the second floor of Webb's Hotel in Murray Street was almost on a level with the belfry across the street, and the first peal went through him like a lightning bolt.

Wyatt was the Claimant's counsel in Australia and he was struggling with his brief. Curzon Allport, his briefing solicitor, was all but scuppered by the news that Holmes had resigned and his client would not, after all, be joining them. Just this last week, Wyatt had seen Allport lose a whole armful of quires—copies of exhibits for the commission—crossing Davey Street on his way from the printers. Caught by the wind tearing up from the docks, the folded sheets had flapped and skirled around the solicitor, and he hadn't even tried to gather them up. That was left to Wyatt and William Chrisfield, the clerk.

Wyatt, who'd taken on the high-profile case as a challenge, was inclined to think it hopeless now. But the impulse that kept him and Allport going was a snaking fascination with what turn it would take next. Wyatt had an inkling that his part in this case, whatever its outcome, would give him tap-room kudos with his wig-wearing colleagues at the Mitre Tavern in Melbourne.

On Friday, 30 April 1869, the Hobart Town *Mercury* had made a last call for 'Any person acquainted with Arthur Orton, who followed the occupation of a Butcher, in Hobart Town and elsewhere in Tasmania, between the years 1853 and 1855.' The Australian commission began its sitting three days later, in the side parlour of Webb's Hotel, directly beneath the room with the belfry view. Wyatt's role in Hobart was primarily as a cross-examiner, since the plaintiff's (that is, the Claimant's) side would call only one witness here to the defendants' fifteen. Hobart, of course, had not featured in the erstwhile Tom Castro's account of his Australian career—and on this point the Claimant remained unequivocal—so the focus here was necessarily on Arthur Orton.

The commission had to rely, in the absence of the Claimant himself, on photographs and other exhibits, and on the strength of these the defence witnesses all expressed themselves pretty well satisfied that Orton and the Claimant were the same man. Wyatt, cross-examining, did his best to throw doubt on the accuracy and independence of that identification. In particular, he questioned John Mackenzie's role in it. Wyatt called as the plaintiff's sole witness Charles Just, chief reporter for the *Mercury*, who grudgingly admitted that he had been misled as to Mackenzie's authority and that his piece of February 1868 equating Orton with the Claimant was not a 'fair journalistic paragraph.'

Even before the commission began, both sides were agreed as to the bookends of Arthur Orton's Vandemonian sojourn: his arrival on the *Middleton* on 26 April 1853 and his departure aboard the *Eclipse* in November 1855. The commission's business was to flesh out the intervening thirty months.

When last we saw Arthur Orton, he was on the Thames headed seaward in company with two ponies and a business of ferrets. He was eighteen years old, a free man bound for a convict colony. The place for free men was Victoria, the colony upstairs, which was just then in the throes of a gold rush. But Arthur thought he'd give Hobart a go first.

He had a bunk aboard the *Middleton*, but slept instead with the Shetland ponies. He shared his provisions with them, too, and carved their names—Tommy and Polly (only he spelt it Poly)—over their stalls. When the weather was fine and the sea smooth, he exercised them on deck and offered pony rides and lasso tuition to the children of the cabin passengers. He even contrived to exercise the other livestock in his care by staging ferret races in a barricaded section of the hold. Most of them got away, two never to be found. One of the fugitives, when Arthur reached in to retrieve it from a dark corner of the provisions store, sank its teeth deep into his forefinger.

That incident was related at the Hobart sitting of the Australian commission by the man who prised the ferret loose, the *Middleton*'s former bosun, James Peebles. Here was a looked-for point of coincidence, for the Claimant, in his original affidavit, had recollected a Peebles as one of the sailors who'd survived the wreck of the *Bella*. As for the vessel that had plucked them from the Atlantic, he'd been able to name only its captain: an Owen Lewis or Lewis Owens, he couldn't say which. It so happened that Owen Lewis, now resident in Hobart, had been a seaman aboard the *Middleton*. In his evidence to the commission, Lewis remembered Arthur Orton as 'a rather large made young man' with no whiskers or beard, just 'a little down like.'

A soldier of the 99th Regiment saw Orton disembark at Hobart Town. He noticed the lumpen youth's 'light scarlet' hair and the way he frolicked with the ponies as he drove them along. He was headed for T. D. Chapman's house at Newtown, a couple of miles north of the docks. There, despite the missing ferrets, he was offered a job as groom in Chapman's stables, starting the following week. But by the time Sunday came, Arthur had heard such bad reports of Chapman as a master that he declined to join his service after all. Returning to town in the interim, he hung around the stockyards by the docks and soon found himself drinking in familiar company, with butchers and others in the noisome, lively trades.

Arthur wasn't without work for long. Joe Knight, butcher, of Murray Street took him on and trained him up. He might have been raised above a butcher's shop, but Arthur knew next to nothing about slaughtering and dressing meat. Knight showed him the basics and kept him busy carting offal, stripping out fat, poking the pickling tub, running deliveries, and keeping the shop books. Arthur's employer had been something of an athlete in his youth and was still considered 'a very fair specimen of what is known as a "sporting butcher".' He liked the shape of his burly apprentice and introduced him to the use of dumb-bells and boxing gloves. With Joe Knight's coaching, Arthur became quite a promising pugilist—'more reliable as a bruiser than a butcher.' At last he had found a use for his bulk. Even his twitch, in the ring, could pass for a feint.

When he'd been at it six months, Knight lined him up for a prize fight against Brawling Bob Bell, a North Hobart cabman. Perhaps it was in preparation for this fight that Arthur's nickname, Long Arthur, was coined. It was to be a £10-a-side match, with Knight putting up Arthur's stake and Bell backed by the roguish Matt Wilkes, publican of the White Conduit tavern across the street. The engagement never came off: whether because Long Arthur had exceeded the twelve-stone weight limit or from some other cause, Joe Knight couldn't recall sixteen years later. But he was certain that, from his 'many opportunities of observing closely the person of Orton,' he would recognise his former protegé's physique and piano-key teeth anywhere. The Claimant's photographs, showing him fleshed-out, tight-lipped and fully clothed, were not much use to Knight.

About the end of October 1853, Arthur left Knight's employ and found work with another butcher, Sammy Loring, down by the Theatre Royal in Campbell Street. He found this end of town more to his liking. There was the familiarity of the docks for a start, as well as the seedy glamour cast by the theatre. Jammed between the theatre and Loring's right-of-way was Gipsy Poll's concert room, and legend

had it that Long Arthur was there the night of the all-in between a
sailor named Brickey Taylor and Brummy Lockley, 'the Boxiana
Huoner'. Jack Higgins, who worked alongside Arthur at Loring's,
remembered him as tall and rather muscular, with a funny jaw and a
string of yarns about lassoing cattle in South America. He asserted,
though, that Long Arthur's real name was Fred.

Arthur didn't stay with Sammy Loring for long—probably not
much beyond a fortnight. 'He was not as sufficient as he represented
himself,' is how John Delve, yet another Hobart butcher, described
Long Arthur. Delve had been no particular friend of Arthur's but
recollected his appearance and mannerisms in vivid detail:

> His hair was very light, he used to brush it back off his forehead
> and behind his ears; it was very thin and long, and when it
> dropped before his eyes he used to brush it back with his hands.
> He had large thin ears; and another thing, Sir, the top of his
> ears used to droop as if pressed down by a cap. There was
> something peculiar in his speech; he would speak as if he had
> some 'baca or a plum like in his mouth; he spoke thick.

The likeness that best agreed with Delve's memory of Long Arthur
was a recent portrait showing the Claimant heavy-lidded and girthful.
'Looks like a man asleep or half drunk,' Delve remarked. 'That is just
the way he would be.' The same portrait was flatly rejected by others
of the Hobart witnesses. 'That was never Arthur Orton in the world!'
declared one. 'No Sir,' said another, 'I never saw Arthur Orton in
such a gorgeous costume as that.'

Long Arthur went from Loring's to the less exacting employ of
William Wilson, whose butchery and abattoirs were at the foot of
Macquarie Street, hard by the domain where the ships landed livestock.
Wilson had the government contract for supplying beasts to the town's
slaughteryards, and it was one of Arthur's jobs—his favourite—to
ride in the stock from the wharves. If it reminded him of home, he

wasn't the only one: that corner of Hobart Town was called Wapping.

It was the Long Arthur of this period that most Hobart witnesses remembered best. Many recalled his riding and roping skills and that he was a handy fellow when it came to 'pulling about bullocks'. Tom Ham and Tom Hales had been workmates of his at Wilson's. Ham, a ticket-of-leave man, recollected Long Arthur only dimly ('it is a long time to think of a man'). Hales could still picture him, though: 'he was a harum-scarum sort of young chap, and did not care which way his hair went; he had a large nose; rather a broadish face; his face was as smooth as a young woman's.' Hales could trace no resemblance to Orton in the Claimant's portraits, though he conceded: 'if he did fill out he would be a big sized man by this time; his skin was big enough on him.' Under Wyatt's cross-examination, both men stated that Long Arthur's arms were tattooed (Ham said 'tabbooed'), which the Claimant's certainly were not.

Pregnell's Shipping Butchers, Hobart. Formerly a government slaughterman, Pregnell had a poor opinion of Long Arthur's butchering prowess

During his time with Wilson, Arthur became, by his own estimation, 'a thorough good butcher.' Others begged to differ. 'At the end
of that time,' stated Tom Pregnell, a slaughterman at the government
yard, 'he was no better butcher than he was when I first knew him.'
Arthur left Wilson's at the beginning of 1855 to work as a stockrider
for Jemmy Ladds, who had the contract to supply meat to Port Arthur
and other convict establishments on the Tasman Peninsula. Arthur
lodged at Ladds' place in town, but in the course of every fortnight
he made a round trip between Hobart and the stock-run and killing-
yard at King George Sound, on the 'gulp' above Eaglehawk Neck,
the land-bridge to the prison peninsula.

Strange though it seems, this out-of-the-way job brought him into
regular contact with a distant relative of his. Frank Jury, brother-in-
law to Arthur's sister Lizzie, was a coxswain at Port Arthur. He and
Arthur had first met in Hobart; now they caught up once a month
when Frank came to the Sound for meat. It was from him that Arthur
learnt that his father's old friend, Captain Angell, was in Hobart:
'i came a bout 80 miles from the run to see him but i only see him
once after all, he was so busy with one and other that he had no time
to speak to me.'

Nor had Captain Angell any letters for him, which was the real reason Arthur had hurried back. He'd barely heard a word from home since
he left. A letter came from his sister Mary Ann in March 1855. Arthur
wrote back warmly, eager for more news ('Let me Know how my Dog
is getting on'), and sent an equally affectionate letter to his other sister,
Lizzie, by the same post. Having mentioned that he'd heard from Mary
Ann, he added a postscript: 'I dont mean Mary Ann Loader.'

He'd been as attentive a sweetheart to Mary Anne Loder as one
could be at such a distance and among such company as he'd been
keeping. By September he'd written to her six times and had not one
word in reply. Undeterred, her boxing beau wrote Mary Anne these
'fue' lines:

My Dear girl I hope you will be comforteble until i come home
that will be in about 15 months…I ham very Glad my Dear
you did not come out when i wanted you because this is a
dreadful place to live in. I should not have been able to have
made you comfitable, and i would sooner luse all i got than
make you un so. i suppose you have quite forgot me now but i
have not forgot you yet, nor wont until i get reasons for it

He signed himself 'your affectionate Lover' and urged her in a postscript to 'Write when you can Dear.'

When Detective Whicher tracked down Mary Anne Loder fifteen
years later, this was the only one she'd kept of Arthur Orton's Hobart
letters. Whether it was simply that Arthur never heard from Mary
Anne or whether word reached him that she was walking out with a
Thames lighterman, he wrote her no more letters after the end of
1855. As for his promised return, it was already three months overdue
when he told his sister in March that year, 'I shall never go to England
again Dear Lisy. I have made my mind to that.'

TWENTY-ONE

UNWHOLESOME MEAT FOR SALE

No local sweetheart surfaced in the evidence of Long Arthur's time in Hobart. In fact, women didn't rate much mention at all. We know he spent time at Gipsy Poll's, whose 'concert room' may well have been euphemistic. (A sailor, calling at Hobart in the early 1850s, mentioned Poll's in the same breath as the town's strumpetry, 'unrivalled' in his travels.)

He didn't get on with Mrs Wilson, the commission heard, and the wife of Ladds, his next employer, was referred to in passing as 'the notorious Tin-dish Bet.' The woman who featured largest in Hobart—at the commission, if not in Arthur's life there—was Frank Jury's Irish-born wife, Mina.

Mina Jury had come to Van Diemen's Land at Her Majesty's pleasure, but by the time Arthur met her she had a ticket-of-leave and four children. As a newly discharged convict, she would probably not have chosen to live at Port Arthur. Every couple of months, she would assert her freedom with a visit to Hobart, at which times she and Arthur met almost daily. When he knew he'd be seeing Frank at the Sound, he'd take down something special for Mina and the youngsters: a crate of new apples, a couple of fowl or a tin of wrapped sweets. Mina, in her turn, would send him any letters she'd had from home.

In May 1855, Arthur decided to set up a shop of his own in town, but he lacked the cash for stock and fixtures. Frank and Mina agreed to lend him £14 and, when Mina next came up to Hobart, she gave him the money in exchange for a three-month promissory note. It was raining hard when they met outside the savings bank and Mina, with her arms full of a squirming infant and a cauliflower, mistook a £5 note for a £1, so that Arthur ended up with £4 more than he signed for.

Mina spoke against the Claimant at the Australian commission. Now widowed and living in Melbourne, she had barrelled up to Sedgefield & Allport's offices in that city's Chancery Lane and demanded payment—with interest—of the money Arthur Orton owed her: 'he went away and cheated me and my orphans.' She was in no doubt, she said, that the Claimant was Orton, having seen his portrait in the *Illustrated Australian News*. Mina's part in the Tichborne case would eventually more than repay the £18 and her years of grudge-bearing.

With the borrowed money, Arthur had taken a stall at the New Market, under a casual sort of arrangement with the lessee, an old-lag butcher and poulterer named Jackie Dight. Two of the £18 went on painting a sign to hang above the stall. *A. Orton, Quality Butcher*, it read; but it lied. His offerings were palpably inferior to those of the other butchers in the New Market. His mutton was bruised and dead-smelling, with tufts of wool still attached. There was a surplus of butchers in Hobart at the time and those who could afford to were pushing up prices at the livestock sales. Arthur's solution was to buy or beg dead sheep off ships at the docks. The skins he sold on to a tanner and the carcasses, if at all presentable, he put out as 'aged mutton' on his stall at the market.

One Tuesday when Arthur was six weeks behind with the rent, Dight paid his stall a visit. Arthur had promised to have a week's rent for him, but he'd only sold a pair of kidneys and a few shanks all day, and had just threepence ha'penny in the tin. Dight agreed to take an iffy side of mutton as payment in kind of a week's rent—and bore it straight to the office of the City Surveyor. Two ribs and a shin of it (presenting a 'most disgusting' appearance) were produced in the

Mayor's Court a week later, when Arthur faced a charge of offering
unwholesome meat for sale. Dosseter, the government stock inspector,
deposed that he had examined Dight's half of the carcass and found
it to be black and sticky inside, indicating that the cause of death was
disease, not slaughtering—'and if it had been killed, it must have been
to save its life.' But Arthur eluded conviction on a technicality. Since
Dight was still the lessee of the stall, Arthur could not be held answer-
able for the condition of goods on sale. Dight had, in effect, informed
against himself. The case was dismissed and the remnants of the poor
wether finally laid to rest.

The informality of their sub-letting arrangement prevented Dight
from prosecuting a claim for the rent owed him. Instead, he swore
to 'lag Orton, right or wrong.' Twice more over the ensuing months
Dight laid information against Arthur—for allowing stock to roam
and selling sheepskins that were not his property—and twice more
the attempt backfired. Finally, when he was £40 out of pocket, Dight
resorted to direct action. Observing Arthur apparently buying a horse
(which Dight's appraising eye valued at £30), he contrived to 'borrow'
the animal, then withheld her, claiming her as part of his back-rent.
Alas, the mare wasn't Arthur's— the money that had changed hands
was a hire fee—and Dight was ordered to reinstate her.

Jackie Dight presented at the Australian commission as an altogether
mellower character than the firecracker he'd been in his Hobart years.
He'd shipped north to Gippsland in 1857 and had his own butchering
business at Tarraville, a short way inland from Port Albert. He and
Orton had met again there in 1858, he told the commission. Dight
studied all nine of the portraits shown to him, dismissing some as
nothing like, but singling out one as a striking ('though stout') likeness
to the 'raw-boned but roomy' Orton of his recollection. 'I could pick
him out of a thousand,' he declared. Unlike Mina Jury, though, Dight
made no mention of monies owed. Had a settling-up occurred
somewhere along the line? In Gippsland? Orton was driving cattle

when they met there and might perhaps have 'mislaid' a head or two, to Dight's advantage. The latter's circumspect performance at the commission suggests that there was something in the acquaintance that Dight himself wished to conceal.

After Dight seized his borrowed mare in September 1855, Arthur must have known the game was up. He unslung his sign and vamoosed to the 'low regions of middle Liverpool-street,' where George Paynter and Dick Lord took him in. Theirs was one of a straggle of butchers' shops up near Harrington Street, with Tommy Ware's Emu public house at the corner acting as a virtual guildhall. It was only four blocks to the west of the market, but it felt land-locked by comparison. Liverpool Street butted up to the Mount Wellington foothills and Sullivan's Cove, coppiced with ship's masts, was scarcely to be guessed at across the intervening town blocks of tight-set brick and stone.

Long Arthur was back in his lazy element, odd-jobbing and drawing a wage. But he was restless, and for a good while now had talked of leaving Hobart for Victoria. Not, as you might expect, for the goldfields but to join one of the regular drafts bound for Gippsland. Squatters like John Foster and John Johnson, having garnered as much land as they could in Van Diemen's Land, had, over the past fifteen years, extended their holdings into Gippsland, the isolated south-eastern portion of the Victorian colony. For their workforce, they relied on restless Vandemonians such as Arthur Orton had become. Many among his acquaintance had either left for Gippsland or been there, and he liked what he'd heard of the place: plenty of saddle-work, good money, a frontier camaraderie, and a hell of a lot of country between a stockman and his overseer. And moving on, as Arthur already knew—even if he didn't admit it—always held the possibility of re-invention.

He answered an advertisement, early in November 1855, calling for splitters, fence-riders and stockriders on John Johnson's Mewburn

Park station. After cursory inquiries around the Hobart meat trade, Johnson's agents signed Arthur up as a stockrider starting at the end of the month. He shipped out on Johnson's schooner *Eclipse* on 17 November.

The week before Christmas 1855, Van Diemen's Land was renamed Tasmania and a letter for Arthur Orton lay unclaimed at the Hobart Town post office.

The evidence presented at the Hobart sitting of the Australian commission wasn't the full story. Contradictory versions of Arthur Orton's Tasmanian sojourn would continue to emerge over long-subsequent years. Five years after the Australian commission, Henry Hollis swore that the Claimant was not Arthur Orton, whom he had known well in Hobart in the early 1850s, and remembered as 'one of Nature's nobility.'

'Orton, in youth, received a highly respectable education,' asserted Hollis. 'At one period of his life he held the post of editor to a highly influential religious journal in England. In Hobart Town I knew him as a gentleman. We were both engaged at the same office, wrote together, attended the law courts together.' Could anything sound more improbable? And yet, twenty years on, in 1895, an old Hobart identity writing as 'The Vet' remembered 'Arthur Orton frequenting the coffee rooms then known as "Money Morgan's", Murray-street, kept by Mr Henry Edward Rothwell Hollis.'

Cast in such a light, Hollis' homage to Orton takes on a cryptic aspect. The 'office' they were both engaged at—did he mean 'Money Morgan's'? Hollis said they'd attended the law courts together, making it sound as if they'd been barristers' clerks. But he might equally have kept the strife-lit Arthur company at his regular court appearances; and, for all we know, Arthur may have done the same for him. As for the rest of it—Arthur's 'highly respectable education' and his editorship of a religious journal—aren't they just the kind of stories he might have spun? Even so, it's hard to reconcile Hollis' assessment of him as 'one of Nature's nobility' with the Long Arthur of common recollection.

Mistaken identity was at the heart of 'The Vet's' lively rendering of events. In an attempt to explain why some Hobart witnesses recalled Arthur Orton as pock-marked and tattooed, with rings in his ears, while others swore otherwise, 'The Vet' contended that it wasn't Arthur who'd arrived in Hobart with the ponies in 1853, but his brother Thomas. It was Thomas, he said, who had worked for Wilson and Jemmy Ladds, had kept a stall in the market, 'and was well known to hundreds of people.' Arthur, meanwhile, had sailed from Wapping back to South America where he met Roger, heir to the Tichborne baronetcy. Arthur had joined the crew of the ill-fated *Bella* and, like Roger, had survived the wreck; but the two men were saved by different ships. Roger had been picked up by the *Osprey* and taken to Melbourne, while an American whaler had conveyed Arthur to Hobart. There he'd found his brother and worked for a short time with Joe Knight and Sammy Loring before shipping out for Melbourne aboard the schooner *Gold Seeker*, in company with Tom Ham.

Of all the Ortons, Thomas was said to be the one whom Arthur most resembled. But since Thomas was married and his father's partner in business, it seems unlikely that he'd have voyaged across the world to deliver a couple of ponies—and then stayed on in Hobart as a jobbing butcher. Thomas would have been almost thirty-five years old in 1853, and the man described by witnesses from the *Middleton* and Hobart was a good fifteen years younger: Arthur's age, in fact. Moreover, Long Arthur inquired after his eldest brother's health in one of his letters home, his sister having mentioned that Thomas was 'rather ill.' Thomas Orton died at Wapping, London, in about 1865.

As for Tom Ham and the *Gold Seeker*, they formed part of an elaborate tale spun by a Melbourne man, Walter Fossey, in about 1880. As Fossey told it, the *Gold Seeker* had cleared out for Melbourne 'on a dark night' in November 1853, with two in the steerage: Ham travelling under the name 'Henry Bailey' and Long Arthur disguised as a woman! Just two months earlier Arthur had written to Mary Anne Loder that 'the Gold diggers and solgers are fighting like Tagers in Melbourne as soon as they have done i shall go over and try my luck.'

Fossey's cross-dressing clue chimes with one particular of a story peddled, from the mid-1870s, by a queerish, vociferous chap named John Dettmer Dodds Jackson. Jackson's version of events placed both Orton *and* Tichborne in Tasmania: Arthur arriving with the ponies and Roger being landed at Hobart by his rescuers. Jackson asserted that he had known both men at Launceston in 1855, as lodgers at the Royal Oak public house. The Oak's landlady at the time, Jackson swore, had been Arthur Orton's sister, Mary Ann Tredgett. In vain was it pointed out to Jackson that the Royal Oak's licensee had been a Mary Ann *Hedger* and that Mrs Tredgett had never in her life set foot outside England. He merely modified his story: 'I remember her name being painted up over the entrance in place of the former licensee, Mrs Hedger.'

In their Launceston days Orton and Tichborne (calling himself Edward Souper) had been inseparable companions; in fact, said Jackson, 'we used to call them a pair of hermaphrodites.' It was commonly known, he said, that Orton had a 'peculiar formation', whereas Souper had kept his surtout coat buttoned, even in warm weather, to conceal, Jackson surmised, that 'the usual appendages of man were wanting.' That, he said, would account for 'the effeminate voice…and his excessive politeness.' Souper had been addicted to tobacco, brandy and piano-playing and, said Jackson, had made no secret of the fact that he was actually Roger Tichborne. Having returned to England, Souper was now private secretary to Lady Ogle of Withdeane Court, Brighton, at which genteel address Jackson plagued him over many years with accusations as to his 'true' identity.

Jackson had taken particular notice of Souper's skill on the piano, since he himself was a piano tuner. Edward Souper of Withdeane Court was indeed an accomplished pianist, while Roger Tichborne's only instrument when he left England had been the honky French horn. Had he mastered the piano in the course of his South American travels, or in a semi-coma aboard the *Osprey*? Nobody ever came forward in support of Jackson's story; nowhere else did there emerge even a suggestion that Arthur, let alone Roger, had ever been in Launceston.

Jackson would champion his delusion for more than twenty years, until his death. And its source? The *General Directory of Hobart Town* for 1854 lists among the occupants of Collins Street 'John Dettmer Dodds, pianoforte and musical instrument maker.' His shop lay close by the New Market and Arthur Orton's watering-hole, the Hope and Anchor tavern. The piano tuner took his business north to Launceston shortly afterwards.

One final Tasmanian link deserves notice. In the Claimant's sworn account of his arrival in Melbourne, he said he'd lodged in Elizabeth Street, at the Roxburgh Castle. In July 1854, Elizabeth Street, Melbourne had no such public house; but Elizabeth Street, Hobart did.

TWENTY-TWO

THE CHIMERICAL OSPREY

INSTEAD of following Arthur Orton's trail to Gippsland, the Australian commission made Melbourne its next stop. The venue was the chambers of Klingender, Charsley & Liddle, counsel representing the Tichborne estate, on the third floor of a grey-faced pile in Bank Place, the hub of the city's legal quarter.

The commission was in Melbourne to test the Claimant's assertion that his rescue vessel, the *Osprey*, had landed him there three months after the wreck of the *Bella*. Five witnesses were called—four for the defendants, one for the Claimant—all of whom, in July 1854, had been in the business of noticing shipping movements in the port of Melbourne. John Tyler, collector of customs, deposed that a schooner named the *Osprey* had arrived on 26 July 1854 (the Claimant had said the 24th). Her manifest listed a crew of just six, all discharged in Melbourne, and no passengers. By the Claimant's account, he'd been one of eight *Bella* survivors picked up by the *Osprey*. Moreover, at sixty-six tons burthen, the schooner *Osprey* was nothing like the three-masted vessel reckoned by the Claimant to have been six times that capacity.

Agents for the *Osprey* in Melbourne had been Wharton, Caird & Little, of whom only Dugald Little survived to give evidence. He recalled the vessel and knew for certain that her captain had made no report of shipwreck survivors, as he'd have been bound to do had he picked any up. In contradiction of the customs records, however, Little stated that there had been a passenger aboard the *Osprey*—a man named Baird, who'd boarded with cargo at the Cape. He and Little had lodged in the same house for a year or more afterwards, during which time Baird ('a very talkative man') said nothing about there having been castaways among his shipmates. Baird himself was no use to the commission, having died twelve months before.

The books of the Immigration Office had been scoured for any trace of shipwrecked crew or passengers delivered up at Melbourne in 1854. Goodman Teale, a clerk in that office, told the commission he could find no mention of either *Bella* or *Osprey*. The defendants' final witness was John Sutton from the *Argus* office, who had searched his files for shipping arrivals in July 1854 and could find only the schooner *Osprey*, with the notation 'No passengers' overlooking the talkative Baird. The *Argus'* records showed that the schooner had sailed from Glasgow via Capetown—a route, it is true, which would have placed it in the same ocean as Roger in his hour of need. But at that hour, late in April, when the *Bella* was foundering somewhere near the equator, the *Osprey* must have been more than a thousand miles to the south, approaching the Cape of Good Hope.

Counsel for the Claimant produced a witness, John Shillinglaw, who in 1854 had been inspector of Melbourne's water police. He asserted that the port had been so inundated with shipping that year that it was possible for a second *Osprey* to have been overlooked. With the rush to Victoria's gold diggings at its peak, said Shillinglaw, more ships had arrived at Melbourne in 1854 than in any year before or since. To add to the congestion, 'almost universal desertion to the diggings prevailed,' so that the bay had been choked with ships stranded for want of a crew, and the water police, who were supposed to board every ship entering port, had been busy chasing deserters instead. Shillinglaw further stated that, until the introduction of a poll tax in 1855, captains had been under no obligation to report shipwreck survivors or list them as passengers.

It was conceivable then that Roger Tichborne could have arrived in Melbourne unnoticed. But even Shillinglaw, the Claimant's sole witness, sounded far from persuaded by the chances of two *Ospreys* having arrived in port within days of each another—one being comprehensively remarked upon, the other (six times the size *and* carrying shipwreck survivors) unheeded.

Even the vessel's name continued to be a matter of conjecture—a circumstance well kept from the Claimant's opponents. That memory of his was to blame, of course. Sunburnt and brine-soaked after three days in a lifeboat, he had been in no state to observe every little detail of the ship that picked him up, or even to be sure of its name. It might have been called the *Osprey*…but he could have been wrong.

Of all the wild goose chases John Holmes undertook on his client's behalf, the search for the chimerical *Osprey* was the most exasperating.

The Claimant first named the *Osprey* in his Sydney affidavit of July 1866. Holmes, when he took the case on, had immediately sought proof of the vessel. In January 1867, the pair went to Lloyds of London to search the shipping brokers' books for the *Osprey*. All they turned up was the schooner. Holmes urged his client—was he certain about the *Osprey?*—at which the Claimant had to concede that he was only 'pretty certain.'

Holmes himself considered the *Osprey* an unlikely prospect. At the beginning of February, he hired Charles Bridger, an inquiry agent, to track down the Claimant's rescue ship and, if possible, to trace the fate of other *Bella* survivors. Many a long hour Holmes spent with the Claimant, 'going through lists of ships supplied by Mr Bridger to refresh your Memory if possible.' At Lloyds and elsewhere, Bridger examined the logs and passenger lists of more than a thousand ships which might conceivably have picked up Roger Tichborne on their way to Melbourne. The *Resolution of Newcastle* looked promising, as did the *Lucette*; but neither rang a bell with the Claimant. When Bridger submitted a passenger list for the ship *Chowringhee*, however, the Claimant pronounced that 'the names were not altogether unfamiliar.' The *Chowringhee* had arrived at Melbourne on 29 June 1854 and Bridger unearthed certain 'peculiar coincidences' which gave him cause to hope, towards the end of 1867, that he had found the Claimant's saviour. That was until he traced two lady passengers in Birmingham who swore that the *Chowringhee* had not picked up anyone at sea on that voyage. Bridger scratched the ship from his list.

Replacing her as prime candidate was the *Themis*, which had arrived at Melbourne on 1 July 1854 with fourteen steerage passengers and a mixed cargo of portable houses, brimstone, anvils, zinc plumbing fixtures, Dutch timber, picks, pans and shovels. The widow of the *Themis*' Captain Nicholls told Bridger that her husband had picked up crewmen and a passenger off a shipwrecked vessel on his way to Melbourne in 1854. Out of gratitude, the rescued passenger had presented the captain with a watch-key bearing a hind's head insignia, which Mrs Nicholls still had. The Claimant had described a ring of similar design—a winged hind's head being the Tichborne family crest—as his only possession to have survived the shipwreck. Now Bridger's discovery seemed to tweak the Claimant's erratic memory. There *was* something familiar about the *Themis*, he believed, and he *had* owned a crested watch-key. Bridger borrowed (or rather, hired) the key from Mrs Nicholls; but the insignia turned out to be an ordinary hind's head—unwinged—and the Claimant disowned the key.

Undeterred, Bridger sought out the *Themis*' passenger list and 'curiously enough' (Holmes informed the Claimant) 'it contains the names of four Females, that being the number of Ladies that you have always represented as being on board the Ship that saved you.' This was November 1867 and, since the end of February, Bridger had been conducting the investigation on his own account, in the expectation that eventually there would be something in it for him. He pursued the *Themis* well into 1868. His discovery of her former mate, James Hansord, in Bombay, caused fleeting jubilation. But over months of correspondence, the intractable crewman refused to divulge what—if anything—he knew of the *Bella* survivors unless he was well paid for it. In July, Bridger succeeded in finding three of the fourteen passengers—a family living near the Welsh border—in whom his questions stirred a hazy recollection of castaways. The Claimant met with them at Shrewsbury and came away 'perfectly satisfied' that it was the *Themis* that had picked him up. But in the first week of August, Bridger found in the office of a defunct Liverpool shipping agent the long-sought log of the *Themis*' 1854 voyage to Melbourne. It made no mention of shipwreck survivors—not a word.

For all that he had been hopeful of the *Themis*, Bridger had not been one-eyed. For much of the past year, he had also been searching for North American ships that might have landed the Claimant at Melbourne in 1854. Now all his hopes were fixed in that direction. Over time, the Claimant's *Osprey* would evolve into a 300-ton black-painted barque hailing from Baltimore, via New York.

At Lloyds, Holmes and the Claimant had glanced at the *Bella*'s record, too. Afterwards, in the affidavit which would form the basis of his claim, Holmes' client was able to recall the names of four of the *Bella* crewmen with whom he'd been rescued: 'Sheers, Williams, Dobbin, and Peebles.' Charles Bridger's inquiries confirmed that there had been a Shears and a Dobner aboard the lost *Bella*, and that a Williams had jumped ship at Rio. But Peebles confounded him.

Bridger traced every one of the *Bella* seamen, visiting their hometowns—from Southampton to Rotterdam—and their families. At Yupton in Sussex, the parents of Thomas White told Bridger that their son had returned home for a time in 1856, from Melbourne, and in recent years had written from Ballarat. Holmes telegraphed Sedgefield & Allport to seek out White, emphasising his 'immense importance' to the case and authorising his fare home. But Thomas

White of Ballarat denied all knowledge of the *Bella* and refused to give particulars of himself. His photograph drew a blank with the Claimant.

Equally perplexing was the story related by the widow of the *Bella*'s Captain Birkett. Three years after the ship's disappearance, she told Bridger, she had received a letter, postmarked Bristol, warmly enjoining her to take care of herself and her children. The letter had borne no signature, but was in her husband's hand—she would swear to it. But Birkett's widow had remarried by the time the letter arrived and its implications so alarmed her that she'd put it straight in the fire.

The Claimant himself continued to have scant recollection of his landing at Melbourne: 'I do not know what report the captain made. I went away the next day, and did not even let the captain know I was going. I do not remember what became of my fellows who were saved from the Bella.' George Jacobs was one of the multitude of witnesses whose collective testimony, over the years, would fill the holes in the Claimant's account. In June 1854, Jacobs had been employed at Sandridge (now Port Melbourne), carting goods unloaded from the *Osprey*. Twenty-one years later he could still remember rolling barrels branded 'Osprey, New York' along the pier. And he'd contributed ten shillings to a subscription taken up at the Sandridge Hotel for seven or eight shipwrecked men brought ashore in a 'deplorable' condition; but whether they had come off the *Osprey*, he couldn't say.

A former Sandridge draper claimed that the *Bella* survivors—Roger Tichborne among them—had been outfitted with clothing from his store. They'd stayed in Melbourne for three weeks, he said, after which five of them sailed for home, each bearing a £30 promissory note for having saved Roger's life. But, as grim chance would have it, their ship struck a rock near the Cape and, twice-wrecked but once-lucky, the five *Bella* shipmates never made it home. Roger himself had left Melbourne for the goldfields in company with the *Bella*'s cook, a bulky fellow known as Doctor. That was the substance of the

Sandridge draper's 'portion of the Tichborne mystery'—except for a veiled reference to cannibalism aboard the *Bella*'s lifeboat, a notion that cast Roger's bond with the ship's cook in a rather interesting light.

A shipping clerk claimed to have boarded the *Osprey* to find that all but one man had deserted for the diggings. The sole occupant—ragged and wild-eyed—had confided that he was heir to an English baronetcy on the run from 'troubles' at home. A woman living in Richmond offered up a treasured memory of having 'Sir' Roger Tichborne, just landed off the *Osprey*, pointed out to her at the post-office corner in Elizabeth Street. She still remembered him, years after the event, as 'the first live lord' she'd ever set eyes on.

On the other side of the ledger, Thomas Prickman, who in 1854 had run a provisioning business at Sandridge, scoffed at the idea that a second *Osprey* with a cargo of castaways could possibly have escaped the notice of reporters from the *Herald* and the *Argus*. What then should we make of the testimony of Isaac Beeby, late of the Nine-Mile Creek diggings? Beeby would relate how a heavy fall of snow had confined him to his tent for four or five days at the end of July 1854, with only a week-old copy of the *Herald* for company. In the thin grey light of his snowbound tent, he read and re-read the close-printed broadsheet until he knew the whole of it by heart. Even twenty years later and back home in Glasgow, Beeby would claim to have perfect recall of that newspaper's contents and would swear that on page two—not under 'Shipping Arrivals' but in the fifth column—there was a detailed account of an American *Osprey* landing at Melbourne with rescued crew and passengers from the *Bella*. And yet a thorough search of the *Herald* (as well as the rival *Argus*) brings no such report to light.

There was a paragraph in the *Herald* of 28 June 1854, about a month before Beeby's blizzard, concerning an *Osprey* and a shipwreck—or, to be exact, a shipwrecked *Osprey*. A trading schooner, this *Osprey* had shuttled for more than ten years between Melbourne, Launceston, Hobart and her home port of Geelong. Her career ended when she ran aground in a gale on 18 June. Was that Isaac Beeby's *Osprey*?

Picture the Claimant in Sydney in 1866. He'd just shed his Tom Castro skin, and the first thing that everyone asked about was the shipwreck. Either he didn't remember or knew nothing to begin with; but hardly a block from Arthur Cubitt's office in Pitt Street was the School of Arts, with its lofty-ceilinged reading room and earwiggy stockpiles of newspapers. Suppose that the Claimant went there as the guest of the grasping Cubitt and asked to see copies of the *Argus* for the month of July 1854. Did he start with the 24th, that being three months from the supposed date of the *Bella*'s sinking? The *Argus* had noted the arrival of the sixty-six ton *Osprey* on 27 July. But there were plenty of other vessels to choose from. Why choose the *Osprey*? The obvious answer is that he had been picked up at sea by a ship of that name, or something like it. But in that case why would he later equivocate when presented with the *Themis* and *Chowringhee*? Perhaps the Claimant had simply settled for the first likely-sounding vessel that met his eye. Or perhaps the name *Osprey* recalled to his mind a schooner which used to call at Hobart and which, if he remembered right, had met a fate not unlike the *Bella*'s.

TWENTY-THREE
THE NEW MAN

BY the Claimant's account, the antipodean Tom Castro was born, full-grown, at Row's Yard, Bourke Street, Melbourne, on or about Saturday, 26 July 1854.

There he was, just off the *Osprey* in stiff new moleskins, a China blue shirt and his first pair of elastic-sided boots. He'd been led to the saleyard by a stream of rough-looking fellows (whom he would soon distinguish as 'bushified') on flash, toey mounts. The streets were all clay and mud, with slush-filled potholes deeper than his boot tops. Horses and bullocks—he'd never seen so many. With the riot of building in progress and the rowdy folk crowding what passed for footpaths, it was noisier than parts of London he could have named. There seemed to be a public house on every corner, with restaurants interspersed, all of them busting with diggers—men dressed like him but with the stiffness rubbed off and a coating of grime and brazen clay laid on. They wore battered wide-awake hats and wild whiskers. Some of them sported fistfuls of gold rings, others dangled a nugget from an earlobe. At the front of the big stores the footway was made unnavigable by stacks of tin dishes and buckets, picks, shovels, wooden tubs and billy-pots. In every shop window was a set of gold scales beside an untidy pile of the genuine article, serving in lieu of a notice: Gold Bought Here.

Having waded through Elizabeth Street, he eventually arrived at Row's Yard. He was leaning on a fence-rail and sizing up a couple of

Frederick Grosse's engraving depicts just the kind of antics that would have drawn the Claimant to Row's Yard, adjacent to Kirk's Horse Bazaar (shown here) in Bourke Street West

Jingellic brumbies, when William Foster offered him a job and 'a very jolly life' in Gippsland. Shaking hands on it, Foster's new man gave his name as Tom Castro. He'd thought of it on the spot, he said.

Asked at the Chancery hearing why he'd changed his name, the

Claimant would cite 'private reasons' and 'because it suited me to do so.' What did not suit him, apparently, was the idea of returning home. It never occurred to him, he said, to send for money to Glynn's, the Tichbornes' London bankers. As for contacting his family: 'I had no particular reason for not writing any more than I did not wish people to know where I was.' Why? 'Because I was not inclined to do so.' Questioning the Claimant never got anybody very far.

Castro started for Gippsland at 5.30 next morning, riding in company with Foster and three other stockmen. Between them they drove a draft of eight or nine horses—'return' horses, they called them—in place of the cattle that Foster and his men had brought up to town. From Melbourne, they rode south-east then dead-east, drizzled on by misty rain. They spent days crossing lush grassy hills, others weaving through dripping gum forests and nearly bushwacked in tangly scrub that grew just high enough to confound a horseman. There was no road to Gippsland then, barely a track. Only a handful of squatters used it, since most traffic went by ship. By the Claimant's recollection, the 145-mile journey took eleven days. For long stretches they saw no one but themselves. At intervals along the track, they'd come to a stockyard knocked together out of bush timber, with a boxy bark hut pushed on a lean by the firewood stacked against it. Inside, these huts were half fireplace, but the travellers were glad of it. Lines slung from the rafters gave their damp gear a chance to dry a little before the next day's early start.

Ten days' travelling brought them to the township of Sale, formerly Flooding Creek. The approach to the town had been slow going, as the roadway wove and plunged through the low, swampy ground bordering a network of coastal lakes. It wasn't the ideal site for a settlement. But scenic it was. The town's dozen-and-a-half scattered habitations were made near-strangers to one another by the intervening stands of swamp gums, sheoaks and native cherries. A traveller, it was said, 'could hardly see more than a gun-shot ahead of him'—

just far enough, in fact, to bag himself a brace of the wild fowl which massed wherever a waterhole pushed the forest aside. Castro and his fellows watered themselves at Bob Fitchett's ramshackle Woolpack Inn, crossroads of the Gippsland backwaters, then pushed on from Sale to arrive by nightfall at The Heart, head station of John Foster's extensive Gippsland pastoral empire.

Foster himself lived in Hobart, leaving the day-to-day running of his Victorian properties to resident managers, among them his nephew and Castro's travelling companion, William Foster. In the early 1840s, John Foster had secured contracts for the supply of beef to the civil service, army, and convict settlements in Van Diemen's Land, and for provisioning homebound ships with salt beef. His successful trade with the Gippsland pastoralists contributed to the development of Port Albert and the establishment of Flooding Creek as a staging-point. Before long, Foster determined to capture his own slice of the near-virgin country and within ten years his pastoral holdings in Gippsland totalled 180,000 acres carrying 21,000 head of livestock, spread across seven runs: The Heart, Tangel, Glenfalloch, Boisdale, Dargo, Glencoe and Erinvale.

As the Claimant told it, he and his companions stopped a night at The Heart, before pushing on next day to their destination, twenty miles to the north. For it was as a stockrider on Boisdale station that Tom Castro had invented himself and signed on at twenty-five shillings a week.

Fifteen years later, the Australian commission took evidence in a private room of the Club Hotel in Foster Street, Sale. Alfred Wyatt was there for the Claimant, well worded-up by Curzon Allport as to difficulties he might expect in turning the Gippsland evidence to their client's favour. It was in this neck of the colonies that their opponents' detective, John Mackenzie, had met with his warmest success in securing evidence against the Claimant. For all his bold talk, Allport's own detective, Otto Berliner, had made little headway in Gippsland; had, in fact, ended up offering his services to the opposition. Allport himself had since made evidence-gathering forays to Gippsland and had a local man acting as agent, taking in the talk around the pubs and stockyards. Their combined lack of success was reflected in the split of witnesses at the commission's Sale sitting: twenty-six for the defendants and just six for the plaintiff.

The main problem was that nobody could remember a man named Tom Castro. There wasn't a trace of him in the Boisdale station books, tendered to the commission as exhibits. Those books, you will recall, had been in the possession of William Foster's widow, now Mrs Macalister, and her husband Matthew. The Claimant's side suspected that the Macalisters or their good friend John Mackenzie had tampered with them. William Montgomery, manager at Boisdale from 1854–56, had intimated as much to Allport. Asked at the commission if a man named Castro had been employed at Boisdale, Montgomery replied ambiguously, 'I do not remember him, as the books are now.'

Sara Macalister was the defendants' star witness. She not only produced the Castro-less station books but swore that William Foster had not been in Melbourne in July 1854. Family events at the time— a sister's marriage and a brother's death—made her recollection especially sharp, she said. Her late husband had been at home in Gippsland from early June until at least the end of July. Moreover, 'home' for William Foster at that time was Erinvale, a sheep run forty miles south of Boisdale. Even supposing her late husband had been in Melbourne in July 1854, said Mrs Macalister, it would have been William Montgomery's responsibility to recruit a stockrider for Boisdale station. But Montgomery himself told the commission that 'it would have been within the scope of [Foster's] duty to engage a man for Boisdale if a man was required.' A former stockrider, William Higgins, testified that he'd driven a mob of Boisdale-bound horses from Melbourne with Foster in 1854, although he couldn't name the month.

Aside from Higgins, only one of the old Boisdale hands was brought before the commission. Andrew Hutton, better known as 'The Highlandman'—'a lugubrious looking individual…whose face looked as if it required cleansing with a ship's scraper'—appeared as a witness for the defence. Hutton was a Gippsland veteran, having been of the party that drove the first mob of cattle into the district in 1838. The point of Hutton's evidence was meant to be that he had no recollection of Castro. Under cross-examination, however, he swung around to assert that there had been a man called Tom ('I think') who'd come down from Melbourne with Foster one time. This Tom might have stayed at Boisdale two months or two years—Hutton couldn't say. But, 'I think he was a good horseman.'

Another of the pioneer Scotch settlers, Dr Alexander Arbuckle, declared that he'd known every man in the district in 1854 and there'd been no Castro among them. The Claimant dismissed Arbuckle as 'an old Doctor who knocked about there was constantly drunk used to stay a week at one station and then at another.' As to the doctor's statement that he'd known all the Boisdale station-hands personally, the Claimant remarked, 'Arbuckle though a drunkard was a Gentleman above associating with the Stockmen.'

The Claimant's side produced Harry Kemmis who, like William Foster, had come to Gippsland in the early 1850s to manage a station belonging to an uncle. Due to 'intense mental excitement, indeed madness' resulting from 'a long course of constant dissipation,' he had committed the crime of bigamy and now had to be fetched out of gaol in order to appear before the commission. Alone of all the witnesses, Kemmis spoke with utter conviction of having known Tom Castro at Boisdale. They were introduced, he said, by William Foster at a muster in 1854 or '55, and he had later seen Castro at Dargo. Foster alone had used the name Castro, said Kemmis; the other men had known him only as Tom. He had noticed nothing in Castro's accent or manner to suggest that he was a Frenchman. What had stood out was Castro's skill with horses, in particular his ability to throw a lasso.

Six years after the Australian commission, Kemmis' evidence would be amplified by Mary McMillan, whose late husband Angus had held the Bushy Park run, adjoining Foster's Boisdale. The two station homesteads stood on opposite banks of the Avon River and there had been constant communication between their inhabitants via a ford in a shallow bend of the river. Mrs McMillan swore that she recognised the Claimant's photograph as a likeness of Castro, or 'the gentleman known on our Bushy Park Station as the French Lord.' Her late husband had met him on a muster at Dargo and, during their ride down-country together, Castro had confided to McMillan 'the full history of his past life, birth, and parentage, and the reasons for assuming his false name.' A firm friendship had developed between the squatter and the 'young lord' and Castro had become a frequent guest at the Bushy Park table. Angus McMillan was four years dead when the Australian commission came to Sale, and not a peep of his household's familiarity with Castro made its way into evidence. The fact that the Claimant should have failed to mention such a significant connection suggests that something other than actual recollection must have prompted Mrs McMillan's belated contribution.

It was sixteen months after the Claimant's supposed ride into Gippsland that Arthur Orton came across from Hobart. The *Eclipse* set him down at Port Albert on 22 November 1855. A posse of men from Mewburn Park, who'd brought down a mob of cattle, had a horse saddled ready for him. Heading inland along the deep-rutted track worn by bullock drays, Arthur's way took him through the seedy hamlet of Tarraville, then across Foster's Erinvale pasturage to Merriman's Creek, where he and his fellows stopped at Greenwood's bark tavern for refreshment. Fourteen miles more brought them to Sale, whence they continued north to Maffra, the main stockyard on the Boisdale run. West of there lay Mewburn Park, Arthur's destination. Fate, if the Claimant was to be believed, thus found the two men—Tom Castro and Arthur Orton—on neighbouring stations, bunked down ten miles apart but, as yet, strangers.

TWENTY-FOUR
A VERY JOLLY LIFE

MATTHEW Macalister, at the Australian commission, summed up the principal duties of a stockman as: 'to ride through the cattle, know where to find them, and muster them.' A cattle station like Boisdale was divided into numerous outstations or runs, a different stockrider taking responsibility for each. For weeks or months at a time, the stockman would keep to his run, living alone in an outstation hut and watching over his stock—like a shepherd on horseback. But at mustering time, he'd have company aplenty.

Mustering was the great business and excitement of station life, as one Gippslander recalled:

> wild cattle from the hills brought in, in mobs, amidst much shouting of men, cracking of whips, barking of dogs, yelling of blackfellows, frenzied and unending lowing of the cattle themselves, galloping of horses, and general excitement everywhere. (*Harrison, p. 23*)

Once a year, every hand would be engaged, from daybreak to dark for six or eight weeks at a stretch, in rounding up the stock from every fringe and corner of the station. This was where the stockrider got his thrills, chasing down rogue cattle through timber, scrub and gully, all at a flat gallop. The hubbub at the stockyard—the muster's focal point—more than made up for the stockriders' weeks of solitude. Here they were employed, all together, in branding the young cattle, doctoring the ailing, and separating the lot into classes: for breeding, for export, for eating, and bullocks for market.

'Stockdriving is hard work,' the Claimant would recall, 'but there is a great deal of fun and amusement in it.' The engrossing nature of the job was to blame for his not writing home, as he explained: 'I got into the saddle at six in the morning, and didn't leave it until eight or nine o'clock at night. I used to feel tired, and even on Sunday I was often obliged to go to neighbouring stations. So the time passed on, and I never wrote at all.' To begin with, though, he was employed close in to the homestead, working with the horses. He ate his meals at the homestead kitchen and shared a hut with others of the regular station-hands. Like them, he took his turn at killing meat—his introduction to butchering, said the Claimant. After a month or so, he was sent to one of the outstations, where he spent eight or ten weeks with an experienced stockrider before being given charge of the run.

Arthur Orton's situation was much the same as that described by the Claimant. And, like the Claimant, Orton evidently found himself with no time for writing. After he left Hobart, his family never heard from him.

Orton was one of six stockriders, one of twenty-five or thirty men altogether, employed on Mewburn Park. His mates in the 'men's hut', two hundred yards from the homestead, included Aleck Neilsen, Billy the Groom, Walter and John Luckman, George Gregory, Tom Toke, and Mickey the Frenchman, most of whom, like him, had come across from Hobart. The butchering skills that had looked third rate in that town qualified Arthur as a virtuoso among the stockman–butchers of Gippsland, so that pretty soon he was called on to do all the station's slaughtering. Not that he was always close in to the homestead. Several times he drove mobs of fat cattle to port, and he spent weeks up along the Macalister River, trailing after vealers.

In contrast to the mostly blank responses elicited by the name

Tom Castro when the Australian commission came to Sale, a good few witnesses remembered Arthur Orton. One of his Mewburn Park hut-mates recalled how Orton had reneged on a £20 prize-fight: 'he said he had a lot of young horses to ride and he did not want to knock himself about.' Different ones sketched him as 'a jolly sort of fellow,' raw-boned but promising to be stout, and with hair 'not curly nor exactly straight' which he used to 'chuck' back off his forehead. A witness who recollected Orton vividly—his moleskin trousers, blue shirt and kneeboots, even calling him 'my mate'—was the former Mewburn Park overseer, Jacobus (Jack) du Moulin. The brother of Sara Macalister of Boisdale, du Moulin declared the Claimant's photographs to be undoubted likenesses of Arthur Orton. But then, so did most of the Gippsland witnesses.

Unlike the Boisdale station books, the records of Orton's employment at Mewburn Park were not submitted as exhibits to the Australian commission. Nor did John Johnson (son of Orton's former employer) shed much light on them in his evidence. He confirmed that he'd found Arthur Orton's name in the books, but couldn't recall the dates and had left the books at home. Although he appeared as a witness for the defence, Johnson had made his search of the station books at the request of Curzon Allport and had sent detailed extracts to the Claimant's lawyers showing that Orton left Mewburn Park on 4 June 1856.

Orton's whereabouts during the next five months were not so clear. It was on one of his last trips to Port Albert with cattle that he'd met up with his old Hobart landlord, Jackie Dight, now butchering and horse dealing at Tarraville. But Dight told the Australian commission that he'd seen Arthur just that once in Gippsland. William Higgins and Jack du Moulin swore that they'd seen Orton in October, splitting timber and burning charcoal on the backwaters of Flooding Creek. Du Moulin had sought his old mate's help in navigating the track through the rain-swelled morass. Orton may well have odd-jobbed around Sale for a time in the latter part of 1856. But there's a better than even chance that his immediate destination after Mewburn Park was the Omeo goldfield.

Three years had passed since he'd written to his London sweet-heart that he intended trying his luck at the diggings. Now, after six months in Victoria and with a goldfield a couple of days' ride to the north, could he have resisted taking a look? Already several of his hut-mates had headed in that direction and word of their success—or that gold-digging was better than wage-work, at any rate—had filtered back to Mewburn Park.

Gold had been found at Omeo, high up in the mountains that form Gippsland's northern boundary, as early as 1851; but five years later the goldfield was still in its infancy. Its isolation was partly to blame: that and the tricky nature of the gold deposits, which favoured experienced hands over novices. At any rate, Omeo had so far failed to attract diggers in the kind of numbers that would constitute a rush. In 1856, it boasted four hotels but no church, post office or police station. For some, though, the absence of a police station was its main point of attraction. In fact, Omeo was already established as a staging-point on the migratory route known as 'the Vandemonian trail'. Station workers—many of them ex-convicts—brought over from Van Diemen's Land to work on the Gippsland runs in the 1850s formed the foundation of a loose-knit cadre whose stock-thieving and bushranging operations would span thirty years and the three hundred-odd miles of the Vandemonian trail: across the mountains, over the Murray River and into the Riverina.

If Arthur Orton did try his hand at digging, he didn't keep at it for long, since he was back working for wages on Gippsland's central plains by November 1856 at the latest. According to the maligned Boisdale station books, Orton was paid in mid-December for six weeks' sheepwashing, after which he took his place on the regular payroll as a stockrider. Just like the Claimant, he was engaged at twenty-five shillings a week by William Foster.

Foster's widow, now Sara Macalister, remembered Orton well. She'd once nursed him through a bad sore throat. He was 'a peculiar looking man,' she said; 'the lower part of his face was very heavy, and he had large ears; he had a very noticeable peculiarity in his mouth; it was a very heavy hanging underlip.' The Claimant was scathing of Mrs Macalister's evidence, retorting, 'She never did such a thing in her life as nurse a Stockman.' He had rather a lot to say about her, actually; she was 'very pretty,' she'd flirted with the 'half bred swell stockmen who said they had come down in the world and were too lazy to work,' and she had at one time 'run away' with her own uncle.

Orton had stuck in the memory of other Boisdale witnesses as 'the best butcher on the station.' A butcher who'd known Long Arthur in Hobart and had met him again in the men's hut at Boisdale swore to his missing front teeth and his preoccupation with lassoing. Moreover, the Claimant's Wagga and Sydney photographs were generally agreed to be fair likenesses of Arthur Orton.

The Claimant contended that he and Orton had met when they both were employed on Boisdale station at the end of 1855—precisely when Orton arrived at Mewburn Park. By his account, they were together only a few days before being posted to different parts of the run. Early the following year the Claimant spent three weeks in Orton's company, after which he left to take charge of the Dargo out-station, in a remote valley forty miles to the north. 'Some mountains intervene,' he recalled, 'but as the crow flies, it is not far.'

While he would, in time, shift the date of his and Orton's meeting from late 1855 to early the next year, and its venue from Boisdale to Dargo, the Claimant would stoutly maintain that he had gone to Dargo in the early part of 1856 and had remained there until April 1857. But according to the Boisdale station books, the lone stockman at Dargo during that period was a Peter McColl, an early resident of Gippsland who was still in the district at the time of the Australian commission. And the Boisdale books show that McColl's successor at Dargo, in May 1857, was none other than Arthur Orton.

Boisdale homestead was set well back on the Gippsland plains, with the foothills of the Great Dividing Range pushing up on its north, west and east. Alpine ferns flourished among the tea-tree and wattle that fringed the snow-fed Avon River within sight of the Fosters' timber house. From Boisdale, tracks led west to the Maffra stock-yards, south to Stratford and Flooding Creek, and north-east to the high-country runs. Most of the lowland cattle stations had a corre-sponding mountain run. Boisdale's was Dargo. Originally meant only for summer grazing, by the mid-1850s Dargo and the neighbouring Cungmungi run (attached to Bushy Park) carried stock all year round. Peter McColl was the first permanent stockrider on Dargo. Arriving there in 1856, he found the station-hut already occupied by his Cungmungi counterpart, Norman Nicholson, whose own run offered no such amenity.

Arthur Orton set off for Dargo early on a Tuesday in May 1857, leading a pack-horse with two months' provisions. His own flapping saddlebags held only three and a half pounds of tobacco, spare clothes, a few books from the station 'library', and food enough for the two-day journey. His ride took him high above Boisdale and the plains to where the fertile flats of the Dargo River's lower reaches threaded between ranks of unmapped mountains. Thus hemmed in, the valley made a sheltered pasturage at that time of year, but the trapped heat in summer could be stifling. More than six hundred head of Boisdale cattle, young stock, were grazed on the Dargo run. It was the stock-rider's job to 'tail' them on horseback by day and drive them into pens at night. After a month or two, the cattle would get used to the run and no longer required constant tailing. Still the stockman kept to his saddle, on the look-out for stragglers, since the numberless creeks and tributaries snaking out from the main valley into dark

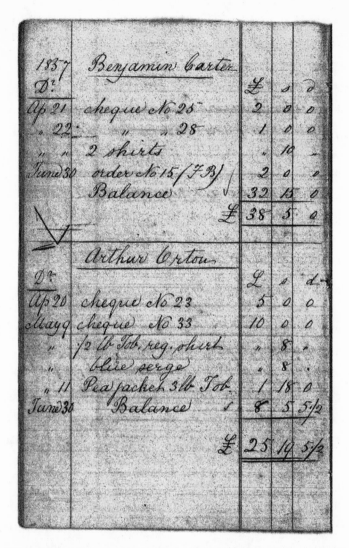

A page from the Boisdale station books shows that Arthur Orton stocked up with clothing and tobacco in preparation for his posting to Dargo in May 1857

creases in the ranges made for no end of places to lose a heifer—or one's self.

The isolation of the Dargo run wasn't to every stockman's taste. Orton accepted the job only when he was offered a wage of £80 a year, or £100 if he stayed at it for more than six months. By the time

Arthur arrived at Dargo, Norman Nicholson had a hut of his own, about a mile the other side of the river. They kept close company until September when Nicholson left for Bushy Park. According to the Claimant, though, there was a third hand—his—at their candlelit card games. He had shacked-up with Nicholson in the Cungmungi hut for some months after leaving Foster's employ, he said, and, 'I saw a good deal of Arthur Orton when he went to Dargo.'

Norman Nicholson remembered things differently. 'Orton was a man of sallow complexion,' he recalled, 'rather fairish hair; big ears; I think greyish eyes; he had a peculiar twitching about the eyes when he spoke; no beard; no whiskers; no moustaches.' All of Orton was hairless, in fact, except for his scalp—so Nicholson observed when the pair took an icy dip in the river once during their winter together. He further recalled how Orton had talked incessantly of lassoing and had seized any opportunity to demonstrate his skill with a hide rope, even lassoing the horse Nicholson was riding. But of Thomas Castro— the ex-Dargo stockman who had supposedly shared his hut—Nicholson could tell the commission nothing.

Cross-examined by Alfred Wyatt, however, the old Cungmungi stockman recounted how, over the course of many long evenings in one or other of their huts, Orton had talked of surviving a shipwreck on his way from South America, of a quarrel with his father, and of the large estate in England which he stood to inherit. Moreover, he'd sometimes spoken French (at least, it had sounded like French to Nicholson). 'Clearly from this,' the Claimant would remark, 'it is apparent he thinks he is speaking of me and is confusing me with Orton.'

Norman Nicholson was succeeded, both at Cungmungi and in the witness seat, by Archie McDonald. He and Arthur Orton had been together in the Dargo River valley from September 1857 until Orton's departure the following June. Like Nicholson, McDonald told of river bathing and his companion's endless talk of South America and the lasso. For sport, the pair of them sometimes used to ride downriver to Tabberabbera, twelve miles from Dargo, to shoot wild bulls. 'He told me his father was a butcher in London, and...was supplying the navy with beef,' McDonald declared. 'As near as I can recollect he said he was a butcher in Tasmania.' 'All of this is true of Orton, not me,' was the Claimant's comment. Yet McDonald's physical description of Orton, son of a shipping butcher, exactly matched Nicholson's of Orton, the shipwrecked heir—and incidentally bore a pretty fair resemblance to Tom Castro of Wagga.

In the course of his evidence, Archie McDonald recalled Orton's fondness for the seafaring novels of Captain Marryat. His brother Donald was the next witness. Exhibit D2, a battered copy of *The Rivals*, an 1829 novel by Gerald Griffin, was produced. Inside the back cover was an inscription:

> This day I have received a letter from Donald MacDonald with the Seal Broken I Arthur Orton here make a vow on this Book. Although not a Bible. It bear a cross That has I am a man of Bone Blood and flesh. That I will find out the man if possible. That broke the said seal. And that I will punish him according to the laws of My Country.
> Sined Arthur Orton
> Dargo
> 11 March 1858

Donald McDonald explained that he used to pack rations up from Bushy Park to his brother at Cungmungi and that, on this occasion, he had also carried a few supplies for Orton, including the letter in question. 'The seal was broken when I got it,' said McDonald, 'and I told him so.' But while he remembered the commotion Orton had made over it, he couldn't recall the letter itself. All he knew was that Orton had made a great play of secrecy over the contents.

Sara Macalister was also questioned about Exhibit D2. 'We had a good library,' she said:

Nearly all the men generally got books from me [but] Arthur Orton was the only man, I think, that ever did scribble in books. The writing at the end I noticed when he returned it, from the peculiarity of the vow and the language. There were two or three others the same, but the books he got were of no value. Library novels—railway novels. He was very fond of writing, Arthur Orton. I think I might say I read all he wrote; it was worth reading.

The Rivals must have come back to Boisdale with Orton in the first week of July 1858. He'd had enough of Dargo. William Foster was displeased that his stockman had returned without permission, leaving the Dargo run untended. Orton resumed his old stockriding duties at Boisdale, but was discharged three months later 'for insubordination and want of skill in his occupation.' ('He was too heavy a weight,' noted Foster at the time, 'and could not ride in timber.') Orton demanded a week's wages in lieu of notice. Foster refused. Orton then lodged a list of claims against his former employer, the principal one being that, although he'd stayed more than six months at Dargo, he hadn't been paid at the promised rate of £100 per annum. But, in papers produced as Exhibit D47 at the Australian commission, the arbitrators in the wage case ruled 'that the Plaintiff Orton has failed to produce any evidence' that Foster had offered him a higher rate, and his claims were rejected.

Ten pounds of Orton's last Boisdale wage packet went as down-payment on a horse. He bought the stallion—a bay, with black points—from John Johnson of Mewburn Park and stabled him at the Royal Exchange Hotel in Sale. Under an arrangement with the publican, Duncan Clarke, Orton ran the hotel's livery stables. This was at the end of 1858, and a number of witnesses recalled Orton's horse. According to one account current in Gippsland at the time of the Australian commission, but not set in print until some years later:

The animal was…tolerably well bred and spirited, and like most horses broken in by stockmen in those days, given to the pastime of bucking with strangers. Orton was warned of this little peculiarity, but remarking that 'he would cure him of that,' sprang quickly into the saddle, and was quickly deposited on the turf again…after a prolonged struggle for mastery, with the same result, 'Ah,' said Orton…'You've got some pluck in you, and some of the right blood, I'll call you Tichborne.'

After a couple of months Orton gave up the Royal Exchange stables and went into the business of horsebreaking. Some witnesses knew his partner as Jack the Devil, others as Jack the Shepherd. At any rate, his name was Jack and the pair ran their operation out of a carter's yard at Sale. Orton boarded at the Turf Hotel, where the landlord would remember him as 'a rowdy fast sort of fellow [who] would just as soon fight as not.' That was quite a contrast to Daniel Sayer's impression of him as 'remarkably quiet and the essence of good-nature.'

Sayer 'built' two saddles for Orton, one of them with 'monstrous' knee pads which Orton assured him were just the thing he'd been accustomed to in South America. Another of the Sale witnesses, William Parker, swore that Orton had given his 'real' name as de Castello and had claimed his mother was a titled Spanish lady. 'His conversation was mysterious,' mused Parker with what might have been hindsight; 'once he said we should hear something of him some day.'

Orton's partnership with Jack, if it ever existed, appears not to have lasted long. He shifted next into an iffy branch of horse dealing. He would obtain a young, half-wild animal on a small down-payment, promising to pay the balance in five or six weeks, by which time, if all went well, he'd have trained up his investment and sold it at a profit. Inevitably though, all did not go well. By the end of May 1859, Arthur Orton was a marked man, as evidenced by the following notice in the *Victorian Police Gazette*—

ARTHUR ORTIN is charged on warrant issued at Sale, with stealing on the 22nd ultimo, there, a chestnut mare, the property of one Thomas Blacker. Description of the offender:—About 5 feet 9 or 10 inches high, stout built, pale complexion, fair hair, small fair whiskers, one front tooth wanting in upper jaw, by trade a butcher, and is a good jockey and horsebreaker.

He had defaulted on his payment for the mare. The *Police Gazette* notice concluded: 'He is supposed to have proceeded to Melbourne, per the steamer *Shandon* on the 25th ultimo.'

Arthur Orton never was apprehended. Thomas Blacker's chestnut mare was recovered a month later not far from Port Albert, where it was 'supposed to have been turned loose by Arthur Ortin, who is still at large.'

TWENTY-FIVE
OUTLAWS OF THE WASTE

BUT where was Tom Castro? Nobody knows. The Claimant offered several different renderings of the two or three years after he left Dargo in August or September 1857—all of which would defy corroboration and leave many months unaccounted for.

From Dargo, he said, he returned to Boisdale for a short time, followed by six months at Sale. He headed east in about May 1858 and, passing through Macleod's Bairnsdale station on the Mitchell River, fell in with a team of horsebreakers. Fred Burrows and Robert Burnett had been contracted to break-in forty-eight horses for Macleod and, according to the Claimant, hired him to 'handle' the animals. He was employed that way for three or four months, he said. Burrows was not to be found in 1869, but Burnett appeared as a defence witness at the commission's one-day sitting in Bairnsdale. 'I knew this man well and so did he know me,' the Claimant would note alongside Burnett's evidence. But Burnett had no recollection of him. ('I should be called *Tom* probably,' was the Claimant's explanation, 'because Castro would never be mentioned.') Moreover, Burnett asserted that it was in 1856, not 1858, that he and Burrows had been horsebreaking at Macleod's. Norman Macleod, the station owner, checked his books and confirmed that the horsebreaking contract had run from May to September 1856—months when *Arthur Orton* was drifting between jobs.

In his original statement to Chancery, the Claimant had spoken of being 'well known to Mr Smith of the Landino Station.' John Smith, owner of Lindenow station (a five-mile ride from Macleod's), was called as a defence witness at Bairnsdale and took less than a minute to deliver his evidence—that he had never known a man named Thomas Castro. 'I *was* well known to Mr Smith,' protested the Claimant, and as proof offered a tale about a black snake dropping onto Smith's dinner table. Had such an interjection been whispered to his counsel while the witness was on the stand, it might have been of some value. But coughed up in England six months later, it was useless. Alfred Wyatt had no questions for Smith.

According to the Claimant's original statement, after all the colts were broken in he and Fred Burrows had left together for Omeo. At the Chancery hearing, however, he said that he'd left Macleod's on his own, meandering all over Gippsland on his way to Omeo where he spent six months or so from the latter part of 1858. He was cagey (even for him) as to how he'd been employed at Omeo: 'knocking about doing one thing and another' was how he summed it up. He said nothing about gold-digging, but did mention driving horses for Joe Day and Tom Sheean, publicans of the Diggers' Arms and Diggers' Rest hotels respectively. At Day's, he broke his horse's neck jumping a six-foot bar for an ounce of gold. (Only his calling the wager '20 penny-weights' betrayed the fact that he'd never dug for gold himself. Ounces were hard won and no digger would have counted them as pennyweights.) Giving evidence at Bairnsdale, Joe Day remembered Fred Burrows well enough, but Tom Castro drew a blank.

There were three witnesses for the Claimant's side, however, who swore that they'd known him at Omeo. Mary and James Andrews and their friend Alexander Neilson described a tall, gentlemanly, fair-haired man with twitching eyebrows and a strong accent, who'd been spoken of as 'the Foreigner' but called Bob to his face. (Here the Claimant noted on his copy of the evidence that he'd sometimes been called Bob to differentiate him from some other fellow called Tom.)

Before Omeo, Neilson and the Andrewses had worked at Mewburn Park and, having known Orton there, they were able to state with certainty that the Foreigner was quite a different man. In identical detail, each testified as to his prowess with pick and shovel, his iron-grey horse and his digging partners—among whom were some of the ripest scoundrels ever to embark on the Vandemonian trail. The three witnesses identified the Claimant's Wagga and Sydney portraits as the Foreigner without a flicker of hesitation. Yet all that they related had taken place in the early part of 1856, a good two years before the Claimant's professed arrival at Omeo. Moreover, another witness, reciting a list of foreigners he had known at Omeo, happened to mention a tall, fair digger who went by the name of Bob the Swede.

After Omeo, the Claimant's account of himself sank almost completely into shadow. For the best part of a year, he said, he had 'roved about different parts of the country' with no other occupation than 'buying a few horses at one station and selling them at another.' Later, though, he would remember that he'd been in Arthur Orton's company, the pair of them crossing back and forth to Beechworth, on the northern side of the alps. There was a decided similarity between the Claimant's shady rovings and the operations of the horse and cattle thieves who were rife in eastern Victoria. They would cut fat cattle and horses from outlying herds and drive them to market on the other side of the mountains, using tracks 'only known to the outlaws of the waste, or their confederates the stock-riders in charge of rarely visited cattle-stations.' Arthur Orton would have known such tracks, and so, by the Claimant's account, would Tom Castro. And either would have been well placed at Dargo to play the part of confederate to one or more of the bandit-chiefs who plied the Great Dividing Range.

In the Claimant's time, the two captains of the local stock-thieving industry were Jack Paynter and Tom Toke. Both made their base at Omeo, the legitimate gateway through the mountains. Paynter was a butcher, formerly of Hobart, where his uncle George had employed Arthur Orton for a time. In his criminal capacity, Paynter was better known as Bogong Jack, and was talked of as a gentleman bushranger and a peerless bushman. Tom Toke, on the other hand, was an old lag of the blackest dye. A graduate of Port Arthur and Norfolk Island, he'd clocked up a dire record during his years of incarceration. Upon receiving his ticket-of-leave at the beginning of 1856, he answered an advertisement for stockriders on Mewburn Park station. Toke arrived in Gippsland shortly after Arthur Orton, but stayed almost no time on Johnson's station. The infant Omeo goldfield was more his kind of place.

At nearly fifty, Tom Toke was an old man by gold-rush standards. He was swarthy and thick-set, and barbed with scars and tattoos. Only his voice offset the impression of menace: some impediment made him speak with a gurgling lisp. Like Arthur Orton, he was London-born, literate, and the son of a butcher. But only Toke wore a platypus-skin hat.

Toke was the Claimant's likeliest connection with the 'business' side of the Vandemonian trail. In 1857–58, Toke was living on the Upper Livingstone Creek, twenty miles from Omeo in the direction of Dargo station. Ostensibly he was digging for gold, but really he made his living by pilfering stock. He knew tracks into the Wentworth and Upper Dargo rivers—country that could kill horse and man—and he knew a track that would bring him to Dargo station, or back, in less than two days. Toke's track to Dargo would be the means of linking the story of the Tichborne Claimant with one of Gippsland's most enduring legends: the disappearance of Ballarat Harry.

It was Sara Macalister who made the connection. Arthur Orton's explanation for his unauthorised return to Boisdale in July 1858, she told the Australian commission, had been that 'he could not stay alone at Dargo after the reported disappearance of a man named Ballarat Harry.'

Three weeks before Orton left Dargo, Tom Toke had been remanded at Omeo on suspicion of murder. Ballarat Harry had been a digging mate of Toke's on the Upper Livingstone Creek. He was a steady man, the sort who kept hold of his gold rather than drinking it. All up, he was said to have £300 in gold and sovereigns about him, besides a decent watch, a steel-grey mare, and a devoted Newfoundland bitch. In March 1858, Tom Toke invited Harry on a prospecting trip to a place he knew, away over on Glenmaggie Creek. Glenmaggie was only about twenty miles west of Boisdale station, but it was treacherous country: all tangled spurs and dead-end gullies and scrub too thick to ride in. And Harry was no bushman. Nonetheless, he agreed to go.

They set off from the Upper Livingstone on 17 March, Toke on his bay colt and Harry on his grey with the Newfoundland trailing behind. Within a day the dog returned without its master, and about three weeks later Toke was back, leading the grey mare, and with Harry's saddle slung off his own. Anyone who asked was told that Harry had decided to go his own way and, 'We parted remarkable good friends.' Toke set himself up as a storekeeper and people noticed him flashing around a swag of sovereigns and nuggets and a gold watch that looked like Harry's. When rumour firmed into suspicion, Toke was taken into custody.

On 17 June, the police magistrate at Omeo commenced hearing evidence into the disappearance of Ballarat Harry. Witnesses identified from amongst Toke's possessions Harry's watch and a gold nugget shaped like an eagle's head, to which the missing man had been particularly attached. Harry had sold him the prized nugget, Toke insisted, along with his horse, the watch, and others of his valuables. He and Harry had stopped in the hut on Dargo station for better than a fortnight on their way south, he said. Toke told the magistrate that 'During the time we were at Dargo we used to have a game of cards in the evenings, playing for pistols, whips, coats, carpet bag, with the storekeeper Philip Newton of Foster's station.'

There never was a Philip Newton at Dargo; but there was an Arthur Orton. And—call it a coincidence—he had received that letter with the broken seal just a few days before Toke and Harry happened by. They'd eventually continued south, said Toke, but at the Macalister River, just short of Glenmaggie, he and Harry had parted ways.

Evidence concerning Ballarat Harry's disappearance was heard over three and a half weeks. On 7 July 1858, the case was dismissed for lack of evidence. A year later, however, Toke would finger one of his own confederates for the murder of an Omeo gold buyer, and when a death sentence looked inevitable, the accused, William Armstrong, would tell the court a thing or two about the Crown's key witness. Toke had boasted to him, said Armstrong, of how he'd 'settled' Ballarat Harry:

> I asked him where. He told me down on a river right away the other side of Dargo. I asked him what he did with him. He said he had chopt him up almost in pound pieces and burnt him. I says, 'Then there's no fear of them finding him,' and he said, 'No, for I don't think I could find the place myself.'

But Armstrong's word would count for nothing. He was condemned to hang, while Toke swaggered free.

When his case reached court in London—at a safe distance from Tom Toke's last-known address—the Claimant would state unequivocally that Toke had murdered Harry and would admit that, yes, he and Toke had 'at one time' been on friendly terms. But to Mrs Macalister's assertion that Orton had fled Dargo upon learning of Harry's fate, the Claimant retorted, 'I know for a fact he knew nothing of the disappearance of Ballarat Harry until he came down to the Head Station Boisdale...he declined to *go back* again on account of the disappearance of Ballarat Harry.'

How did the Claimant *know for a fact* what Arthur Orton had known? And what should we make of the statement's substance? It seems pretty certain that Toke and Harry stayed at the Dargo hut on their outward journey. Not only did Toke himself say so, but a Bushy Park stockman told the Australian commission that he'd seen them there with Orton. Moreover, Toke had returned—alone—by way of Dargo. Orton must have wondered then (if he didn't already know) what had become of Harry.

Toke was detained for questioning on 12 June 1858. Arthur Orton left Dargo on 1 July. Had he heard? Toke told the Omeo police court six days later, 'I believe there has been word from Dargo that me and the said Harry was there.' It's a moot point whether it was fear of Toke or of being called as a witness that made Orton unwilling to return to Dargo. At Boisdale, however, Orton seems to have relished his reflected notoriety, boasting that he was surprised he hadn't been subpoenaed, since Ballarat Harry was last seen alive in his hut. And the idea took root. Ten years later—a hundred years later—people in Gippsland would still be saying 'that he and Toke had something to do with it.'

TWENTY-SIX
STILL AT LARGE

THREE days after the paddle steamer *Shandon* berthed at Queen's Wharf in Melbourne, Arthur Orton took a Union Line coach to Kilmore, forty miles up the Sydney Road. The fare must have beggared him: after a fortifier at the Red Lion, he walked the eighteen muddy miles to the Reedy Creek diggings. He arrived next day, 1 June 1859, and, as plain Arthur, landed himself a job before dinnertime.

That, at least, was the contention of the defendants in the Tichborne case, and the reason for a two-day sitting of the Australian commission at the bluestone Royal Hotel in Kilmore in the spring of 1869. It was almost a month since the last evidence was heard in Gippsland. Of the five witnesses to appear at Kilmore, not one came from the Claimant's side, since he swore that he'd never been near the place.

The Reedy Creek goldfield had been at its peak in June 1859, with three public houses and an unanchored population of close to two thousand. Rugged, steep and unwatered, boxed in on three sides by ranges, it would never amount to much as a goldfield.

The man testified to by the Reedy Creek witnesses had been employed from June to November by the butchering partnership of Soraghan and McManus. Patrick McManus still had the account book to prove it; although 'in the book he is only put down as Arthur' and McManus alone claimed any recollection of the name Orton. For five and a half months Arthur had lodged with McManus and his

wife, and had told them, McManus recalled, that he was a native of
Chile. 'He told me he bought some horses in Gipp's Land and they
turned out to be stolen; he said he was afraid there was a warrant out
for him.' One of the Reedy Creek witnesses recollected that Arthur
had sported a large beard. Or rather, 'as far as nature had given him
a beard it was allowed to grow'—making it sound rather like an attempt
at disguise.

After leaving McManus' employ about the end of November,
Arthur had been seen knocking around Reedy Creek for two or three
weeks—driving horses and carting, that kind of thing. His departure,
as McManus remembered it, followed the disappearance of a couple
of horses belonging to a storekeeper. A £10 reward having been posted,
Arthur declared with apparent certainty that the missing horses would
be found near Bendigo and set off in that direction. Nothing more
was heard of him, but eight days later the horses returned, seemingly
of their own accord.

Take a long last look as Arthur mounts the ridge. Orton or otherwise, that's the last we'll see of him for certain.

Just after New Year 1860, Tom Castro applied to Collie & Reid of
Bendigo for a job as a bullock driver. Their staple trade was in wholesale produce and provisions—stockfeed, flour, tea, spices—but they
also trafficked in labour (disgruntled diggers, in the main) for their
customers on the land. A farmer named Campbell was in need of a
man who could handle bullocks and make himself generally useful.
'Must be sober and steady' the advertisement had stipulated. Tom
Castro was that man—or the nearest approximation to be had at that
awkward time of year. He left Collie & Reid's with a fat roll of empty
feed bags and directions to Campbell's farm on the Campaspe, north
of Bendigo, where the river widened out on its run to the Murray.

Alexander Collie hadn't explained that those feed bags would be
Castro's bedding, and the new bullock driver wasn't impressed when

he found out. Moreover, the stock route to the Murray River port of Echuca and beyond to the Riverina ran close by Campbell's boundary. Castro would ride out to the dusted-up paddocks along the road's edge of an evening and smoke a reeky pipe with the Riverina stockmen bivouacked there on their way to market or back. After not many weeks at Campbell's, Tom Castro headed north on that road, going someplace.

The account of Castro at Campbell's farm would emerge almost thirty years after the Australian commission, but it works here to connect two bitten-off strands of the narrative. Evidence of the undoubted Tom Castro was first heard at Deniliquin, the commission's next stop after Kilmore.

On a map of New South Wales, Deniliquin—175 miles north of Melbourne and nearly three times as far inland from Sydney—looks a lot like the south end of the back end of nowhere. But already, in the 1860s, it was at the heart of one of the world's finest wool-growing districts, and was the funnel through which stock routes from all over the Riverina converged on their way south to the ravenous markets that fed Melbourne and the Victorian goldfields. Deniliquin was the *someplace* that Tom Castro came to when he followed the stock-trod road north. Passing out of Victoria when he crossed the Murray River at Echuca, he pushed on for another forty-five miles to this great confluence of stockmen and stockyards and jostlery.

The Australian commission heard evidence at Deniliquin's Royal Hotel from eight witnesses—four a side. In his original affidavit to Chancery, the Claimant had placed himself at Deniliquin for the whole of 1859. John Burrows, formerly a butcher at North Deniliquin, consulted his old shop-books and found that Tom Castro had been in his employ for eighteen months from 4 June 1860. He recollected, however, (as did others) that Castro had earlier worked for another butcher, Charles Lucas of South Deniliquin. The Claimant took this as corroboration for his 1859 arrival in the town, noting alongside

Burrows' evidence: 'I was with Lucas about 9 months' and 'Orton is traced to be at Kilmore till Decr 1859'—ergo, he could not be Arthur Orton.

John Burrows, it transpired, was the elder brother of Fred, the Claimant's supposed horse-breaking partner on Macleod's station in Gippsland. Yet no one questioned John Burrows about his brother's present whereabouts or friendship with the butcher Castro. In 1860, Fred had kept a public house at Deniliquin, dealing in horses, with his brother, on the side. According to one witness for the plaintiff, it was in Fred Burrows' company that Tom Castro had arrived in Deniliquin. 'This confirms my statement' the Claimant would note with satisfaction—about his having left Gippsland with Burrows in 1858, he meant. But in June 1858, when he ought still to have been horse-breaking in Gippsland, Fred Burrows, innkeeper, was marrying a lass at Conargo on Billabong Creek, fifteen miles out of Deniliquin.

Both John Burrows and Jane, his wife, remembered their employee as reserved—'a quiet inoffensive man with very little to say'—but with eyes that swivelled wildly if he got excited. Mrs said that Castro couldn't spot a heifer at twilight—she called it 'moonblindness'—while Mr stated just the opposite: 'he could skin a sheep at night without light as well as he could in the day.' (The Claimant would dismiss both notions as 'chaff'.) Besides butchering, he had broken in colts for Burrows and had performed his usual stunts with the lasso. 'He was a very good hand at it,' said Burrows, although he added that Castro had ridden 'more like a trooper than what we call a rough rider.' Jane Burrows scoffed at the idea. 'He used to swing his arms too much [and] his legs projected too far,' she said. 'We used to laugh at his riding.' Both saw Castro's likeness in the Claimant's Wagga photograph, however, and agreed that he'd been a big, raw-boned man who'd walked 'as if his feet were tender.' He'd alluded to travelling in 'Spanish America', they recalled, and sometimes had spoken in a foreign tongue. Moreover, like others of the Deniliquin witnesses, the Burrowses remarked on a certain 'pecularity of accent.' 'I don't know what countryman he was,' said Jane Burrows, 'but he was not English, Irish or Scotch.'

Evidence for the defence at Deniliquin was characterised by the use of 'Spanish America' for South America, which the Claimant's side took as a mark—like 'de Castro'—of John Mackenzie's infiltration. (The same term had been used by the partisan Macalisters of Boisdale.) It was at Deniliquin that the detective Mackenzie had struck his first public blow against the Claimant, when the local newspaper ran a report in August 1867 denouncing 'de Castro' as an impostor. The *Pastoral Times* had subsequently recanted, even quoting with approval the Claimant's retort that Mackenzie, not he, was the impostor: 'We can only say that we wrote according to the information supplied us by Mr Mackenzie, who alleged here that he was sent out by the Court of Chancery to gather evidence for both sides, and that he was therefore neutral.'

Neutral? The original report had composted the Claimant as 'a man of low cunning—a master of deception,' and his wife as 'a girl of very low habits and character.' Called to account by the commission, the editor of the *Pastoral Times* lamely defended his presentation of pernicious hearsay as fact. 'I am only putting it as a newspaper writer,' he said.

An old Deniliquin acquaintance, Cornelius Haxall, appeared as a witness for the Claimant. He had helped Tom Castro most evenings at the slaughteryard, shooting the cattle for him because, he said, 'he was nervous and apt to miss them.' The man described as reserved by other Deniliquin witnesses had been an open book to Cornelius Haxall. In their 'great many conversations,' Castro had given 'two or three contradictory histories' of himself, which Haxall took delight in outlining for the commission. One was markedly Tichbornish: that Castro's mother was a Spanish lady, that he had been an officer in the Guards, and that he'd been the sole survivor of a shipwreck off the coast of South America—'the thought struck him when he was wrecked what a good joke it would be to stay away some years, and go home and surprise his family.' Haxall recalled how Castro, when lathered with filth from the slaughteryard, had laughed: 'I'd look a pretty picture now to walk into my mother's parlor!' Another of the 'histories' that Haxall related had Castro as the nephew and apprentice of a Whitechapel butcher; in a third he was son of a South American army officer who had died at his side in battle. Asked by Alfred Wyatt, for the Claimant, if he'd ever remarked to Castro on the inconsistency of his tales, Haxall replied: 'Oh! yes, often, and when I did he would give me some other account of his life.' Haxall's evidence would be heavily annotated in the Claimant's hand: 'This is all concocted…I never said so…all imagination.'

Haxall offered as his *pièce de résistance* an account of a conversation that had taken place one evening, late in their acquaintance, when he'd found Castro looking 'cull':

> I asked him what was the matter. He said,—I was just thinking what a fool I am to remain here, and me a baronet in my own right. I asked him what title he gave himself, or what title may I give you, he said 'Sir Roger Tichborne'…He said that his father was dead, and that he did not like to go home and disturb his brother in possession, or some such words. He would sooner let them think he was dead, as they always had done, but that if anything were to happen to his brother he would go home and claim his own. He said that…all the other tales were a parcel of gammon…

This latest parcel came wrapped in a copy of the *Illustrated London News*, which, at Wyatt's prompting, Haxall recalled that Castro had been clasping at the time. Here the Claimant's side was plainly trying to link Castro's alleged outpouring with the publication in that journal of Sir James Tichborne's obituary. But their timing was out. Sir James had died in June 1862 so that the news would have reached Deniliquin, at the soonest, nine months after Castro was proven to have left the town.

The case for the plaintiff was perhaps better served by the evidence of James Fegan. A foot-constable formerly stationed at Deniliquin, he swore that he'd seen Castro perform the sword exercise—part of an army officer's drill—and had heard him boast of being heir to a property and that 'he would be able to help us all.' As far as Fegan knew, Castro had ignored his urging to see a solicitor about his inheritance. But the Claimant's London lawyers had learnt from a local informant that Tom Castro *had* taken a Deniliquin solicitor into his confidence. Thomas Robertson was the man in question, and John Holmes had duly sought particulars of his client's disclosure. Robertson had not deigned to reply, instead passing on Holmes' letter to the detective Mackenzie, who had at that time been rattling Deniliquin to see what fell out. Once Mackenzie moved on, Robertson took on the role of local agent, gathering and garnishing witnesses for the Tichborne defence. But, in a letter tendered to the commission, he admitted to a colleague, 'there was some truth in the statement as to Castro having boasted to me of his gentle blood (which he did after the close of a case in which I had prosecuted him unsuccessfully under the Cattle Stealing Prevention Act).'

Actually, the charge had been one of false pretences and was, in effect, a counter-charge laid by a man accused of illegally taking and using Castro's horse. Both charges concerned Goldie, a bay mare that Castro had bought from Jack Gibson in January 1861. Gibson had borrowed back Goldie in April and had failed to return her for seven months. When finally Castro regained possession, the mare had been branded *JG* on the near shoulder. Gibson contended that Goldie was still his property, since Castro had paid for her with a promissory note that had proved next to worthless. Supposedly it had entitled its bearer to claim £14 of Castro's wages from his employer; but when the note was presented to him, John Burrows had only £2 of his journeyman's funds in hand. After three months, Gibson had contrived to reclaim the mare, figuring that Castro had had his £2 worth of her.

The charges were heard in the Deniliquin District Court at the end of November 1861, with Thomas Robertson representing Gibson and Castro acting for himself. Both cases were dismissed and, though the judge singled out his conduct as 'very reprehensible,' Castro was granted possession of the mare on the condition that he give Gibson £1 a week until Goldie was paid for. That was on a Thursday. Five days later, he left John Burrows' employ and, in rather less than the twelve weeks it would have taken to clear his debt to Gibson, Tom Castro was gone from Deniliquin—cantering north on his waggle-arsed mare.

TWENTY-SEVEN

NECK-OR-NOTHING

SUMMER was not the best time of year to be crossing the Old Man Plain, seventy-five miles of saltbush and reedy cane grass stretching north from Deniliquin to Hay, on the Murrumbidgee River. Chances are that Castro had stayed on at Deniliquin for the 1862 New Year races and so had fallen in with Parramatta Jack Ward, a butchering jockey from Hay. In any case, it was to Hay and Ward's employ that Castro was headed when he pointed Goldie, slung about with water-bags, at the Old Man Plain.

Like Deniliquin, Hay was a town on the rise. Its situation on the bank of the broad Murrumbidgee made it a key junction and crossing-place for stock routes from the north and east. The flash-riding Parramatta Jack had his shop at the upper end of Lachlan Street, complete with piggery and stables and two sausage machines. Castro was employed by Ward in the usual capacity—slaughtering, shop-work, deliveries—but seems to have found more than the usual opportunities to show off in the saddle. To cultivate the rough-rider image he tried new barbate variations; but his moustache never amounted to much and the slender tuft of a Yankee beard looked shipwrecked at the bottom of his jowly face.

When he'd been about six months at Hay, Castro sought to make a hero of himself. Johnny, the son of Parramatta Jack and an Aboriginal woman, was wanted by the police, and Castro offered his services as a bounty hunter. Henry Shiell was police magistrate at Hay in 1862, and seven years later appeared as a witness at the Australian commission. The Claimant had written to him from London:

> You must remember me I am the party who went out and run
> the Black boy down who had committed an assault on a little
> child and who the police could not catch. You must remember
> making a promise to me with Sub Inspector O'Neal that if I
> went and caught him you would not summond me at the trial.

But Shiell claimed to remember neither the incident nor its protagonist. 'It is hardly possible I should have forgotten Castro if I had known him,' he told the commission. ('I lived within 50 yards of his house,' the Claimant would insist, '[and] used to see him nearly every day.') Moreover, Shiell said he knew nothing of Johnny Ward's capture: he'd been out of town at the time. The case book at the Hay police court was consulted. It showed that Johnny had been apprehended by Sub-Inspector O'Neill and that Tom Castro was not among the witnesses called. Either O'Neill had kept his word or the Claimant was lying.

The Claimant's letter to Shiell had continued: 'I am also the party who wrote the letters Mr Sinclair left in your charge in case I should die.' Before he went in pursuit of Johnny, he said, he'd deposited a package with Shiell's chief clerk, Charles Sinclair, to be opened in the event of his (Castro's) death. Inside had been letters to Sir James and Lady Tichborne, along with a note revealing his identity and asking Shiell to inform the Tichbornes of their son's fate. But upon his safe return, the Claimant said, he'd had trouble recovering his papers. 'I have no doubt you remember,' he wrote to Shiell, 'I had to write to Mr Robenson before you would give them up to me.' This 'Robenson' was the same Thomas Robertson of Deniliquin to whom Tom Castro had earlier confided his blue blood. He was also a friend and colleague of Shiell's. When he received the Claimant's letter in 1868, Shiell wrote to both Robertson and Sinclair, canvassing their recollection of events. 'I have not the faintest recollection of any one of the name of Castro leaving any letters in my charge or of my giving them over to you,' Sinclair replied, 'although the name appears to me as if I had heard it somewhere.' Robertson, then acting as an agent for the Tichborne defence, likewise claimed to know nothing of the affair. There was no one, it seemed, who could (or would) corroborate the Claimant's story.

With Parramatta Jack dead and many of Castro's acquaintances moved on, only three Hay witnesses were scheduled to give evidence at the Australian commission. Rather than take the caravan all the way to Hay for just one day's sitting, the commission fetched them down to Wagga and Deniliquin. Alexander MacDonald—a bushman, known to his friends as Mac—testified that he had known Arthur Orton in Hobart, but when they met again at Hay the Claimant had importuned him: 'Mac, don't say anything about it, I have changed my name. Call me Tom, Tom Castro.' Mac played to his audience. Shown the Claimant's Wagga portrait, he said: 'Ah! poor Tom, that's the same as he used to be in his bush dress.' Though a witness for the defence, Mac swore that Orton/Castro had 'told me even in Tasmania he was a baronet and a peer of the realm of Great Britain, he said his mother was a duchess and fasted on Lent, Ember days, and Vigils.' The Claimant's counsel, unimpressed, asked the witness how much brandy he had drunk that day. None, came the affronted reply—'but I have had three glasses of beer.' The Claimant himself would dismiss Mac's evidence with the remark: 'I don't know this man, and to the best of my knowledge I never did.'

He would say the same about another of the Hay witnesses, a bootmaker named James Anderson. 'I knew Thomas Castro,' Anderson told the commission, 'he was a fellow townsman of mine, a customer of mine, and he was courting a step-daughter of mine. He did not marry her,' he added. The courtship had ended with Castro's abrupt departure from Hay—something to do with an unpaid debt.

James Gormly said nothing to the commission, but years later Tom Castro would animate an entire chapter in his memoirs. As a mail contractor in the 1860s, Gormly ran a network of coaches and mail-riders across the Riverina, employing dozens of skilled drivers and horsemen. His business often took him to Hay where Castro would boast of his horsemanship and badger the contractor for a job. Castro's tenacity paid off. Visiting Hay late in 1862, Gormly offered him work in his 'paddock' at Wagga. He had some young horses that wanted breaking to the saddle. Castro grabbed the offer and within days was on his way to Wagga, upstream on the Murrumbidgee, 175 miles from Hay.

Gormly had visitors out at his place on Marshall's Point when Castro arrived, eager to start work in the breaking yard. The contractor picked the most vicious colt from the mob as Castro's first mount. Even with his gaucho-style saddle ('so huge,' jeered Gormly, 'that any man with ordinary practice could keep his seat'), Tom was thrown twice and was going back for a third rattling when Gormly jumped the fence and made short work of breaking the horse's spirit. 'That,' declared Gormly as he dismounted, 'is how an Australian can ride.'

The taunt evidently hit its mark, since Castro, hitherto proud of the fancy tricks he'd picked up in South America, began to claim that he was an Australian native, born near Sydney. The rough-riding reputation of native-born bushmen—the likes of Gormly and Castro's old friend Fred Burrows—was at that time on the ascendant, while 'Mexicans or those coming from any part of South America as riders were looked upon with contempt.' But Gormly thought enough of Castro's horsemanship to give him a job on the mail run—driving a two-horse gig on one of the minor routes, between Narrandera (midway between Hay and Wagga) and Boree Creek, to the south.

From November 1862, Castro made his base at Boree, sharing a tent with an Irishman by the name of Joe Madden. Twice a week Madden drove the mail from Hay to Boree, and Castro took it on from there to Narrandera, twenty-five miles up a red road sugar-dusted with quartz gravel. Like Gormly, Madden was nowhere in view when the Australian commission came calling, but three years later he would reminisce long and loud about 'my old friend Tichborne, with whom I have spent many a hard wet night.' Although a decade had passed, he remembered like yesterday their earnest conversations at Boree Creek. 'We were both together in this tent: the Claimant lay on a bunk reading a book, and I was mending a green hide halter, made fast to the doorpost, when I said to him, "I don't think, Tom, you are a native of this country."' And out it all had tumbled: his real name, title and prospects, the falling-out with his family, the shipwreck. Castro had owned a pewter brandy flask, said Madden, which each of them carried on his leg of the mail run. That same day, to signify the secret they shared, Castro had scratched his 'proper' name, Roger C. Tichborne, on one side of the flask and his assumed name, Tom Castro, on the other.

Madden recalled another name, a nickname, by which Castro had been known on the mail-run: Neck-or-Nothing—derived, he said, 'from a narrative of Castro's own, too long to write.'

Tom Castro rode the Boree–Narrandera mail for something like four months. He still had Goldie and he fancied her chances in the £1,000 Champion Race to be run at Wagga in March 1863. James Gormly called the mare 'a small weedy thing,' quite unfit for a man of Castro's bulk, and declared that 'he had no chance to win a race with such an animal'—an assessment evidently shared by the race stewards, since Goldie didn't get a run. Nevertheless, on the last afternoon of the three-day meeting, Castro was to be seen at the course, bragging that his mare could outrun any hack in the Riverina. Eventually his challenge found a taker and poor Goldie found herself matched against Sailor, a strong, wiry stallion, for a lap of the paddock. Castro's only stipulation was that both horses should carry the same weight and, when he taxed the scales at sixteen stone, the job of piloting Sailor fell to Charlie Buffrey, 'the biggest man in Wagga.' Even so, Goldie struggled home a good furlong behind.

Castro left Wagga just a few days after the race, and followed the Murrumbidgee eastward. In the middle of April he was at Adelong, heart of the mountainous Snowy River gold diggings and close to the northern end of the mountain chain that sweeps all the way to Boisdale in Gippsland. Adelong was past its gold-rush peak of three or four years earlier, still lively in character but more settled in appearance: which is to say that grog shanties had been replaced by public houses.

Edward Stidworthy, a blacksmith, produced at the Wagga sitting of the Australian commission a paper signed 'Tomas Castro' and dated 17 April 1863. It was a receipt for the sale of Goldie—whose full name, it turned out, was 'Gold-finder'. The two men had met at Riley's public house a few days before the Adelong races. Stidworthy had a colt entered for the Maiden Plate and Castro was eager to give Goldie another run. The blacksmith took one look at the 'weedy little mare' and laughed. But seeing that Castro was in earnest, Stidworthy implored him at least to get the poor animal shod first, 'as I could see she had not been shod for six months, and there were two or three inches of hoof to come off.' He did the job himself, for Goldie's sake (Castro being unable to pay), and two days later she ran in the Selling Stakes, winning her heat but finishing well back in the final field. Stidworthy bought her from Castro next day for £20.

The transaction was sealed over breakfast, the first Castro had eaten (he said) in three days. Between mouthfuls of lambs fry and strong tea, the name John Peisley came up. It was Castro who raised it, said Stidworthy—

> He meant by the name of Piesly a man who was a notorious bushranger, and was hanged. He said he and Piesly were mates at one time; he did not say in what way he was a mate, whether

it was bushranging or not...He spoke a great deal about Piesly, and seemed to know all about him.

Peisley had been hanged the previous year, after several seasons bailing up travellers and mail coaches all the way from Bathurst to the Victorian border. He had worked with some of the big names in bushranging—John Gilbert, Frank Gardiner—and, like Ned Kelly after him, had publicly defended himself against his supposed victimisation by the police. In September 1861, Peisley wrote boldly to the *Bathurst Free Press*:

> I am no doubt a desperado in the eyes of the law, but never, in no instance, did I ever used violence, nor did I ever use rudeness to any of the fair sex, and I must certainly be the Invisible Prince to commit one-tenth of what is laid to my charge.

He may have had a way with words, but Peisley was an ugly drunk and ended up shooting a man in a fight, for which crime he was hanged.

'I knew Johnny for years,' the Claimant told his lawyers. 'He was a native, and came from Stratford-on-Avon in Gippsland.' But the John Peisley who'd lived at Stratford, eight miles from Boisdale station, was a different man. Peisley the bushranger had been in Parramatta gaol, serving a five-year sentence for horse stealing, when Peisley of Stratford was listed as a voter in the Legislative Assembly elections of June 1856—the same period at which he had drained nobblers with the Claimant at Mrs Lane's Shakespeare Hotel. Whether or not Castro really believed that his old acquaintance and the 'celebrated' bushranger were the same man, the Peisley connection served as a standard in his blowhard repertoire during the latter years of his colonial career.

After breakfast in Adelong, Castro took a coach thirteen miles further up the Snowy Mountains road to the town of Tumut. There

he sank what remained of his £20 into a one-third share of an enterprise known as the London Butchery. His partners were brothers,
Phil and John Davis, about whom nothing is known beyond the fact
that Castro left them to face the music when the business went bad.

He cut loose from Tumut in October 1863, leaving debts left and
right, then took a coach south to Albury and proceeded to work his
way back in the direction of Wagga. In late November he was stock-
riding at Yarra Yarra station on Billabong Creek, halfway between
those two towns. Nothing would be known of Tom Castro's brief
career at Yarra Yarra were it not for the evidence of an itinerant 'photographic artist' named William Fearne. He'd been taking portraits at
Yarra Yarra when one of his horses went missing, the photographer
told the commission, and Tom Castro had found it for him. Fearne
had tendered five shillings as a reward, which Castro refused, instead
accepting the photographer's offer of a portrait. When he came that
evening for his sitting, Castro had explained that he wanted just a
single *carte-de-visite* portrait 'for his own use' and asked whether the
photograph could be processed while he waited, so that he might be
certain no additional copies were made.

> I said No. He then said he would not have it done as he did not
> want any chance of his portrait being about the country…he
> said, Mr Fearne, I will give you a reason why: my family at
> home hold position, and they believe that I am dead, and I have
> no wish for them to think otherwise. He remarked that very
> likely a number of the family's friends and connections were in
> the country, and my travelling with a portrait of his, it might
> be recognised by them.

It was agreed that Fearne would instead take a 'glass picture'—an
ambrotype, a single image on glass which could not be replicated. ('I
only kept this portrait a short time and then destroyed it,' the Claimant
would state upon reading Fearne's evidence. 'It was a bad one.')

Fearne had been intrigued by Castro's request, he said, and had doubted the truth of his explanation. In fact he'd rather suspected it was another kind of detection that Castro wished to avoid. 'The police make great use of the photographic portraits in the hands of photographers,' Fearne told the commission.

Castro was at Yarra Yarra until early in the new year of 1864. His next stop—his last as Tom Castro—would be Wagga Wagga.

TWENTY-EIGHT
I NEVER MADE SAUSAGES

Tom Castro was approaching his thirtieth birthday. He was unmarried, an incorrigible wanderer. But when he surfaced at Wagga early in 1864 there was a woman with him. Her name was Annie Hume, but at Wagga they'd remember her as Gentle Annie.

On Castro's second day in the town, Edward Stidworthy, Goldie's new owner, hailed him from the Prince of Wales' billiard room. 'He asked me,' Stidworthy recalled, 'if I knew where he could take his wife into a quiet family.' But the blacksmith was not to be deceived. 'I saw the person he called his wife,' he told the Australian commission. 'She was not his wife.' Harry Moxham, the retired circus clown who ran the Prince of Wales, wasn't particular about Annie's marital status: he hired her as a servant that very day.

They didn't stay together for long, Tom and Annie. According to Stidworthy, she left him. But she stayed on at Moxham's, which might explain why, in spite of its proximity to his own place of work, the Claimant would insist that 'I was not in the Prince of Wales 3 times whilst Moxham kept it.' Records show an Ann Hume marrying a William Gentle later the same year, so that Gentle Annie's nickname probably postdated her alliance with Tom Castro.

Among the myriad Tom Castro stories that John Mackenzie caught hold of when he was poking about at Wagga in 1867 was one that touched on some peculiarity—undefined—of Castro's 'sexual formation'. William Gibbes, the solicitor, told Mackenzie of Castro's relief at the birth of his daughter and how he waggled his little finger when asked why his mother would be surprised that he'd fathered a child. Since then, said Gibbes, he'd become aware that the Claimant's supposed malformation was 'a matter of public notoriety' in Wagga. Might there be anybody (Mackenzie must have asked) who could verify the matter? Gibbes (or somebody) must have suggested a name, for the Tichborne lawyers exhorted Mackenzie to obtain a statement from 'the girl Annie Hume': 'as to Castro's sexual formation…she could surely set that question entirely to rest one way or the other.' But Annie was long gone.

Tom Castro had found work in the butcher shop attached to Robert Higgins' Australian Hotel in Fitzmaurice Street. Opinion at the Wagga sitting of the Australian commission, as elsewhere, was divided as to Castro's skill as a butcher. Higgins, his former employer, called him 'a very good butcher,' as did Edward Smith, formerly an auctioneer in the town. Castro told Smith he'd learnt his trade in London, where he had 'cut up' for Newgate Market. Smith had relatives who were stall-keepers at Newgate and, to his delight, Castro recalled them well. 'It is a custom in the colonies,' Smith explained to the commission, 'when a person says he knows a certain place, to test him and see whether he knows it.' Castro, he said, had passed the test.

Others of the Wagga witnesses took a contrary view of Castro's butchering prowess. Yet there was general agreement that he'd been a first-rate sausage maker, an accolade which, in his annotations on the Wagga evidence, the Claimant firmly and insistently refuted. 'This is not true—never made sausages…I never was a small goods man or ever made sausages or black puddings…I deny that I made sausages.'

Evidently, he had given up trying to pass himself off as an Australian native. At Wagga he was either South American or, more often, London-born. William Beeson, a bootmaker, had bought hides from Castro. Born in Holborn, Beeson reckoned himself 'a judge of a cockney' and declared, 'I should take Castro to be one.' Another witness, John Perrin, felt sure that Castro was no London-trained butcher. At first, said Perrin, he'd claimed to be a Londoner, 'then he afterwards told me he belonged to Hampshire.' Calling himself a Londoner, he told Perrin that he'd suffered as a lad from St Vitus' Dance, 'and that it was a fright that gave it to him, and a fright that cured him. I asked him what fright, and he said when he got shipwrecked.' And Perrin and Beeson both heard him talk of having been an interpreter at the Mansion House in London. As a Hampshireman, Castro's story was that he'd fled England in disgrace after being swindled out of £1,600 by Johnny and Harry Broome ('the fighting men') in a game of cards at Brighton. It was true that Johnny Broome, one of the prize-fighting Broome brothers, had been gaoled in 1851 for a sensational card swindle at Brighton; but his victim was the son of a Herefordshire clergyman. This famous affair was undoubtedly the same 'card case at Brighton' cited by Castro as a point of identification ('things which can only be known to you and me') in his first letter to the Dowager Lady Tichborne.

These confidences of Castro's had sprung from an incident in which John Perrin asked him to witness a receipt in Walsh's butchery: 'he seemed to be flurried, and picked up the pen, and in witnessing the receipt he signed like an R.C. on the receipt, and smudged that out with his hand and signed Tom Castro, laughing as he did it.' Perrin was vague about dates, but Castro had kept the books at Walsh's shop only after he left Higgins' at the end of 1865. His conversion from Londoner to Hampshireman, then, had occurred in those teasing months leading up to his departure from Wagga, during which he'd been torn between keeping his 'real' identity a secret and shouting it down Gurwood Street. Even so, the commission had heard a good few witnesses swear that Castro had spoken of a shipwreck, his titled family and his prospects long before that notice appeared in the *Australasian* in August 1865.

Among the Claimant's opponents there were some who were beginning to think that Castro 'and his conspirators' had hatched their scheme of deception at the time of the Dowager's original notice in *The Times*, two years earlier—or even upon seeing Sir James' obituary in the *Illustrated London News* a year earlier still. It was true that Castro had never been out of range of the 'home' papers. Even riding the mails, newspapers would have formed part of his cargo. In the backblocks, a newspaper from home had extended currency, weathering repeated readings and passing from hand to hand. Since the news, when it arrived, was already on the stale side, a few months more didn't make much difference.

Owing to their suspicions, the defendants sought to ascertain the availability at Wagga, during Tom Castro's residency there, of those journals from which he might have gleaned information about the Tichborne family. The evidence of storekeeper William Love served up just what was required. At the arrival of every English mail, Love told the commission, Castro had come begging a loan of *The Times* or the *Illustrated London News*. 'I never borrowed the Times or Illustrated News or knew he took it in,' the Claimant would retort indignantly. 'I did not see 4 English Newspapers during the whole of the time I was in the Colony.'

The defence had to establish Castro's access to published material about the Tichborne family before August 1865, in order to counter evidence like that of the travelling photographer, William Fearne. Having settled himself for a longish stay at Wagga in July 1864, Fearne told the Australian commission, he'd met up again with that mysterious fellow from Yarra Yarra. Over the next five months they saw a lot of each other and Castro confided, among other things, that his family was 'about one of the most ancient Catholic families there is in England.' But that wasn't all. Fearne delivered a plot-thickener that would germinate speculation and tall stories for decades to come.

At the time of which Fearne was speaking—1864—Dan Morgan,

the bushranger, was abroad. His bushranging career had been at a
gallop since early in 1863, with hold-ups and outrages attributed to
him weekly or oftener. His bushranging operations were centred on
that part of the eastern Riverina bordered by Billabong Creek and
the Sydney road. Holding-up travellers kept him in cash, clothing
and trinkets, while raids on stations also yielded food, fresh horses,
and other necessaries. Having been a superlative stockman himself,
Morgan found favour with many station-workers who admired his
riding and his daring. But by the time Fearne and Castro met at
Wagga in July 1864, Dan Morgan had crossed from mere banditry
to outlawry. He was twice a murderer and had a £1,000 reward on
his head. The two men often talked of his exploits.

One evening, towards the end of the photographer's season at
Wagga—about November 1864, he thought it was—Castro had come
to his rooms, 'by appointment':

> The subject of conversation was Morgan again; that was what
> he wanted to see me about…He told me he had made up his
> mind to attempt to take Morgan. He said he had no hesitation
> in saying he could go direct to him, and he believed Morgan
> would have no suspicion of him, in consequence of having met
> him so many times camped on the Yarra Station. He said there
> was a little matter to consider before he went. He said,—I want
> to place some confidence in you…

Castro told Fearne about a packet that he always carried about him,
'whereby I should be recognised in case of my death':

> He said,—If I die by Morgan's hand what I have about me will
> be destroyed, or made away with, or never come to light…He
> said,—If you'll swear to return a packet to me in the same state
> as I give it you, if I return, I will carry out my idea. If by accident
> I should get killed, you can open the packet and get your instruc-
> tions what to do.

'With regard to the packet,' the Claimant would note alongside Fearne's evidence, 'I did the same to this witness as I had done to Sinclair [at Hay] and Gosford before I left home.'

For about a fortnight, said Fearne, Castro had continued to plan his pursuit of Morgan, seeing to the preparation of his horse 'and other matters.' He intended to inform the Wagga police magistrate before setting off; 'otherwise if the police met him armed he might get into a mess himself.' At the very last moment, though, six weeks before Christmas 1864, Castro was thrown by his horse at North Wagga. That's when he was laid up at the Black Swan Inn, convalescing and courting Mary Ann Bryant. By the time he mended, he was all but a family man and chasing Morgan was out of the question.

It's worth dwelling for a moment on the idea of a link between Tom Castro and that baddest of bushrangers, Dan Morgan. Castro told Fearne he could go straight to Morgan, and that the outlaw 'would have no suspicion of him, in consequence of having met him so many times camped on the Yarra Station.' Yarra Yarra was indeed a particular haunt of Morgan's and the station's owner, James McLaurin, a particular target. Once, Morgan bailed up the station wagonette, seizing a new coat intended for McLaurin and throwing his tattered one to the driver. 'Give that to old McLaurin,' he said, 'and tell him I'm coming for him soon.' He used to make free with McLaurin's horses, taking his pick of them and shooting the rest or driving them up into the hills. It was McLaurin who'd sent Castro out to find Fearne's horse, and both McLaurin's choice and Castro's success suggest that he'd carried out the same duty before. It's possible— even probable—that Morgan and Castro had met in the hills or about the station or in one of the inns that Morgan frequented on the Sydney road near by. Castro may well have been, if not exactly an associate, at least a sympathiser or a lackey of the quicksilver Morgan—much as Arthur Orton had been to Tom Toke of Omeo. A letter to the police from a prisoner seeking a share of the Morgan reward named several station-workers who had given shelter and assistance to the outlaw, among them a certain 'Long Tom'.

But whatever admiration Castro felt for the bushranger evaporated in June 1864 with the news of Morgan's outrage at Round Hill station, not far from Yarra Yarra. The overseer had been killed and another man, an acquaintance of Castro's, injured by gunfire. Elaborating on William Fearne's evidence, the Claimant would state: 'The reason why I formed an intention to go after Morgan was that at the Round Hill Station he had shot a friend of mine named Herriott—son of the owner of the Station—through the hand.' In fact, John Heriot was shot in the knee. The overseer, John McLean, was riding to fetch a doctor for Heriot when he was felled by Morgan's second bullet. Within a day or two of the shooting at Round Hill, a posse of local men were deputed special constables and set off in fruitless pursuit of Morgan. It was a Sergeant Maginnity who had the bad luck to meet the outlaw on the road. By way of greeting, Morgan shot him dead.

That was when the reward was posted for Morgan's capture. Four months later, Castro determined to join the hunt. Other adventurers had gone out alone, taking employment on the stations along Billabong Creek and waiting for Morgan to surface. One such fellow, posing as a stockrider, was indiscreet in the station hut one night—next day Morgan rode up and shot him in the groin, telling him, 'That's what I think of spies.' Reading of that grim encounter on his sick bed at the Black Swan, with romantic (or, at any rate, lustful) possibilities looming offstage left, Castro must have flinched. In a unique occurrence, the doctor who treated him after his fall billed Castro one guinea and received two.

Castro and Mary Ann were married the following January, an event which some of the Claimant's opponents would later point to as the sternest proof of his imposture. It was impossible, they said, that Roger Tichborne could ever have made such a marriage. They likewise took it as proof that Castro had not yet dreamt up his bold scheme. Even a rogue, they said, must have apprehended Mary Ann's unsuitability as a consort to any manner of gentleman. They pinpointed the genesis of Castro's imposture to the ten weeks between his marriage and 13 April 1865, on which date the following letter left Wagga addressed to Mr James Richardson of High Street, Wapping, London:

> Sir,—Although a perfect Stranger I take the liberty of addressing you and as my residence at present is in this distant Colony I trust you will pardon the intrusion and oblige me by granting the favor I seek.
>
> I believe there was some years ago living in your neighbourhood a man named *Orton*. To this man I wrote several letters none of which has been answered. The letters were of importance to Orton or his family and to no other so that I must conclude he has not received them as I am certain they would be answered—besides as the district is or lately was in a very disturbed state through a lawless set who styled themselves Bushrangers and who respected neither life nor property I concluded my letters perhaps fell into their hands—If *Orton* or his family live near you still or if you have or can give any information respecting them I shall for ever feel grateful. I beg to say here with pleasure that one of the most notorious of the Bushrangers has fallen by a *Rifle ball* and that on the news of his death and doings being properly chronicled I will send you the paper containing such.
>
> I trust you will not fail to oblige me by sending any information whatever respecting *Orton* or his son Arthur.—I am, Sir, your obedient servant, Thomas Castro.

What was Castro up to? The letter wasn't in his handwriting; according to the Claimant, it was written for him by a schoolmaster—whose name he'd forgotten but who 'was always in my office'—in order to determine the whereabouts of his old friend, Arthur Orton. But the schoolmaster, he said, had misunderstood his instructions, inquiring instead about Orton's father. Why hadn't Castro written the letter himself? 'I thought he would do it better than I,' was the Claimant's explanation although Castro, elsewhere, had shown that he was proud of his writing ability. Far more plausible is that he had not wanted his handwriting to be recognised. But why?

James Richardson had been Wapping's parish treasurer, a tailor and outfitter with a shop in the High Street, three doors up from the Ortons. But he was dead by 1865 and it was his brother David who took Tom Castro's letter down to the Ortons to ask what reply he should make. Old George Orton seemed to apprehend that it was his youngest son, not himself, about whom the writer was inquiring, and told Richardson that the last his family had heard of Arthur was a letter from Hobart, dated 9 June 1854. George Orton added that he'd be obliged if this Thomas Castro, should he see or hear from Arthur, would ask him to communicate with his family. On 15 July 1865, David Richardson duly replied to Castro. But the Claimant would deny ever receiving any such letter.

Tom Castro's letter to Wapping didn't figure in the inquiries by the Australian commission, as it hadn't yet come to light. David Richardson would hand it to the Claimant's opponents soon after-wards. Later, both sides would attempt to establish Castro's motive for sending it. His opponents believed that Castro—really Orton—had sought to satisfy himself, before launching his imposture, that his own family had given him up as dead. Moreover, they surmised, he had hoped to ascertain which of his relations were still living and might pose a threat to his scheme's success.

As for the letter's gleeful references to Dan Morgan, their significance was anybody's guess. Morgan had finally been cornered and killed just four days before the letter's date, at Peechelba station near Wangaratta in northern Victoria. Castro's jubilation at the outlaw's downfall comes as no surprise. But why should he have chosen that moment to seek out his old comrade, Arthur Orton? Or, supposing him to *be* Arthur Orton, why write home in so obscure a manner, after more than ten years' silence, trumpeting the news of a slain bushranger?

Arguably the chief significance of the letter's swaggerings over Morgan is that they were utterly characteristic of both the out-to-impress Tom Castro and the excitable Arthur Orton. Many interested in the Tichborne case, however, would infer that Castro or Orton or both had been in league with Dan Morgan. The Claimant, when questioned to that effect, would maintain that his letter to Richardson had been nothing more than an attempt to locate Arthur Orton; but for what reason, he refused to say.

One of the last witnesses to be heard at the Wagga sitting of the Australian commission was Pat Reardon, who'd joined Higgins' employ in April 1865—the same month the Richardson letter was sent. Reardon announced: 'I have a book,' and Exhibit P6 was produced.

It was a ready reckoner—a little book of tables for quick calculations in pounds, shillings and pence—that had been used in Higgins' shop. On one of the blank pages at the back , Tom Castro had twice written: *R.C.T., Hampshire, Eng.* 'I saw him write it,' said Reardon: 'He said—That's my name. I leave it to you to guess it…After he wrote the top R.C.T. he wrote something else and cut it off with his pocket-knife.' The vital question was: when had Castro written those *R.C.T.*s? Reardon stated, with apparent certainty, 'These words were written in the same month as I went to Higgins, that is in April 1865'— the same month he made Tom Castro's acquaintance.

Reardon was followed into the makeshift witness stand (a comfortable chair in a private room of the Commercial Hotel, Fitzmaurice Street) by William Hopwood. A butchering stockman by trade, Hopwood related a long and leery tale of having met Arthur Orton in Gippsland in the 1850s and again at Wagga in 1864. That second time, said Hopwood, Orton had been going by the name of Tom *de* Castro and had cautioned his old acquaintance not to mention that other name. The Tichborne defence made much of Hopwood as the crucial link between Orton of Gippsland and Castro of Wagga. But the Claimant, in his margin-notes, dismissed Hopwood's evidence as 'made up and garbled almost from beginning to end,' and the witness himself as a stranger to him.

Then came the testimony of the Claimant's former solicitor, William Gibbes. Mackenzie had scared Gibbes, threatening him with a charge of colluding in a fraud. Gibbes told the commission, 'I greatly feared that I had been victimized'—by the Claimant, he meant. Called now as a witness for the Claimant's side, he planted his words carefully, referring to his former client not as 'Sir Roger', but as 'the Claimant of the Tichborne baronetcy.' There was a pained, dignified aloofness that told you he was no longer the Claimant's man. The defence pelted him with questions about things he allegedly had told Mackenzie, to all of which he responded: 'I decline to answer that.' He didn't refuse: he *declined*. William Gibbes was that kind of man. Calling to mind the old adage about pots and kettles, the Claimant would note: 'This Witness Mr Gibbes was a man rather given to drink and not much to be depended upon for accuracy.'

When the counsel and commissioners gathered up their papers and vacated the room at the Commercial, there was one key player in the Wagga act who hadn't occupied the witness seat. In fact, Dick Slate's name hadn't even been mentioned, let alone hailed down the corridor.

From Wagga, the Australian commission headed to Sydney, just as the Claimant had done three years earlier. And, just like him, the commission made its headquarters at the Metropolitan Hotel in Castlereagh Street—the same hotel which the Claimant had once proposed to buy. Nothing startling or new emerged in evidence there. In fact there was little to distinguish witnesses for the defence from those for the plaintiff. All sounded equally peeved and recriminatory. Arthur Cubitt spoke bitterly of 'a person who called himself Roger Charles Tichborne.' Michael Guilfoyle, the former Tichborne Park gardener who'd sworn that the Claimant was the missing baronet ('I could swear to him as I could to my own child'), now swore to the contrary—and swore, moreover, that he had never been deceived. Andrew Bogle junior, whose father had accompanied the Claimant back to England, contradicted Guilfoyle's evidence but complained that the Claimant owed him £200. Also appearing for the Claimant's side was Stephen Butts, former landlord of the Metropolitan. He could muster no warmer description of his former celebrity resident than 'a person who passed in my hotel by the name of Sir Roger Tichborne.'

Truth Butts, the Claimant's erstwhile secretary, had only recently returned from England. Questioned about a visit to Guilfoyle's house in the Claimant's company, he recollected one or two incidents, before concluding: 'It is possible something else may have passed in that half hour which I do not now recollect, but.' Counsel and commissioners insisted on knowing what Truth Butts had meant by that terminal *but*:

Oh! 'but', that is nothing. The sentence was finished.

Will you swear that you did not intend to follow up that word 'but' by anything else?

Yes, I will swear I used the word 'but' without meaning anything by it…I am not in the habit of using the word 'but' without meaning anything by it. This is the sole occasion on which the word escaped me without meaning anything by it.

Except for that one exchange, the Sydney sitting was a bleak way to end the Australian commission. Six months, two weeks and four days it had taken, from Hobart to Sydney, from first witness to last.

It was 22 November 1869. Alfred Wyatt took a hot bath at his Pitt Street hotel. In his room down the hall, papers were piled high. The printed evidence would amount to just 179 pages. Now, thought Wyatt—his job done, his bathwater just right, his steamer ticket booked—let *them* see what they can make of it all.

PART THREE

TWENTY-NINE
NO WORRIES WHATEVER

THE Claimant's *them* no longer included John Holmes. He had quit the case ten months ago upon his client's returning, unrepentant, from his costly pleasure trip to South America. About that time, the end of January 1869, James Dobinson, solicitor for the Tichborne family, met Holmes in the street and asked if he was ready to admit that his client was an impostor. Holmes replied, 'Pretty well,' then added, with rather more heat, 'Whoever he is, he has behaved in a most heartless manner to me.'

Two weeks later, Holmes presided over a meeting at the Swan Inn, Alresford, at which the Claimant was confronted by others of his now-hostile supporters. They demanded that he explain—to their satisfaction, this time—not only his failure to appear at the Chilean commission, but certain other matters, such as his visit to Wapping on Christmas night 1866 and his naming acquaintances of Arthur Orton in the will he made at Wagga. The Claimant's explanations were rejected as 'deliberate untruths' and all those present resolved to withhold further support from him.

Returning to London, Holmes finalised his bill. It came to £5,711 18s. The voluminous 'bill of costs', itemising Holmes' services on the Claimant's behalf since 3 January 1867, read like a sustained indictment against him: *I urged upon you…you assured me…your defective memory…your dishonoured Bills…the great damage you were doing your case*. The final entry recorded that, following Holmes' departure from

Alresford, the Claimant had sought to placate his supporters by giving them 'certain information and explanation…with reference to Arthur Orton and the motives for concealing your true history abroad which you had never previously confided in any one.' And if he'd not exactly convinced them that he was telling the truth, he had at least under-mined their certainty that he was lying. He had lost Holmes and the money-lender Hingston, but held on, for now, to his key Hampshire supporters: Baigent, Bulpett, Rous, Dr Lipscombe and Colonel Lushington. Guildford Onslow and Harry Bloxam, who had the most money riding on him, had not flinched from their investment. Conferring with the Claimant prior to the tense Alresford meeting, Onslow noted that 'he looks and acts as though he has no worries whatever.'

Holmes' successor was Frederick Moojen of Southampton Street, Bloomsbury. Baigent, who'd been highly critical of Holmes, conceded after his first meeting with Moojen that Holmes was 'much the best of the two men.' Moojen, he said, 'talked very big and a lot of nonsense about the case.' Holmes refused to relinquish any papers or infor-mation until his bill was paid. He did, however, agree to meet with Moojen and was astounded to read the statement which the Claimant had made to his new solicitor. 'It was simply,' Holmes told a colleague, 'a narrative of what myself and my agents discovered respecting the Ship *Themis*, which he now believes to have conveyed him to Melbourne.' Moreover, Moojen considered the evidence from the Chilean commission 'quite favourable' to the Claimant's case—so much so, he said, that 'we cannot conceive there can be the slightest doubt as to success.' Holmes must have snorted at that.

The Chilean evidence, which arrived in England soon after the Claimant, had beaten the last nail in the coffin of Holmes' convic-tion. After reading it through, he concluded 'that no one but Arthur Orton could have written the letters you sent to the Castros, there-fore that you must be Arthur Orton.' He told the Claimant, 'It is monstrous you should put your opponents to the expence of at least £5,000 to execute the Australian Commission and if you had any sense of Justice left you should at once take steps to prevent so serious an outlay.' Holmes submitted his bill the next day.

Edward Rous, landlord of the Swan Inn, had been among the Claimant's first and staunchest supporters. But not any more. Several times he'd borne the blast of the Claimant's temper and, living in the same street, had seen him and his wife at their worst. The Claimant wrote to him in March, complaining that 'Hingston and them…they all go with Holmes, who is trying to do me all the injurie he can,' and condemning as 'scoundrels' and 'partisans' those who'd withdrawn their support. Rous forwarded that letter to Francis Baigent who, although he continued to believe—or not entirely to disbelieve—agreed it was 'very nasty indeed.'

In April, the Claimant moved house. Colonel Lushington, although ostensibly still a supporter, had ceased to be responsible for the Claimant's rent, servants and his wife's allowance. Worse, Lushington had announced his own intention to live abroad and to relinquish Tichborne House to Lady Teresa and her son, the infant heir, thereby ceding to the Claimant's 'enemies' the advantage of occupancy. Baigent called it 'the worst thing that could happen.' Harry Bloxam now took on the burden of housing the Claimant and his family, installing them as his neighbours in Harley Lodge, a big white house just off the Fulham Road, in the smart London suburb of West Brompton. Baigent was there to help them settle in, and he sketched the scene for Rous:

> That wife of his will never leave him alone…She keeps on at him and makes him grumble about a pair of missing pigeons while she herself was lamenting the breakage of either the bread pan or picklepan. I forget which. It was quite sickening to hear them go on harping at such trifles and caring nothing about the loss of friends and difficulties ensuing.

Shortly afterwards, Rous handed over to Dobinson & Geare, solicitors to the Tichborne estates, all the Claimant's letters to him. Opponents of the Claimant gloated about 'rats leaving a sinking vessel.'

Piecemeal accounts of the Australian commission made their way to England throughout the second half of 1869; when the evidence was collated and printed in early 1870, both sides declared it a triumph for their cause. From the Claimant's headquarters, Baigent wrote: 'The Orton theory has been scattered to the winds... The opposition does not have a leg left to stand on.' The opposition, in the person of Sir Pyers Mostyn, one of the trustees of the Tichborne estates, was perplexed by reports of jubilation on the Claimant's side. 'How the fellow can get over his own evidence which appears very conclusively to condemn him, I am at a loss to imagine.' Both sides continued to gather witnesses and evidence in preparation for the trial, due to commence later in 1870. In Australia, the Claimant's agents were still searching for Arthur Orton.

The Claimant was out of funds and hopelessly in debt. A year earlier his supporters had voted him an annual allowance of £1,400. Not only had he managed to (over)spend that amount, but he'd blown a further £5,000 in loans. In the event, he skirted bankruptcy for another year and, though he contested Holmes' bill in court, he was ordered to pay it.

Bloxam's stewardship seems to have done nothing to stem the Claimant's extravagant tastes, which, in 1870, ran to thirteen pints of Irish whiskey and 150 cigars 'of the largest size' each week. Twice a week or more he went fly-fishing or pigeon-shooting. He wrote to an acquaintance in March: 'I have been down at the Grounds to day and made the best score that been made by any one for some years. Killing 42 pigeons out of 53. Extraordinary. I killed 13 out of 14.

Tomorrow I have a match to shoot at Ilford.' Whilst effective, the Claimant's technique lacked finesse: he'd fire his second barrel, even if his first had killed the bird. That very next day at Ilford he was spotted by a Wapping man, Fred Whitbread, who was 'paralyzed' at recognising his old playmate, Arthur Orton, on the end of a shotgun. Later, in court, Whitbread would claim to have been besieged in the days that followed by calls from Robert Jury, Orton's brother-in-law, imploring him not to denounce the Claimant.

By and large, though, the Claimant's talent for killing small verte-brates and the bonhomie he exhibited at the shooting-grounds gained him a good deal of support. The influential Guildford Onslow had been won over to his cause upon observing, during a grouse hunt, that the Claimant exhibited the same hunting tics as Sir James Tichborne. And there was money in pigeon-shooting. Sometimes he was paid to appear at an exhibition match; other times he competed for—and often won—a prize of £100 or more.

But the odd cash prize was nowhere near enough to keep the Claimant in silk socks and whiskey *and* run his legal case. In April 1870, Bloxam and Moojen, the lawyer, conceived of a scheme that promised to put an end to the Claimant's money troubles. They drew up a legal document headed *Tichborne Estate Mortgage Debenture*, had the Claimant sign it, and printed 1,500 copies. These were the Tichborne bonds. Each bond entitled the holder to exact £100 from the Claimant within a month of his gaining possession of his estates. The issue price was £65, by which means it was proposed to raise £100,000 towards the cost of the Claimant's case. To begin with, the bonds were targeted at supporters and their acquaintances, but before long they were being hawked around public houses, market places, and amongst crowds at sporting events. They rarely sold at the full issue price, generally fetching only £20 or £30 each; but they did sell, all of them, raising the very welcome sum of £40,000 by the end of 1870.

Aside from being lucrative, the Tichborne bonds were a public

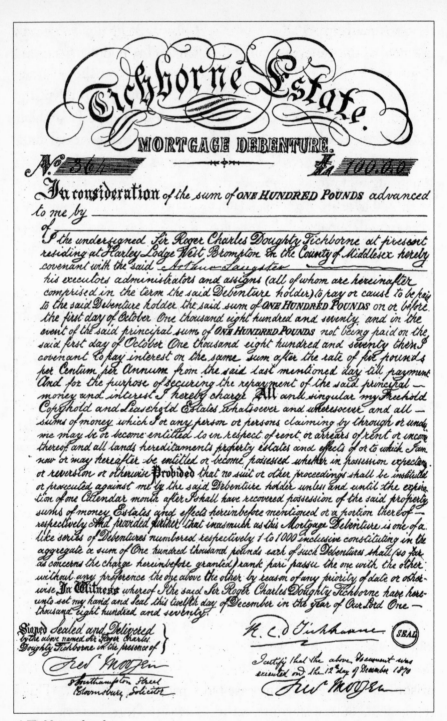

Tichborne Estate.

MORTGAGE DEBENTURE.

N°. 364   £ 100.0.0

In consideration of the sum of ONE HUNDRED POUNDS advanced to me by _____

of _____ I the undersigned Sir Roger Charles Doughty Tichborne at present residing at Harley Lodge West Brompton in the County of Middlesex hereby covenant with the said ~~Arthur Saugster~~ his executors administrators and assigns (all of whom are hereinafter comprised in the term the said Debenture holder) to pay or cause to be paid to the said Debenture holder the said sum of ONE HUNDRED POUNDS on or before the first day of October One thousand eight hundred and seventy and in the event of the said principal sum of ONE HUNDRED POUNDS not being paid on the said first day of October One thousand eight hundred and seventy then I covenant to pay interest on the same sum after the rate of five pounds per Centum per Annum from the said last mentioned day till payment And for the purpose of securing the repayment of the said principal money and interest I hereby charge All and singular my Freehold Copyhold and Leasehold Estates whatsoever and wheresoever and all sums of money which I or any person or persons claiming by through or under me may be or become entitled to in respect of rent or arrears of rent or income thereof and all lands hereditaments property estates and effects of or to which I am now or may hereafter be entitled or become possessed whether in possession expectancy or reversion or otherwise **Provided** that no suit or other proceedings shall be instituted or prosecuted against me by the said Debenture holder unless and until the expiration of one Calendar month after I shall have recovered possession of the said property sums of money Estates and effects hereinbefore mentioned or a portion thereof respectively And provided further that inasmuch as this Mortgage Debenture is one of a like series of Debentures numbered respectively 1 to 1000 inclusive constituting in the aggregate a sum of One hundred thousand pounds each of such Debentures shall (so far as concerns the charge hereinbefore granted) rank pari passu the one with the other without any preference the one above the other by reason of any priority of date or otherwise **In Witness** whereof I the said Sir Roger Charles Doughty Tichborne have hereunto set my hand and seal this twelfth day of December in the year of Our Lord One thousand eight hundred and seventy.

Signed Sealed and Delivered
by the above named Sir Roger Charles
Doughty Tichborne in the presence of

     Fred Moyer
     8 Southampton Street
     Bloomsbury, Solicitor

R. C. D. Tichborne   (SEAL)

I certify that the above Instrument was
executed on the 12th day of December 1870

     Fred Moyer

A Tichborne bond

relations masterpiece. By appealing to the sporting (i.e. gambling) instincts of the general public, the Claimant gained the dedicated support of a greater number and a more varied class of people than he could otherwise have hoped to reach. Throughout England and beyond, thousands now held a stake in the outcome of the Tichborne case. The country's legislative and propertied classes, however, were alarmed at this dangerous precedent. Such a scheme could enable any scoundrel to finance a bogus claim against another's possessions. At this point the Tichborne case may be said to have entered a new stage. Its progress became a matter of interest—and not a little disquiet—in circles extending far beyond its immediate complicitants.

Although the Tichborne bonds bore Frederick Moojen's signature, his connection with the case was severed almost before the ink was dry. The manner of his departure is unclear, but his £3,000 bill must have swallowed the initial income from the sale of bonds. (Perhaps he had proposed the scheme precisely to ensure that his bill would be paid.) In his place the Claimant's supporters retained Markham Spofforth, a partner with the firm of Baxter, Rose & Norton, in preparation for the trial which was scheduled to begin in November 1870. But the Prussian army's siege of Paris, late that year, prevented the departure of several witnesses for the defence, causing the trial's postponement until they were free to travel.

There had, during the foregoing year, been discussion on both sides as to whether a compromise of some sort might not be preferable to the 'exposure and scandal' of a public trial. The success and audacity of the Tichborne bonds put an end to such talk for good. During a period in 1869 when the Claimant had been beset by debtors, his opponents feared that he might either do a flit or find himself in prison, thus preventing the case from proceeding to trial. 'This I think would be a misfortune,' wrote Sir Pyers Mostyn:

272

for it would leave it open to the scoundrel's son to bring the question on again at some distant period when all the present important Witnesses have gone to another world. I should like to see Arthur Orton worried in the Witness Box…afterwards prosecuted for perjury then for forgery for which he would probably get 20 years penal servitude. This would be certain to scuttle the question for ever and I fear without some such record there would be a possibility, perhaps a probability, of its being reopened many years hence.

Perhaps, had he read Mostyn's words, the Claimant *would* have made himself scarce. As it was, in February 1871, waiting for the trial to begin and seeing no way out of the ordeal he had brought upon himself, he wrote to Guildford Onslow: 'Were it not for my friends and children I should like to die. I am so tired of this worry; besides, it is hardly worth while living in this world now, for I see nothing but law suits before me, even if the Case was settled, for years to come.'

THIRTY
THE ORDEAL HE HAS TO GO THROUGH

WHEN he took on the case, Markham Spofforth assured his client that the trial would last no more than four or five weeks. By the time the case was called, though, it was generally acknowledged that the trial's duration would be measured not in weeks, but months. Things got off to a bad start when, on the first day of sitting—Wednesday, 10 May 1871—only three jurors turned up amongst the crowd at the Court of Common Pleas, one of several law courts clustered within the ancient, hammer-beamed Westminster Hall, contiguous to the Houses of Parliament. A panel of twenty-four prospective jurors had been summoned: where were the rest? Sir William Bovill, Chief Justice of the Common Pleas, fumed and waited, then finally instructed that fresh summonses be issued and, further, invited journalists (of whom there were many in court) to make it known that recalcitrant jurors would be fined, progressively, £10, then £20, then £50 for each day they failed to appear.

At ten the next morning there were seven jurors in the court; two more arrived shortly after. None of them was happy to be there. The prospective jurors—professionals, businessmen, men of property—had been hand-picked as men capable of grasping the complexities of the case. But men of that sort little relished the prospect of serving on a jury for a prolonged period and for almost no recompense. At noon on the second day both sides were asked—and refused—to accept a jury of just nine. During the luncheon break, two more candidates

The Claimant during his long occupancy of the witness box

were hunted down. One presented a medical certificate, which was rejected; the other was a member of the Queen's Own Guard and protested that the Queen was expecting him to attend her the following day. The Chief Justice assured him that by serving on the Tichborne jury he *would* be attending the Queen. Whereupon a reluctant jury of eleven was hastily empanelled and the trial began.

As instigator of the case, the Claimant's (or plaintiff's) side was the first to present its evidence. His counsel, Serjeant Ballantine, promised to present eighty-five witnesses. With his wry, lugubrious face, Ballantine somehow looked just the right man to represent the Claimant. At their first meeting, he had observed that his client's manners were 'not those of a person who had ever moved in good society', but that nonetheless 'a great likeness was discoverable in him to many members of the Tichborne family.' The point at issue, Ballantine told the jury, was whether or not the Claimant was entitled to the Tichborne baronetcy and estates. But there was, he added, a second, 'subordinate' question: 'whether the gentleman whom I represent is in reality heir to the baronetcy.' Was Ballantine suggesting his client might be entitled to what he claimed and yet *not* be Roger Tichborne?

Ballantine, who was himself raised in Wapping, introduced the jury to the spectre of Arthur Orton, whom he characterised as 'a butcher, of the butcher type—the butcher type of Wapping.' Could such a type, he asked jurors, ever have contemplated a 'substitution' from butcher to baronet? Ballantine's speech occupied Thursday afternoon and half of Friday—a mere blink, in the scheme of things— and he ended by assuring the jury that 'Sir Roger Tichborne knows the punishment of detection in falsehood. He has no fear and no alarm; he has perfect self-confidence, and knows right well the ordeal he has to go through.'

The following Monday morning, before the trial began in earnest, the Chief Justice sought to clear up a few things. He and others involved in the trial had been inundated with requests for tickets of admission. No such tickets were necessary, he explained: the court was open to as many people as could squeeze in without overcrowding. But the present court, he conceded, was 'so inconveniently small' that the use of the larger Court of Queen's Bench had been granted for the duration of the trial. He had also found it necessary to request a staff of police 'to preserve the arrangements'—to control the crowds seeking entry to the court. From start to finish, Monday would be the gala day at the Tichborne trial. Not even the larger court could accommodate all who sought admission, though the Chief Justice would do his bit to increase the court's capacity by inviting acquaintances and dignitaries (including, on one occasion, the Prince and Princess of Wales) to sit beside him on the bench.

Thirty-four witnesses were called by Ballantine during the first fortnight of the trial. He took a roughly chronological approach, so that his first witnesses were those who'd known Roger Tichborne as a boy, followed by schoolmates, Carabineers, and so on. These witnesses all swore that Roger Tichborne and the Claimant were the same person. Under cross-examination, however, the basis for their certainty proved less than compelling. The evidence of John Moore, Roger's servant on the first leg of his South American journey, was an exception. Against all his expectations, and his fealty to the Tichbornes, Moore had recognised the Claimant as his old master. He had tested him on matters known only to himself and Roger. For instance, he'd drawn up a list of dogs' names: Juno, Spot, Bounce, Dash, Pie Crust, Jumper, Harkaway, Tear Coat, Tumbler and Carlo. Which, he asked the Claimant, was the name of Moore's 'elephant-skinned' dog at Santiago? The Claimant had correctly chosen Tear Coat. Moore further related that Roger Tichborne's mastery of French had already begun to slip on the voyage to South America. But Moore's evidence owed its potency to his initial scepticism and his links with the Tichborne family.

Anthony Biddulph, a Tichborne relation, likewise overcame a strong prejudice in favour of the infant heir to recognise the Claimant as his cousin. Admittedly Biddulph had met Roger just once, but, like Moore, he was won over by the Claimant's recalling things known only to the two of them, as well as by his resemblance to other stout-grown family members. Asked about the Claimant's inability to speak French, Biddulph replied that Roger's grasp of his native language had never been better than parrot-like. 'The more I see of him,' he declared, 'the more I am convinced he is my cousin.'

Several servants were called to the stand, including the saucy laundress from Upton, who testified as to Mister Roger's queerly patterned shirts and the Claimant's recollection of same. These witnesses, like the rest, attested to similarities between Roger's ears, eyebrows and turned-in knees and those of Serjeant Ballantine's client. Under cross-examination, they were quizzed about the colour of Roger's hair and whether it curled at his collar. Dr Lipscombe of Alresford had been the Tichborne family doctor and, shortly before Roger left for South America, had treated him for a chronic sore throat. Soon after the Claimant's arrival in Hampshire, Dr Lipscombe had been called to treat *him* for the same ailment. Casting an eye over his patient, the doctor had observed that his eyebrows twitched (just like Roger), that he walked with an 'in-knee' (just like Roger *and* his uncle Henry), and that he had scars high on his left arm, behind one ear, and on his right ankle (all just like Roger). But, Dr Lipscombe was asked in cross-examination, what about a tattoo?

Shortly before the Claimant's arrival in England, the doctor had been visited by the Tichborne family lawyer, Frederick Bowker, and had described his recollection of a tattoo on Roger's left arm. There had been his initials, RCT, and 'a ship or a mermaid, or some other device, over it.' His impression was that 'the person who did it must have been either a novice or drunk,' and Roger had admitted it was the work of a schoolfriend. Not long after making the Claimant's acquaintance, however, the doctor had told Bowker that he believed he'd been mistaken about Roger's tattoo; it must have been somebody else's left arm he had been thinking of. Now, to the defence counsel's question, Dr Lipscombe replied categorically that the Claimant bore no trace of a tattoo.

The doctor's evidence brought the trial to the end of its second week. Next morning, 30 May, the Chief Justice voiced the jury's request that 'at this advanced stage of the case' the Claimant be put in the witness box. It took less than five minutes for the star witness and Chief Justice Bovill to clash. Ballantine began with a question about his client's childhood in Paris, eliciting the reply: 'I remember that we lived in the Rue de Ferme.' The Chief Justice, to test the Claimant's knowledge of French, interrupted: 'Is it *du* or *de?*' The

Claimant spelt the preposition correctly, but was pulled up a minute later over his pronunciation of Rue des Pyramides. 'If you want me to hear your evidence you will pronounce more clearly,' commanded the Chief Justice, to which the Claimant retorted, 'I will pronounce it five hundred times if you wish.' Once more was enough for the Chief Justice; but then, for the amusement of those beside him on the bench, he asked 'Can you spell it?' 'I don't know that I can't spell it,' replied the Claimant with dignity, 'but I would prefer not to do it. I might make a mistake, and I don't wish to be laughed at.' And he called for a glass of water.

He weighed twenty-seven stone, but he refused a seat. He was hung-over and exhausted (he had difficulty sleeping), riddled with intestinal parasites, and suffering from cigar-smoker's chest and (probably) gonorrhoea. And, being hopelessly addicted, he was dying for a drink.

Again and again that first day, the Chief Justice, jurors, and defence counsel complained that they couldn't hear his evidence, that his voice trailed away at the end of sentences. Ballantine blamed the Claimant's bad chest, as well as the 'little difficulty' of the ill-fitting dentures which replaced his missing front teeth. In the course of the afternoon, the Claimant's seat (he had at last grown tired of standing) was moved about the courtroom—now closer the jury, now directly in front of the judge—in an effort to make him better heard. Proceedings were delayed next morning while a sounding-board was erected behind the witness box. Having nothing else to do but watch the carpenter at work, those in court were afforded 'extraordinary merriment' by the fact that the framework, before the board was mounted, somewhat resembled a gibbet.

By eleven o'clock on Friday morning, 2 June, the Claimant's examination was complete. In less than three days, his counsel had guided him through a halting narrative of his childhood, army career, travels and shipwreck, his life in Australia, and the progress of his claim to date. Now for the cross-examination. Sir John Coleridge was his interrogator, by default. Coleridge originally had been retained as the defendants' number two counsel, to assist the formidable criminal barrister, Henry Hawkins, QC. But when Gladstone's Whig government was elected in 1868 and Coleridge became Solicitor-General, he was promoted to leader in the Tichborne case, relegating Hawkins to the junior position. Hawkins could have spat, as indeed could the Tichborne trustees. Of the two, Hawkins was by far the more effective cross-examiner—deadly, in fact—and it had long been his boast that, had *he* cross-examined the Claimant at the Chancery hearing, the case would have gone no further. But Coleridge it was.

In a bantering exchange with the Bench a few days earlier, he had assured the Chief Justice that 'The cross-examination, my lord, will be rather disagreeable.' Coleridge's idea of disagreeable, however, was nothing like Hawkins'—more long-winded than lunging. Take the following specimen:

> Surely up to sixteen you can tell me what you learned in Paris. Did you ride?—Very little.
> Did you ride at all?—No, I don't think I did.
> Did you ride in Paris during the sixteen years you were there?—I might have done, but I don't recollect whether I did or not.
> Then you never crossed a horse in Paris?—Not to my recollection, but I might have done. No doubt I rode when there.
> Then what is your recollection?—To the best of my belief I did. No doubt I did.
> Did you ever learn to ride in Paris?—No, I learned at Tichborne.
> Did you ever go to school in Paris to learn to ride?—No, I did not go to any school to learn, but I might have gone to one for an hour or so.
> But did you go to one?—No, I can't recollect that I did.

> Surely you cannot forget whether you went to a large
> building week by week, or day by day, to learn to ride?—You
> have got my answer.
> You don't remember, then?—I don't remember.

Typical of Coleridge's flaccid style was his habit of prefacing questions with *Would you be surprised to hear…?*—to which the Claimant invariably replied, 'Nothing you can say, sir, would surprise me.' After three weeks, Coleridge had to concede a grudging regard for the Claimant's tenacity. 'A cleverer and more slippery scoundrel I never had to do with in all my life,' he confided to his diary. 'He will kill me before I do him.' What was more likely to kill Coleridge was his plan to call 253 witnesses.

The Claimant would later produce a scorecard of his performance in the witness box: 'I was 29 days under cross-examination, during which time I had 11,900 questions put to me, and…out of that number I answered 9,300 correctly.' Obviously he counted as correct an inability to remember. He was quizzed on particulars of his schooling at Stonyhurst College. Latin, Greek, geometry: all were a blank to him:

> What is the meaning of the letters A.M.D.G., that were put
> up in every room at Stonyhurst?—No, I cannot say. It don't
> flash across my memory just now.
> Is it a fact that those letters were printed in every book, and
> stood at the head of every exercise at Stonyhurst?—All I can
> say is that I don't remember it.
> Do they not mean, 'Ad Majorem Dei Gloriam'?—No doubt
> it does. The last two words are 'God's glory'. I don't know
> what the others mean.

The exposure of such ignorance Coleridge considered a triumph. However, former schoolfriends of Roger's—witnesses for the defence—would later betray the same lapses.

The years that followed Stonyhurst were less of a blur to the Claimant. He was able to tell the court a good deal about his time in the army. Questioned about his postings at Dublin and Cahir, he supplied precise details of landmarks and parade grounds and barracks:

> Where was the orderly room at Portobello [barracks]?—
> I don't think there was any room called the orderly room.
> Where was the business of the regiment done?—In the
> office. I suppose you call that the orderly room.
> Where was the office?—The fourth door from the right.
> Who used to go to the orderly room, or the office, as you
> call it?—The sergeant-major.

Yet, for all that, he couldn't distinguish between a squadron and a troop. And he had forgotten how to play chess and read music. He blamed his missing teeth for his inability to play the French horn, but stated that he could play 'almost any other instrument.'

Onlookers in court were often stunned by the Claimant's unvarnished ignorance of Roger Tichborne's early life. But looked at another way, the very brazenness of his not-knowing made it more plausible that he really was Roger. After all, he'd had six years to prepare for this trial; six years to refine and rehearse, and even invent, every single thing he might be asked about in court. There was no shortage of well-placed informants, loyal to his cause, who might have coached him until he was word perfect. But the Claimant brandished ignorance and knowledge as equally valid credentials. After all, hadn't he stated from the start that the shipwreck and hard living in the colonies had impaired his memory? His unpolished performance in the witness box might be seen as confirmation of the one thing he knew for certain: that he was Roger Tichborne.

One thing he professed to know was the contents of the sealed packet Roger had entrusted to Vincent Gosford in 1852. Questioned in court by his own counsel, the Claimant had declined to reveal the packet's contents, saying only that he had 'very strong reasons' for his silence. Serjeant Ballantine, being acquainted with the gist of the note locked up in the Bank of England—the Claimant's version of the sealed packet—did not press him. Coleridge, however, was not inclined to let the matter pass. After the Chancery hearing, at which the Claimant had likewise refused to be drawn about the sealed packet, he had, however, made an affidavit relating in cryptic terms the broad nature and circumstances of the document. Coleridge summarised: 'In your affidavit you say that…you sealed up and placed in the hands of Mr Vincent Gosford a sealed document written by you and relating to your cousin, Miss Katherine Doughty. You requested Gosford not to open it except in certain events, one of which you know has not happened, and the other you hope has not happened. What is the event which you say has not happened?'

The Claimant replied, 'I think it was my death.' The side of his face twitched like a telegraph. 'I feel sure of it.'

Then: 'What is the event you *hoped* had not happened?' The Claimant prevaricated and Coleridge repeated the question.

'I do not wish to answer it publicly,' said the Claimant, adding, 'It is not for my own sake I do not answer.' Again the question was repeated. 'You ought not to compel me,' the Claimant warned. 'It must be on your own head.'

Once more the question resounded: 'What is the event you hoped had not happened?'

'The confinement of my cousin.'

> Do you mean to swear before the Judge and jury that you seduced this lady?—I most solemnly to my God swear I did. (Sensation)
>
> This lady (pointing to Mrs Radcliffe, who sat by the side of her husband, immediately below counsel)?—Yes, that lady.

That '(Sensation)', noted by a reporter, signified the uproar in court. After Judge Bovill gavelled it down, Coleridge pressed on, gingerly drawing out the circumstances of the alleged seduction. It had occurred, the Claimant told the court, at the mill on the edge of Tichborne Park in July or August 1852, six months after he had been banished by his uncle, Sir Edward. When next he and Kattie met, in Tichborne village some two months later, she'd confided her fear that she was pregnant. With no hope of being allowed to marry his cousin, the Claimant explained, he had written a letter, sealed it well, and handed it to Vincent Gosford, directing that it be opened only in the event of his own death or Kattie's confinement. Here the court adjourned while the Claimant's lawyers produced the document that had been festering for four years in the Bank of England. Coleridge took hold of it and read:

> Cheriton, Nov. 1852
> If it be true that my cousin Kate Doughty should prove to be enceinte, you are to make all necessary arrangements for her going to Scotland, and you are to see that Upton is properly prepared for her until I return or she marries. You are to show great kindness to her, and let her have everything she requires. If she remains single until I come back, I will marry her.

Mrs Radcliffe—the former Katherine Doughty—sat just feet away. During the brief adjournment, her husband Percy had urged her to leave, but she shook off his solicitous hand and stayed put, still as glass, her face hidden by a veil. Coleridge had one last question for the Claimant: 'Did you leave this country in March 1853, uncertain whether the young cousin, whom, as you say, you had seduced, was about to have a child or not?' The Claimant replied, 'I never thought she was, myself.'

The court-day ended at four. It was now a quarter-to. Addressing the Bench, the Claimant said, 'I feel very exhausted now. I do not

feel capable of going on,' and Judge Bovill let him step down. Guildford Onslow would ever after relate how it was he who steered the
Claimant from the crowded courtroom that day. Once in his brougham,
said Onslow, the Claimant had collapsed in tears, sobbing, 'Now I
am disgraced forever!' And he was right. Thereafter, opposition to
the Claimant sharpened steeply in pitch and determination. From
being merely an uncouth adventurer, he was now condemned as
the most depraved of villains. Like wildfire, moral outrage tore
through the ranks of Radcliffes, Doughtys, Tichbornes and their
influential ilk. The packet was no longer sealed, but the Claimant's
fate was.

Even taking Onslow's account to be true, the Claimant can hardly
have grasped the enormity of what he'd done that day. And why?
Why ever had he done it? If he meant to punish Kattie and her mother,
Lady Doughty, for refusing to acknowledge him, then he'd grasped
the serpent by the wrong end. The story itself cast discredit on him,
the telling of it more so. His claim gained nothing by it. Yet, for some,
the Claimant's embrace of dishonour only confirmed his authenticity.
No impostor, they reasoned, would dare be so reckless with the good
name to which he aspired.

The crowd vying for admission next morning was more vast and
sharp-elbowed than ever. Once the last spectator had been jemmied
into the courtroom, the Chief Justice reiterated that he was in no
position to reserve seats or issue tickets. 'From the time I begin to
dress,' he lamented, 'to the time I go to bed I am made miserable by
the applications which are poured in on me, I may say by hundreds.'
The clamour of the shut-out crowds was felt too by *The Times* of
London. For a month now, that newspaper had devoted two long
columns each day to coverage of the Tichborne trial, and readers
wanted more. Only by printing a literal report of every word uttered
and document produced, *The Times* responded, might it give anything
like a fair notion of 'this extraordinary trial':

We might if we adopted this course fill at least one sheet of *The
Times* every day, and even then it is impossible to convey to our
readers a faint idea of the manner of the witness, the withering
sarcasm of the Solicitor-General, the tone of his voice, the
sensation in court, and the general effect of the proceedings.

Strained anticlimax was the 'general effect of the proceedings' on
the day after the sealed-packet revelation. As the morning wore on
and Coleridge nipped and bullied him for mundane particulars of
Roger's boyhood in Paris, the Claimant grew visibly distressed. Finally,
to Coleridge's barked command to 'Brush yourself up and tell me',
he replied—

> I feel that I am entirely incapable of giving evidence. I said so
> before I came into court, but I was told that the impression of
> the public would be bad if I did not come today. When I got
> up this morning I didn't know whether I was in my room or
> not, my head was so bad.

The judge then adjourned for an early lunch. An hour later, the
Claimant reappeared looking, if anything, worse. 'My head is very
light,' he pleaded, 'and I hardly know what I am saying.' It being a
Thursday, the judge thought it best to adjourn until the following
Monday, giving the Claimant—and all of them—three days' rest.

Chief Justice Bovill had been privy to a confidential medical report
submitted, during the luncheon break, by the Claimant's lawyers.
According to Dr Henry Johnstone of St George's Hospital, the
Claimant was suffering from pain in the bladder, feeble heartbeat,
tapeworm infestation and swelling of the penis and scrotum, 'a swelling
which is sequel no doubt of the severe attack to which I referred in my
certificate of the 3rd ultimo':

> What with his obesity and the condition of his heart, he obtains
> little natural sleep. He passes his nights propped up by pillows,

and unable even to take such rest as that for more than three or four hours. Nor is his state by day very much better. He cannot stand long, nor walk fast, on account of his excessive weight, nor can he sit long without much discomfort by reason of the pain in the region of the bladder and of the tendency to swelling of the scrotum. These infirmities are aggravated, and have perhaps been due to habits, the not unnatural fruit of a life of adventure and excitement.

He informs me that he is in the habit of partaking largely of stimulants, but that such excess never produces any intoxicating effect, but on the contrary, raises him from a state of depression to a condition that renders his intellect clear and precise.

Adjournments might be minimised, Dr Johnstone suggested, if his patient were permitted to take 'a certain amount of stimulus' during cross-examination, as well as regular breaks to relieve his bladder and rest his sluggish heart.

The Claimant was still in the witness box at the end of June. It was summer now and the ancient courtroom, packed to the pilasters, was hot and airless. Counsel for both sides complained to Judge Bovill of the pressure, from within the court and without, to get the thing finished. The jury had long ago surrendered to despair, and the Chief Justice himself conceded, 'I have felt exhausted and have suffered in my health from the bad atmosphere of this court.' It had been anticipated that the trial would be over by 10 July when Judge Bovill was due to hear a case in the Old Bailey. But there were more than three hundred witnesses yet to be sworn. It was agreed that the Tichborne trial would adjourn on Friday, 7 July, to resume in November upon His Lordship's completion of the spring circuit. Coleridge obligingly finished with the Claimant just as Big Ben pealed its brassy noon on the day of the adjournment.

The progress of the Tichborne case had convulsed the public imagination. On stage and in the street, Coleridge's flannel-boned *Would you be surprised to hear?* and the exclamatory *Just like Roger!* were the catchcries of the season. Besides its saturation coverage in the mainstream press, the case was the topic of countless broadsides, songs and pamphlets, most of them barracking for 'Jolly Sir Roger'. Among a certain class, his popularity had swelled immeasurably since he confessed to seducing his cousin. His rakish reputation, combined with his fondness for a joke and prowess in the manly arts of shooting, gambling and drinking, cast him in favourable contrast to the perceived dour rapacity of his opponents. Many were impressed, moreover, by the monolithic powers of endurance and steadfast talent for evasion he had demonstrated in the witness box.

To feed the public appetite for things Tichborne during the long break in proceedings, John Heywood of Manchester rushed into print a record of the trial so far, under the title of *The Tichborne Romance*. It sold in its thousands at railway kiosks up and down the country. Its author was rumoured to be William Heysham, a remote relative of the Tichbornes, who'd attended every one of the trial's first forty days and had been observed taking copious notes.

There's no saying exactly how the Claimant felt at the end of his ordeal. His supporters, loudly confident, did a fair amount of back-slapping and he seemed to go along with it. That was at the Waterloo Hotel in Jermyn Street, in a private suite that served as his supporters' clubhouse and where, for its proximity to the court, he passed most of his nights now. But once he was alone, and when he sat up drinking in the small hours of the night, it must have been relief that he felt the most. For though the thing wasn't over yet—not by a long chalk—for him it was. He'd done his utmost, hadn't he? Forty days in that stinkhole, twenty-nine in the witness box, baited and sneered at and disbelieved. Well, they could believe him or they could be damned, but they'd never get him back in that box.

There was a prize shoot at Epsom next day. The close season for trout had lately ended and grouse season soon would begin. Four whole months he'd got: all of summer and the best part of autumn. He reckoned he deserved a rest.

THIRTY-ONE
WHERE IS ARTHUR ORTON?

Over the course of the trial so far, Coleridge had strafed the court with the name of Arthur Orton. It can be taken as a mark of his success that the Chief Justice several times had addressed the Claimant as 'Mr Orton' instead of 'Sir Roger'. In cross-examining the Claimant, there was a good deal that Coleridge had sought to learn about Orton: not just what name he had used to render himself invisible, but how he and Tom Castro had fitted together. Step by step, Coleridge had drawn out a chronicle of their acquaintance:

> Have the goodness to tell me, as near as you can, the dates and places at which you have met Arthur Orton?—I think it was in the latter end of 1855 I first met him.
> Where?—At Boisdale.
> How long did you know him then?—…three days.
> When was the next?—About six months after…
> Where?—In Boisdale again.
> For how long?—Three weeks.

And so on. The gist of it was that Castro and Orton had met on and off, at Boisdale, Dargo and elsewhere in Gippsland, over the space of a couple of years. Then, meeting up at Stratford around the middle of 1858, they rode together to Omeo and remained in constant company for about eighteen months. ('He only left my company for a short time the whole time,' said the Claimant, probably to dissociate himself from the charge of horse stealing laid against Orton at Sale in May 1859.) The pair occupied themselves in 'crossing the country' between Gippsland and Beechworth, 'buying a few horses at one station and selling them at another.' They parted late in 1859 at Deniliquin whence Orton had continued northwards. Here the Claimant not only refuted the Australian commission evidence that placed Orton at Reedy Creek during the second half of 1859, but contradicted his own earlier assertion that *he* had been at Deniliquin for the whole of that year—an assertion which itself had relied on Orton's Reedy Creek sojourn as proof that Tom Castro of Deniliquin was a separate individual.

In the Claimant's latest account of his arrival at Deniliquin, it is possible to detect a clue to the manner in which the colonial Arthur Orton was 'constructed'. The Claimant had told the Chancery hearing, four years earlier, that it had been his horse-breaking partner, Fred Burrows, with whom he'd ridden to Omeo in mid-1858. Then, in evidence to the Australian commission, a witness had recalled Castro's arriving at Deniliquin in company with Burrows. The Claimant had noted in the margin, 'This confirms my statement,' meaning his state- ment about riding to *Omeo* with Burrows. From that point, he seems to have spliced the Omeo ride with the Deniliquin arrival, filling the gap with vague 'roving about' and transmogrifying Fred Burrows into Arthur Orton.

Some of his other encounters with Orton, as detailed by the Claimant in his testimony to the Common Pleas, appear also to have sprung from events described in the Australian commission evidence and elsewhere. For instance, two witnesses at the commission swore that they'd met Tom Castro at the Myer's Flat diggings, on the outskirts of Bendigo, early in 1858. He'd been selling horses, they said, in company with a man named Pearson, and the pair of them had stopped a few nights at Moorhead's Hotel. Until that evidence met his eye, the Claimant had never mentioned Myer's Flat; but a year later, under oath, he was able to recall, 'I was a short time at a place called Myer's Flat in 1858…Orton was with me there. There was a hotel in the place.' Similarly, by the time of the trial, the Claimant's side had a statement from Joe Madden, his hut-mate at Boree Creek. 'Once a man shorter than Castro came to the hut,' Madden recalled, 'and inquired for Castro and they recognised each other.' Madden now 'supposed' that the stranger must have been Arthur Orton. And sure enough the jury of eleven heard that, after parting at Deniliquin, Castro and Orton had next met at Boree Creek. Orton had come down from the Lachlan River, said the Claimant, and after a few days they had gone together to Wagga, then parted once more.

Apart from a brief meeting some months later, the Claimant said, he and Orton had not seen one another again until shortly before he left Wagga for good in 1866. It was Orton, he explained, who suggested the names of Captain Angell and John Jarvis as executors of the will he made to satisfy his Wagga creditors. By nominating strangers, he had thought to render the will invalid. Asked by Sir John Coleridge why he hadn't simply inserted the names of 'two persons out of the street', the Claimant replied, 'I should have put in your name if I had thought of it.' 'Then,' Coleridge rejoined, 'I should have declined the honour.'

'I saw him on two occasions—on the first occasion for three days, and on the second for four or five days…I saw him in the town and brought him home with me, and he stayed that night.' The exactness of the Claimant's latest account of his acquaintance with Orton suggests he wasn't describing a figment but a real, solid *somebody* besides himself. But there wasn't a reliable sighting of Orton and Castro together anywhere, ever. So who *was* the sporadic other of the Claimant's colonial narrative?

Not one person perhaps, but several grafted together—Fred Burrows and the diabolical Tom Toke among them. Toke was known to have visited Orton at Dargo, and the Claimant admitted to being acquainted with the wily blackguard. He and Toke had a friend in common at Bruthen, on the Omeo road: an old Mewburn Park hand who kept a store there. The Claimant, in a letter, recalled a time he was bushwacked on his way from Dargo to Bruthen—'which place I reached (Mickey the Frenchman's) in an exhausted state, after having been days without food or water.' Now, in court, he stated that he had once met Orton at Bruthen, whence they'd ridden back to Dargo together. But Tom Toke's appearance didn't much tally with the Claimant's description of Orton as tall, sharp-featured, long-faced, pock-marked and drill-eared.

And at Wagga—who of his acquaintance at that place might he have cast in the role of Orton? For a start there was Harry Osborne, whom he'd passed off as Orton to the gullible Jack Cater. Osborne had worked with Castro at Higgins' butchery, and Cater well remembered selling bread to the lanky butcher with the pock-marked face. Cater's corroboration had fallen in a ditch, however, when he'd admitted that he only had the Claimant's word that Osborne was really Orton. Cater must have misunderstood him, the Claimant had then demurred: Osborne was a different fellow altogether.

The Claimant now maintained that 'Alfred Smith' had been Orton's Wagga alias. Hadn't he directed a letter from Orton's sister to a person of that name? The Claimant even asserted that he himself had written to Smith, via their mutual friend Joseph Robins, the Wagga wheelwright. Robins, at the Australian commission, denied having received the letter or knowing any such person as Alfred Smith.

The most obvious candidate for Orton's Wagga incarnation was the man who'd put the Dowager Lady Tichborne's notice under Tom Castro's nose in the first place—Dick Slate. Suitably itinerant, he had driven stock for Robert Higgins on at least one occasion, and was avowed by the Claimant 'a very great friend.' And, like Orton, Slate was something of a shape-shifter. His fittest qualification for the role was that he was nowhere to be found. But then, nobody seems to have looked very hard.

Arthur Orton, on the other hand, had been hunted for high and low. 'Are you yourself Arthur Orton?' Coleridge demanded, on his eleventh day cross-examining the Claimant. 'I am not,' came the calm reply. Asked by Coleridge, though, whether he had ever taken any name other than Tichborne and Castro, the Claimant made the interesting reply that, when he worked on Yarra Yarra station, he'd called himself Morgan.

> What made you drop Castro and take Morgan?—I decline to answer the question.
> Why?—Because it might have a tendency to criminate myself.
> The Chief-Justice: Do you mean in the sense that it would render you liable to a criminal prosecution?
> The Claimant: Yes, my lord.

At that, the tempo of Coleridge's interrogation quickened.

> Was Arthur Orton in the same place as you were when you changed your name from Castro to Morgan?—He was, just previous.
> Was Arthur Orton accused of any crime at that time?—He was.
> Of what?—Bushranging...
> Were you charged with the same crime that Arthur Orton was charged with?—I decline to answer that question.

What could have possessed the Claimant to take the red-hot name of Morgan at *that* time and place? In court he was evasive, merely saying, 'It was the first that came.' Coleridge asked then about the real Morgan, Dan Morgan, the bushranger.

> Did you ever meet with him?—Yes.
> When?—On several occasions.

In the bush?—Yes.

Ranging?—Well, he was in the bush.

Where was this leading? Sir John Coleridge had an idea. In sending immediate news of Dan Morgan's death to James Richardson, a friend of the Ortons at Wapping, had the Claimant meant to imply that the notorious bushranger who had fallen by a rifle ball had been Orton? The Claimant denied it; but he'd led Coleridge down this track for a reason.

Having already acknowledged that Orton had been accused of horse stealing in 1859, he now stated that *he* had been charged at the same time. But it wasn't the horse at Sale he was talking about. The charges had been heard, he said, at the police court in the goldfield town of Castlemaine, south of Bendigo. He'd been charged in the name of Castro, Orton under his own name, and their accuser had been a gold digger called Burgess. 'I may as well say,' he added, 'that we proved them to be our own horses, and we got discharged,' so that clearly this was not the incident from which he feared incrimination. Even so, ears pricked up in the bewigged portion of the courtroom. Charges laid, a court hearing—that meant there must be records.

Francis Jeune and Henry Purcell sailed for Melbourne within a fortnight of the Tichborne trial's adjournment in July 1871. Jeune was a lawyer for the Claimant's side, Purcell for his opponents. Both were charged 'to advise on evidence and clear up certain matters.' By the time they arrived at Melbourne, local agents had already searched the police charge books at Castlemaine for the horse stealing case of 1859, with no result. Purcell himself spent a couple of days up at Castlemaine, scouring the charge books from 1858–60 without turning up a trace of Castro or Orton. He applied to remove the books to England as evidence. The local court was willing, but the Victorian solicitor-general withheld permission; his decision was overturned by the premier, who in turn was overruled by parliament. Purcell had to settle, in the end, for a certified copy of the charge books.

Francis Jeune, the Claimant's man, disembarked in Melbourne to the news that, although the Castlemaine records had proved fruitless, an eyewitness to Orton and Castro's day in court had come forward. William Lock claimed to have been serving as a detective at Castlemaine in 1859 and expressed himself not in the least surprised that there was no record of the pair's trial, given 'the loose way things were done there in the excitement of the times.' But by 1859, goldrush towns like Castlemaine were soundly run and regulated. That horse stealing charges were treated anything but loosely can be seen in the *Mount Alexander Mail*'s coverage of the local police court, which devoted many more column inches to accused horse thieves—on the rare occasions they faced court—than to the usual cast of drunks and street brawlers.

Nonetheless, Jeune and the Claimant's Australian lawyers seized on Lock's explanation and sought further eyewitnesses to the trial. A dozen or more came forward, of whom several vied for the honour of having owned the horses allegedly stolen by Castro and Orton. At least two men claimed to be the Burgess named in evidence by the Claimant, causing the *Melbourne Leader* to remark that 'Burgess, after a bit, will be as difficult of identification as Tichborne.' But the most vivid account of the phantasmal trial emerged not in the colonies but in the seaside town of Eastbourne where 'Professor' Anderson ('The Great Wizard') was resident for the season, performing 'feats of prestidigitation and marvels of mechanical science.' The Great Wizard had himself been in Castlemaine in July 1859, for a two-week season at the Theatre Royal. At a loose end one wet afternoon, he had stepped into the courthouse where the trial of Castro and Orton was in progress. Duly acquitted, they had repaired in high spirits to the professor's digs, the Supreme Court Hotel on the corner opposite.

The showman's last performance had been scheduled for the following evening, the 22nd, but he'd mislaid the whip he always used in his grand finale, a scene from *Rob Roy*. Hearing of this, Castro had insisted that the professor accept as a gift the fine-looking whip slung round his swag.

'And I have it still!' announced Professor Anderson twelve years later. Ever the showman, he simultaneously leapt to his feet and reached inside his coat, producing his trophy with a flourish. This took place in the London offices of Baxter, Rose & Norton, but Spofforth, the Claimant's solicitor, barely blinked as the skirling lash winged a light fixture. Nothing surprised him anymore. He examined the whip handle minutely, however, for any mark that might identify it with his client. 'I was in the habit of writing my initials everywhere,' the Claimant had said of his years in the colonies. But no such luck. And the old necromancer shook his head when Spofforth showed him a recent photograph of the Claimant, clean-shaven and primly garbed. Taking up a pen, though, he inked in a moustache and heavy beard, then added a broad-brimmed hat and a dark, muffly coat. Now *that*, he pronounced, was Tom Castro.

As for Arthur Orton, during the years when evidence fixed him firmly in Hobart or Gippsland, he had been promiscuously sighted (according to witness statements now forthcoming) all over Melbourne, at the McIvor diggings in company with a one-eyed man named Blind Geordie, as a suspected murderer on the Avoca diggings, sporting a 'light amber' goatee at Myrtleford, carousing with the bushranger Harry Power at an inn on the Murray River, dead in the snow on his way to Omeo, and ditto with a bullet through his brain at King William Gully, Daylesford. Roger Tichborne, since his disappearance at sea, had been spotted buying cigars in Sydney, posing as a mineralogist on the Rokewood diggings, camped out on the Mount Alexander road, trying on a truss in a Beechworth chemist's shop, stockriding near Wangaratta, and near starvation at Ballarat. In the fat sheaf of half-baked apocrypha that made Francis Jeune's eyes and valise bulge were plot lines enough for a dozen novels, but nothing that added a wafer of substance to the Claimant's case.

Henry Purcell had better fortune. He retraced the Claimant's purported steps to Bendigo and thence via Echuca to Deniliquin and Hay. There he was approached by Charley Cox, publican of the Caledonian Hotel—formerly of the Squatter's Hotel at Wagga, a watering-hole of Tom Castro's. Cox had in his possession a pocket-book which he claimed to have found in Fitzmaurice Street about the time that Castro left Wagga. Like the book earlier produced by Pat Reardon, this one was full of scribble, most of it scrappy memoranda of accounts and meat orders. But amongst the scribble was much to interest parties concerned with the Tichborne trial—particularly the Claimant's opponents. Inside the cover, for instance, was the dual inscription:

> Tomas Castro, Wagga-Wagga
> Roger Charles Tichborne, Tichborne Hall, Surrey, London

Other entries in the pocket-book included these:

> Melipilla, South Amerika, Rio de Janeiro, Rio de la Plata, Buenos Ayres, La Bella

> La Bella, R.C.T. arrived Hobart Town July 4, 1854

> Lost 13 Septr. This day in Wagga-Wagga. Those That found it Are Welcome to keep it Two cases in the Small Debt Court. One of 6 pound and one for three pound sixteen shillings.

> Some men has plenty money and no brains. And some men has plenty brains and no Money Surely Men with plenty Money and no brains were Made for Men with plenty brains and no Money.

> Sir James Tichborne, R.C. Tichborne, Bart., Some day I hope.

Tichborne Hall, Newmarket, London

Richard Nevill Slate, Tomas Castro, Rodger Charles Tichborne

Stephen Butts Metrop.

I Tomas Castro Do hereby certify my Name is not Tomas Castro at all. Therefore those say it is, dont know any think about it. R.C.T.

There were, in addition, a sketch of a three-masted ship and a crude portrait in profile with *R.C.T. Bart.* beneath it and the name *Richard Nevill Slate* repeated on the same page. On the last page was this: *Miss Mary Ann Loder, 7 Russells Buildings, High-street, Wapping, London,* and what looked like the words *Own Dear Fair one.*

The pocket-book contained a calendar for the year 1860, but the final entry was dated 4 June 1866—two days after the Claimant reckoned he'd departed Wagga. Purcell was able to verify that 'Lost 13 Sept[r]...Two cases in the Small Debt Court' referred to actions brought against Tom Castro in 1865, suggesting that the wishful 'R.C. Tichborne, Bart. Some day I hope', further on in the book and dated December, was written that same year. *La Bella* was the name given to the missing ship in the Dowager's advertisement; it ought to have been plain *Bella.* As for *R.C.T. arrived Hobart July 4, 1854*—who could say?

The pocket-book's contents appeared to be written in two or more different hands, and the Claimant's side would allege that parts of it were 'the rude work of some detective.' Joseph Shaw, the Claimant's inquiry agent at Tumut, warned, 'that if it is not altogether a *forgery* it has most certainly been *tampered* with. We have kept a true copy of that book, and it has been carefully photographed page by page.' A copy had been made by Tom Castro's Wagga solicitor, William Gibbes, to whom Cox had first shown the book. When called on later to state which of the contents were in Castro's handwriting, Gibbes would declare himself 'not sure' of perhaps half—the more damaging half.

Cox had declined to show his face, or his book, at the Australian commission because the hearing had been held at a rival hotel. Now he was asking £1,000 for the book. He had offered it first to the Claimant's side, but they refused to meet his price. Purcell too baulked, but agreed that the Tichborne defence would pay for Cox to convey the pocket-book to London in person. Departing Melbourne by mail steamer at the end of October, the man they called 'Pocket-book' Cox was cock-a-hoop, declaring that the book and his evidence would decide the Tichborne case. But the Claimant's friend Joe Madden of Hay predicted, 'I don't think it will terminate in a very judicious trip for him.'

From the Riverina, Purcell proceeded to Sydney, then sailed back to Melbourne and paid a flying visit to Gippsland before boarding a steamer that would see him back in London by Christmas. A week or two ahead of him, Jeune had pursued his own inquiries along a similar trail, stopping also at Tumut, where he was apprised of a fresh and promising lead in the search for Alfred Smith. Joseph Shaw—the Claimant's man at Tumut—had been talking with Pat Reardon, Tom Castro's one-time offsider at Wagga, now butchering at Tumut. Having read the Claimant's own evidence as to Orton's Wagga persona, Reardon found himself persuaded that he recalled Alfred Smith:

> shortly before Tom Castro left Wagga Wagga a man came there who knew him, and was much with him. He wore a peculiar leather coat…Smith stopped at Castro's place…he was helping Castro to smoke some beef for the journey…For two days before Castro left the two were inseparable, walking the town together…

He told his tale to Shaw, who 'with much trouble and letter-writing…traced this man, Alfred Smith's history' and welcomed Jeune to Tumut with the words: '*I found him.*'

The man he had found was an inmate of the lunatic asylum at Gladesville in Sydney, and his name was William Cresswell. Cresswell had been a familiar figure around Tumut until recently, and a 'peculiar leather vest' had been listed among his effects on admission to Gladesville. He'd arrived there from Darlinghurst gaol with a letter setting out the 'particulars as to his insanity': namely, 'that he was continually writing extravagant letters to Lord Belmore, talked nonsense, and was very violent and abusive.' At the end of August 1871, Dr Manning at Gladesville had commenced Cresswell's file with the following observations: 'He constantly asserts that he has considerable property rightfully belonging to him in England…but it is difficult to separate the wheat from the chaff of his conversation, or to ascertain exactly what is delusion.'

It was also rumoured that the new inmate had stated his real name was Arthur Orton. A paragraph to that effect appeared in the *Goulburn Herald* in September, following which 'the lunatic Cresswell' was examined by a succession of lawyers connected with the Tichborne case. 'His *writing* is very unlike,' conceded a rueful Joseph Shaw, 'his history does not coincide with Orton's, neither do the marks upon his person.' All Cresswell's visitors reached the same conclusion: that he was not Arthur Orton. In fact, 'quite rational' now, he told them so himself. But he had known Tom Castro well, he said; the pair of them had been together as far back as Boisdale.

Cresswell, it appears, was at least as calculating as he was deluded in the statements he made. There *was* some property in his home county of Hampshire—part of the late Duke of Wellington's Strathfieldsaye estate—to which he believed himself entitled, and doubtless he saw his implication in the Tichborne case as a chance to advance his own claim.

The Claimant's side obtained letters of Cresswell's that showed a close familiarity with the Riverina, Wagga in particular, and with many figures—publicans, storekeepers, squatters—who were likewise known to Castro. But the likelihood of a glancing association between the pair brought Francis Jeune no closer to finding Arthur Orton. The most he could salvage from the Cresswell episode was the word of a lunatic that Tom Castro *had* been in Gippsland.

Purcell, on the other hand, had not only secured Pocket-book Cox and the Castlemaine court records, but was able to report that his search of the colonies for Orton or Alfred Smith had yielded 'not the trace of either.'

THIRTY-TWO

AND HAST THOU SLAIN THE WAGGAWOCK?

CHEERS greeted the Claimant outside Westminster Hall on 7 November 1871. Since the middle of that year, Claimant-spotting had been the fashionable sport of London wags. One sighting that could always be relied upon was his effigy in wax, newly installed at Madame Tussaud's, dressed in clothing from the Claimant's own wardrobe.

That Tuesday morning, a bigger-than-Monday crowd clamoured outside the court for the resumption of the best show in town. Chief Justice Bovill, though still not issuing tickets, made room at the bench for the American ambassador and the Emperor of Brazil. The Claimant looked well, it was generally agreed; the more so considering his poor state of health at the time of the adjournment. Several observers remarked that his hair appeared to be growing darker as the trial progressed. Some believed that, with the aid of the cosmetician Madame Rachel, he was cultivating a head of hair more like Roger Tichborne's.

It was acknowledged, that first day back in court, that the trial would not be finished by Christmas and might well drag on until Easter, nearly five months hence. 'Some elderly persons,' if you believed the *Illustrated London News*, 'have now resigned themselves to die before knowing the verdict.' There were fifty witnesses yet to give evidence for the Claimant's side and more than five times that number for the defence.

As things stood, it looked as if the expense of the marathon trial would defeat the Claimant long ahead of any verdict. Before calling witnesses, Serjeant Ballantine informed the court that his client could no longer afford to pay half the weekly cost—£700—of taking short-hand notes of the proceedings. Sir John Coleridge accused his learned friend of shedding crocodile tears, pointing to the Claimant's brougham and livery as clear evidence of his solvency. The judge was equally scornful: he'd heard that the plaintiff had recently paid two hundred guineas for a horse. Besides, he said, the Claimant had five counsel representing him; Serjeant Ballantine surely didn't expect the court to believe that he and his colleagues were appearing without pay! *For* (quoth the Chief Justice) *lawyers have more sober sense / Than to argue at their own expense.*

Ballantine replied stiffly that he and his colleagues considered it a matter of honour to complete any case they undertook, regardless of whether or not their fees were forthcoming. If the Chief Justice was surprised at their situation, Coleridge wasn't. The defendants' resources were likewise being drained at such a rate that *The Times* predicted 'that not much beyond shells will be left to the Tichborne baronet when the oyster is opened.'*

Having made his point, Ballantine commenced to call the rest of his witnesses. Of the fifty-odd, only three or four would provide evidence of any substance. Chief among them was Francis Baigent. Noble, worthy, unlucky Baigent. His prissy particularity of manner and expression made him an easy target for ridicule, and he had the misfortune to be cross-examined by Coleridge's second, the brilliant, voracious Henry Hawkins. For two whole weeks, Hawkins hammered and mocked him. Baigent exhibited 'an extreme and delicate dislike to be so rude as to give point-blank answers even to rude, point-blank questions.'

* At its conclusion, the trial was estimated to have cost the Tichborne estate more than £90,000.

Hawkins' aim was to show that the 'historian and picture-cleaner' to the Tichborne family had been in the perfect position to coach an impostor. Moreover, he sought to suggest that Baigent harboured some malice against the Tichbornes. Was it not true, asked Hawkins, that the witness was connected with the Tichborne family by marriage? Baigent admitted it was so, and that he and his wife—the former Miss Plowden, a cousin of Roger's and antagonist of the Claimant's—had separated a short time after the ceremony. But, despite Hawkins' spirited efforts, no one could quite make out what Baigent stood to gain by allying himself with the Claimant, especially after Hawkins read out passages from Baigent's letters to Edward Rous.

The jury heard of Baigent's distaste for the Claimant's wife ('*Lady T. seems more stuck up than ever*') and his complaints against the Claimant ('*The Baronet is acting more foolish every day…I have been for a long time dissatisfied with him*'). These did not sound much like the machinations of a conspirator. In fact, all Hawkins' hounding failed to shift Baigent one whit from his insistence that he *knew* the Claimant was Roger Tichborne. The Claimant smiled with Roger's smile, he said, and there was in his manner something—a wistful melancholy was part of it—that was unaltered and unmistakably Roger.

After Baigent, two of the Claimant's financial backers, William Bulpett and Harry Bloxam, took their turns in the witness box. Both were vigorously cross-examined as to how much they had staked on the Claimant. For that reason, Guildford Onslow was *not* called, as the value of his testimony on the Claimant's behalf would have been far outweighed by the exposure of his heavy bets on the trial's outcome.

The Claimant's case wound up on Wednesday, 20 December 1871, upon which the trial was adjourned until mid-January. While the Claimant spent the festive season embosomed with his family at West Brompton, *The Times* reported that 'a person passing himself off as Sir Roger Tichborne and possessing a strong resemblance to the claimant to that title'—an impostor, no less—had been apprehended in Cardiff.

Sir John Coleridge was busy during the break, making ready the case for the defence. Before Christmas he had given the jury notice of his intended contribution to the length of the proceedings. 'My speech,' he told them, 'will be endless.' In fact Coleridge's opening address ran for twenty-six sitting days, the longest speech ever made in an English civil court. He denounced the Claimant as 'a cunning and dangerous conspirator, a perjurer, a forger, an impostor, and a villain.' For more than five weeks, he picked over 'the miserable scraps of testimony fitted up by the Claimant.' His account of the so-called sealed packet was singled out as 'the most infernal lie that ever villain told in a court of justice':

> It is not for me to sing her praises but I know this: that, all my life long, when I want to point to an example of how a woman can be modest and courageous, and can mingle gentleness and firmness, I shall point to the conduct of Mrs Radcliffe.

At that point on Day Three of Coleridge's opening address, the Chief Justice adjourned for an early luncheon.

Outlining the defence case on Day Fourteen, Coleridge promised that it would expose hundreds of facts inconsistent with the evidence currently before the court, any one of which, he said, would serve to convict the Claimant of 'a fraud, a lie, and a crime, on a scale of depth and wickedness unequalled in the annals of the law.' On Day Twenty-one, he arrived at the question of the Claimant's identity. The defendants' only duty, he told the jurors, was to contest the plaintiff's claim that he was Roger Tichborne; they were not required to show who he really was. Nonetheless, 'I will not conceal that I have a great body of evidence'—here he indicated the Claimant and paused for a titter from his audience—'to show that the plaintiff probably is Arthur Orton.' In this connection, Coleridge alluded to 'a curious discovery', namely Cox's pocket-book, which was now lodged with the court's clerk as an exhibit for the defence. Only on the last of his twenty-six days in the spotlight did Coleridge reveal that he would be calling numerous witnesses who would testify that Roger Tichborne's left arm was tattooed. He brought his address to a close at 3.07 that afternoon, with a vow to unmask 'this detestable imposture…so that it shall require no second doing.'

Coleridge's first witness was Lord Bellew, who had been a fellow scholar of Roger's at Stonyhurst. Roger had arrived at the college, Bellew told the court, already sporting a large tattoo. The witness produced a sketch of the tattoo as he remembered it: a cross, a heart and an anchor, signifying faith, hope and charity. Roger had taught him how it was done—using three needles mounted on matchsticks— and, as his first attempt, the young Bellew had added a wobbly 'RCT'

The modestly courageous Mrs Radcliffe

to the original tattoo on Roger's left forearm.

Mrs Radcliffe was the next to take the stand. 'There is not one word of truth,' she said, exhibiting just the kind of modest courage that Coleridge had led the court to expect, 'in what the Claimant has said of his intimacy with me. It is completely and absolutely false.' She denied intimacy with the Claimant, not with Roger. And the tattoo? Yes, Mrs Radcliffe told Coleridge, she had seen it more than once when Roger had rolled up his sleeve to catch minnows or to retrieve his chisel from the river at Tichborne. Her recollection of the tattoo was much the same as Lord Bellew's, as was that of her mother, Lady Doughty, who followed her into the witness box. Approaching her eightieth year, her Ladyship was stout and infirm, but her features and her manner had lost none of their sharpness. Her memory, apparently, had grown sharper with age, since she admitted to Serjeant Ballantine that in 1867 she only *thought* Roger had been tattooed: now she felt certain of it.

After Lady Doughty came a succession of Tichborne aunts and cousins and a priest or two from Paris, all attesting to the tattoo. Roger's aunt, Mrs Nangle, went further still, insisting that he had offered to tattoo *her* arm and those of other female relatives.

The point, of course, was that the Claimant was not tattooed. A doctor conceded that a circular, depressed scar on the back of his left forearm was consistent with tattoo excision. But it was no bigger than a sixpence; Roger's tattoo had, by all accounts, measured more than two inches in length. What was hardest to credit about the tattoo, though (besides the witnesses' failure to pipe up about it five years earlier), was that Roger's mother, the smothersome Henriette Tichborne, had apparently known nothing of it. Several witnesses were adamant that Roger had been tattooed during a holiday in Brittany at the age of eleven—and that his mother had never found out.

Over the course of ten days, seventeen witnesses swore to their certainty that the Claimant was not Roger Tichborne. Ballantine dutifully cross-examined each of them, but was unable to muster much spirit now for a case that looked like sending him to the poor-house and to which he could see no earthly end.

On Monday afternoon, 4 March 1872, the jury requested permission to confer in private, and when they emerged their foreman handed Chief Justice Bovill a note, to the following effect:

> We have now heard the evidence regarding the tattoo marks, and, subject to your lordship's directions and to the hearing of any evidence which the learned counsel may desire to place before us, I am authorised to state that the jury do not require any further evidence.

In this situation, it was up to the plaintiff to decide whether to let the trial run its course or to declare himself 'non-suited'—that is, to drop the case without a formal verdict. The court was adjourned until Wednesday.

The journalist G. A. Sala had long taken an interest in the Claimant as a species of curiosity. On the occasions when the pair had met socially, Sala had 'watched him narrowly,' intrigued not so much by *who* as *what* the Claimant was. It is to Sala that we owe the best disinterested observations of the Claimant in his milieu:

> He stood with his back to the fireplace, looked quietly round, and made that peculiar 'maultasche', or 'pouch-mouth', movement, accompanied by a slight gasp or two, and a gesture of his hands with the thumbs extended, as though to place them in the pockets of his waistcoat...

As luck would have it, Sala was attending a meeting of the Claimant's supporters at the Waterloo Hotel in Jermyn Street when word arrived that the trial had been stopped. There were wine, biscuits and cigars laid on, of which the Claimant took his fill before announcing: 'I've some rather curious news (puff—pant—puff) for you, gentlemen.'

He read the jury's note aloud, then looked blandly around, said Sala, 'like an affable seal, with nothing whatever on his conscience.' He left to confer with his lawyers, returning hours later as calm and unruffled as ever—'to all appearances as torpidly happy as if he had been drawing dividends at the Bank.' Sala professed himself 'utterly baffled and bewildered':

> I could trace neither the bravado of a desperate villain, foiled and exposed, and doggedly determined to brazen matters out, nor the pardonable anguish of an innocent man unjustly branded with crime...The claimant looked simply unmoved, and as though he would like a little brandy-and-water, or, in default of that stimulant, a nap. What was passing within his mind, not I nor any man living can tell...

On the Wednesday morning, 6 March—the trial's 103rd day—the judge sought to ascertain whether the jury's decision had been based solely on the evidence concerning Roger Tichborne's tattoo (as their note suggested) or on the whole of the evidence presented. Taking the hint, the jury foreman replied that they'd based their decision on the evidence in its entirety. Serjeant Ballantine thereupon informed the judge that his client had elected a non-suit. Actually, the Claimant had expressed no view, one way or the other. His counsel had disagreed over it, Ballantine arguing for a non-suit while his second believed they should hold out for a verdict. Ballantine had got his way. Technically, a non-suit left the Claimant free to commence proceedings afresh—but, in the event, his energies were to be otherwise directed. For, in a development which Ballantine had not anticipated, Chief Justice Bovill declared that he believed the Claimant to be guilty of wilful and corrupt perjury, and ordered his immediate arrest.

The Claimant had been too 'unmoved' to bother coming to court that day, so that it was in his sitting-room at the Waterloo Hotel that police officers served him with the warrant for his arrest. That document committed 'Thomas Castro, alias Arthur Orton, alias Sir Roger Charles Doughty Tichborne' for trial at the next criminal sessions, until which time he was to be detained in Newgate gaol. The accused perjurer received these tidings with characteristic nonchalance, complaining only mildly of the 'inconvenience'. He drove to Newgate in his own brougham, accompanied by a police superintendent and shouts from the street of *Sir Roger!* and *Arthur Orton!* and even of *Wagga Wagga!* Once inside the gaol, he gave his name as Roger Charles Doughty Tichborne, but the registrar put 'Thomas Castro' in accordance with the warrant. The prisoner surrendered his valuables (a gold watch and chain, several ditto rings and a snuffbox, all engraved with the Tichborne coat of arms) and emptied his pockets of £73—the exact amount he had purloined from the Dowager Lady Tichborne's chamber on the morning she died.

For nine months and more, the leader-writers had had to contain their indignation. Now the trial's sudden end let them off the leash. The orgy of outrage in the *Weekly Dispatch* was as typical as its opening line was paradoxical. Its full-page feature began: 'The world will never more desire to hear another syllable concerning the unblushing pretender.'

> The question was not one of simple identity. It amounted to more than that. It was whether an ill-bred adventurer, by telling a plausible story and enlisting on his behalf a host of easily-gulled believers, could wrest a title and estate from their legitimate possessors, ruin the hitherto stainless reputation of an English lady—a wife and mother—and intrude himself as a great landed proprietor of England, to indulge his sot's and slaughter-man's habits to the offence of decent society.

Mrs Radcliffe's ruination was at the heart of every diatribe. In fact, it was arguably at the heart of the Claimant's current predicament.

The Chief Justice's final act, having closed the trial and signed off the arrest warrant, had been to express ('amid loud applause') his absolute belief in the evidence of Mrs Radcliffe. 'That lie,' declared the *Illustrated London News*, 'has been utterly and for ever trampled out.'

Or had it? One of the charges of perjury laid against the Claimant related specifically to Cousin Kattie's ruination, so that the alleged lie might be trampled, but it wasn't dead yet. Nor had Coleridge lived up to his vow that he would settle the question of the Claimant's identity so that it should require 'no second doing.' The Junior Gun Club, when it met to consider the Claimant's expulsion from its ranks, declared itself far from satisfied with the balance of evidence on which the trial had been decided:

> The members were of the opinion that the evidence of the eighty-five witnesses for the plaintiff was as reliable as that of the seventeen for the defence; and, in the absence of any witnesses to prove that he was Arthur Orton or any other man than Sir Roger, it would not be just to expel him.

Also dissatisfied with the trial's outcome was a posse of Australian police who were rumoured to be in London awaiting conclusive proof that the Claimant really was Arthur Orton. According to the *Globe*, the nature of the offence which he had refused to spell out for fear of incrimination was 'a murder in the bush, near Melbourne.'

The squibbed ending of the trial had left punters up in the air, too: did the jury's decision count as a verdict against the Claimant, or not? Most bets laid on the trial's outcome were not paid out, but were carried over pending the verdict of the perjury trial.

At *Punch*, the trial's satirical potential boiled forth in creations such as 'Waggawock': *'Beware the Waggawock, my son, / The eyelid twitch, the knees incline...'* Out on the streets, the sellers of broadsides let fly with racy doggerel—

Now I wonder what he thinks of,
As in Newgate he does stop,
Whether he'd like to be at Wapping,
In a large butcher's shop.
I wonder if before he goes to bed,
He offers up his prayers,
Or wishes most devoutly
He'd got Mrs Radcliffe there.

The Claimant's bed at Newgate was a stout wooden one, not the pouchy canvas hammock endured by most prisoners. No hammock could bear his 27-stone frame. He languished in Newgate for seven

"THE MONSTER SLAIN."
"AND HAST THOU SLAIN THE WAGGA-WOCK?
COME TO MY ARMS, MY BEAMISH BOY!"

Punch's *take on Lewis Carroll's Jabberwock*. Through the Looking-Glass *was published while the Tichborne trial was in progress*

weeks—'cheerful and confident,' according to a warder, 'and maintaining that he has been the victim of an infamous conspiracy'— while his supporters outside toiled to raise the security for his bail. Ten thousand pounds was the amount they had to find.

And the bail was the only the beginning. Nobody could say how much his first trial had cost the Claimant's side, but the next trial would cost much more.

THIRTY-THREE

A KING AMONG THE ROUGH CLASS

A CROWD of thousands was outside Newgate on 26 April 1872 to see the Claimant released on bail. But they jostled and craned their necks in vain, as he was smuggled out through an underground passage to the Old Bailey. From there he took a cab to his marital home, having no 'business' to keep him near Westminster just now; besides which the Waterloo Hotel had refused him further credit. Half his bail had been stood by four wealthy backers, to the tune of £1,250 apiece. The other half—the Claimant's own recognisances—was largely accounted for by public subscriptions.

From Newgate a fortnight after his arrest, he'd written an open letter to readers of the *Standard*. As the penniless victim of an 'infamous conspiracy', he had been persuaded, he said, that he must appeal to the British public for money to conduct his defence. Professing the greatest reluctance, he gave the address of his London solicitor and, from that day forward, subscriptions arrived in torrents. 'To be sure,' remarked a journalist who had cast an eye over the paperwork, 'the majority of the signatures are of a character to excite a smile...but they represent a class.'

'But for the working classes,' Guildford Onslow told the crowd outside Newgate, 'Sir Roger would still be in jail.' Although a banker and a parliamentarian, Onslow was in his element at the racetrack and looked a perfect fit for a bookmaker or music-hall impresario: loud checked suit, bowler hat, curly waxed moustache, and fat cigar.

*'A mass of tastefully-ornamented whale-blubber in broadcloth': the Claimant,
looking every inch—and every ounce—the showman*

George Whalley, member of parliament for Peterborough, was new to the Claimant's band, but played a fervent second fiddle to Onslow's lead. These two, more than any, would shape the rhetoric of the Claimant's campaign in the lead-up to the perjury trial. The keynote was conspiracy: that the Claimant had been disinherited and was now to be prosecuted at government expense for violating the established social order by having lived like a common man. It was a surefire rouser among British working men, many of whom had been granted the vote only a few years earlier.

By the time the Claimant was bailed, branches of the Tichborne Defence Fund Committee were active in towns and provincial cities up and down England. Hampshire was his stronghold, and there he headed in May on his first fundraising tour. Alresford could not have welcomed him more fervently had he won his trial and title. He was fetched the three miles from Onslow's home at Ropley in a bedecked wagonette sent by the new landlord of the Swan Inn. Along the way, the huntsmen and whips of the Hampshire Hounds formed a guard of honour and folk sang out, 'Glory to you, Sir Roger!' as he rattled past. A group of Tichborne tenants wearing blue rosettes met the wagonette on the Alresford outskirts, liberated the horses, and hauled their hero up the hill into town to the brass-band encouragement of 'Auld Lang Syne' and 'Home Sweet Home'. Broad Street was jammed with an estimated three thousand people waiting to hear the Claimant speak—which he did, to great effect. The lustiest cheers came when he implored *Is working men's evidence not as good as that of Lord Bellew?* and the Alresford crowd booed whenever Sir John Coleridge's name was uttered. Afterwards there were fireworks and tunes from the band until midnight, while the cause of all the excitement revived himself at the Swan.

More bands greeted him the following day at Southampton, where he spoke beneath a banner declaring 'THOU SHALT NOT BEAR FALSE WITNESS AGAINST THY NEIGHBOUR.' An indoor meeting that evening drew close to two thousand people, and the same again the next night—quite a turnout in a town of less than a hundred thousand. Even more astounding, those attending paid between one and three shillings a head to see the 'show', all proceeds benefiting the Tichborne Defence Fund.

In the months ahead the Claimant clocked up thousands of railway miles and proved a fundraising phenomenon. Twenty thousand people paid to see him at the Pomona Gardens in Manchester, seven thousand at that city's Free Trade Hall, and eight thousand at St George's Hall in Bradford. A more usual turnout was between one and three thousand,

'The Beggar's Petition'

A confident-looking Guildford Onslow

and it was to paying audiences of that size that he gave ten performances at Leeds, six at each of Newcastle, Nottingham, Birmingham,

Plymouth, Swansea and Leicester, five at Huddersfield, Shields, Sheffield, Hull, Glasgow and Sunderland, and a great many more besides. At every place he stopped, he'd be met by crowds at the railway station, cheered along the streets to his hotel, and mobbed whenever he showed himself out of doors. At Newcastle's Central Station, his swarming supporters knocked down a cast-iron pillar box.

Sir John Coleridge had called him 'a mass of flesh.' 'Probably it is so,' the Claimant told an audience in Preston, 'but I am as nature formed me, and I am very well satisfied with what I am.' For all his bulk, his ill-health and his addiction, he kept himself impeccably groomed. It was common knowledge that he wore only stockings of the finest silk, a fresh pair each day, and that his outsized suits were tailored by London's best. His soft, slender hands and elegantly shod feet—so at odds with those of the 'slommicking' Arthur Orton of Wapping—always excited particular notice. When he appeared at a Spennymoor shooting-match, for instance, in 'enormously wide trousers of guano colour,' the local press remarked that 'there is still a nimbleness of foot which is in strange contrast with the superin-cumbent structure his feet have to move and bear.' He still spoke with the accent of a working man, but more and more he comported and expressed himself like a gentleman—his speeches were 'most country-gentlemanlike in their bold and ungrammatical inconse-quence.' It was a combination that worked powerfully on those who heard him speak. Women, it was said, found him irresistible.

Onslow or Whalley generally acted as his chaperone. Four years earlier Baigent had written, 'I don't like his going away by himself...not only because of his great size and liability to be ill but there is the danger of his getting into mischief,' and his chief supporters held the same misgivings still. Besides being there to steer the Claimant straight, they would speak before him at meetings, spreading thick their endorsement as the men who'd stood his bail and warming crowds to the mighty themes of conspiracy and injustice. After the Claimant would come a third speaker, brought up from the audience by pre-arrangement. Nearly always it was a man who'd been in the colonies and either had known Tom Castro there or, at least, could vouch for his version of bush life.

At one of the Southampton meetings, a fellow named John Fasham, lately returned from New South Wales, advanced a novel explanation for the Claimant's having forgotten how to speak French:

> On a horse-run of 300 miles in the bush he might see a white man or two perhaps once in a few months, and these speaking a broken language, partly English and partly the language of the aboriginal natives of the bush—a style of speaking used in all parts of that wonderful, almost unknown land. The most frequent sounds he would hear would be the abominable howling of the wild dogs, the squeaking of the various kinds of parrots and cockatoos, the jabbering of the wild, naked savages…and this for many years, shut out entirely from civilized society in the wild grandeur of the Australian bush.

The Claimant himself later expanded on the same theme, declaring at the Victoria Hall in Leeds that, though he had uttered not a word of French during his years in the bush, he'd mastered four Aboriginal dialects. An audience in Birmingham heard from John Dyke, formerly a carpenter at Wagga, that the Claimant's work at Higgins' butchery had been a far cry from the lowly occupation depicted by Coleridge. It was nothing for £1,000 or more to pass through Castro's velvety hands every month—and as soon as he left, the business had collapsed. Elaborating on Dyke's testimony, the Claimant added that he had several times saved enough for his fare to England and had even gone to Melbourne, intending to embark on a steamer home. Each time though, he had blown his savings—at the races, on a horse, on he couldn't remember what—and had ended up back in the bush.

Another to vouch publicly for his colonial bona fides was the Great

Wizard, 'Professor' Anderson. He told a meeting at Bournemouth that he'd first set eyes on the Claimant as a commanding figure on horseback in a busy Melbourne thoroughfare. Castro had been renowned not just as the finest horseman in the colonies but as 'a sort of "King" among the rough class, amongst whom he had cast his lot.' The Great Wizard's testimonial inspired George Whalley to declare—

> that there never went forth from England to the wild part of the Empire a man who did more good, promoted more happiness, prevented more misery, or carried into the darkest part of the Empire the powers of civilization in a more benevolent and beneficent system of action…

In fact, said Whalley, the Claimant had been nothing less than 'the good angel of the Australian bush.'

As 1872 progressed and the Claimant's performances gained in length, steam and polish, the support role was regularly filled by 'Captain' William Jackson Barry, an adventurer of long and varied colonial experience. Most recently he'd made a living—but a poor one—by lecturing on mining and minerals. A born showman, Barry lent vim to the public meetings and his highly coloured yarns appeared to bear out some of the more improbable aspects of the Claimant's avowed colonial life. Like the Claimant, Barry half-confessed to acts of bushranging, and swore that he'd known both Castro and Orton in Gippsland in the 1850s, and that the Claimant was indisputably the former.

But Barry and the rest were paid (yes, paid) to lend colour more than veracity. The Claimant's own performance was shaped to whip up outrage against his 'persecutors'. 'Allow me to say I am not come here to ask you to believe I am Sir Roger Tichborne,' he would begin. 'That we will leave to be decided by the courts of law. What I do ask is to say and insist on my having a fair trial like any other Englishman.'

And it worked. At Swansea the following resolution was passed:

> That it is the opinion of this meeting that the whole of the proceedings against Sir Roger Tichborne…forms one of the grandest conspiracies against a private gentleman to swear away his name, rob him of his inheritance, his fame, his title and respectability ever attempted in this country.

The same meeting demanded 'every explanation and information relative to this gigantic government prosecution now being carried on at such enormous cost.' A special resolution at Bristol protested that a government so miserly as to cut back the number of quill pens issued to civil servants had engaged six counsel to prosecute the Tichborne case. Guildford Onslow was a master at lathering up crowds. By his reckoning, he told an audience at Greenock, Sir John Coleridge (a government minister, no less!) had been paid six shillings and fourpence *a minute* during the late trial, while the Claimant's counsel had struggled on empty-bellied.

Within government ranks there was growing alarm at the elevation of the Claimant's case to a popular political cause. Almost certainly he'd contravened the conditions of his bail—if not with his incendiary conduct, then by travelling to the Channel Islands for a public meeting—but the government knew that returning him to Newgate would merely fuel the accusations of conspiracy and injustice. Imposing a fine would be futile, too, since he was bankrupt. But Onslow and Whalley—members of parliament both—could and should be held accountable for their behaviour and were charged, at the end of 1872, with contempt of court. Onslow had been cited for declaring that the Claimant was victim of 'the greatest conspiracy which had ever been known to the laws' and for referring to Mrs Radcliffe as Roger Tichborne's 'traitorous former lover.' Whalley's contemptible statement had named the parties to the alleged conspiracy: from the Tichborne–Doughty enclave, on through the government, the judiciary and the Catholic church, right up to the royal family. Found guilty in January 1873, the pair were fined £100 each and were barred from attending public meetings until the trial was over.

The Claimant gave evidence in his friends' defence, pointing out that contemptible utterances at his meetings amounted to feeble retaliation for the prejudicial onslaught mounted against him in the newspapers. As an instance, he read aloud from that week's *Saturday Review* in which Sir John Coleridge (now attorney-general) was quoted using 'the most uncontrolled language' about him. The judge conceded the impropriety, but declined to take action. Of the major dailies, only the *Morning Advertiser* remained steadfast in its support for the Claimant, so that his cause largely relied on its own newspaper, the monthly *Tichborne News* ('an Anti-Oppression Journal'), to carry its message to the reading public. Priced at a penny, it was brimful of just the kind of inflammatory language for which Onslow and Whalley had been arraigned. It also listed subscribers to the Tichborne Defence Fund, many of them pseudonymous and 'of a character to excite a smile,' as exemplified by this selection from February 1873:

> A few Lovers of Justice and three Servant Girls—12s
> All Men are Fools—10s 6d
> A few Cutters and Warehousemen at Cookson & Co's,
> St Mary-axe—£1 3s
> Lizzy, Stepney—2s 6d
> Flashing Sword—1s 6d

Almost a year after his arrest as a perjurer, it seemed no exaggeration to state that the Claimant 'is Arthur Orton in almost every drawing-room, while he is Roger Tichborne throughout all England.'

THIRTY-FOUR

INSPECTOR DENNING'S CIRCUS

WHILE still in Newgate, the Claimant had declared that he'd get no justice if the jurors at his trial were drawn from the same class of 'half-bred swells' as those at the first trial. He ought to have been pleased then with the twelve men eventually selected: two hosiers, a bootmaker, a hairdresser, a milkman, a lodging-house keeper, two publicans, a butcher, a clerk, a draper and a maker of rubberised floor coverings.

To reduce the likelihood of an appeal, the trial was to be conducted 'at bar', presided over by three judges: Sir Alexander Cockburn, Lord Chief Justice of England, assisted by Justices Mellor and Lush, judges of the Queen's Bench. Cockburn was an obvious choice, but not an uncontentious one. He had publicly denounced the Claimant as an impostor as far back as 1868 and showed no sign of having moderated that view, having recently announced to a hock-and-pheasant luncheon that the Claimant could look forward to seven years in prison—the maximum sentence for perjury.

It was April 1873 before the trial was set to begin. Getting hold of witnesses had been the main cause of delay. The prosecution would end up calling 212 witnesses and the defence 256; but as the trial commenced, both sides were still signing up new witnesses daily. The Claimant, of course, had to raise the money to cover witness costs—statements, subpoenas, travel expenses, and the rest. All the prosecution's expenses would be met by Treasury. Moreover, since the depositions from the Australian and Chilean commissions were not permissible evidence in a criminal trial, witnesses had to be brought over from those countries. Neither side had the power to compel off-shore witnesses to attend; they had to be lured to London, which, for the Claimant's side, was rather out of the question. In spite of all the fundraising, there was not money enough in the coffers to import a single witness for the defence.

The most glaring absence from the witness box, however, would be the Claimant himself. The criminal law prevented an accused person from giving evidence in his own defence. He would have to sit by dumbly while counsel and judges pored over his evidence from the civil trial, half-guessing what he had meant by this answer or that. Still, given the confounding nature of his testimony to date, the Claimant's enforced silence was not necessarily a bad thing for his defence.

Sir John Coleridge had originally been retained to lead the Crown's legal team. But the Tichborne Defence movement had so demonised him that his appointment would only have reinforced the impression of a government plot. Instead, Henry Hawkins took the helm. In the afterglow of the civil trial, Coleridge had ventured the opinion that the case against the Claimant was a simple one, the whole affair amounting, he said, to 'an insult on the commonsense of mankind.' He ought to have known better. 'Instead of the work diminishing as we proceeded, it increased day by day and week by week,' Hawkins would later write. 'It seemed absolutely endless and hopeless.'

Leading counsel for the defence was Dr Edward Kenealy. Like Hawkins, he had not been first choice. Serjeant Ballantine had offered his services for a fee of £1,000 up front, but the Claimant refused to have him. Ballantine's second, Hardinge Giffard, fell out of contention after declaring that it would take £10,000 to secure his services. Eventually the brief went to a Serjeant Sleigh, who dropped dead two months before the trial's commencement. With just five weeks to go, Kenealy accepted the brief.

Taking a very serious view of things—the messianic Dr Edward Kenealy

A note scribbled by him during the course of the trial—*'One is ready to suspect everybody and everything'*—sums up Dr Kenealy. Under his superintendence, the supposed plot against the Claimant sprouted fantastic new curlicues, most of them implicating the Jesuits. The Popish-conspiracy angle was nothing new. The ardently Protestant George Whalley had already connected most of the dots: the Tichbornes were among England's most powerful Catholic dynasties and endowed the Church a percentage of their wealth annually; Sir John Coleridge's brother was a Jesuit; even Gladstone, the prime minister, was so High Church as to be practically a Papist. But it took Kenealy to trace 'the unseen, invisible, almost universally permeating influence of Stonyhurst,' the Jesuit college, all the way up to the royal family.

Kenealy was, in many respects, a bewhiskered Dowager Lady Tichborne. Like her, he was capable of a strangulating devotion and demanded utter loyalty in return. But his delusions were of megalo-maniac proportions beyond the Dowager's imagining. Kenealy saw himself a Messiah—the twelfth in a line that began with Adam and progressed on through Christ, Mohammed and eight more down to himself. His Messianic destiny was spelt out in five self-published volumes of biblical dimensions. He had the temper of a Fury, clenched and bull-roaring with righteous intensity, and a set of side-whiskers that rendered him ludicrous. Kenealy was clever, but clueless. And the Claimant's case lay in his hands.

The trial of *R v. Castro* commenced on Wednesday, 23 April 1873 in the Court of Queen's Bench. Admission was to be strictly regulated this time, with tickets issued by application to Inspector Denning of the House of Commons police. By this means, the Claimant's side believed, the courtroom was stacked with 'enemies'. 'Get near the Court, see one of the numerous detectives who are continually about, and then set to and abuse me. He will take you in at once.' That was the Claimant's advice to a supporter as the best way of gaining admission. For the duration of the Tichborne trial, Inspector Denning would find himself one of the most wooed men in London, importuned for the favour of tickets by peers, celebrities, even foreign royalty. Even so, the court was no less packed than it had been during the last trial. Barristers struggled through to the bar seats, their wigs knocked sideways and sleeves half torn off. Two women fainted during the first day's proceedings. But the Claimant never complained about the crush.

'Tomàs Castro, alias Roger Charles Doughty Tichborne, Baronet, aged 42, of no occupation and of imperfect education' faced two counts of wilful and corrupt perjury: one arising from his statements under oath at the Chancery hearing, the other from his evidence at the civil trial. The two counts comprised thirty-three separate charges of exceptional specificity; for instance, that he had lied about having lived in Paris until 1845 and having been charged with horse stealing at Castlemaine. Foremost among the charges, however, were his claims that he was Roger Tichborne, that he was not Arthur Orton, and that he had seduced Katherine Doughty in 1852.

Kenealy was at a disadvantage in, among other things, having no copy of the evidence from the second half of the civil trial, after the Claimant was unable to keep up his share of the shorthand writer's fee. Justice Mellor, with an eye to posterity, was pleased to lend his copy to the defence. 'I propose to keep it as a curiosity eventually,' he told Kenealy that first day in court. 'You may make any notes you like. I shall rather value it on that account.' Among the prosecution's many advantages over the defence, as the trial began, was its possession of 'very voluminous' papers subpoenaed from the Claimant's former solicitor, John Holmes, who had never been paid. Long and bitterly would Kenealy curse Holmes for supplying the Claimant's opponents with 'all the munitions of war.'

Henry Hawkins endeared himself to the jury with an opening address that lasted just four days. On the fifth he called his first witnesses. Hawkins was a fine, measured performer, who knew when humour was called for, when to cue pathos or indignation, and how to carry his audience with him. Unlike his counterpart for the defence, Hawkins knew how to act.

In cross-examining members of the Tichborne family and their circle, Kenealy affected a sneering deference which belied the things he said about them. 'All the men were Rogues,' he would later write, 'and all the women were Unchaste.' He dealt roughly with Lord

Bellew, forcing him to admit that he'd once committed adultery with the wife of a fellow officer, as if that negated his Lordship's evidence concerning Roger's tattoo. With Lady Radcliffe (now that her husband Percival had been knighted) Kenealy was no less snide, but even he had the sense to know that her handling called for a degree of delicacy. Instead of leaning on the question of her alleged seduction, he focused on her knowledge of Roger's tattoo. She had claimed to have seen it when her cousin was catching minnows by hand in the river at Tichborne Park. It was the first time he'd heard, said Kenealy, of a person minnowing that way. Had Roger succeeded in catching any? She believed so, Lady Radcliffe replied. Kenealy feigned wonderment, musing that he had once caught carp by hand—at which the Lord Chief Justice broke in with his own account of trout-tickling, Justice Lush added that he'd heard of squeezing goldfishes, and the whole exchange concluded with a juror telling the court, 'I saw a couple of carp the other day which had been sent through the post. They were alive.'

Kenealy pestered the prosecution's Carabineer witnesses with a fusillade of questions about Dublin landmarks, seeking to corroborate statements made by the Claimant at the civil trial. Kenealy was pestered in turn by Dickins, the jury foreman, who several times corrected him on points of military etiquette. 'Mr Dickins,' Kenealy would later write, 'prided himself upon his vast military knowledge—though we never could find out why, except that he sold hosiery to some military men.' Edward McEvoy, who'd been in Roger's regiment, was unrattled by Kenealy's gunmetal sarcasm. The Claimant, said McEvoy decidedly, was 'altogether a much better looking man than Roger Tichborne.'

The defence scored a few minor points. Jules Barraut, the servant who'd seen Roger aboard the *Bella* at Rio, felt certain that the Claimant was not his old master, yet was equally insistent that Roger had not been tattooed. The prosecution's handwriting expert, Chabot, conceded that Roger had been not much better than the Claimant at spelling. Chabot had counted 165 different words misspelt in Roger's correspondence and 190 in the Claimant's. The handwriting and mode of expression in Arthur Orton's letters from Hobart was also analysed and found to bear strong similarities to the Claimant's. Kenealy suspected (as he would) that Orton's letters were forgeries, and later would name Joseph Redding, a Treasury clerk 'and the second-most expert forger in the world,' as the perpetrator.

Both sides made a liberal harvest of witnesses from Wapping, the most Tichborne-obsessed parish in the country. Of the sixty or more public meetings the Claimant had attended in London since the middle of 1872, two-thirds had been held within a stone's throw of Arthur Orton's birthplace. He had, moreover, been 'exhibited' six times at the Pavilion Theatre in Wapping, and the same at Creighton's White Lion Tavern in Shadwell.

Wapping teemed with witnesses aligned with one side or the other in the Tichborne case. Having signed their affidavit, they were offered a fee for each new witness they recruited. Forty-eight Wappingites were eventually called by Hawkins to identify the Claimant as Arthur Orton, and fifty-eight by Kenealy to refute them.

Alfred Schottler had not long returned from the colonies himself. Facing the Claimant in court, he had no trouble recognising the boy with whom he'd run about Red Mead Lane. Arthur, he said, had always been 'the best sample' of the Orton family. William Willoughby likewise identified the Claimant as Orton, but told Hawkins, 'I have had many opponents down in my own neighbourhood.' Too right he had. The same day Abraham Bush gave his evidence for the prosecution, he collapsed and died during a fight in a Wapping public house over the question of the Claimant's identity. A petition refuting that the Claimant was Orton had amassed 6,333 signatures in Wapping.

Captain Henry Angell was not himself a Wappingite, but had been a good friend of the Ortons, young Arthur included. Moreover, he'd

Mary Orton

George Orton

been the last of his countrymen to clap eyes on the undoubted Arthur, having seen him briefly at Hobart in 1855. But the prosecution's real interest in the captain was that he'd been named as an executor to the Claimant's Wagga will, a circumstance for which he could offer no explanation besides the obvious one: that the Claimant was Arthur Orton. The captain recognised him for his likeness not only to the young Arthur but to George and Mary Orton, whose portraits were shown to the jury. 'There is one thing I do not believe,' added Captain Angell. 'I do not think he knows it himself…It is just possible he may not know he is Arthur Orton, he might forget his own identity…There may have been such things in the history of the world as a man not knowing himself.'

Those who ought to have known Arthur Orton best did not appear at the trial. His brother Charley, who professed to have received hush money from the Claimant, was now on the payroll of the Treasury, which had inherited the liability from the Tichborne trustees. Inspector Denning had instructions to advance Charley 'subsistence money' of a guinea each week. Not that the prosecution had any intention of calling him as a witness: they paid him so that he wouldn't change his story, not because they believed it. The Orton sisters, Mrs Jury and Mrs Tredgett, were considered too unreliable to put in the stand. John Holmes, in his dying days on the case, had made a note on the file: 'Mrs Jury begged me not to call her as a Witness as she could

Mary Anne Loder

not say whether you were her Brother or not, altho' she was strongly inclined to believe you were not.'

Common sense insists that Mrs Jury must have known whether or not the Claimant was her brother; but since both sides were afraid of what she might say under cross-examination, neither was willing to subpoena her. The prosecution did, however, call her estranged husband, Robert, who declared himself certain that the Claimant was his brother-in-law, Arthur Orton.

One person who should have known Orton better, in some respects, than his own sisters was Mary Anne Loder, who took the stand for the prosecution on the twenty-second day of the trial. She was a worried-faced, sturdy woman of thirty-seven who had never married. Quietly spoken, she answered every question—even Kenealy's impertinent ones—without a hint of prevarication. She was candid about the trickery employed by the Claimant's opponents to obtain evidence against him. In 1867, she'd handed over Arthur's Hobart letters to Detective Whicher, believing that she was doing her old sweetheart a service. A few months later, she'd accompanied Whicher to the Dowager's funeral and 'directly I saw him I recognised him.' Saying so in court, Mary Anne looked steadily at the Claimant; occupied with pen and paper, he did not meet her gaze. Had she been in any doubt whatever, the witness assured Hawkins, the Claimant would have had the benefit of it. In reply to Kenealy's questions, she couldn't recall Arthur's feet having been especially large, nor had he been tattooed or worn rings in his ears. His hair, she was certain, had been fair. And no, she told Kenealy, she had not been paid for her evidence.

Had Coleridge been leading the prosecution, doubtless he'd have asked Mary Anne Loder *Would she be surprised to hear?* that her name appeared on the last page of the pocket-book handed in by Charley Cox. The civil trial had ended without calling on Cox and he'd since returned home to find his hotel burnt down—the 'injudicious termination' prophesied by the Claimant's friend, Joe Madden. The pocket-book itself had stayed behind as an exhibit for the prosecution and, on Day Twenty-five, formed part of Hawkins' examination of William Gibbes, the single witness brought over from Wagga for the trial. Only the prosecution could afford to pay his passage; but, even had the defence been able to, it's unlikely they'd have called him. His evidence for the Claimant at the Australian commission was ambivalent, to say the least. He didn't *know* the truth of the matter, that was plain. But one thing he was certain of. 'I have been so fearfully bored the last seven years with this abominable affair,' he said, 'that I was only too glad to get rid of everything to do with it.' Like Holmes, he'd handed all his papers over to the Crown.

Common gossip had it that William Gibbes drank too much, but it's hard to doubt that he was an honest man. For a short time early in the affair he'd hoped to gain something from Tom Castro's changed fortunes; and he'd been disappointed. But Gibbes had shown the Claimant no ill-will and, more than anyone, had been philosophical about the way things seemed to be turning out. The £600 the prosecution paid him he took as his reward for seven years' aggravation.

Hawkins led Gibbes through Cox's pocket-book, page by page and line by line, to ascertain which parts were in Tom Castro's handwriting. By Gibbes' reckoning, at least half the entries—including the one about Mary Anne Loder—were attributable to the Claimant. Of the rest he was uncertain, except for a few entries that were plainly in a strange hand.

> R.C. Tichborne Bart—Yes.
> La Bella, R.C.T. arrived Hobart Town July 4, 1854—Not sure. Written in up-and-down hand.
> Stephen Butts—Not in same hand.
> I Tomas Castro Do hereby certify my Name is not Tomas Castro at all. Therefore those say it is, dont know any think about it. R.C.T.—Some yes, some not sure.

Richard Nevill Slate—Not sure. I do not know who he is at all.
Some men has plenty money and no brains. And some men
has plenty brains and no Money Surely Men with plenty
Money and no brains were Made for Men with plenty brains
and no Money—Not sure.

That last entry, the prosecution had discovered, was a paraphrase, in
'vulgar vernacular', of a line from Mary Braddon's sensation novel,
Aurora Floyd. In the novel, said Hawkins, the words had issued from
the mouth of 'a very crafty and guilty person, who turns out to be a
great scoundrel.'

One entry in the pocket-book was written in Rosicrucian cipher.
Justice Mellor had already given the prosecution his interpretation;
now Hawkins asked Gibbes to decipher it. Gibbes was thrilled. 'I can
show you the clue to it,' he kept saying. 'I have had that given to me,'
said Hawkins, wearily. 'Just put it on the back of the piece of paper.'
Gibbes arrived at the same result as Justice Mellor: viz, *Sir Roger
Charles Tichborne, Bart*. In a letter to his friend Lord Rivers, the
Claimant as much as admitted that the pocket-book and its contents
were his, boasting that he'd taught the cipher to other 'outlaws' in
the bush, so that they might correspond in secret. 'To the best of my
knowledge,' he said, 'there are not now twenty people in the colony
who understand it.'

On the last page of the pocket-book, beneath Mary Anne Loder's
address, appeared an odd doodle, something between a scarab beetle
and an algebraic equation. William Gibbes didn't recognise it, but
the jury did. They'd seen the same quirk at the foot of Miss Loder's
letters from Hobart. It was Arthur Orton's rubrica.

The other witnesses imported by the prosecution to reprise their
Australian commission testimony were Sara and Matthew Macalister
of Boisdale, and Mina Jury. Mina was paid £500 for her trouble and

passage. Kenealy's cross-examination of her was larded with the insinuation that she would say anything for money. When, after the trial, her criminal antecedents came to light, he was furious he hadn't been able to use them to discredit her.

The Macalisters were so long in coming from Australia that the end of the prosecution case had to be delayed to await them. Finally their ship berthed and they were scheduled to give evidence the following day. But, when the court resumed at ten next morning, there was no sign of the Macalisters. Eleven o'clock passed: still nothing, and a clerk who'd been sent to find them reported that they'd left the Charing Cross Hotel—half a mile from Westminster Hall— at a quarter to ten. There was consternation in court, until it emerged that they'd fallen into the hands of a London cabman, who, discovering their ignorance of the metropolis, conveyed them to Westminster by the scenic route. Instead of five or six minutes, the journey took an hour-and-a-half and shaved an entire guinea off the Macalisters' £1,000 appearance fee. London cabbies being among the Claimant's fiercest followers, there may well have been more than a pecuniary motive for taking a couple of his sworn enemies for a ride.

Not all the Crown's Australian witnesses had to be paid as much or travel as far. There were plenty of ex-colonists in England with stories to relate. Richard Redman was one. Now a wharfinger's clerk in Deptford, he professed to have met Arthur Orton in Victoria in 1858. Redman had been sheepwashing on a property called Nowhere-Else, deep in the mallee country of the colony's north-west, and vividly recalled the hut-keeper, a fellow by the name of Arthur. In the three weeks they'd shared a hut, Redman had heard all about Arthur's father (a shipping butcher of Wapping) and his travels in Gippsland and South America (Redman was sure he'd mentioned Melipilla). This Arthur had been in possession of a stolen horse and had boasted of his acquaintance with the bushranger, Dan Morgan—a curious thing, since Morgan was unheard of at that date. 'I may as well say,' Redman admitted, 'that reading the accounts of the trial has reminded me of those names.' Nevertheless, he ran on about this Arthur's 'staring eyebrows,' his laziness, his bad cooking. 'There he sits,' he declared, levelling a finger at the Claimant.

The Boisdale station books for 1858, sworn to by the Macalisters when they finally made it to court, fixed Arthur Orton more than three hundred miles from Nowhere-Else—supposing, of course, that such a place ever existed.

THIRTY-FIVE

NOT A BED OF ROSES

If I had the gold of the Treasury at my back I might bring witnesses here who might immediately annihilate the sort of evidence brought before you. I might bring people here to prove there is no such place as Nowhere-Else. I can do nothing. Representing him I am like a person bound with fetters.

That was Kenealy, opening for the defence. The prosecution case had run for twelve weeks, winding up on 19 July 1873. Kenealy was playing for sympathy—and not just from the jury. To mount a case with even a fraction of its six hundred potential witnesses, the defence needed to keep subscriptions rolling in. More wary of a contempt charge once the trial was under way, the Claimant had scarcely trod the boards since Easter. He still competed at the occasional shooting match, but any prize money he pocketed for personal use.

Kenealy's hand-wringing backfired. A short way into his opening address, the Lord Chief Justice announced that the Crown *would* pay witness costs for the defence after all—but only when the trial was over, and only for those witnesses judged to have been 'properly brought forward.' In other words, Treasury could withhold payment for any witness deemed 'frivolous' by the bench. Guildford Onslow called it 'a concerted trick,' and it worked. Cockburn's announcement had the effect of a tourniquet on the flow of donations to the Claimant. Within a fortnight, a postal order for six shillings from 'some working friends in Shropshire' was rare enough to warrant a mention from Tichborne Defence Fund headquarters.

The defence's cheapest course was to keep Dr Kenealy talking, an undertaking that presented him with no difficulty whatever. In vain did the jurors request that he limit himself to 'a short sermon':

> Gentlemen, it has been one of the unhappy incidents of this Case that the rights of this Defendant have been sought in a great measure to be destroyed by language and vituperation calculated to excite public passion and prejudice against him. Instead of the minds of our countrymen coming to a case of this description in a calm, judicial, and unimpassioned manner, language of the most violent description ever known, and objurgations of the most cruel character, have been used against a man who was to stand his trial at the bar of criminal justice. He has been called by a person of high authority a Conspirator, a Perjurer, a Forger, a Slanderer, and a Villain, and my learned friend here opens his case to you as that of a man charged with crimes as black and foul as Justice ever raised her sword to strike...

Kenealy's opening address tested the endurance of everyone who had to sit through it. It lasted a month, and coincided with the height of the London summer, making the atmosphere in the Court of Queen's Bench doubly unbearable. On a Monday towards the end of July, one of the jurors took a fainting fit, causing proceedings to halt for several days. 'Had a juryman died after months of the trial had passed,' Hawkins would later write, 'the Government must have abandoned the prosecution. This was the last hope of the defence.' Certainly the juror's misfortune occasioned glee in the Claimant's camp. Hearing of it, Lord Rivers exalted, 'I have never doubted that either now, or very soon, that will be the Finale of this great Trial.' But the juror recovered and Kenealy's speech resumed.

He dwelt at length on the Dowager Lady Tichborne. If her recognition of the Claimant was to count for anything, Kenealy needed to counteract the prosecution's depiction of her as an unhinged, vindictive harridan. As usual he tried too hard. She was, he said, 'one of the most beautiful women in France when this Mr James Tichborne, with his brutal ideas, married her.' Moving on to the Claimant's emergence in Wagga in 1865, Kenealy spun a fancy around the coincidence of his client writing to 'My dear Mother' at the very time she was telling Mr Cubitt of the Missing Friends Office: 'I shall expect an answer from him.'

> There would seem to be what the French call a kind of rapport between this mother and her son because they both hit on precisely the same idea. I do not want, Gentlemen, to take you into the region of the supernatural, but we know that there are astonishing things which happen every day in the world that cannot be accounted for by merely material or terrestrial explanations. Now, is not this a singular thing that the same idea seems to have shot across the minds of the son and mother, both separated by such a vast continent?

An ironical smile from the Lord Chief Justice licensed the jury to laugh aloud. And Kenealy's protesting, 'I assure you, gentlemen, I am perfectly serious,' only made them laugh the harder.

The Claimant's opponents had always been at pains to emphasise his lack of education. Rather than challenge that contention, Kenealy sought to show the jury that his client was more than just unlettered. 'Tichborne is the greatest Hypocrite or the weakest Fool in the world,' he declared. 'I have preferred taking the latter view of his character.' He disparaged the Claimant before the court and the watching world as an 'idiot' with 'the mind of a hippopotamus.'

Kenealy began the demolition of his client's character with a short treatise on fatness. 'In the majority of cases persons who in their early youth were fat, as they get older grow thin; and the opposite rule prevails.' Men like the Claimant, to whom that opposite rule applied, were characterised by 'mighty passions' and excesses proportionate to their size. Most significantly, 'fatness is supposed by many persons who have thought deeply on this subject to be a thing that impairs the memory; it is thought to cloud the understanding to a certain extent.' Nor was it the Claimant's size alone that militated against a clear head. A doctor had stated that the enlargement of his earlobes— they were pendulous, while Roger's ears, in the Santiago portraits, were lobeless—was indicative of brain deterioration, the result of sunstroke and dissipated habits. Kenealy enjoined jurors to imagine themselves in the Claimant's 'remarkably gross habit of body': the whiskey commixed with his bloodstream, the tapeworm strangling his vitals, and 'the brain diseased and rotten from excesses and misuse, and poisoned by the use of mercury, syphilis having got into the system.'

All this was leading somewhere. Everyone knew, said Kenealy, that impostors were possessed of artifice, foresight and cunning from which they rarely blundered. By contrast, his client's performance bespoke a headlong recklessness. 'No man who has rationality,' said Kenealy, 'no man who has any particle of common sense, would have done what he has done, if his case be true.' A substantial part of the Claimant's evidence Kenealy dismissed as 'absurdities…Why, if he stood up in Court and said he was Arthur Orton, it would make no impression on my mind—not the slightest…Yet you are asked to believe this man to be a criminal because he is a fool.' He urged the jury, instead, to reverse that equation: the Claimant was unbeliev-able, ergo, he could not be an impostor. If he had not committed *wilful* perjury, they couldn't find him guilty. 'You should judge him as he is,' declared Kenealy, 'a man among a million of men.'

Still, the Claimant's imagination, however 'grotesque', could not have dreamt up the things he seemed to know about Arthur Orton's life. Kenealy was in no doubt that, during his years of vagabondage in the colonies, the feeble-minded Tichborne had come under Orton's sway:

> When he and Arthur Orton were in the woods miles and miles away from any human being, sitting up the greater part of the night under the magnificent and cloudless skies of Australia, by the fireside, talking over ancient times, I can imagine Arthur Orton, a man probably of stronger mind, impressing vividly on the mind of a weaker man relations and anecdotes of persons who belonged to him in the past...Am I departing from the strict path of reason, or logic, or argument, or common sense, if I put that to you as a thing that may have occurred, and may account for a great many of the absurd things he did?

Absurd things like writing Mary Anne Loder's name in his pocket-book, like naming Orton family friends as executors of his will, like alluding to the *Jessie Miller* as the ship that carried him to South America, or like passing off a photograph of his own wife and child as Arthur Orton's.

> This is what, as Arthur Orton, this man is said to do; but it is not what Arthur Orton, claiming to be Roger Tichborne, would ever have been absurd enough to do.

Kenealy's own demons prevented him from including under the heading of 'absurdities' that most kamikaze of the Claimant's stories, his account of the sealed packet's contents. But it ought to have been clear to him, as it was to everybody else, that neither jury nor judges were going to exonerate his client if he persisted with the story of Lady Radcliffe's seduction. Kenealy charged right in.

The question of 'Miss Doughty's chasteness,' he contended, ought not to have been the subject of a perjury charge, that lady's character having been vindicated quite sufficiently by Chief Justice Bovill at

the conclusion of the last trial. It was a charge calculated to perpetuate passion and prejudice against his client, said Kenealy. The
prosecution, in seeking to convince the jury of the unlikelihood of
Roger's having seduced his cousin Kattie, had pitched a chaste, sober
and moral view of his character. 'I have been obliged, therefore,' said
Kenealy, 'to show him as he was: a loose and drunken libertine.'

Kenealy swiped at the 'corrupting influence' of Roger's Parisian
tutors and the Stonyhurst Jesuits, who bred in him the habits of
smoking and snuff-taking and dancing the can-can. He deplored 'the
perfectly polluted and rotten mind' of a young man who would recommend to his aunt the books of Paul de Kock—'one of the most wicked
writers that ever wrote for the French people.' The court was cleared
of ladies on Day Sixty-one of the trial, so that Kenealy might read
'relevant' passages from two of de Kock's novels.

> Could they resist the instructions of their hearts? Could they
> combat against the passion that was devouring them? Frederick
> dared everything and Sister Anne soon surrendered herself to
> her lover without regret—without remorse...She delivered
> herself up to his advances, she abandoned herself to love; she
> shared the burning ardour with which he was inflamed.

And so on until lunchtime. Kenealy's performance inspired the versi-
fying Lord Exmouth, in the court that day, to fifteen stanzas, beginning:

> Said Kenealy, from drinking, and smoking, and snuff,
> Morality suffers a shock;
> But to build up a 'Roger' they are not enough,
> You must call in the aid of De Kock.

Roger's memorandum book from his army years yielded a few
shallow hints from which Kenealy drank deep. In particular it included
a name whose significance Justice Cockburn could not deny. 'Madame
Guerin, 15 Norton-street...one of the most noted procuresses and

prostitutes in London.' In his record of the trial, Kenealy added a footnote: 'Cockburn knows her well.' He drew from the memorandum book one more proof of Roger, the incipient seducer: a 'rather queer' French verse, on De Kock-ian lines:

> *O l'innocence*
> *Dans mon absence*
> *Livre ton cœur*
> *Pour ton bonheur*
> *Car la Pocelle*
> *Elle est si belle*
> *Quand sans ——*
> *Elle vit une nuit.*

Consider that dash, Kenealy bid the jury, and he rendered the foregoing lines in English for them: 'She was a very charming young lady, and particularly so after having passed some time without ——' But, being 'so innocent and modest,' they failed to take his gist and as there were ladies in the court he could not well explain that the missing words were *une vis*—a screw.

Kenealy was winging it. Halfway through his address, in early August 1873, he had practically no idea of how his client's case was to proceed. He claimed that, since taking on the brief in March, he'd received no instructions from the Claimant's solicitor. There was not even any certainty, he said, that witnesses would be forthcoming, and he feared that the case must collapse when his speech came to an end. The Lord Chief Justice privately encouraged Kenealy to give up the case.

Alfred Hendricks had been the Claimant's solicitor since the end of the civil trial. He made it clear from the outset that he viewed the case strictly as a paying proposition. On 15 August, three weeks into Kenealy's opening speech, Hendricks resigned. He could see no hope of being paid. Moreover, he made it plain that he *had* provided Kenealy with instructions—and that they'd been ignored. Kenealy's response was characteristic: 'I am extremely glad to find that Sir Roger Tichborne has at length got rid of you. You have been one of his worst enemies, and I hope that you will get your reward.' Hendricks was replaced by a Mr Harcourt: 'a reliable man' in Lord Rivers' estimation and 'Not such a *flâneur* as the other' in the Claimant's.

The day after Hendricks' resignation—a hot, clear-blue Saturday—Kenealy spent sweltering at the files, trying to plot a path forward. His client, 'habitually careless' to the conduct of his case, was at Chiswick, shooting at pigeons for a purse of £200. He was living, these days, at 34 Bessborough Street, Pimlico, with a pug named Tissie ('the life of my idle hours'). His family was installed in a house at Caversham Road, Kentish Town, which, though not much above four miles from Westminster, he considered too far to travel to court each day. Nor, he said, could he allow himself the distraction of family life: 'when I get near my children I get lazy, and do not come to work, besides,' he wrote to Mary, 'although you may not understand me, the sight of my children completely upsets my brain, that I am not in a fit state to do my business.'

That was one of the countless letters he wrote during his long, mute hours in the Court of Queen's Bench. Each morning he brought to court a small leather bag, from which he methodically unpacked notepaper, envelopes, clasp-knife, pocket dictionary, and a tiny pair of scissors which he used to cut 'exquisite little patterns' out of paper: stars, roses, diamonds. As Kenealy ranted, his client would lay down the scissors and carefully unfold his latest creation, holding it up towards one of the court's high windows so that it cast a lacy shadow across his face. He also sketched—scenes from the courtroom, mainly: portraits, sometimes spiteful, of witnesses, jurors, judges, and anybody else who took his eye. Though far from the masterpieces claimed by Kenealy, the Claimant's drawings revealed a decided talent for carica-ture. One way and another, his hands were hardly ever still.

Sketched by the Claimant in court. His subject was Captain Fraser, a prosecution witness who revealed that Roger Tichborne was called 'Small Cock' by his brother officers

His letters from court were most often addressed to Guildford Onslow, who cared for his family and gave him his beloved Tissie. When the pug died of distemper midway through the trial, the distraught Claimant wrote to Onslow: 'You try and get me another, will you, and I will promise never to blow you up any more.' He wrote letters to Kenealy too:

> Surely penal servitude cannot be worse than having your life torn out of you by your friends. I certainly can't look at it with the horror which is supposed to belong to it. Any place, even hell, can't be worse than the last five years have been to me on this earth. The more I wish to die, the longer I seem to live…

Early in July, George Whalley had rushed off to New York in pursuit of a fresh lead concerning the rescue of survivors from the *Bella*. From there he kept imploring Kenealy, by telegram, to prolong his speech. On 14 August he begged for six or seven days more, as he'd discovered proof 'of vital importance to the success of the case' and was bringing it home.

Kenealy did his best, subjecting the jury to several days of minute comparison between the handwritings of Roger, the Claimant, and Arthur Orton.

> I call your attention to the 'v' in the last line, which I consider a very remarkable, curious 'v', analogous to the 'v' of Roger, with a kind of superfluous dash about it...

By 4.30 p.m. on 21 August, the jury had heard enough. Kenealy's chief antagonist on the panel, Jonas Taylor, spoke up just as the court was set to adjourn for the day:

> You promised us the other day to finish on Friday, then on Monday, then on Wednesday, and yet you are still going on...
> Dr Kenealy: Do not be too hard on me.
> Mr Taylor: This is a sheep pen.
> Dr Kenealy: I assure you mine is not a bed of roses.
> Mr Taylor: I am sorry for you.

Probably Kenealy was right to doubt the sincerity of that last remark. Nonetheless, he wound his opening speech to a conclusion the next afternoon, just before three. 'I call on you, in the name of that divine maternal instinct which pointed out that man to her to be her son, to find—and no doubt by your verdict you will find, and delight the whole country of England by that verdict—that this is Roger Tichborne.'

After the briefest of adjournments, his assisting barrister, Patrick McMahon, led off the evidence for the defence.

THIRTY-SIX

NEVER SURPRISED AT ANYTHING

THE defence called most of the same witnesses who'd appeared for the Claimant at the civil trial. Francis Baigent was a notable absentee. He'd baulked at submitting a second time to Hawkins' ferocious cross-examining. Besides, Kenealy considered Baigent a liability, contending that his past performance in the box had weakened the Claimant's case. Roger's servant and travelling companion, John Moore, had been among the solidest witnesses at the last trial. This time, however, he decided 'to serve my own interests' and shipped himself beyond the reach of subpoena-servers.

One who did take the stand a second time was Andrew Bogle, the old Tichborne retainer who'd accompanied the Claimant from Sydney. Arguably, Bogle was one of the most important witnesses for the defence. A great deal of folklore had built up around him, many people crediting the former slave boy as the Claimant's svengali: the one who, in the first place, had schooled him and drilled him in Tichborne family lore, without which preparation his claim could not have endured a week in England. Among a certain class, Bogle represented that most dangerous and unnatural of creatures: the loyal servant turned bad. He was sixty-seven years old and, far from leading the 'more sociable' life he'd dreamt of in Sydney, found himself cooped up with the Claimant's foul-tempered wife and an ill-assorted bunch of spongers in the house at Kentish Town.

Nobody looked forward to Bogle's turn in the witness box more than did Henry Hawkins. Thanks to what he regarded as timidity on the part of Coleridge, the old valet's credibility had been little shaken at the last trial. Now Hawkins greeted him as the Claimant's 'murky satellite' and counselled the jury to distrust his evidence: 'I do not like, as a rule, to abuse whole classes of men, but I cannot forget that there are some portions of the negro race who are not proverbial for truth.'

But Bogle proved more than a match for the prosecution's leading counsel. He politely answered every question, no matter how sneering or impertinent, and while Hawkins grew hot from his exertions Bogle remained supremely cool, never for a moment letting his dignity or his discretion slip. Hawkins even resorted to Coleridge's old line, asking whether Bogle had been surprised to hear that the Claimant had bought the Metropolitan Hotel in Sydney. 'No,' replied Bogle, 'I am never surprised at anything myself.'

'You are never surprised at anything?' Hawkins sounded incredulous.

'Never in my life,' said Bogle, with such blank equanimity that it was hard to doubt it. 'I never recall that I was.' Nothing Hawkins tried could shift him a whisker from his avowal that the Claimant was Roger Tichborne and no other. What Bogle wasn't asked was if, when he met the Claimant in Sydney, he'd happened to mention the *Africa*, the ship that had borne him from England in 1854—and how she'd called first at Melbourne, on 24 July, the very same day as the alleged, untraceable *Osprey*.

After the young-Roger witnesses came the defence's fifty-eight Wapping witnesses. Nearly all of them were in trades connected with shipping: lighterman, shipsmith, sailmaker, shipping butcher, barge builder. Wapping was a small place by any reckoning—its half square mile embraced a community as tight as the Claimant's collar—and it was obvious that six years' untrammelled gossip and the past year's recruitment drive had well and truly 'contaminated' the witnesses.

Those awaiting their turn in the box were able to follow their neighbours' evidence closely, either in court or via the newspapers, which reported each day's proceedings almost verbatim. A dozen or more of the defence's Wapping witnesses used the same term, 'splaw foot', to describe Arthur Orton's walk, and nearly all gave a word-for-word rendition of his high cheekbones, his gruff voice, his 'huge' hands and feet, and the rings he wore in his ears.

Like others of the Wapping witnesses, George Sallaway showed himself to be of a literal—or possibly comic—turn of mind. Asked by Kenealy whether the Claimant's were the same sort of boots as Arthur Orton had worn before he went to sea, he replied, 'Oh no! I should think they would have been worn out.'

Next he was asked about Orton's earrings. 'Do you recollect the last time you saw them?'

'In his ears,' Sallaway replied.

Henry Hawkins, cross-examining, indulged in some fun with the Wapping witnesses. One, for instance, insisted that the Claimant could not be Arthur Orton because he was not fat enough. 'Did you expect to see an elephant in a frock-coat then?' Hawkins loved this kind of thing.

'Well,' said the witness, 'if Arthur Orton, I should have thought he would be bigger.'

Most of the Wappingites were testifying with apparent certainty to events which had taken place more than twenty years before. To test their memory for dates, Hawkins commonly asked them to state the year of their birth. Edward Wakeling replied that he was forty years old. Hawkins pressed him. 'You were born in the year 1833?'

'I suppose that would be about it.'

'You do not know?' asked Hawkins.

'I was there at the birth,' replied Wakeling, 'but I cannot swear to it.'

Another witness, attesting to the reputed naivety of Wapping youths, declared, 'They are born very young down there.'

Dr Kenealy preferred his witnesses, like himself, to be taken seriously. The trouble was, nobody laughed louder than his client. The Claimant's dark moods were fleeting. The notes he passed to his counsel typically contained riddles, such as 'How many cow tails reach to the moon?' Finding a caricature of himself in the latest edition of *Punch* gave him no end of 'vague, unmeaning pleasure'; and Kenealy being incapable of seeing the joke, he would pass it along to the prosecution end of the bar table. Indeed, his good humour in court was such that even Hawkins was inclined to think the better of him. 'The Claimant himself not only gave me no offence from first to last,' he would recall in his memoirs, 'but was at times in his manner very amusing, and preserved his natural good temper admirably, considering what he had at stake on the issue of the trial.'

The Claimant's good humour was the more remarkable because (according to Kenealy) he lived in fear for his life, the Tichborne trustees having posted a £1,000 reward for his murder. Kenealy even claimed that attempts had been made on his own life: several times on his walk to and from Westminster and once via the agency of a fresh-killed pheasant delivered to his home. Suspicious of the anonymous gift, Kenealy had it thrown out in the yard where even the cats had refused to touch it.

Kenealy's half-hour walk to court each morning, while it made him an easy target for assassins, did much to fortify him for the day's ordeal. The Claimant travelled the short distance in his famous Wedgwood-blue brougham. Both men were met by a crowd that more than filled Palace Yard, the forecourt to Westminster Hall. On a typical Monday—'the Tichborne gala day of the week'—between eight and ten thousand people gathered outside the court, morning and afternoon, to catch a glimpse of their champion, the Claimant. 'It was a grand sight,' wrote Kenealy, 'like a vast sea of humanity rallying round this unhappy victim of papal rage and cold-blooded

Fashion.' They were kept in order by Inspector Denning's special contingent of 150 police, who formed double lines at the gateways each afternoon to prevent the crowd chasing after the Claimant's carriage. The Palace Yard mob was dismissed as riff-raff by London's leading newspapers, but the *Morning Advertiser*, sympathetic to the Claimant, noted of a Monday's crowd in October: 'In the main it was a well-dressed assemblage, composed largely of respectable-looking females, whose conduct and demeanour were pledges of their respectability.' The reporter estimated that, from their headgear ('billy-cock hats, wideawakes, and other low-crowned tiles'), only one in twenty of those assembled could be 'classed amongst the London roughs.'

All of England, the Australian colonies, even America followed the progress of the trial assiduously. The thing was every bit as picaresquely contrived as a novel; in fact, one newspaper declared it 'a case exceeding any three-volume novel in interest, fuller of mystery and artifice than fifty novels by Wilkie Collins himself—fifty *Women in White*.' Even George Eliot, whose own novels were paeans to realism, was caught up in the Tichborne fever. She spent a day in the court's public gallery and called it 'an experience of great interest to me.' Her next (and last) novel, published two years later, bore an uncharacteristic epigraph: 'It is a part of probability that many improbable things will happen.'

In October 1873, when the defence case had been running eleven weeks, Kenealy introduced a line of evidence that raised his client still higher on the scale of fabulous renown. It was so risqué that the newspapers could allude to it only in the vaguest of terms, leaving imagination and hearsay to fill in the details. Something of the sort had been rumoured for years. As Serjeant Parry, assisting counsel for the prosecution, had put it to Kenealy one day in the Westminster Hall lunch room: 'We hear your client is made like a horse.'

It was an interest in phrenology that had led Dr David Wilson to seek the Claimant's acquaintance. It might be just the thing, the doctor had suggested, to confirm him as the undoubted Roger Tichborne. In the course of 'reading' the Claimant's bumps, Dr Wilson had inquired about his health in general and heard that his bladder was giving him some difficulty. Shifting his attention from skull to trunk, the doctor made a thorough examination. Now Kenealy asked him to tell the Court of Queen's Bench what he had discovered inside the Claimant's trousers. The answer was 'nothing'—which is to say, nothing where the Claimant's penis ought to have been.

To begin with, Dr Wilson had supposed that the appendage was merely obscured by the great expanse of fat sagging over it. With both hands he lifted the apron of flesh; still he could see nothing. He asked the Claimant then to hold up his own stomach but, seeing him unequal to the task, had propped the back of a chair under it. Then the doctor crouched down and peered in close. Above the Claimant's scrotum was a circular recess with just the tip of a penis discernible at its opening. 'Ah,' the Claimant had said, self-conscious. 'That is my malformation.'

'Am I to understand the member was not at all protruding?' asked Kenealy.

'Not at all,' agreed Dr Wilson, 'nothing but the orifice was to be seen.' The rumours were true: the Claimant was made like a horse.

The court was cleared of ladies as soon as the thrust of the doctor's evidence became apparent. He went on, at Kenealy's prompting, to explain how the absence of the Claimant's penis was connected with his bladder problem. The bladder, it seemed, was of such an unusually large capacity that he could, and frequently did, go for two or three days without emptying it. 'He did not do it as a matter of choice,' Dr Wilson explained, but because 'the water did not come.' When finally he did relieve himself, he might pass as much as several quarts of urine. The doctor believed that the weight of his full bladder, combined with the absence of a muscle connecting urethra to pubic bone, caused the Claimant's penis to retract like a horse's. Unlike a horse's, however, it did not emerge when he urinated, although the doctor assured the court that he had found it 'more turgid' on other occasions.

The Claimant sat through Dr Wilson's evidence as unconcerned as if it were his hat-size that was being discussed. He had his little scissors out and was working on a clover-shaped design which, when complete, he mounted on three dead matches and waited for a breeze to knock it down.

In corroboration of Dr Wilson's evidence, Kenealy tendered to the court a report made by Dr Lipscombe of Alresford in 1869: 'The penis and testicles are small; the former so much retracted (when not excited) that it rests upon the upper part of the scrotum, like a bud, about an inch-and-a-half in height.' From there, Kenealy made a backwards leap to contend that Roger Tichborne had possessed the same malformation. Hadn't Captain George Fraser, a prosecution witness, admitted that Roger had been dubbed 'Small Cock' by his tormentors in the Carabineers? Now William Privett, a nephew of the Dowager's, was put in the stand to depose that three years after Roger's disappearance his aunt had sent him a detailed physical description of her son, in case Privett should meet with him on his travels abroad. Among other oddities, she had listed 'a peculiar malformation of person called by those attending on him his seal, or God's mark.' Then there was the withered leaf sent by Roger, at his most misanthropic, to his aunt, Lady Doughty, as a symbol of his prospects. Kenealy preferred to interpret it as a reference to the youth's withered member. Here, he said, was the meaning of the Claimant's assertion that the Dowager would have difficulty believing him the father of a child. Hadn't he waggled his little finger as he said so? According to Kenealy, the Dowager had insisted on seeing the Claimant's penis before acknowledging him as her son, a suggestion the Lord Chief Justice dismissed as 'monstrously indelicate.'

Nevertheless he granted permission for the Claimant to drop his trousers in the robing room so that jurors might inspect the malformation for themselves. This was curiosity at work, not the law. But the Claimant made no objection; in fact, he seemed to enjoy the attention as if it wasn't the first time he'd made a sideshow of himself this way—nor would it be the last. He wrote to Onslow a short time later that he had made arrangements with Dr Wilson 'to have my photo taken in a particular way for some scientific purpose.'

'The important service rendered to the cause of justice by the art of photography' was widely acknowledged during and after the Tichborne trial. The principal exhibits in the case—hundreds of letters, Roger's and the Claimant's pocket-books, and many dozens of portraits— were all photographed by the London Stereoscopic Company for examination in court. The same enterprising company produced, and sold, thousands of *cartes de visite* of the protagonists in the case. A shilling would buy a William Gibbes, a Dowager Lady Tichborne, a Guildford Onslow, a Justice Mellor or even an Inspector Denning. Portraits of the Claimant himself came in dozens of different poses, while his wife and children featured in a further five.

The trial also played a role in developing new scientific applications for photography. William Matthew, 'celebrated scientific photographer' and honorary secretary of the Bristol Science-Test Tichborne Committee, invented the Identiscope and its by-product, the Tichborne Photographic Blend. The Identiscope took two portraits and, by 'geometric admeasurement', compared their subjects' features. Using the technique, the Tichborne Photographic Blend overlaid a current portrait of the Claimant on Roger Tichborne's daguerreotype to reveal that, despite their apparent differences, the position and dimensions of the features in the two were identical. Matthew declared it 'a process that cannot err.'

No such exalted claim attached itself to a sheaf of photographs produced as trial exhibits by the defence. These murky vistas, the work of Guildford Onslow, purported to depict a tree-shaded grotto beside the Itchen River at Tichborne—allegedly the scene of Miss Doughty's seduction. (The infamous spot had shifted: at the last trial, it had been a mill-house nearby.) Kenealy seems to have had great hopes for the persuasive power of these photographs; instead, they were the subject of ridicule. He had himself done a similar demolition job on a portrait of the Claimant shown to witnesses by the prosecution. 'It is as much like me as it is like the Defendant,' he snorted. 'In fact, it is more like the King of Ashantee, or a person who has just descended a chimney.'

But the grandest photographic squib of the trial centred on the Santiago daguerreotypes of Roger Tichborne. There were two of them, almost mirror images: one held by the prosecution, the other by the defence. The prosecution's daguerreotype—originally Lady Doughty's—had travelled with the commission to Chile and had been badly rubbed and scratched on the train journey from Valparaiso to Santiago. The worst of the damage was around the edges, making the top of Roger's hat and his hands indistinct. It was the hands that troubled Kenealy: in particular, one of the thumbs. In the defence's daguerreotype, Roger's right thumb was just visible in the corner. Kenealy produced experts to swear that a large portion of the thumb-nail appeared to be missing and to observe, moreover, that the Claimant's right thumb bore the same deformity. It was a fixation of Kenealy's that the prosecution's daguerreotype had been deliberately damaged to conceal this mark of identification, and he was unmoved even by evidence from his own experts that it was not uncommon for fingers or thumbs to appear greatly distorted in photographs, or even for hands to acquire extra digits. Nor were Kenealy's claims supported by medical evidence. The doctor who'd first examined the Claimant's thumbnail, in 1871, deposed that the injury seemed to be of recent occurrence—and that the Claimant himself had confirmed as much.

Kenealy came last—or almost last—to his Australian witnesses. Some swore they'd seen the *Osprey* arrive at Melbourne, others reworked bushy tales from the Castro–Orton miscellany. But the defence had to make do without the valuable evidence of 'Professor' Anderson. He was in the middle of a three-week engagement on the Isle of Man when he was subpoenaed as a witness at the Tichborne trial. As the writ carried no force under Manx law, he declined to comply.

At the close of the prosecution case, back in July, a London journalist had reflected that 'we have all suddenly become familiar with Australian geography, and talk glibly of Gundagai, and Gippsland, and Tumut.' For many, the Tichborne trial served as an introduction to the Australian bush. 'That expression "in the bush",' observed the London correspondent for the *Argus*, 'seems to have exercised a powerful sway over the imaginations of persons concerned in the trial'—none more than Dr Kenealy. Rhapsodically he evoked the splendour of life in 'the bush': 'You are under the most delightful climate in the world— nine months of uninterrupted sunshine. You have all the Arab independence of the desert; a beautiful climate, glorious nights of stars and moonlight such as are never seen in Europe.' It was the kind of place that could seduce a man, could make him forget his family and everything that was proper, luring him into a 'vagabond life, pleasant but wrong.' There was no question, said Kenealy, but that life in the Australian bush, with Arthur Orton as a tutor, could trans- form an aristocrat into a butcher.

Kenealy's notion of life in the bush ranged from hazy to delirious. His 'most delightful climate in the world' referred to Gippsland in July. He blamed 'struggling through the bush' for the scars on his client's ankles. He even proposed that a ditty from Rapino's *Song of Andalusia*, sung by Roger in a concert at Stonyhurst—its verses alluding to highway robbery, drunkenness and wenching—had served as 'a preparation for bush life.' The Lord Chief Justice was quite right to ask, 'What sort of bush life?'

Justice Cockburn fancied that he knew a thing or two about the bush. 'Suppose,' Kenealy surmised at one point, 'that he lived on the kangaroos that he shot...' 'Or the emu,' interjected his Lordship, whom his close friends knew as 'Cocky'. But the word 'Australia'—drawled by a former colonist—tripped him up on one occasion; he misheard it as 'horse-stealers'. It was evidence relating to the goldfields, though, that most mystified Cockburn and the court. Charles Janes' assertion that he had 'followed the diggings' was too much for the Lord Chief Justice. 'The diggings do not move; they are stationary,' he snapped.

Charles Janes had followed the diggings as a vendor of sly grog and claimed that Castro and Orton also had shifted about from goldfield to goldfield—Castlemaine, Fryers Creek, Tarrangower—in their bushranging capacity. With their cohorts, they'd often gathered at Janes' campfire and partaken of his grog. Orton, he remembered, had pierced ears and used to wear gum leaves poked through the holes. Questioned about his own activities, Janes (now a greengrocer at Hornsey) maintained that he'd never been in trouble of any kind—had never been caught, in other words—in light of which Hawkins dubbed him 'a highly respectable sly-grogsman.'

Janes was succeeded in the witness box by Jean Luie, a Danish sailor. It was Luie whose information about the rescue of survivors from the *Bella* had sent Whalley scurrying to New York for corroborating evidence. Luie had presented himself at Number 2, Poets' Corner, Westminster—headquarters of the Tichborne defence—at the beginning of July. He had only recently returned from a long stretch at sea, he said, and had read in the papers of the Claimant's case and his supposed rescue by the *Osprey*. 'I set vitin myself,' Luie told the court, 'dis iss de yong mann who vas in my bert on de *Osprey*. I like to see him moch.'* He claimed to have been steward on the

* As rendered by London's *Daily Telegraph*.

ship that picked up Roger Tichborne after the wreck of the *Bella*. The young man had been wearing an outfit of striped calico when they hauled him aboard the *Osprey* and, once he surfaced from his delirium, had given his name as Rogers. Luie had shared a berth with him, bathed his salt blisters, and put clean clothes on his back. Three others of the *Bella* survivors he could also recall: Lewis, Jarvis and 'Doctor', the ship's cook. When the *Osprey* reached Melbourne, Luie had deserted for the goldfields with two of the *Bella* men and spent almost a year at Ballarat. As for the castaway Rogers, Luie had seen no more of him from the time he jumped ship in Melbourne until four months ago when he spotted the Claimant's portrait on a railway newsstand. He was certain it was the same man.

Luie confirmed the Claimant's statement that the *Osprey* was a barque-rigged vessel, painted black, and that she'd arrived in Melbourne in July 1854. Most importantly, Luie identified her point of origin (New York), her owners, ship-brokers, and the names of a dozen others who could attest to her voyage to Melbourne. The defence was secretive about what Whalley had actually discovered in New York. It was rumoured that he'd obtained the *Osprey*'s log, but no such thing ever turned up in court. Certainly he'd brought back no witnesses, but he must have seen or heard something that bore out Luie's story, since he and his friends at Poets' Corner regarded the genial Dane as the Claimant's trump card. Kenealy wasn't so sure.

Jean Luie made a steadfast and credible witness, strong on detail and cool under pressure. Onlookers were charmed by the 'indescribable twinkle of merriment in his voice, as of one who…views the world from its comic side, and finds it a most amusing farce.' But Hawkins smelled a rat and declared Luie's evidence 'a tale which, if such a thing were possible, would be still more incredible than the Defendant's.' Before Luie had finished in the stand, the prosecution had its own agent on the way to New York to check the bona fides of the *Osprey* and the defence's prize witness.

Luie's evidence concluded the case for the defence. The prosecution then obtained an adjournment for the entire month of November, to await its agent's findings in New York. When December began, the prosecution produced rebutting evidence to show not only that the *Osprey* was untraceable in New York, but that Jean Luie was not who he claimed to be. John or Carl Lundgren, alias Lindgrew, alias Petersen, alias Sorensen, alias Smith, had been at Hull when he was supposed to have been at Ballarat and in Chatham prison, serving time for fraud, until shortly before he showed up at Poets' Corner. On 2 December, the same day Kenealy was due to commence his closing address, Jean Luie was arrested for perjury.

'It would not have happened,' said Luie upon his arrest, 'if I had not been encouraged and made up to do what I have done.' Encouraged by *whom*? The prosecution would hardly have sent an agent to New York if it already knew the *Osprey* evidence to be bogus. And Inspector Denning of the Palace Yard flying squad had learned of Luie's previous conviction only in the first week of December, when Chatham prison forwarded the record of his release, complete with a photograph. As for the suggestion that the Claimant's side had put Luie up to it—'Nobody,' said Kenealy, 'but people red-hot from Bedlam would ever have thought of calling a ticket-of-leave man as one of their staple witnesses.' Luie would be sentenced to seven years for perjury, and a further three on a bigamy charge that had caught up with him at last.

There was bad blood in the Claimant's camp after the unmasking of Luie. George Whalley bore the brunt of blame for the debacle; yet he persisted in his folly. Not only did he defend Luie's evidence but he did so publicly, in letters to the newspapers, for which he was charged with contempt of court. He turned on the Claimant, spreading rumours amongst his supporters that their hero had misspent on women funds raised for his defence. Whalley and the Claimant came close to fisticuffs in a confrontation at Poets' Corner. 'We all know how it goes,' Whalley accused him: 'You get the poor people's pennies, and you do not apply it to your defence. If you were not a bigger man than me, and if I were not convinced that you were Sir Roger Tichborne, I would try to knock you down!'

'Go! go! you little Jew,' blazed the Claimant. 'You took up my cause not for *my* sake, but to get notoriety. And it was *you* who brought that villain Luie upon me. You are the worst enemy I ever had!'

Even Whalley's own friend, Lord Rivers, turned against him, telling Kenealy, 'Whalley is the man *I* most distrust in all the various phases of the Trial.' Upon his conviction for contempt, the man they called 'Folly' would elect three months' gaol rather than pay the £250 fine. But he would never shift in his belief that the Claimant was not only Sir Roger Tichborne but 'a thoroughly generous and kind-hearted man.'

That the Claimant's generosity extended to lavishing money on women was not just Whalley's contention. Kenealy would later state that during the trial—'when the outside public thought that his whole heart and mind were concentrated in getting evidence'—his client's evenings had been spent 'in making assignations with women, whom he introduced into the gallery.' Outside of his own circle, it was widely rumoured that what kept him away from his family was not business, but his attachment to a 'former actress' who kept house with him at Bessborough Street.

THIRTY-SEVEN

HE MUST BE SOMEBODY

KENEALY could not afford to be sidetracked by the business with Whalley and Jean Luie. He had yet to deliver his summing-up for the defence. On 2 December 1873 he got to his feet:

> I commence my observations in defence of the Accused by reverently invoking the Supreme Judge of the Universe, that in this mighty Trial He may guide us by wisdom, by impartiality, by the spirit of justice unto a true verdict on the issue before us; that we may not be misled by any temporal consideration—by fear, by favour, by affection—to deviate in the least degree from the glorious path of sunbright rectitude; but that we may all of us bear in mind that according to the justice that we mete out here, so shall be the justice administered to ourselves in the dread Hereafter.

Taking that supplicatory threat as his starting point, Kenealy kept talking for twenty-six days, pausing for just the meagrest of adjournments at Christmas and New Year.

He went in hard. 'I don't believe there is one honest man in England who believes this is Arthur Orton.' Then he put to jurors his contention 'that the Defendant is Roger Tichborne, and that it is not until I have entirely failed to prove that he is *not* Roger Tichborne that you are entitled to regard him as Arthur Orton.' Here he was equating 'Tichborne until proved Orton' with 'innocent until proved guilty'.

But the Lord Chief Justice begged to differ:

> You have a right to assume that the Defendant is Roger
> Tichborne till the contrary is proved; but it is quite a different
> matter to say that you have a right to assume he is Roger
> Tichborne till he is proved to be Arthur Orton. The Prosecution
> may wholly fail in showing that he is Arthur Orton, and yet
> may prove that he is not Roger Tichborne.

'I cannot think that perjury can be brought home to a man without a clear proof of who he is,' objected Lord Rivers to Kenealy at this juncture. 'To convict, the man must be proved to be somebody.' If Rivers was confused (and he wasn't the only one), Dr Kenealy was at least partly to blame. Serjeant Ballantine, the Claimant's former advocate, was critical of Kenealy for taking on 'the unnecessary burden of proving that the defendant was really Sir Roger Tichborne,' when all that was required was to establish reasonable doubt in jurors' minds. The dubious nature of the tattoo evidence, Ballantine believed, might alone have been sufficient to achieve that. But Kenealy had something to prove.

'If you should convict him,' he told the jury on the first day of his summing-up, the 132nd day of the trial, 'they will have his estates for ever.'

'Who are "They"?' asked the Lord Chief Justice.

'His enemies.'

Kenealy meant the Jesuits. 'The infant heir is seven or eight years old, and may be trained as they think fit,' he said, 'but here is a grown man, who has outburst their chains.' The Roman Catholic Church received £50,000 a year from the Tichborne estates, Kenealy asserted, and stood to get nothing should his client inherit. All the way from Wagga ('The Jesuits have little birds everywhere'), word had reached them of this lapsed son of Rome and they had determined from the outset to crush his claim. Were jurors reminded of Kenealy's own words, earlier in the trial, as they sat through his latest rant? 'One of the signs of insanity,' he had declared, 'is a man fancying everybody is his enemy.'

Halfway through his closing address, Kenealy went looking—too late—for Dick Slate, the Claimant's mate from Wagga. The prosecution's one witness who'd known Slate had said nothing to flesh (or flush) him out: only that he hailed from Hampshire and was 'a very well educated man.' From such scant evidence and his name in Cox's pocket-book, the world was meant to surmise, said Kenealy, that it was Slate, endowed with the entire history of the Tichborne family, who had masterminded Tom Castro's campaign of imposture. 'Where is Slate?' Kenealy demanded:

> These men have gone to the ends of the earth for Witnesses. Where is Slate? Here is the man who taught my Client the A, B, C, the rudiments, the grammar, nay, the whole Case! Where is he? SLATE! SLATE! SLATE! Where art thou? Echo answers, Where art thou?

As his speech drew near its end, Kenealy sought to woo the jurors with visions of immortality. 'Your names,' he told them, 'will be preserved for ever and will be known by generations of men yet unborn, who will be riveted by this amazing story.'

> You must, as it were, judge the whole of this case as a kind of drama passing before you, different from all other dramas that exist, that have ever come within your experience—not to apply to its varied scenes what you would apply to ordinary commonplace things, but regarding them as something extraordinary, something novel, something that probably never happened before, and, in all human possibility, will never happen again.

Finally, he evoked 'the spirit of that departed lady' the Dowager Lady Tichborne. 'In her name and in the name of justice, I demand an acquittal for Roger Tichborne.'

If the Dowager was Kenealy's guiding angel, Hawkins' was Lady Radcliffe.

> You are boldly and audaciously asked by the Defendant's Counsel to discredit a virtuous woman's oath, to stain her maiden name with the taint of impurity, and, stamping her with perjury, to say that she has been soiled and polluted by his Client's filthy, unholy, unnatural touch.

Here, after all, was the heart of the Tichborne trial. The Claimant's acquittal would amount to the conviction of Lady Radcliffe, the sanctioning of his 'foul charge' against her. 'I have no fear of you,' Hawkins crooned to the jury. 'In your hands her honour will be safe.'

Hawkins' closing address lasted a fortnight, long enough for him to damn the Claimant and his counsel a thousand different ways before enjoining jurors to 'fulfil your sacred mission' and relinquishing the limelight to the Lord Chief Justice for his summing-up.

Justice Cockburn was flat-out speechifying for more than three weeks. He reminded jurors at the outset that the onus of proof lay with the prosecution: 'The question…is not so much whether he is Roger Tichborne, as whether the Prosecution has proved that he is *not* Roger Tichborne.' He began and ended his long address by upbraiding Kenealy for his conduct during the trial, but he was not unduly harsh on the Claimant himself. Sceptical, certainly; but not scathing.

He found it 'insupportable' that Roger Tichborne—'a man accustomed to the comforts and enjoyments of a highly civilised and refined life'—would submit to living in a bark hut 'with associates of the rudest, roughest, and coarsest class.'

> When Roger Tichborne, if he was Roger Tichborne, discovered the sort of life he was called upon to lead, would you not have expected that he would have said, 'This is unendurable. I

must write home at once and say where I am. I must obtain funds and get out of this as soon as I possibly can'?

The mirror to that question had been posed by Kenealy in his closing address, when he asked jurors to suppose what his client, had he been Arthur Orton, would have done when bailed from Newgate pending the trial:

> What would Arthur Orton have done when he was thus at large? He would probably have said to himself, 'The game is played out; I have lost it and must look to myself. I shall go back to Australia and hide myself in the wilds. I will ensconce myself in my old haunts, and be made welcome by my old companions.'

Those old haunts and companions, Justice Cockburn believed, held the key to the Claimant's defence. In particular, there were the nine or ten hazy months of 1859, which, evidence suggested, had swallowed Arthur Orton at the one end and spat out Tom Castro at the other. But his Lordship did not buy Kenealy's explanation for the enmeshing of the two men's lives.

> Gentlemen, we have all heard of the transmigration of souls… But I have never heard of the transmigration of mind from one living person to another. According to this theory, the effect of the discourses which had taken place between the two persons under the canopy of heaven and the magnificent and cloudless skies of Australia was that the recollections of Arthur Orton had passed into the mind of Roger Tichborne and, superseding his own and turning it out altogether, had taken bodily possession of his memory.

He did, however, confess himself puzzled by the apparent admixture of identities and the contradiction of the Claimant's being recognised

by one set of witnesses as Roger Tichborne and by another as Arthur
Orton. He was inclined to think, his Lordship said, that 'to a certain
extent both sets of Witnesses are right, and both sets of Witnesses
are wrong,' in that the Claimant bore a likeness both to Tichborne and
to Orton. Here the judge seemed to be hinting at the belief, widespread
among opponents of the Claimant, that he was an illegitimate
Tichborne. It was a view to which Sir John Coleridge, during the last
trial, had privately subscribed while publicly maintaining that the
Claimant was Arthur Orton. Yet the two propositions were not
mutually exclusive. According to 'stage-play-like' reports in circulation, Mary Orton—Arthur's mother—either was an illegitimate
daughter of Roger's grandfather or had shared a counterpane with
Sir James Tichborne.

On the question of the sealed packet and Miss Doughty's seduction, the Lord Chief Justice's guidance of the jury was tempered by
gallantry, but not throbbing with it:

> Here the accused becomes the accuser, in a matter in which the
> honour, the position, the happiness of a woman are concerned.
> You are fathers, husbands, and brothers, and therefore know
> what a woman's honour is, and what it is worth. You are bound
> in justice to give the case your most careful attention! that the
> charge, if a false one, may be pronounced and declared to be so;
> while at the same time, no feeling of sympathy with the woman
> should warp your minds from deciding according to the truth.

Dr Kenealy was absent from court for much of Justice Cockburn's
speech. Like Ballantine before him, his exertions had gone largely
unpaid. Moreover, the Lord Chief Justice's reproaches were nothing
to the enmity Kenealy bore him in return. In footnotes to his published
record of the trial, Kenealy would allege not only that Cockburn was
addicted to French novels 'of the very worst description,' but that
he'd been party to a murder in a Bristol brothel.

In a letter written in court while Cockburn's summing-up was in progress, the Claimant apologised for his poor grammar: 'I am writing under difficulties, hearing this —— all the while.' Calls on his time outside of the court included sitting for a bust, to be exhibited at the Royal Academy in May. 'There is plenty of time,' he told Mr Harrison, the sculptor, at the end of January. Or perhaps not. Two days later, a Sunday, word swept London that the Claimant had cut his own throat. So vast and expectatious was the crowd at Palace Yard next morning that two of Inspector Denning's men had ribs cracked by the mighty surge against the railings when the blue brougham came bowling up Millbank. The Claimant wasn't dead; but he feared he soon would be. At least, that was his latest excuse for so rarely coming 'home' to Kentish Town. Writing in mid-February, he told his wife, 'I cannot possibly have long to live in this World, therefore I am anxious to do what I can during my existence here.'

The twenty-second day of Justice Cockburn's summing-up was a Friday and, when it came time for that day's adjournment, he signalled that he was not far off finishing. He had spared the jurors (and himself) from Saturday sittings thus far, leaving them one day of the working week to catch up on their neglected business. Now he asked if they would mind returning to court the following day to hear the conclusion of his address and commence their deliberations. They consented with alacrity.

'I feel my nerves giving way,' the Claimant wrote to Guildford Onslow that evening, 'although for ten months I have never slept without a piece of iron in my hand, a custom I have had for years from which I find great benefit.' And to Mary, his wife, he sent a note: 'I am too worried and too tired to go so far as Caversham-road to-night.'

A record crowd stuffed into Palace Yard to greet the Claimant the next momentous morning, 28 February 1874. Kenealy, waiting at the entrance of Westminster Hall, basked in his client's glory as he stepped from the brougham with his trademark ungainly grace: 'The winning smile for which he was remarkable passed between his mouth and eyes like a sunbeam, as for the last time he acknowledged, with a sort of kingly grace, the plaudits with which he was received.'

Inside, the court was packed—with foes, said Kenealy, 'who seemed as though they came, as the old Romans did into the amphitheatre, to enjoy a feast of blood.' Immediately behind the Claimant, in the seats usually reserved for the press, two stern, burly fellows stood out as plainclothes policemen. 'They came to Court with handcuffs in their pockets and revolvers in the breasts of their coats ready for action.' For once, Kenealy's sinister imaginings weren't far off the mark. Precautions had been taken after an anonymous letter tipped off Inspector Denning that the Claimant might, if pronounced guilty, take poison rather than submit to imprisonment.

At ten o'clock, the Lord Chief Justice resumed his summing-up, assuring the jury that, notwithstanding the unprecedented interest which the case had excited, their verdict would find acceptance with all 'except fanatics and fools.' Shortly after twelve, he was done. He directed them to withdraw—which they did, after a moment's delay. (The foreman thought it unnecessary even to leave the box; the others assured him it would look better if they did.) Kenealy and his client exchanged a few words, the Claimant trying to hearten his counsel. 'Cheer up, Doctor, all will be right.' But he took a sheet of quarto and wrote to his wife: 'I am afraid they will give way. If so, take my advice: remain quiet for a little time, and have nothing to do with anybody.'

At 12.35 p.m., the jury filed back in and the tipstaff positioned himself beside the Claimant. 'This looks bad,' he said to Kenealy, and hurriedly unfastened his watch-chain. The jury foreman pronounced him guilty on both counts of perjury. 'All is lost,' the Claimant scribbled before he struggled to his feet to be dealt his sentence.

Justice Mellor had the sentence ready; but first came a lengthy preamble. The jury's verdict met with the unanimous approval of the court, Mellor told the Claimant. 'Indeed, it is difficult to conceive how any person who has considered the intrinsic improbabilities of your story, and has intelligently considered the evidence which has been adduced in the course of this trial, could have come to any other conclusion.' The judge's 'somewhat rosy countenance' bloomed darker when he came to the charge concerning Lady Radcliffe's seduction.

> Wicked and nefarious as it was to impose yourself upon society as Roger Charles Tichborne, and to attempt to deprive the lawful heir of his inheritance, that offence sinks almost into insignificance when compared with the still more infamous perjury by which you sought to support your scheme. I refer to your attempt to blast the reputation of Lady Radcliffe. No more foul or deliberate falsehood was ever heard in a court of justice.

From there, it was a quick-march to the sentence itself.

> I believe I am speaking the sentiment of every member of the court when I say that the punishment about to be assigned by the court is wholly inadequate to your offence. The framers of the Act of Parliament that fixes and limits the sentence which the court is authorised to pass upon you, never dreamt of circumstances so aggravated as exist in your case.

Those unimaginative law-makers had set the maximum sentence for perjury at seven years' imprisonment; moreover, it was customary for multiple sentences to be served concurrently. But Justice Mellor, in sentencing the Claimant to seven years on each of the two indictments, directed that the sentences be served consecutively—a total of fourteen years' imprisonment.

When Mellor had finished, the Claimant's voice was heard in Court of Queen's Bench for the first and last time, 'May I be allowed to say a few words?' 'No,' came the answer, and the tipstaff gripped him at the elbow as bench and jury converged in mutual congratulation.

The Claimant was led out via the Houses of Parliament to a waiting police van, its windows whitewashed. 'It is not necessary, gentlemen,' he said, with a sad glimmer of a smile, when the detectives brought out handcuffs. 'I know how to behave.' He was silent in the van. He had a bad cold and, according to one of his escorts, 'began to show symptoms of depression.' The valuables that he'd handed over on his last admission to Newgate had never been returned to him. This time he emptied his pockets of only six shillings, a few postage stamps, a comb, his paper-knife and an eyeglass. Next his hair was cropped short and his whiskers shaved by a warder. He was allowed to keep his own clothes, there being no prison suit large enough for him; in time, he'd be set to work to make his own. Within less than an hour of the verdict, the Claimant was sitting on the wooden bedstead in the same tight, grey cell he'd occupied two years earlier.

His supporters averred that, in his poor state of health and with his spirit crushed, the penalty was, in effect, a death sentence. Amid the riot of gloating that swelled the newspapers after his conviction, however, one writer proposed the audacious idea that the Claimant might be feeling 'not disappointment, rage, shame, grief, remorse, but simply…a sense of gratification that the acting season was at an end.' After all, they calculated, 'For at least three-fourths of each day of twenty-four hours during the last six years he has been persistently trying to play the part of Roger Tichborne, or, at all events, of somebody who was not Arthur Orton.' It was actually more than eight years.

Two decades later the Claimant himself would look back on the guilty verdict as 'one of the greatest reliefs I had ever felt in my life.'

PART FOUR

THIRTY-EIGHT

NOT ONE HAS TURNED AGAINST YOU

ON the night of the verdict, two servants were killed when a cannon exploded during festivities at Wardour Castle, the seat of Lord Arundell, uncle of the young Tichborne heir. Dr Kenealy only regretted that no member of the family had been killed: 'it would have been more like a judgment.'

Sir Henry Tichborne was seven and a half years old. Before he was eight, his inheritance would be made inviolable by the Tichborne Estates Act. Moreover, heeding Justice Mellor's remarks in sentencing the Claimant, parliament passed the False Personation Act, whereby anyone 'falsely and deceitfully personat[ing] any person, with intent fraudulently to obtain any land, estate, chattel, [or] money' would be liable to imprisonment for life. Inspector Denning was showered with gifts and testimonials in gratitude for his felicitous seating arrangements.

The two Tichborne trials had together lasted 291 days, making the case the longest ever tried in England.* It was a *cause célèbre*, ubiquitous throughout the English-speaking world and beyond. 'Certainly,' said *The Times* in its verdict edition, 'no one human career has ever been so universally and thoroughly known as either that of the true or false Roger Tichborne.' The journalist Henry Labouchere called the Claimant 'the town's talk, the country's talk, the world's talk':

---

* The Tichborne case held the record until 1996, when it was outdone by the 'McLibel' case—which has itself since been exceeded.

the daily newspapers owed to him a larger circulation than they have ever known save in the most exceptionally exciting times. The great man was to them a Bulgarian Atrocity, an Indian Famine, a Franco-German War, a Paris Besieged, a Welsh Mining Disaster, a Prince's Visit, a Great Exhibition, a Ministerial Crisis, a City Panic, an International Conference, a 'Gladstone's resolutions', all rolled into one. Infants lisped his name; women of every degree gossiped over his 'rights' and wrongs; men found in him a fertile source of interest, and his affairs were an unfailing solace to the tedium and worries of workaday and pleasure-taking lives alike.

The *Daily News* agreed that 'Many people will not know what to do with their thoughts' now that the trial was over:

> We find it hard to believe in a time when we shall hear no more about tattooing, and the Sealed Packet and Mr Bogle and Mr Baigent and the Rio witnesses and the Wagga Wagga witnesses, and woman's powers of memory, and man's capacity for oblivion, and the Orton family and the relative size of boots, and hands, and heads, and all the rest of the various topics which have been our daily food…

Australian journalists were less scandalised by the case than were their British counterparts. It wasn't that colonial writers and readers were more inclined to believe the Claimant (quite the opposite); but, unlike the Lord Chief Justice, few among them had difficulty in believing that a gentleman might willingly trade rank and privilege for a life in the bush. A writer in the *Argus* claimed to have encountered three such fellows inside forty-eight hours of bush travel: a civil engineer turned well-sinker, a horsebreaker who'd thrown up an army commission, and a former medical student living contentedly as a shepherd and composing novels in his idle hours. Such stories were commonplace in the colonies; as a rule, their hearers gave their tellers the benefit of the doubt but were none too surprised to learn that they'd been 'taken'. Being familiar with the Claimant's type, Australian colonists were not so much provoked by his cheek as amused that it had got him so far.

The Tichborne case promoted a new image of Australia as mystical and engulfing, its 'bush' possessing strange, transformative powers. Places whose names had never been heard beyond Port Phillip Heads or Middle Harbour became familiar to half the world—and none more so than Wagga Wagga. Sneeringly pronounced by his detractors, the syllables seemed to encapsulate the ludicrousness of the Claimant's pretensions. Conversely, his barrackers would sing out 'Wagga Wagga!' when their hero bagged a pigeon or as they chased his brougham down a London street. And its steam-piston euphony gave the name rich comic possibilities, as instanced in a penny broadside entitled 'Poor Roger Tichborne's Lamentation':

> When the Jury said I was not Roger,
> Oh! how they made me stagger,
> The pretty girls they'll always think,
> Of poor Roger's Wagga-Wagga.

A scene in Act Four of *Tichborne: or is he Butcher or Baronet?*, a melodrama produced for the London stage, had Roger Tichborne tied to the railway tracks in 'the Dargo Hill Tunnel...with the 11.40 express due.' Other theatrical offshoots of the trial included *The Claimant: or the Lost One Found*, *The Wreck of the Bella*, *The Butcher Baronet: or the Wagga Wagga Mystery*, and a bogus-sounding Neopolitan opera, *La Causa Ticciborni*, featuring as principal characters Sir Ruggiero Ticciborni, Arturo Ortone and Caterina Dauti. 'Fat claimant' and 'wopping butcher' became topical insults, and the trial popped up in the lyrics of all manner of pantomimes and burlesques, Tichborne being made to rhyme with rich-born, twitch-born, and so on.

Photographs of the Claimant continued to outsell those of royalty. Some folks framed their worthless Tichborne bonds, revering them as souvenirs or as a caution against folly; others burnt theirs. Tichborne dinner sets were for sale in the Tottenham Court Road, along with china figurines of the leading players, tablecloths printed with scenes from the trial, even bedroom slippers with 'The Claimant' in long-stitch on one toe, 'Roger Tichborne' on the other. A satirical broadside announced a 'Sale of interesting relics of the great Tichborne trial. To be sold by auction without reserve, by Messrs Gammon & Spinach, on Wednesday next, at the Hearty Joke Tavern.' Lot 1 was listed as 'A Hempen Necktie worn in Australia by Orton's friend,' and Lot 5 an 'Egyptian Mummy, which it is supposed Lady Tichborne would have recognised as her son.' In like vein, the Melbourne *Herald* adverted to the existence of a spade used by Tom Castro to dig potatoes, 'but in consequence of the notoriety attached to the implement, it is only exhibited on Gala days at Wagga.'

As a sign of that town's progress, the Claimant's 'far-famed residence' in Gurwood Street had been pulled down while the trial was in progress. The structure in question was indeed far-famed, thanks to

The mythic 'Castro butcher shop' at Wagga, mocked up by a postcard photographer, c.1867

a *carte de visite* that circulated in both hemispheres; but the Claimant's it was not. The sign in the picture—'T. Castro, Butcher'—had been strung above the door by the photographer. Nevertheless, the *Wagga Wagga Advertiser* made it known that 'the place where Lady Mary Ann's washing-tubs stood will soon be devoted to other and more elegant purposes.' The hut itself was advertised for sale in the English papers, evidently in the same spirit as the spoof auction at the Hearty Joke Tavern—but maybe not.

> The house is made of logs, has a brick chimney and a bark roof. On the door still remain pencilled accounts of sales of meat, written by the Claimant himself. The whole structure can be easily pulled down, the door, chimney, and sheets of bark (roof) packed in cases, and, by the aid of plans and photographs, re-erected anywhere. The logs will be numbered, and also the sheets of bark, and everything close to render its erection an easy matter. This remarkable specimen of an Australian bush-house, rendered particularly interesting through the most remarkable trial of modern times, will be sent some 400 miles by bullock waggon, and put on board a ship bound direct to London for the sum of £2,400.

The supposed vendor, G. B. Allen, called it 'A splendid investment for speculators.' He was a Melbourne journalist. When the real 'Tichborne butchery', behind the Australian Hotel, was demolished seventy-five years later, a slab of red gum would be salvaged and fitted as a mantelpiece at the Wagga Wagga Golf Club. The club relocated in 1980 and the talismanic slab, now badly warped, failed to survive the move.

A relic of the Tichborne trial would surface in the making of another myth. Returning home to Hay after the civil trial to find his public house in ashes, Charley 'Pocket-book' Cox moved a hundred miles south to Jerilderie, where he took up the licence of the Royal

Mail Hotel. In a cashbox behind the bar he kept, among other valuables, a gold chronometer watch engraved with the Tichborne seal. He'd often show it off to customers and regale them with the story of how he had come by it. When the civil trial ended in the Claimant's arrest, Cox had visited his old friend in Newgate. Although the publican had sold evidence against him, the Claimant was overjoyed to see him and pressed on him a pawn ticket, as a keepsake. For £30, Cox then exchanged the ticket for the Claimant's treasured watch, which had belonged to Alfred Tichborne before him. That, at least, was Cox's story. It's more likely that the watch acquired by Cox—perhaps in part-payment for his pocket-book—had been taken from the Claimant upon entering prison. That watch was never returned, nor was it amongst goods seized by creditors under his bankruptcy. Its provenance aside, though, Cox's Tichborne relic was in its box under the bar when the Kelly gang seized the Royal Mail Hotel during their Jerilderie stake-out in 1879. Discovering Cox's box of treasures as he helped himself to the contents of the bar, Dan Kelly took a particular shine to the fine gold watch. 'This'll do for me,' he said, making to fix the chain to his smoke-blackened waistcoat. But his brother Ned, gentlemanly to a fault (so the story goes), was moved by Cox's pleading—'Take anything else, but leave me the watch!'—and made Dan hand it back.

Along with their verdict, the jury had submitted a censure of the intemperate, wrong-headed Dr Kenealy. Following an inquiry, he was disbarred. 'I do not withdraw a word that I have uttered in this Trial,' he declared in response. 'The willow withstood the tempest and lived through storms by yielding to every blast. The oak resisted and was swept away. I am that oak.'

He won a seat in the House of Commons the next year, on a platform demanding a new trial for the Tichborne Claimant and justice for 'the people'. Inside Parliament and out, he continued to spout bile against the aristocracy and the Jesuits, the latter of whom he still insisted were trying to poison him. In April 1875, he sought a Royal Commission into the conduct of the Tichborne trial; but his three-hour diatribe in parliament resulted in a vote of 433–1 against the motion.

All over the country, scores of thousands (Kenealy said a million) belonged to chapters of the Tichborne Release Association—the old Tichborne Defence Fund Committee—and Kenealy's newspaper, the *Englishman*, had a weekly circulation in excess of 150,000. 'There is not another bold or truthful journal in the kingdom,' trumpeted its editor; but then Kenealy's idea of truthfulness was not everyone's. In an early number of the *Englishman*, he gloated over 'the dread punishment…coming upon the conspirators in that awful crime against Sir Roger Tichborne':

> Mr Henry Danby Seymour was cut off, almost in an instant, after enduring two years of horrible agonies.
> The wife of Dickins, the [jury] Foreman, died of a most horrible disease, howling in agony for the part she had taken…
> Ballantine, the traitor, I hear, is almost begging.
> Bellew's son blew his brains out; Lady Radcliffe has taken to drink; and Gibbes, the Australian lawyer, was also carried off.*

As an adjunct to the *Englishman*, Kenealy published the entire proceedings of *The Trial at Bar of Sir Roger C.D. Tichborne* by monthly instalments. Described by its editor as 'Probably the most interesting work in the world,' *The Trial at Bar* ran over five years, for three of them at a heavy loss.

When Kenealy was swept into parliament on a wave of public

---

* Gibbes was widely rumoured to have drowned himself in the Thames after the trial; in fact, he returned to Wagga and died there in 1877 'from bodily ailments of long standing.'

support for the Claimant, *The Times* branded him 'the spokesman of an insane delusion,' the extent of which, it said:

> is evidence of something worse than a low state of education among large masses of the people; it brings into unpleasant prominence…a degraded condition of morality, such as we are accustomed to associate with the rowdy population of other communities rather than with our own countrymen…It warns us that there is in this sensible, sober, and calculating England, a stratum of society about as unaccountable and as little to be depended upon as a quicksand or a quagmire.

Such views were harvested by Kenealy and the Tichborne Release Association as further proof that the law-making classes despised 'the people' and that one law existed for the rich, another for the poor— of which latter class 'Sir Roger' was an honorary member. Throughout the 1870s, branches of the Tichborne Release Association met weekly in London and the larger towns. Besides raising money and gathering evidence towards a retrial, they met to keep the faith alive. Every Easter Monday for six years saw a procession in London, headed by one of the Claimant's children bearing a banner—PRAY RELEASE MY DEAR FATHER—and attended by tens of thousands who scattered the pigeons in Trafalgar Square with a massed rendition of the Association's anthem:

> Rise men, rise, and let your rulers know,
> For Law we will have Justice, and not a legal show;
> Rise, men, rise, and let the nation see,
> We know that he is Tichborne, and mean to set him free.

By the end of the 1870s, support for the Claimant's cause was waning. Repeated attempts to mount an appeal or a retrial had come to nothing. In the general election of April 1880, Kenealy lost his seat. 'It is better to be a sausage-seller,' he concluded bitterly, 'than the greatest scholar on earth.' But there was not much bitterness—not much of anything—left in Kenealy. He died just a fortnight after the election. His spirit lived on, though, in his son Maurice, by then editor of the *Englishman*, who blamed his father's death on Jesuit assassins.

'Out of all your friends and witnesses not one has turned against you,' Guildford Onslow assured the Claimant in 1877. Onslow, Harry Bloxam, Lord Rivers, and others of the Claimant's big-ticket backers, still saw a chance of victory and stood firm for the Claimant's cause. So long as there was agitation for an appeal or a retrial, those—like Onslow—who'd laid heavy bets on the trial's outcome refused to settle their losses on the grounds that the case was yet to be decided. Others of the Claimant's old supporters sank into the shadows. Francis Baigent had lost a good deal by his advocacy of the Claimant and, while he never stopped believing, kept himself aloof from the Tichborne Release movement. Old Andrew Bogle likewise remained quietly loyal until his death in 1877. Made homeless by the Claimant's imprisonment, for his last three years he eked a bare living out of fifteen shillings a week sent him by Lady Radcliffe—a partial reinstatement of his lost annuity. (Kenealy called it proof that she acknowledged Bogle's truthfulness.)

Onslow, Lord Rivers and the rest continued to keep the Claimant's family. Mary was illiterate, but in a letter to the Home Secretary in 1876, she protested her husband's innocence and lamented 'the miserable hours I am doomed to pass…the anguish I suffer from his awful position.' The words and penmanship were probably Onslow's. Mary already had formed an alliance with another man and would give birth to a daughter the following year. The Claimant stopped sending her his love after that and, before long, their children were taken into the care of his Hampshire friends. Agnes, the eldest, went to a family in Lymington. 'My mother,' she would later say, 'had neither the inclination nor the desire to stand up against ill-fortune.' And so Mary fell—and kept falling, all the way to the workhouse.

THIRTY-NINE

THOMAS CASTRO—UNDER PROTEST

AFTER six weeks in Newgate, prisoner A1139 Thomas Castro was transferred to Millbank prison, on the Thames-side, upriver of Westminster. His former daily drive from court to his digs in Bessborough Street must have dipped him in the prison's shadow a hundred times before he passed through its gates chained up in a Black Maria.

On account of his obesity, he was excused at Newgate from scrubbing out his cell each day. But at Millbank a long-handled scrubbing brush was found for him and he was made to shift for himself. To keep the charismatic Claimant separate from other prisoners, he was not required to take his turn in cleaning the passages. Later, he would boast of his privileged treatment at Millbank: 'I was placed in a large cell, larger than that given to ordinary prisoners, and it was fitted up on purpose for me.' Not true, but it pleased him to think so—or to have others believe it.

Set to work in his cell, making prisoners' flannel underclothing, he never saw his fellow inmates except at chapel. He professed to be untroubled by the confinement and isolation, and found the work 'beneficial' to his spirits. In fact, when illness caused his work to be taken from him for a time, he felt the loss very much: 'I really felt as if I should go mad if I was not allowed to have my work.' On the prison doctor's orders, his sewing was returned to him, 'and after that I got on very nicely indeed.'

His probation period over, he was moved in 1875 to the foggy damp of Her Majesty's Prison Dartmoor. He'd been regarded as a well-conducted prisoner until then, but at Dartmoor he got a reputation for insolence. The Home Secretary, who had responsibility for prisons, took a vigilant interest in the welfare of prisoner A1139. The slightest cause for complaint, he knew, would be seized on and broadcast by the Claimant's friends on the outside as further evidence of their hero's persecution at the hands of the government. Well aware of his leverage, the Claimant lodged frequent complaints, resulting, in 1876, in a magisterial inquiry and a directive to exercise even greater caution in the handling of this ticklish inmate.

The governor and warders at Dartmoor were expected to give the Claimant kid-glove treatment without appearing to do so. He constantly pushed at the rules—giving cheek to warders, talking in chapel— 'apparently with the object of establishing a belief...that he is a privileged person and therefore not subject to the same rules as other men.' Warders faced the choice of ignoring his incursions or reporting them, knowing the latter course would lead to questions in parliament. More than once, his 'prejudicial' treatment by the prison doctor was the subject of investigation.

'The complaints he makes,' reported the prison governor to the Home Office, 'are just such as the Fenian prisoners used to concoct— i.e. on a slight basis of fact some little addition is made which converts a commonplace incident of prison life into an act of tyranny or impropriety.' Michael Davitt and others of the Fenians were serving out their treason sentences when the Claimant arrived at Dartmoor. According to Davitt, '"Sir Roger" soon became the lion of the place...To settle an argument on any topic—legal, political, or disciplinary—required but the assertion, "Sir Roger Tichborne says so."' Notwithstanding, Davitt judged the Claimant's intellectual capacity to be 'exactly on a level with that of the ordinary magsman.'

He worked in the tailoring shop, sewing coat-linings for the uniforms of prison warders and the Metropolitan Police. He took to wearing spectacles, but neither they nor his muddy-yellow prison slops were the reason that Henry Labouchere had trouble recognising '*the man*' when he visited Dartmoor in 1877. 'In a word,' wrote Labouchere, 'those physical attributes which made Thomas Castro what he once was have simply ceased to exist.' Denied his weekly intake of thirteen pints of Jameson's and comestibles in proportion, the Claimant had shed three stone in Newgate, six more at Millbank, and after eight months at Dartmoor had (in the words of Guildford Onslow) 'sunk into the condition of an Egyptian Mummy.' At twelve stone, his weight was less than half what it had been upon conviction. So weakened was the Claimant by his loss of flesh that, at the beginning of 1876, the doctor ordered that his diet be fortified with extra bread, beef tea and ('at his own request') a double helping of treacle. By the time Labouchere spied him at his treadle, the Claimant's weight had steadied at about eighteen stone, lubberly enough by most standards but almost cadaverous by his own.

Extra rations notwithstanding, Dartmoor continued not to suit him. He complained that the damp made him rheumaticky, the warders ('a set of brutes') ogled his malformation, and the governor mishandled his good-conduct marks and allowed him to be exhibited, he said, 'to my most bitter and virulent enemies.' (He believed that Chief Justice Cockburn had spied on him in his cell.) His agitations bore fruit in October 1877 when he was removed to Portsea prison on the Hampshire coast, where the 'less bleak air' and kindlier officers were more to his liking, and where he would serve out the remainder of his sentence.

The Claimant would later state that, through all his time in gaol, 'I never made any friend of any prisoner.' For all that, he 'jawed' with his fellows whenever he got the chance, and was observed to seek the company of 'low class' prisoners in the exercise yard. Alone in his cell, he turned for company to *Chamber's Journal* and *Leisure Hour*, and to books like *Explorations in Africa*, *Voyage of the Fox*, and *Life with the Esquimaux*, all borrowed from the prison library. But he was not the avid novel reader he'd been in Gippsland, nowadays preferring the Old Testament to the works of Captain Marryat and R. M. Ballantyne.

He kept up a regular correspondence with his friends on the outside, of whom Guildford Onslow was the most fervent and the most favoured. His letters from the Claimant were printed in the *Englishman*, so that Onslow was not the only one to observe 'the most wonderful change in his mental capacity in language, pronunciation and intelligence.' When at liberty, the Claimant had struggled with the word 'erysipelas' (a skin complaint he suffered): writing from Dartmoor, he spelt it right for the first time ever. In his published letters, he quoted from the scriptures in Latin and generally expressed himself in an articulate, high-minded manner:

> Has Justice, then, gone for a tour on the Continent, or left the island altogether? I know that my friends and supporters have gone to the extreme limit in a legitimate way. God forbid they should take any other, is my nightly prayer. They will soon have it in their power to retaliate for the contempt that has been shown them, and I feel sure they will not then forget me.

According to Michael Davitt, some of the Claimant's letters were written for him by another prisoner; but many of those published in the *Englishman* bore a striking resemblance to the pompous and declamatory style of Guildford Onslow himself. Evidently the resemblance was noticed at the time for, in his report of a visit to Portsea in 1878, Onslow let it be known that the Claimant 'regretted that people should accuse me of forging his letters, as all who knew me must know I was incapable of doing so.' But that they were not all his own work is pretty apparent from a letter the Claimant wrote to the Prisons Department in 1880: 'Now Gentlemen, has the delay has taken place to oblige the Government and being a matter of a few days only I should feel extremely oblige if you will excuse my hair being cut untill the case is decided one way or the other.' Untouched by Onslow, that sounded more like the Claimant of old—rogue *h* and all.

Years later, he would say of his time in prison that 'I would not allow anything in connection with the trial to occupy my thoughts for a moment.' His letters say otherwise. Certainly he never showed the slightest sway in his insistence that he was Roger Tichborne, nor once willingly gave his name as Thomas Castro. At Dartmoor, he scored a small victory over the governor when the Home Office agreed that he need not give his name as Castro, provided he answered to it when spoken to. His letters he signed 'Thomas Castro—under protest' or 'R.C.D. Tichborne (Thomas Castro)' or even 'Roger Thomas Castro'.

Every letter and visit he received gave him cause to believe that his verdict would soon be reversed. His hopes were fed their richest fare by Onslow, whose letters proved him to be not just a stakeholder but, as he signed himself, 'Your devoted friend.' Onslow wrote to him in 1877:

> In case of my death I have bequeathed you an enormous tin box to be placed in your hands on the day of your freedom, and if I am in another world I shall feel gratified in knowing that you will find in that box rouleau of 100 sovereigns, 1000 cigars, a box of Tobacco, your gold chain and watch and a complete bound library of all your case trials, and private and public letters that will be of inestimable value to you and yours in future years, a locked box and something that will cheer you besides, together with fresh statutory declarations that will win you a verdict at any new trial…
>
> So bear up my dear Friend. God's ways are not our ways. He will work as he thinks best and I feel sure the day is not far distant when right will triumph over might and that your release will be effected in a manner that will gratify you and astonish the world.

FORTY
THE PARRAMATTA LUNATIC

WHAT Onslow had in mind when he talked of astonishing the world was the appearance of the 'real' Arthur Orton. He personally had put up more than half of the £2,300 reward on offer towards that end.

In Australia, reports were as thick on the ground as ever. From the town of Yea, not far from Reedy Creek, came several accounts of Orton having been involved in the shooting of a horse thief thereabouts in 1862, and fresh reports of Orton's death were also bruited in different parts of the country. Two men in Melbourne made their pitch for the reward with a yarn that fixed Orton in New Zealand, breeding greyhounds.

Then, out of the tiny gold-mining settlement of Red Jacket, stranded high on the western flank of the mountain range severing Gippsland from the rest of Victoria, came a curious report of Roger Tichborne. Its source was Annie Alexander (*née* Gray), a married woman with a family of five. Her husband, Charles, owned two hotels and had mining interests in the district; Annie herself helped out as sewing-mistress at the Red Jacket school. According to her story, she and Roger had been lovers in England when he was still a schoolboy. A secret was here alluded to—a pregnancy, perhaps—as a result of which she'd been sent away to an uncle in the colonies. While living as a governess on a Victorian pastoral station in 1855, she happened to meet her old flame, then going by the name of Thomas Castro. He

Truth compels me… *Annie Alexander, photographed many years after her brush with the Tichborne case*

told her of his falling-out with his family, the wreck of the *Bella*, and his intention to hide himself in the colonies for a year or two. 'I remonstrated,' wrote Annie Alexander, 'but you might as well speak to the wind as to Roger Tichborne when his mind was made up.' She knew for a fact he had no tattoos on his arms, she said, 'for I had seen him wash many times.'

For all that she lived in one of the remotest of Australia's settled districts, Mrs Alexander was well-connected in England—her mother's family were bankers in Chichester, her brother a high-ranked clergyman admired by Prime Minister Gladstone—and Guildford Onslow seized on her as a witness of just the right sort. (Significantly, none of her family could be persuaded to vouch for her, though a former Stonyhurst boy swore that he remembered posting letters from Roger to a Miss Gray of Chichester in 1848.) Onslow sent her a selection of the Claimant's *cartes de visite*, upon receipt of which she replied: 'I should have been pleased if they had been the likeness of a man who was a stranger to me…instead of which, truth compels me to say that the photographs are of Roger Tichborne, and of no other man.'

Her letter, forwarded by Onslow to the *Englishman*, deplored that 'the true heir of Tichborne' should be 'herded amongst felons and convicts':

> Now I, who felt little or no compassion for him when he was driving in his brougham in London, yet from such an unmerited and shameful fate, to save this man who is, notwithstanding all his faults and follies, the true Roger Tichborne, I here avow myself willing to come to England and give my evidence, without fee or reward.

It's tempting to hear something of Onslow in the tenor of Mrs Alexander's letter, of which there is much more in the same vein. However, she repeated many of the same expressions in a letter to the *Gippsland Mercury*, together with the hope that she might find a publisher for the novel she proposed writing on the subject. Perhaps she was not being entirely candid when she told Onslow that giving evidence to 'save' the Claimant would be 'a great sacrifice on my part, and gain for me a notoriety for which I have not the slightest ambition.'

Whatever the truth of her story, Annie Alexander evidently viewed the Tichborne case as her ticket out of Red Jacket. Her present situation she described to Onslow as 'locked in, in the mountains of Gippsland, with the daily cares of a large family.' The family grew smaller not long after that, when her husband took his own ticket out of Red Jacket, leaving for the Queensland goldfields and taking their eldest son with him. Perhaps an escape from her marriage was the liberation Annie had really been seeking, in which case it looked as if her public avowal of support for the Claimant had done its job. Let us hope so for, though Onslow extolled her evidence as 'conclusive', the hinted-at advance for her passage to England never materialised. And when Onslow alluded, in 1877, to evidence that would astonish the world, he had his sights fixed instead on the Parramatta asylum.

William Cresswell, the putative Orton whom the Claimant's agent at Tumut had turned up in 1871, was now an inmate there. He'd been reinstated to the list of potential Ortons with the advent of the £2,300 reward, and by 1876 was again the hot favourite. William Lock was the man angling for the honour of discoverer. He visited Parramatta asylum and 'almost' swore that Cresswell was the same Orton with whom he'd seen Tom Castro tried for horse stealing at Castlemaine. At Lock's instigation, Orton's sister, Mrs Jury, was sent out to Sydney in 1877, but failed to recognise Cresswell as her brother. Undeterred, Lock declared that 'the likeness between Mrs Jury and the lunatic was the marvel of all.' He sent Onslow a full account of the meeting together with half a dozen photographs of Cresswell, which Onslow promised to take with him when next he visited Dartmoor.

Cresswell's portraits were enlarged to life-size so the Claimant could see them across the eight-foot gap that separated him from his visitors. In the next issue of the *Englishman*, Onslow declared that the Claimant had recognised Orton in an instant 'and he expressed in the strongest terms his surprise that any one who ever knew Arthur Orton could doubt it.' Strange then that the Claimant's wife didn't recognise the portraits, having stated in her petition to the Home Secretary the previous year, 'I was long and intimately acquainted with Arthur Orton in Australia, before I ever made the acquaintance of my husband.' Strange too that the Claimant pointed out as 'unmistakable' a scar on Cresswell's face and bore-holes in his ears, neither of which existed, according to the doctor at Parramatta asylum.

Guildford Onslow and the Tichborne Release Association began campaigning 'to bring Arthur Orton home.' Kenealy, however, opposed the enterprise, insisting that:

> Arthur Orton is dead, & has been dead for many years. Tichborne & his wife have their reasons for stating that he was alive at a certain period—but the truth is *he came to a violent death*; and it is really not right to get money from the People to bring home a man who is dead.

Kenealy seems to have based his belief on the slim evidence of the note sent by the Claimant to his wife just before the verdict, in which he counselled her to 'remain quiet for a little time.' Kenealy rendered the note as 'You ——, keep your own Counsel!' Preferring to be guided by his own delusions, Onslow ignored Kenealy's objection.

In March 1878, William Lock formally lodged a request for the release of Cresswell—on behalf of Charles Orton of Paradise Street, Rotherhithe, who claimed him as his brother Arthur. Proving as amenable to inducement as ever, Charley wrote to the Home Secretary, recanting his earlier 'confession'. Only now, in the portraits of William Cresswell, he declared, did he truly recognise his long-lost brother. That scar (the one that didn't exist) was identical with Arthur's; had he ever been permitted to see the Claimant face-to-face (he had), he could have ascertained in a moment that he was not his brother. 'I was but a dupe,' said Charley.

The New South Wales Colonial Secretary refused Lock's application, stating: 'It is not in the interests of the lunatic himself that this liberation is desired, but in the interests of a felon now serving a sentence in England.' Lock's cause, and the quest for the reward, was subsequently taken up in the New South Wales parliament by Joseph Eckford, a Sydney publican and member of the Legislative Assembly, who instigated a parliamentary inquiry into the matter in October 1878. The medical superintendent at Parramatta asylum offered compelling evidence that Cresswell was not Arthur Orton, for which he was accused by Eckford of being complicit with the Claimant's enemies. A porter from Redfern railway station recognised 'the lunatic' as the same William Cresswell he'd known at Bathurst twenty years earlier, and produced a book Cresswell had given him as a keepsake. Inscribed in the front was Cresswell's name and place of origin— 'Balksdown Farm, Bramley, Hants'—which fitted with the lunatic's jumbled account of his family's connection with the Duke of Wellington's Strathfieldsaye estate. Unmoved by Lock's own submission, the inquiry reiterated the Colonial Secretary's decision: that Cresswell 'should not under any circumstances be delivered up to the person making this application.'

The case of William Cresswell was revived four years later. William Lock had faded from the scene, but Joseph Eckford had replaced him as colonial agent for the Tichborne Release Association. Guildford Onslow and Lord Rivers were dead by this time, but filling their shoes—financially speaking—was Miss Georgiana Baring, eccentric daughter of a wealthy Hampshire family. Thanks to her, Charley Orton was still drawing a livelihood from the Tichborne case. Arriving in Sydney in 1882, he renewed his attempt to have Cresswell released to his care. With Miss Baring's backing, Eckford sent to Mexico in search of Edmund, another long-lost Orton brother, that he might lend corroboration to the mercurial word of Charley.

Early in 1883 the New South Wales attorney-general directed that any application for Cresswell's release should be 'vigorously opposed.' To that end, urgent inquiries were initiated by police in both that colony and Victoria into the background and identity of the inmate at Parramatta asylum. The New South Wales inspector-general of police told his district inspectors: 'This is important.'

Information already to hand led police to make inquiries at Tumut, Wagga and Bathurst, and over in Gippsland where Cresswell claimed to have kept company with Tom Castro. Cresswell's supposed alias of Smith muddied the waters; different witnesses reckoned to have known him as George or William or just plain Smith, but not one (besides the Claimant) had ever heard him called Alfred. Witnesses recalled Cresswell's unusual bowling style, his playing cornet in a circus band, that he had been struck dead by lightning in 1872. A list of informants compiled by a Victorian policeman even included a Madame von Halle, 'business clairvoyant' of George Street, Sydney. Altogether, it took upwards of a year for police in the two colonies to gather up the information and winnow out the blatant furphies.

Born in 1826 to a farming family in Hampshire, William Cresswell had come out to Sydney with a consignment of bulls in 1855. His family heard of his safe arrival and that he intended escorting the livestock to their new owner at Bathurst—then nothing, until his letter from Gladesville asylum sixteen years later. He stayed some months at Bathurst before moving on, nobody knew where. Down in Gippsland though, witnesses recalled a butcher named Smith— George, some thought—at Sale in 1858, who had been a mate of Arthur Orton's. Descriptions of this Smith varied, but Cresswell's portrait was considered not unlike him. At the other end of the alps, in the Monaro district of New South Wales, somebody remembered a George Smith working in a butcher shop at Araluen in 1860, freshly arrived from Gippsland.

The following year a William Smith was hired as a groom and coachman at nearby Ginninderra, where he made a name as a cricketer and a boozer. His performance at the crease caught the interest of Ellen Clarke, a widow who kept the Cottage of Content public house at Gundaroo. Smith assumed—or resumed—the name Cresswell on their wedding day in 1863, saying that he did so in honour of Sir Cresswell Cresswell, judge of the English divorce court. After that inauspicious start, the marriage expired within a year, during which Cresswell knocked his wife about, squandered her savings, and consumed more liquor than she sold across the bar of the Cottage of

Does a beard count as a likeness? 'The Lunatic' Cresswell (left) poses at Parramatta Asylum with the Orton brothers, Charley (centre) and Edmund

Content. Old residents of Gundaroo recalled him as reserved but eccentric, 'and when in *that* mood he would constantly exclaim, "I will make a stir some day; they don't know who I am."' Gaoled in 1864 for 'throwing a shepherd in the fire,' he was described as stoutly built and swarthy, with prematurely grey hair. His distinguishing marks—a large scar on one hand and two moles on his back—exactly matched those of the man in the asylum.

Upon his release from prison in 1865, Cresswell went with a mob of cattle to Wagga, where Deborah Simpson, then landlady of the

Black Swan Inn, recalled him being an 'intimate friend' of Tom Castro's. He left Wagga for Tumut late in 1865 and knocked about that district for several years until his increasingly erratic behaviour tipped him into the lock-up and thence, by lapse and relapse, to the asylum. At Darlinghurst Lunatic Reception House in January 1871 the admitting doctor noted: 'Gave little or no trouble and conversed rationally, and said his name was Orton, and that he was a butcher.'

Cresswell's history was presented in evidence by fifteen Crown witnesses at a court hearing in 1884. Edmund Orton had been traced to a silver mine in central Mexico and was now in Sydney, where he joined with Charley in petitioning for the release of their brother Arthur—a.k.a. the lunatic Cresswell. Cresswell himself appeared at the hearing, 'in a lucid interval,' and gave an account which followed closely the narrative formed by the other Crown evidence. He had never called himself Arthur Orton, he said, but he had gone, for a time, under the name of Smith. Only with difficulty did he recollect a person named Orton at Wagga: a butcher who kept racehorses and was 'heavy with crime.'

Balanced against the Crown's account was the testimony of thirteen witnesses who swore that the lunatic was Orton. They included Henry Edwards, who claimed to be the same Ballarat Harry supposed murdered in Gippsland in 1858. A Tumut police sergeant deposed that he'd received letters—alas destroyed—written by Cresswell but signed 'Arthur Orton'. And James Peebles, second mate of the *Middleton*, told the court he recognised Cresswell as Orton by a scar on his right forefinger, where a ferret had bitten him on the voyage to Hobart. (Peebles was presently living at Joseph Eckford's hotel, having been delivered from a Sydney poorhouse in return for his evidence.) Two former Wappingites attested to the 'peculiar' blue eyes of the youthful Arthur Orton, identical with those of Cresswell.

Representing the Ortons at the hearing, Edmund Barton, Australia's future prime minister, submitted that his clients' application sprang from brotherly affection and a wish to relieve the public purse of Cresswell's upkeep—contentions scoffed at by the Crown counsel. Charley and Edmund Orton were in the pay of 'an old lady with a craze,' he said, and should their application succeed the liberated Cresswell would be used 'to rake up the dying embers of an almost forgotten lawsuit.'

Late in the hearing, the Ortons won a three-month adjournment to procure one further witness: Tom Cresswell, brother of William. Tom had told Miss Baring's representatives in London that his brother's eyes were brown and that he was a good two inches taller than the man in the asylum. Moreover, he agreed that letters he'd received from Parramatta corresponded with the Claimant's handwriting. But, shipped out to Sydney at Miss Baring's expense, Tom Cresswell identified the blue-eyed lunatic as his brother. His eyes and nose were very like their father's, said Tom, and the discrepancy in height he accounted for by William's former fondness for high-heeled boots.

Making his ruling in October 1884, the judge declared that never had his confidence in evidence been so rudely shaken as in this case. He was not prepared to say that the lunatic was *not* Arthur Orton; nor was he persuaded that he was. So saying, he elected to 'leave the matter *status quo*': Cresswell would remain at Parramatta. As for Tom Cresswell, though he recognised his brother, he did not seek his release. His sole interest in the affair, it appeared, had been to establish William's identity and whereabouts with a view to inheriting his share of the family property when he died.

Edmund Orton returned to Mexico, but Charley stayed on in Sydney. 'It would be rash for anyone to suppose,' the judge said in closing, 'that the last has been heard of the pretensions of the Ortons that the unfortunate man is their brother.'

FORTY-ONE

NO OTHER PERSON

ONCE shot of Dartmoor, prisoner A1139 amassed enough good-conduct marks to pare more than three years off his sentence. As of 22 October 1884, the Tichborne Release Association was redundant. He was free.

Death, defeat and forgetfulness had gutted the ranks of the Claimant's supporters. There was no Guildford Onslow to welcome him out—only his tin-trunk legacy of sovereigns, cigars and 'something that will cheer you besides.' At the Southampton workhouse, the trustees wondered if they might be relieved of responsibility for Mary Ann Tichborne now that her husband was at liberty. But he would have nothing to do with her or the two children born while he was inside. Of his own children, only Agnes—now eighteen—had really known their father, and she was among the small party that met him upon his release. Later, she wrote:

> No one had thought to prepare me for any change and I frankly admit I was struck with horror of my own father; the man with the awful clothes, rough hands and voice and manner seemed an utter stranger, nothing in the least resembling the Daddy I remembered. I could not endure him to touch me or be near me, nor had I the least affection for him.

His surviving friends—the Hampshire stalwarts—found a house for him at Southampton, where his three younger children were at school.

The Claimant, barely recognisable after his release from prison in 1884

A new suit of clothes, the attentions of a hairdresser, and the lubrica-tive action of liquor did much to smooth out his rough edges, so that young Roger, Hetty and James were spared the shock their elder sister had suffered.

In any case, their father was rarely at home. Immediately upon his release, Sir Roger (as he still insisted) signed a twelve-month contract with one Sanger, music-hall agent and proprietor of a travelling circus. The scheme was pitched to the Claimant as a means of rebuilding his public support, but its real attraction was the stipend—a hundred guineas a week. Five evenings a week, in towns all over the country,

Sanger's headline act delivered a half-hour rendition of his sensational career, distilled down to a few bushy yarns and an appeal to
outraged justice, all overlaid with smoke from one of his big cigars.
Sometimes, for a change, he featured in an illusionist's routine, being
made to vanish from a chair swinging in mid-air. In the same troupe
was Harry Relph, a rolypoly comedian of about four feet high who,
trading on 'Sir Roger's' fame, billed himself as Little Tich.*

The Claimant had worked outdoors during his final years in prison
and, at a shade over sixteen stone, he was in his best shape for nearly
two decades. But now he excited a good deal less curiosity than he
had as the spectral victim of a conspiracy. Moreover, it was hard to
take him seriously, sharing billing with dancing bears and a rubber
man. The much-touted breakthrough never came, the 'real' Arthur
Orton remaining stubbornly undiscovered and all traces of the *Bella*
or the *Osprey* either long-sunk or forgotten. The *Englishman* finally
snuffed out in 1886, not many months after its last breathless headline
announcing the 'Expected Arrival of Arthur Orton.' That same year,
the Claimant took a boat to New York. But Barnum's circus didn't
want him and he bombed as a vaudeville act. He ended up bar-tending
in a rough neighbourhood, where his recitations sufficed as some
kind of attraction. The pay was poor, but his drinks were free.

By the end of 1887 he was back in London—and back in the music
halls, though lower down the bill. There he made the backstage
acquaintance of a dancer, Lily Enever, with whom he took lodgings
in Paddington. His sons were both soldiers now, and his daughters
also had made their own lives. Hetty, under an assumed name, was
working in a shop in the West End, while Agnes (as Theresa Alexander)
pursued a career on the stage. In 1888, his own career faltering, the
Claimant refused his Hampshire friends' offer of money. He had
hopes, he said, of getting the management of a public house. No such

---

*   His own subsequent fame caused the nickname Tich (or Titch) to attach
    itself to men of Relph's, rather than the Claimant's, stature.

thing transpired, however, and he continued to rely on his 'lecturing' to keep himself and Lily afloat. He cut an increasingly pathetic figure, with his white beard, and his cuffs and story fraying. Lily gave birth to four little Tichbornes, each of whom died at just a few days old.

In 1895 the Claimant was sixty-one years old—assuming, that is, that he was Arthur Orton. And, in April that year, he confessed as much—'*I am Arthur Orton, and no other person*'—in the first of six weekly instalments in the *People*. He not only repudiated that he was Roger Tichborne, but wrote: 'I have never seen Roger Tichborne in my life, nor had I when I left Wagga Wagga the slightest intention of ever claiming the Tichborne estates. All I was hoping for was to get money.' He'd have stayed behind in Sydney or taken a ship for California, he said, had it not been for the urgings and attentions of his 'infatuated' followers. But to his surprise and with little effort on his part, he had found that 'the story really built itself, and in that way it grew so large that I really could not get out of it.'

The fifteen-thousand-word confession purported to clear up all the mysteries of the Tichborne case. In the main, it amounted to not much more than a summary of the prosecution evidence at the perjury trial. But what more there was had an authentic ring to it, revealing, for instance, a vivid acquaintance with (or imagining of) previously uncharted episodes in the young life of Arthur Orton. In one characteristic digression, the Claimant related how, as a sailor boy, he'd suffered a bellyache from eating too many figs when the *Ocean* called at Tahiti. He told too of jumping ship at Valparaiso and of his sojourn at Melipilla:

> After staying several months in that Town, I left to go to Don Ramon Alcada, a Spanish nobleman, who had a large estate near San Francisco del Monte…I fired a gun for the first time in my life in his presence at a blackbird sitting on a hedge. This he thought wonderful and made me practice every day…Don Ramon made me a present of a very nice horse, and some cattle

being sent to Valparaiso, I went with them for protection sake. I sold my horse at Valparaiso for five dollars. Stayed at the Sailor's Home in Calls de Cockrane. Shipped as an ordinary seaman on board the brig *Jessie Miller*...

The Claimant admitted having 'sucked the brains' of his old Wagga friend, Dick Slate, on the subject of Hampshire. ('I have always been a good listener.') Up to that point, he said, he couldn't even have found Hampshire on a map.

Dick then said to me, 'You know where Basingstoke is, don't you? That's where I came from.'...
I said to Dick, 'I suppose you know the Tichbornes then?'
He replied, 'Oh, yes; everybody knows them.'

'Dick Slate and me were on very friendly terms,' the Claimant wrote; but in the next breath came this: 'I never believed in a man, much less a woman, and never trusted neither.'

Slate was six years dead when the Claimant confessed. Under his own and proper name, he'd lived to a decent old age at Broadmeadows, on the plains north of Melbourne, where the Riverina mobs and stockriders took their last night's spell on the long road to market. As the Claimant had rightly stated, Slate was married, but childless. And it turns out he was London-born. He'd arrived in Sydney in 1848 aboard a vessel that, strange to relate, was carrying seven crew saved from a shipwreck. 'Imagination,' as the Claimant said, 'goes a very long way.'

He was paid several hundred pounds for his confession, but denied that the money had been his object. 'I wish to clear my conscience,' he wrote, 'and to relieve the public mind of any doubt that they may have entertained as to my real identity.' Several times across the six instalments he apologised to the Tichborne family and Lady Radcliffe 'for the great trouble and anxiety that I have for years caused them.' It's not inconceivable that Tichborne connections might have played a part in securing his confession; for although the Tichborne estates were securely vested in Sir Henry, the Doughty estates, lodged in Chancery under the terms of Roger's will, were still up for grabs. The Claimant's confession—'his last card,' *The Times* called it—promised to 'scuttle the question for ever,' extinguishing not just his own pretensions but those of his descendants.

And it might have done so had he not, soon after the final instalment, recanted the thing in its entirety. He had approached the *People*, he said, with the intention of selling his story as Roger Tichborne; but, for fear of libel, they'd persuaded him instead to 'masquerade' as Orton. Now he told a reporter from *News of the World*, 'I am no more Orton than you are.'

When cables bearing news of the Claimant's confession reached Sydney, the serpentine Charley Orton was swift to endorse it, concurring that the Claimant *was* his brother, after all. Soon after, a fresh application for William Cresswell's release from Parramatta asylum contended that Cresswell was none other than Roger Tichborne.

'The man in the asylum is the only one who can assume the title of Doughty.' That was the assertion of Edward Priestman, an accountant in a Sydney insurance office and Cresswell's would-be protector on this occasion. Priestman's application was supported by the daughter of the late Joseph Eckford, MLA, who stated that her father, in attempting to have Cresswell released as Arthur Orton, had all along believed him to be Roger—'But he knew he could not get him released as Tichborne.' Dr F. Norton Manning, who, as medical superintendent at Gladesville asylum, had been present when agents for both sides first visited Cresswell in 1871, agreed that, even at that early date, there'd been a suggestion that he was Tichborne. When a New South Wales parliamentary select committee failed to reach a decision on Priestman's application, a Royal Commission was mounted for the purpose of settling the question of Cresswell's identity once and for all.

Examined from head to heel, the now-demented Cresswell was found to bear no trace either of tattoos or of scars at the ankles, where Roger had been bled during an asthma attack. Moreover, at age seventy-four, Cresswell was still a good inch taller than Roger had been at twenty-four. For good measure, the examining doctor noted that Cresswell's penis (although shrivelled with age) was pendant, not retracted.

Among the dozens of witnesses to appear before the Cresswell Royal Commission were many who'd testified at the inquiries of twenty-odd years before. The same witnesses who'd previously been certain that Cresswell was Orton now declared themselves equally convinced that he was Tichborne. Most curious of all was the testimony of Jean Luie, the man convicted of perjury for his evidence at the second Tichborne trial. Now living in Sydney, he declared that the elusive *Osprey* had been none other than the *Bella* incognito. Her captain and crew had faked the wreck of the *Bella*, then sailed her to New Zealand where she was repainted and rechristened the *Osprey*. The sole passenger, 'young Tichborne', had welcomed the chance to disappear with the *Bella*, said Luie, and on landing at Melbourne had taken to the bush with no backward glance. Luie swore that Cresswell was the very man.

The Royal Commissioners concluded that 'much of the testimony so freely offered was of little value.' They found William Cresswell to be himself and no other; but, persuaded that his confinement was to blame for his continued insanity, they recommended his release— into his own care, not Priestman's. Cresswell, however, had no inclination to leave the asylum which had been his home for almost forty years. It was agreed to let him be.

There came one final attempt at his release, in 1903. This time, the present Lady Tichborne (wife of Sir Henry, the erstwhile infant heir) was prevailed on to stop at Parramatta asylum en route to India. Her visit was held by some suspicious souls to be proof that the

Tichborne family was behind the Cresswell-as-Tichborne campaign. If found to be Roger (the theory went), Cresswell offered the means of restoring the Doughty estates to the Tichbornes. In the event, Lady Tichborne failed to discern in Cresswell any trace of a resemblance either to her husband or to any of the portraits hanging in Tichborne House. She re-embarked for Calcutta, leaving Cresswell secure in the asylum, where he occupied himself sewing handbags until his death the following year.

In the course of the Royal Commission, an alternative theory emerged as to Cresswell's role in the affair. Its plot line ran thus: Cresswell, a by-blow of Sir James Tichborne's, happened to meet his half brother Roger in the bush of Gippsland or the Riverina; Roger met with a violent end, upon which Cresswell and his confederate, Orton, formed a plan to claim the baronetcy; Cresswell had been groomed to play the part of Roger but, slipping a cog, left Orton to proceed with the imposture alone. Offered in support of this hypothesis were a report of a headless body—never identified—unearthed near Wagga in 1867, Cresswell's alleged fixation with decapitation, and his latest response to the mention of Orton: 'There is blood and crime attached to that name.'

The suggestion that Orton had killed Tichborne and assumed his identity was not new. Something of the sort had been rumoured ever since the mystery of Ballarat Harry's disappearance bled into the Tichborne case. But the counter-theory—that Tichborne had killed Orton—had attracted rather less notice. Kenealy was its chief adherent. Why else, he'd demanded in the *Englishman*, had police from Melbourne attended the Claimant's trial, only to skulk away when he was found to be Orton? And why else had the Claimant sworn his wife to silence on the brink of his conviction? Serjeant Ballantine, the Claimant's barrister at the first trial, suspected much the same thing. Perhaps both of them had it straight from the Claimant's mouth.

'I am Roger Tichborne. Arthur Orton, whom I am supposed to be, was my confederate in many exploits in Australia. I shot him dead in Wagga Wagga in 1866 during a quarrel, in which he threatened to expose me!' That's what the Claimant's elder daughter stated he had 'confessed' to her following his release from prison. Orton had been trying to blackmail him, threatening to reveal 'things' about her mother and about Tichborne–Castro's own colonial misdeeds. That was why, when he arrived in London, the Claimant hurried straight to Wapping: to ascertain whether, before his demise, Orton had spilled the beans to his family. He had. It was on that account—not because *he* was Arthur Orton—that her father had paid hush-money to Charley and his sisters, said the Claimant's daughter. It almost sounded plausible.

Back then his daughter had been called Agnes, but in later years she went by her stage name, Theresa. As Theresa Doughty Tichborne she was gaoled in 1923 for writing threatening letters to members of the Tichborne family. Ten years earlier she'd served time in Holloway after threatening to shoot the bride of Joseph Tichborne (son of Sir Henry) on their wedding day. Theresa never lost faith in her father's claim, and upon completion of her second sentence in 1924, she in turn sold her story to the *People*.

Having failed in her stage career, she had worked for a time as a barmaid, after which she 'ran round town for a bit.' One of those with whom she ran round was a young man known as Goldie— properly Sir Henry Tichborne. His attentions and payments for favours had caused her to hope, in vain, that she might yet receive her 'proper' dues. That was in the late 1880s, and Goldie and his assigns were plagued by Theresa for decades thereafter. In old age, she fulfilled her ambition of renown in London's West End, selling flowers and matches outside Joseph Tichborne's flat in Bond Street, with a placard bearing her credentials as daughter of 'The Late Sir Roger Tichborne, Victim of a Wicked Miscarriage of Justice.' She died in 1939, on the day before war was declared.

Mary, the Claimant's Wagga bride, lived more than forty years in the Southampton workhouse, her legendary temper and the brawn that once had fitted her for chimney-building earning her a lifelong post as subduer of rowdy inmates. According to the workhouse matron, 'Mrs Tichborne never spoke of her past.'

With the earnings from his confession, the Claimant opened a tobacconist's shop in Islington. That enterprise failing, he was destined to end his days on parish relief. Publicans took pity on him, letting 'Sir Roger' peddle his tarnished tale to their customers in exchange for a nobbler or a few coppers. But he still carried eighteen stone, and eventually the sluggish action of his heart confined him to his third-floor lodgings in Shouldham Street, off Marylebone Road. At six in the morning on April Fools Day, 1898, Lily woke to find him dead.

Crowds began gathering in Shouldham Street at daybreak on the morning of his funeral. By mid-afternoon, knots of spectators were assembled on street corners all along Edgware Road, and at Paddington cemetery the shrouded hearse might almost have been the blue brougham of old, so familiar was the carnival-like crush that awaited it. The newspapers had obituarised him as Arthur Orton, but when, at the graveside, his broad oak coffin was divested of wreaths, the Claimant's last card was revealed: affixed to the lid was a shield-shaped plaque, inscribed SIR ROGER CHARLES DOUGHTY TICHBORNE. His grave was left unmarked, his epitaph graven in newsprint: 'He almost lied like truth.'

THE END

·◯:◯·

M

THEY are not called con artists for nothing; they are called con artists precisely in recognition of the qualities they share with regular artists, which are: (1) love of solitude; (2) love of freedom; (3) dislike of authority; and (4) extraordinary powers of daydreaming...

That con artists are indeed artists rather than mere journeymen (like burglars) is demonstrated by their love of invention and dislike of repetition. An artist by definition is someone who refuses to repeat himself...

Janet Malcolm, The Crime of Sheila McGough

ACKNOWLEDGMENTS

My thanks are due to the following people, organisations and cat:

Marnie Bertram, for sharing her family's Tichborne archive.

Flo Pearce of Maffra, my generous guide to Boisdale.

Dick and Jill Stone and Donna Slingo, the Alresford connection.

Professor Michael Roe, for encouragement and lunch.

The late Douglas Woodruff for supplying this book's title.

Staff of the Castlemaine, Maffra and Yea libraries, State Library of Tasmania, Baillieu Library (University of Melbourne), State Library of Victoria, and Public Record Office (UK).

Christine Campbell, Local Studies Librarian, Wagga Wagga City Library; Chris Dormer, Burke Museum, Beechworth; Stefan Petrou, Law Library, University of Tasmania; Gerard Hayes, La Trobe Australian Manuscripts Collection, State Library of Victoria; Mark Hildebrand, Dixson Collection, State Library of NSW; Graeme Powell, Manuscript Librarian, National Library of Australia; Tony Marshall and Claudia Valenzuela, Heritage Collections, State Library of Tasmania; John Ross, Crime Museum, New Scotland Yard.

John Winterbottom at Wagga Wagga Historical Society, Margaret Kennedy of Warracknabeal Historical Society, and Jeff Cooper of Omeo Historical Society.

Joe Bugner at the Tasmanian Writers' Centre, Alan Byrnes, Rob Christie, Les Cromb, Anna Lanyon, Ted Lennon of Wagga Wagga Golf Club, James H. McLaurin, Steve Marsden, Cathy Milward-Bason, Pat Riedl, J. G. Rogers, Liz Rushen, Clare Williamson, and the late Ken the cat of Stoneman's Bookroom, Castlemaine.

John Jameson & Son's Bow Street Distillery of Dublin, Ireland, for mine and the Claimant's favourite drop.

The good-but-not-great Michael Heyward, Mandy Brett, Donica Bettanin and Chong Weng-ho at Text, for making a book of this.

David Bannear for eating those curried egg sandwiches, and for his Buchan manifesto. And Rosie Annear for putting up with a strange man about the house.

ILLUSTRATIONS

pp. *xvi*, 113, 133, 274, 315, 317, 378, 396—National Library of Australia

cover, pp. 7 & 73—Mitchell Library, State Library of New South Wales

pp. 6 & 47—Dixson Galleries, State Library of New South Wales

pp. 138, 206—La Trobe Picture Collection, State Library of Victoria

p. 219—La Trobe Australian Manuscripts Collection, State Library of Victoria

p. 186—W. L. Crowther Library, State Library of Tasmania

p. 390—Mr Les Cromb

p. 12—from Lord Maugham's *The Tichborne Trial*

pp. 35, 64, 97, 400—from Douglas Woodruff's *The Tichborne Claimant*

Pictures not acknowledged above are from *The Trial at Bar of Roger C. D. Tichborne, Bart.* (author's collection)

The quote on p. 409, from Janet Malcolm's *The Crime of Sheila McGough*, is reproduced with permission of the author and the Wylie Agency (UK) Ltd

BIBLIOGRAPHY

Anderson, Hugh (ed.) *Baronet or Butcher? The Trials of the Tichborne Claimant*, Red Rooster Press, Hotham Hill, 1999

Atlay, J. M. 'The Tichborne Trial', in *Famous Trials of the Century*, Grant Richards, London, 1899

Ballantine, Mr Serjeant *Some Experiences of a Barrister's Life*, vol. 2, Richard Bentley & Son, London, 1882

Balmer, Lawrence 'Reedy Creek Gold Rush', in *Broadford, A Regional History*, ed. B. J. Fletcher, Lowden Publishing Co., Kilmore, 1975

Barraclough, Linda and Debra Squires, *A Gippsland Chronology to 1899*, Kapana Press, Bairnsdale, 1992

Boisdale Station papers & account books MS6019–MS6022 & MS9619, LaTrobe Australian Manuscripts Collection, State Library of Victoria

Boldrewood, Rolf *Nevermore*, Macmillan & Co., London, 1892

Borges, Jorge Luis 'Tom Castro, the Implausible Imposter' in *A Universal History of Infamy*, Penguin, Harmondsworth, 1975 (first published 1935)

Boxall, George *History of the Australian Bushrangers*, Home Entertainment Library, Sydney, 1935

Braddon, Mary Elizabeth *Aurora Floyd*, Oxford University Press, Oxford, 1996 (first published 1863)

Bradshaw, Jack *The True History of the Australian Bushrangers*, W. J. Anderson, Sydney, n. d. (c. 1911)

Burton, Sarah *Impostors: Six Kinds of Liar*, Viking, London, 2000

Bushby, John E. P. *Saltbush Country: History of the Deniliquin District*, Library of Australian History, Deniliquin, 1980

Carnegie, Margaret *Friday Mount*, Hawthorn Press, Melbourne, 1973

—— *Morgan the Bold Bushranger*, Hawthorn Press, Melbourne, 1974

Christie, R. W. and G. D. Gray *Victoria's Forgotten Goldfield: A History of the Dargo, Crooked River Goldfield*, High Country Publishing, Dargo, 1996

Connell, R. W. 'Wagga's Butcher, Tichborne's Claimant, Kenealy's Cause', *Meanjin*, Autumn 1975, pp. 100–3

Cotton, Leicester *The Sydney Assassins: A mid-Victorian mystery*, Lansdowne Press, Melbourne, 1964

Cowans, Jenny and Katrina Cowans 'History of Thomas Toke' (ms), c. 1984, copy in Omeo Historical Society

Cunningham, James E. 'The Sequel to the Tichborne Case. Arthur Orton or William Cresswell? The proceedings in New South Wales', manuscript for pamphlet, October 1884—National Library of Australia MS 760/16/5

Davis, Natalie Zemon *The Return of Martin Guerre*, Harvard University Press, Cambridge, 1983

Davitt, Michael *Leaves from a Prison Diary; or, Lectures to a 'Solitary' Audience*, vol. 1, Chapman & Hall, London, 1885

Denning papers Two albums of photographs and letters, and a folio of pamphlets and broadsides on the Tichborne case—National Library of Australia FRM NK713

Devant, David *My Magic Life*, Hutchinson & Co., London, 1931

Dexter, Nancy 'Wagga Wagga and the Tichborne Case', in *Walkabout*, August 1966, pp. 19–21

Docker, Edward Wybergh *Furphies: Fact or Fantasy in Australian History*, Hampton Press, 2000

Dormer family papers MS11197 (microfilm copy), Australian Manuscripts Collection, State Library of Victoria—originals in Warwick County Record Office, UK

Duggan, Laurie *The Ash Range*, Pan, Woollahra, 1987

Dunlop, Alan J. *Wodonga: Over river and plain*, Hawthorn Press, Melbourne, 1976

Dyer, Max *Yarns and Characters from the Mountains*, self-published, Bairnsdale, 1997

414

Ellis, S. M.   *Henry Kingsley, 1830–1876: Towards a Vindication*, Grant Richards, London, 1931

Ewart, W. J.   'Reminiscences of the Upper Yarra', originally published as a series in the *Warburton Mail*, 1934; reprinted in Earle Parkinson, *Warburton Ways*, Signs Publishing Company, Warburton, 1993

Examiner and Kilmore & McIvor Weekly Journal

Fairweather, Keith McD.   *Brajerack: Mining at Omeo and Glen Wills*, Bairnsdale, 1983

——   *Time to Remember: The history of gold mining on the Tambo and its tributaries*, Bairnsdale, 1975

Fane family papers   MS842 Reel 1 (microfilm copy) in Australian Manuscripts Collection, State Library of Victoria—originals in Lincolnshire Country Record Office, UK

Fletcher, Meredith   *Avon to the Alps*, Shire of Avon, Stratford, 1988

Freeman, Hilda M.   *Murrumbidgee Memories and Riverina Reminiscences*, 1985

Frost, W. A. (writing as W. A. F.)   *An Exposure of the Orton Confession of the Tichborne Claimant*, Lynwood and Co. Ltd, London, 1912

General Directory of Hobart Town   Huxtable & Deakin, Murray Street, Hobart, 1854

Gilbert, Michael   *The Claimant*, Constable, London, 1957

Gormly, Hon. James, MLC   *Exploration and Settlement in Australia*, self-published, Sydney, 1921

Harding, Eric   *Bogong Jack: The Gentleman Bushranger*, Yandoo Publishing Company, South Melbourne, 1967

Harris, Richard, K. C. (ed.)   *Reminiscences of Sir Henry Hawkins (Baron Brampton)*, vol. 1, Edward Arnold, London, 1904

Harrison, Jessie B.   'Some Memories of Old Gippsland and its Earliest Pioneers'—in Leslie & Cowie

?Heysham, William Nunez   *The Tichborne Romance: A Full and Accurate Report of the Proceedings in the Extraordinary and Interesting*

Trial of Tichborne v. Lushington, in the Court of Common Pleas, Westminster, for Forty Days, From Wednesday, May 1, to Friday, July 7, 1871; including the whole of the examination, cross-examination, and re-examination of the Claimant, John Heywood, Manchester, n. d. [1871]

Hicks, Jenny   *Australian Cowboys, Roughriders and Rodeos*, Angus & Robertson, Sydney, 2000

In the Common Pleas—Tichborne v. Lushington, Australian Commission, 1869—microfilm 93/62, University of Tasmania Law Library; annotated copy at Dixson Library Q460

Jackson, John Dettmer Dodds   *Sir Roger Tichborne revealed: The discovery of Sir Roger Charles Doughty Tichborne alias Edward Caleb Souper, secretary to Lady Ogle of Withdeane Court near Brighton, Sussex, England, and his confederates [and] Lady Tichborne's correspondence with Mr William Gibbes…and Mr Arthur Cubitt…*, 1885

Jones, Graham   *Bushrangers of the North East*, Charquin Hill, Wangaratta, 1991

Keir, Don and Wilma Keir   'Boisdale Estate' notes, Traralgon and District Historical Society, November 1973

Kemp, Doris   *Maffra: The History of the Shire to 1975*, Shire of Maffra, 1975

Kenealy, Arabella   *Memoirs of Edward Vaughan Kenealy*, John Long, London, 1908

Kenealy, E. V. K. (ed.)   *The Trial at Bar of Sir Roger C. D. Tichborne, Bart.*, 9 vols, 1875–1880

Kent, Christopher A.   'Victorian Self-Making, or Self-Unmaking? The Tichborne Claimant Revisited', in *Victorian Review* (Journal of the Victorian Studies Association of Western Canada), vol. 17, no. 1, Summer 1991, pp. 18–34

Kingsley, Henry   *Ravenshoe*, Macmillan & Co., London, 1862

Laughton, Alfred Nelson   *High-Bailiff Laughton's Reminiscences*, S. K. Broadbent & Co. Ltd., Douglas, Isle of Man, 1916

Lawson, Sir John   Correspondence between Sir John Lawson of Brough and A. K. Stephenson, clerk for the Crown case against the Claimant, April–May 1873. M2115 (microfilm copy) in National Library of Australia; originals in North Yorkshire Records Office, UK

Leslie, J. W. and H. C. Cowie   *The Wind Still Blows…Early Gippsland Diaries*, Sale, 1973

Lewis, Janet   *The Wife of Martin Guerre*, Penguin, Harmondsworth, 1983 (first published 1941)

Loney, J. K.   *Wrecks on the Gippsland Coast*, Marine History, Geelong 1968

McGrath, Dr Helen & Hazel Edwards   *Difficult Personalities: A practical guide to managing the hurtful behaviour of others (and maybe your own)*, Choice Books, Marrickville, 2000

MacGregor, Geddes   *The Tichborne Impostor*, Lippincott, New York, 1957

McLaren Collection   The Case of William Cresswell, Baillieu Library, University of Melbourne

Malcolm, Janet   *The Crime of Sheila McGough*, Vintage Books, New York, 2000

Manning, Laurie   *Discovering Briagolong*, Briagolong, 1994

Maugham, Lord   *The Tichborne Case*, Hodder & Stoughton, London, 1936

Mills/Yeoman papers   Papers of Bessie Yeoman concerning her father, Robert Mills of Kilmorey Station, Victoria (supposed to have been Roger Tichborne). In private collection.

Montgomery, Mrs   'Life in Gippsland', written in 1916, ms in Stratford Historical Society—extracts in Leslie & Cowie, pp. 97–117

Morgan, Dorothy & Marjorie Morgan   *Happy-Go-Lucky: A Gippsland Gold Town 1863–1917*, Acacia Press, Blackburn, 1987

Morgan, Patrick   'The Vandemonian Trail: Convicts and Bushrangers in Eastern Victoria', in *Island*, no. 74, Autumn, 1998, pp. 52–62

——   'Tales of Old Travel: Predecessors of David Malouf's *The Conversations at Curlow Creek*', in *Australian Literary Studies*, vol. 18, no. 2, 1997

——   *The Settling of Gippsland: A Regional History*, Gippsland Municipalities Association, Traralgon, 1997

Mount Alexander Mail

Moye, D. G. (ed.)   *Historic Kiandra*, Cooma–Monaro Historical Society, 1959

Murphy, John   *Barr's Creek: A Mystery of the Upper Murray*, Dyer and Murphy, Box Hill South, 1998

National Library of Australia   MS 1415: Arthur Orton—2 letters, c. 1870, to Dr Healy (or Henty)

——   MS 1816: Notes from an old diary found in Retreat Hotel, Westbury, Vic, in 1965.

——   MS 2256: Three letters from or re. the Claimant, 1873–75

New South Wales Legislative Assembly   Parliamentary Papers, William Cresswell etc., 1878

——   Parliamentary Papers, William Cresswell etc., 1883–84

——   *Progress Report from the Select Committee on the Case of William Creswell* [sic], 1899

——   *Inquiry into the Case of William Creswell* [sic], appointed 12/1/1900

Newton, H. Chance   *Crime and the Drama, or Dark Deeds Dramatized*, Stanley Paul & Co., London, 1927

Nicholas, Jeremy   *Victorian Curiosities: Bizarre and Trivial Facts from a Hundred Years Ago*, Little Brown, London, 1995

Nixon, Allan M.   *Stand and Deliver: 100 Australian Bushrangers, 1789–1901*, Lothian, Port Melbourne, 1991

O'Brien, R. Barry   *John Bright: A Monograph*, Smith, Elder & Co., London, 1910

'Old Commercial Traveller (T. F. H.)'   *The Tichborne Case: Being an exposition of the scheme at first intended to be adopted, in order to carry out to a successful issue this extraordinary imposition*, Brisbane, 1882

Ovens and Murray Advertiser

Parry, Judge Edward Abbott   *Vagabonds All*, Cassell & Co., London, 1926

Pearce, Florence   *Boisdale: From Squatter to Settler*, Maffra & District Historical Society, 1980

Peck, Harry H.   *Memoirs of a Stockman*, Stock & Land Publishing, Melbourne, 1942

Phelan, Dave   Interview, 18 February 1961, with N. P. O'Connor and M. J. Officer—National Library of Australia, Oral TRC 2539/69.

Powell, Roy W.   *Back to Boisdale*, April 1968—condensed by Trish Gregory as 'Boisdale', for Traralgon & District Historical Society

Priestman, Edward   *The Tichborne Mystery: On the verge of solution, midst the ashes of a dead past*, W. Dymock, Sydney, 1899

Public Record Office, UK   Prison record of Thomas Castro A1139, 1877–1880 (PCOM 8/173 80941)

Radcliffe family papers   M1900 (microfilm copy) in Australian Manuscripts Collection, State Library of Victoria—originals in Leeds Archives, UK

Rickards, E. C.   *Zoe Thomson of Bishopsthorne and her friends*, John Murray, London, 1916

Robertson, A. J.   *History of Alresford*, revised edn, Laurence Oxley, Alresford, 1969

Roe, Michael   *Kenealy and the Tichborne Cause: A Study in mid-Victorian Populism*, Melbourne University Press, Carlton, 1974

——   'Arthur Orton, the Tichborne Case, and Tasmania', in *Papers and Proceedings*, Tasmanian Historical Research Association, vol. 18, 1971, pp. 115–36

Rogers, J. G.   *Jericho on the Jordan: A Gippsland goldfield history*, Moe, 1998

Sadlier, John   *Recollections of a Victorian Police Officer*, first published by George Robertson & Company, Melbourne, 1913; facsimile published by Penguin Books, Ringwood, 1973

Sala, George Augustus   *Life and Adventures of George Augustus Sala*, Scribners, New York, 1895

Schulz, Mat   *Claim*, Flamingo, Sydney, 1996

Scott, Harold   *The Early Doors: Origins of the Music Hall*, Nicholson & Watson, London, 1946

Smith, Daniel   *The Tichborne Trial: Startling affidavit of Lady Tichborne*, Redfern, c. 1883

Smith, John Thomas   *The Streets of London*, Richard Bentley, London, 1854 edition

Swan, Keith   *A History of Wagga Wagga*, City of Wagga Wagga, 1970

Thomas, Martin   *The Fraud: Behind the mystery of John Friedrich, Australia's greatest conman*, Pagemasters, Richmond, 1991

Tichborne case papers   Dixson Library, State Library of New South Wales—Australia's most extensive collection of original Tichborne case material

Twain, Mark   *Mark Twain in Australia and New Zealand*, Penguin Books, Ringwood, 1973

'The Vet'   *Old Time Echoes of Tasmania*, 1895

Victoria Police Gazette

Wagga Wagga Advertiser

Wagga Wagga Express

Webber, Vic   'A Web that Remains Tangled: Crimes at Early Omeo', in *Gippsland Heritage Journal*, No. 15 (December 1993), pp. 52–54

——   *Taming a Town: Law and Order at Omeo*, Kapana Press, Bairnsdale, 1993

Wilkins, Harold T.   *Mysteries Solved and Unsolved*, Odhams Press, London, 1958

Woodruff, Douglas   *The Tichborne Claimant: A Victorian mystery*, Hollis & Carter, London, 1957

Zencey, Eric   *Panama*, Sceptre, London, 1995

INDEX

430